Inside the Black Box

Third Edition

Inside the Black Box

A Simple Guide to Systematic Investing

Third Edition

RISHI K NARANG

WILEY

Published by John Wiley & Sons, Inc., Hoboken, New Jersey.
Published simultaneously in Canada.

For general information on our other products and services or for technical support, please contact
our Customer Care Department within the United States at (800) 762-2974, outside the United
States at (317) 572-3993 or fax (317) 572-4002.

Wiley also publishes its books in a variety of electronic formats. Some content that appears in print
may not be available in electronic formats. For more information about Wiley products, visit our
web site at www.wiley.com.

Library of Congress Cataloging-in-Publication Data

Names: Narang, Rishi K, 1974- author. | John Wiley & Sons, publisher.
Title: Inside the black box : a simple guide to systematic investing /
    Rishi K Narang.
Description: Third edition. | Hoboken, New Jersey : Wiley, [2024] |
    Includes index.
Identifiers: LCCN 2024018002 (print) | LCCN 2024018003 (ebook) | ISBN
    9781119931898 (hardback) | ISBN 9781119931911 (adobe pdf) | ISBN
    9781119931904 (epub)
Subjects: LCSH: Portfolio management—Mathematical models. | Investment
    analysis—Mathematical models. | Stocks—Mathematical models.
Classification: LCC HG4529.5 .N37 2024 (print) | LCC HG4529.5 (ebook) |
    DDC 332.64/2—dc23/eng/20240515
LC record available at https://lccn.loc.gov/2024018002
LC ebook record available at https://lccn.loc.gov/2024018003

Cover Design: Wiley
Cover Image: © Rishi Narang
Author Photo: Courtesy of Miko Lim
Printed and bound by CPI Group (UK) Ltd, Croydon, CR0 4YY

C9781119931898_310524

Contents

Foreword

In 1992, I joined a large bank with the aim of becoming a quant trader. I had spent the previous seven years working for a financial consulting firm, and when that started to get a little boring, learning to play poker competitively. I had read every paper I could find about exploiting market inefficiencies, and I thought my background gave me a reasonable chance at being successful. And I was, thanks to a combination of luck, hard work, and some fantastic colleagues.

I wish that at the time I started PDT, I had had a book like Rishi's. It would have given me a lot of ideas and saved me a lot of time and mistakes. But let me be clear. Reading *Inside the Black Box* will not teach you how to make money using quantitative techniques in financial markets. Few people have figured out how to do that, and those of us who have are understandably reluctant to share our secrets. On the other hand, this book will provide helpful, accurate information about the different approaches that quantitative traders use, and the myriad of disciplines they need to understand to succeed. For someone new to the field, or looking to invest quantitatively, Rishi has provided a great guidebook.

Most of the people we hire at PDT have backgrounds in physics, mathematics, engineering, or computer science. We provide a finance reading list to get them up to speed in their new domain. The previous edition of Rishi's book has been on that list, and so will this version, which includes great updates in the sections on portfolio construction, risk management, and research.

As a long-term allocator to smaller quant funds, Rishi Narang has seen first-hand a lot of the mistakes quants make, and the challenges they face. *Inside the Black Box* is clearly written, provides a thorough overview of all things quant, and dispassionately presents different perspectives on controversial issues. I hope you enjoy it!

Pete Muller
Founder and CEO, PDT Partners

Preface to the Third Edition

It is hard to believe that it has been 15 years since I wrote the first edition of *Inside the Black Box*. I never could have guessed it would end up being used by quant funds as a training manual, nor as a textbook in grad school classes on quant finance. I wrote that first edition more or less in anger, in the wake of the August 2007 quant meltdown. Investors, reporters, and regulators were asking stupid questions and making stupid statements and generalizations. I was complaining to Steve Drobny at his home in Manhattan Beach about how unfathomable it is that people couldn't understand what quants do, because it's so obvious and transparent. He retorted, "If it's that easy, write a book." All it took was a brief hesitation in response, and Steve had already punched out an email to Wiley Finance, publisher of his legendary *Inside the House of Money*, on his Blackberry, insisting that they publish my then-nonexistent (and not-yet-conceived) book.

About four years later, I reluctantly undertook to update the book to address another annoying, widely misunderstood, but ultimately straightforward topic—high frequency trading. I also updated and upgraded many other aspects of the book, and, in my mind, my work on the topic of explaining systematic investing in plain English was probably done. The principles and concepts remained valid and relevant, so while there might be this minor advancement or that new methodology to solve an extant problem, I saw no need to put out another edition.

So much has changed since then. We've had Brexit, a couple of highly contentious U.S. elections, a global pandemic, continued acts of terrorism and armed conflicts in several parts of the world. We've had a plethora of natural disasters, most of which are spurred by climate change—massive hurricanes, bomb cyclones, atmospheric rivers. We've also had the development of crypto-currencies, decentralized finance, non-fungible tokens, and Web3. A new wave of speculators came (and has now gone?) whose aims seem to have been not-entirely economic in nature—they live by mantras-as-acronyms, such as FOMO, YOLO, and HODL. We've had a few highlights too: the 2015 Paris Accord, the rapid development of a new kind of vaccine and other treatments to ameliorate a pandemic that very much remains with us, the creation of a whole new category of investable assets (crypto-currencies), and the advent of Large Language Models. Much else has changed and happened, but all these events were directly relevant to capital markets and the investors who participate in them.

More to the point, the quant investing industry, too, has had an eventful decade. Acceptance of this approach to investing as a valid and important one is now widespread, and assets under management among quants have grown significantly. Certain business models have become significantly favored by many investors, which has had a direct impact on the competitive landscape of practitioners in the space. And beyond business considerations, the work itself has evolved significantly. Machine-learning techniques went from fringe and cutting edge to ubiquitous. Alternative datasets were also very new a decade ago, and now those too are everywhere. The asset classes and geographies accessible to and traded by quants have expanded dramatically. While none of this really changes the core concepts presented even in the first edition, there was enough to do that I felt it was time to update.

The basic layout of this book is the same as that of the second edition's. Part One (Chapters 1 and 2) contains some introductory material and an overview of the structure of systematic investing strategies. Part Two (Chapters 3–9) contains an explication of the various aspects of that structure. Part Three (Chapters 10–12) presents a practical guide to investing in quantitative strategies. Part Four (Chapters 13–15) contains an explanation of high-frequency trading. And again, we close in Chapter 16 with a look at some interesting current and future topics in this space of innovation and evolution. We have moved the discussion of criticisms of high-frequency trading to an appendix, as this was far more topical in the few years following the financial crisis than it has been since.

And as much as has changed and happened, far more fundamentally, things remain very much the same. Quant investing remains different from traditional, discretionary approaches largely in a different model, focusing on *how* to go about investing, rather than on *what* is being done. The ideas utilized by quants remain mostly driven by an economic rationale that would make total sense to most people. Quants continue to have only modestly-better-than-random odds of success on any given forecast or position and continue to rely on diversification of bets (either across many positions at once, or by taking many bets over time, or both). They still compete with each other to sniff out inefficiencies created by various market participants' varying utility functions or suboptimal behaviors. The bulk of the interesting work in this industry continues to be performed by humans, largely in the framework of scientific research. Egos continue to be negatively associated with the probability of success.

As before, my goal is to explain things in terms as plain as possible. If you have a basic understanding of capital markets, you should be able to understand this book. And, in turn, hopefully, you will develop a better understanding of a corner of the investment management industry that, undoubtedly, will only continue to gain prominence and market share.

Acknowledgments

I want to start by thanking Steve Drobny, without whom I would never have written a book at all. He has been a great friend, and he's a great human being.

I also want to thank my publisher, Wiley Finance, and especially Bill Falloon, Vitusha Rameshan, and Purvi Patel. Wiley took a chance on me some 15 years ago, when I was no one they knew about, solely on the back of Steve's say-so. I thank Susan Dunsmore for her excellent copy-editing and catching so many of my mistakes.

For their help with large portions of this edition, I am grateful to my colleagues Dave Demers and Tim Long. I am also thankful for Samantha Broussard-Wilson's help with updating industry data. Julie Wilson, my colleague since the first day of T2AM's existence, has my gratitude for her partnership all these long years.

Chapter 6 greatly benefited from the input of Stephen Boyd and Kasper Johansson. Kasper also kindly and deftly created the new optimization exhibits in Chapter 6, while on holiday. Mani Mahjouri and Brian Englebert were extremely helpful with Chapter 8—it ended up being a much bigger lift than I anticipated, but they made it possible. I am also thankful to Matthew Rothman, who's been a friend for more than 16 years, and who was an excellent sounding board for Chapter 16. I also want to thank Kevin Plominski for his help with some data on the industry generally.

On a personal note, I want to thank Miko Lim for his photographs. I also want to express how grateful I am to my son, Solomon Narang. He was only three years old when the second edition came out, and he'll be 14 when this one does. I am so proud of you, my little man. Last, and certainly not least, I want to say a huge thank you to Ali Menoutis, who has been a wonderful partner and teacher these past three years.

I could not have known what doors would open and what amazing connections I would make as a result of the publication of *ItBB*. It is clear that it changed my life very significantly. I want to just say aloud how grateful I am for all the wonderful friends I have been lucky to make and experiences I have been lucky to have as a result.

Inside the Black Box

The Quant Universe

CHAPTER 1

Why Does Quant Trading Matter?

Look into their minds, at what wise men do and don't.
—Marcus Aurelius, *Meditations*

John is a quant trader running a mid-sized hedge fund. He completed an undergraduate degree in mathematics and computer science at a top school in the early 1990s. John immediately started working on Wall Street trading desks, eager to capitalize on his quantitative background. After seven years on the Street in various quant-oriented roles, John decided to start his own hedge fund. With partners handling business and operations, John was able to create a quant strategy that recently was trading over $1.5 billion per day in equity volume. More relevant to his investors, the strategy made money on 60 percent of days and 85 percent of months—a rather impressive accomplishment.

Despite trading billions of dollars of stock every day, there is no shouting at John's hedge fund, no orders being given over the phone, and no drama in the air; in fact, the only sign that there is any trading going on at all is the large flat-screen television in John's office that shows the strategy's performance throughout the day and its trading volume. John can't give you a fantastically interesting story about why his strategy is long this stock or short that one. While he is monitoring his universe of thousands of stocks for events that might require intervention, for the most part he lets the automated trading strategy do the hard work. What John monitors quite carefully, however, is the health of his strategy and the market environment's impact on it. He is aggressive about conducting research on an ongoing basis to adjust his models for changes in the market that would impact him.

Across from John sits Mark, a recently hired partner of the fund who is researching high-frequency trading. Unlike the firm's first strategy, which only makes money on 6 out of 10 days, the high-frequency efforts Mark and John are working on target a much more ambitious task: looking for smaller opportunities that can make money every day. Mark's first attempt at high-frequency strategies already makes money nearly 95 percent of the time. In fact, their target for this high-frequency business is even loftier: They want to replicate the success of those firms whose trading strategies make money every hour, maybe even every minute, of every day. Such high-frequency strategies can't accommodate large investments, because the opportunities they find are small, fleeting. The technology required to support such an endeavor is also incredibly expensive, not only to build, but also to maintain. Nonetheless, they are highly attractive for whatever capital they can accommodate. Within their high-frequency trading business, John and Mark expect their strategy to generate returns of about 200 percent a year, possibly much more.

Per the FT, quoting Hedge Fund Research's report, quants managed over $900 billion in assets at the end of October 2017,[1] nearly double the level from 2010, with continued inflows since. Aurum put the number a bit under half that amount in 2022, but even $445 billion is a significant sum, representing about 14 percent of the total assets under management they estimated are in hedge funds (and making quant the second largest category of hedge funds).[2] It is clear that quants are substantial players in the market, and that they're not only here to stay, but growing.

Not all quants are successful, however. It seems that once every decade or so, quant traders cause—or at least are perceived to cause—markets to move dramatically because of their failures, though we have only about four datapoints, the most recent from 2010, at which to point. The most obvious instance is, of course, Long Term Capital Management (LTCM), which nearly (but for the intervention of Federal Reserve banking officials and a consortium of Wall Street banks) brought the financial world to its knees. Although the world markets survived, LTCM itself was not as lucky. The firm, which averaged 30 percent returns after fees for four years, lost nearly 100 percent of its capital in the debacle of August–October 1998 and left many investors both skeptical and afraid of quant traders. Never mind that it is debatable whether this was a quant trading failure or a failure of human judgment in risk management, nor that it's questionable whether LTCM was even a quant trading firm at all. It was staffed by PhDs and Nobel Prize-winning economists, and that was enough to cast it as a quant trading outfit, and to make all quants "guilty by association."

Not only have quants been widely panned because of LTCM, but they have also been blamed (probably unfairly) for the crash of 1987 and (quite fairly) for the eponymous quant liquidation of 2007, the latter having severely impacted many quant shops. Even some of the largest names in quant trading suffered through August 2007's quant liquidation. For instance, Goldman Sachs' largely quantitative Global Alpha Fund was down an estimated 40 percent in 2007 after posting a 6 percent loss in 2006.[3] In less than a week during August 2007, many quant traders lost between 10 and 40 percent in a few days, though some of them rebounded strongly for the remainder of the month.

A best-selling nonfiction book by a former *Wall Street Journal* reporter even attempted to cast the blame for the massive financial crisis that came to a head in 2008 on quant trading. There were gaps in his logic large enough to drive an 18-wheeler through, but the popular perception of quants has never been positive. And this is all before high-frequency trading (HFT) came into the public consciousness in 2010, after the "Flash Crash" on May 10th of that year. Ever since then, various corners of the investment and trading world have tried very hard to assert that quants (this time, in the form of HFTs) are responsible for increased market volatility, instability in the capital markets, market manipulation, front-running, and many other evils. We will look into HFT and the claims leveled against it in greater detail in Chapter 16, but any quick search of the internet will confirm that quant trading and HFT have left the near-total obscurity they enjoyed for decades and entered the mainstream's thoughts on a regular basis.

There was also the Flash Crash on May 6, 2010, during which the U.S. stock market lost some 7 percent in a mere 15 minutes, with about $1 trillion in market capitalization vanishing. Eight large cap companies, including Accenture and Exelon, fell to $0.01 per share—an exceedingly low price. Twenty minutes later, most of the loss had been recovered. Quants were widely blamed for the incident, most notably by Michael Lewis, in *Flash Boys*.

More recently, but less significantly, Bloomberg published an article on November 30, 2023, entitled, "Oil's Wild Ride Is Driven by a Disruptive Band of Bot Traders," which claimed that the trend-following quant strategies add to volatility (and point only to oil prices increasing due to such pressure) by engaging in what humans have always done—follow trends. I am certain that there were no algorithms behind the bubble in tulips in Holland, nor in the roaring 1920s in the U.S. But, yes, let's blame the quants. As an apropos error in reporting, the authors quote a quant from Cayler Capital. While they correctly categorize Cayler as a Commodity Trading Advisor (CTA, for short, and a type of institution that is distinguished only by its trading of futures on behalf of clients—not by being systematic in so doing), they lump his firm in with trend followers. Even more ironically, this article merely recounts an anecdote in which the portfolio manager decided not to intervene in his models, which happened to be positioned correctly for the Russian invasion of Ukraine, vis-à-vis oil prices.[4]

Leaving aside the spectacular successes and failures of quant trading, and all the ills for which quant trading is blamed by some, there is no doubt that quants cast an enormous shadow over the capital markets virtually every trading day. Across U.S. equity markets, a significant, and rapidly growing, proportion of all trading is done through algorithmic execution, one footprint of quant strategies. (*Algorithmic execution* is the use of computer software to manage and "work" an investor's buy and sell orders in electronic markets.) Although this automated execution technology is not the exclusive domain of quant strategies—any trade that needs to be done, whether by an index fund or a discretionary macro trader, can be worked using execution algorithms—certainly a substantial portion of all algorithmic trades are done by quants. Furthermore, quants were both the inventors of, and primary innovators of, algorithmic trading engines. A mere five such quant traders account for about 1 billion shares of volume *per day*, in aggregate, in the United States alone. It is worth noting that not one of these is well known to the broader investing public, even now, after all the press surrounding high-frequency trading. As of 2017, algorithmic trading—which to be clear, represents only the execution of trades, not whether the determinant of that investment decision came via a human utilizing a trading algorithm or a systematic investing strategy utilizing potentially the same kind of algorithm—accounted for about 70 percent of equity trading, 50 percent of futures trading, 40 percent of options trading, 25 percent of foreign exchange trading, and almost 10 percent of fixed income trading.[5]

It is clear that the magnitude of quant trading among hedge funds is substantial. In 2021, SigTech estimated that about 22 percent of the world's hedge funds were entirely systematic. That portion will not likely be declining. Furthermore, another of their surveys from early 2022 indicated that about 95 percent of respondents believed that even discretionary hedge fund managers are increasing their use of systematic tools in their investment processes. While this is hardly an unbiased source, their observations are in line with my own observations of the industry.

Hedge funds are private investment pools that are accessible only to sophisticated, wealthy individual or institutional clients. They can pursue virtually any investment mandate one can dream up, and they are allowed to keep a portion of the profits they generate for their clients. But this is only one of several arenas in which quant trading is widespread. Proprietary trading desks at the various banks, boutique proprietary trading firms, and various "multi-strategy" hedge fund managers who utilize quantitative trading for a portion of their overall business each contribute to a much larger estimate of the size of the quant trading universe.

With such size and extremes of success and failure, it is not surprising that quants take their share of headlines in the financial press. And though most press coverage of quants seems to be markedly negative, this is not always the case. In fact, not only have many quant funds been praised for their steady returns (a hallmark of their disciplined implementation process), but some experts have even argued that the existence of successful quant strategies improves the marketplace for all investors, regardless of their style. For instance, Reto Francioni (chief executive of Deutsche Börse AG, which runs the Frankfurt Stock Exchange) said in a speech that algorithmic trading "benefits all market participants through positive effects on liquidity." Francioni went on to reference a recent academic study showing "a positive causal relationship between algo trading and liquidity."[6] Indeed, this is almost guaranteed to be true. Quant traders, using execution algorithms (hence, "algo trading"), typically slice their orders into many small pieces to improve both the cost and efficiency of the execution process. As mentioned before, although originally developed by quant funds, these algorithms have been adopted by the broader investment community. By placing many small orders, other investors who might have different views or needs can also get their own executions improved.

Quants typically make markets more efficient for other participants by providing liquidity when other traders' needs cause a temporary imbalance in the supply and demand for a security. These imbalances are known as "inefficiencies," after the economic concept of "efficient markets." True inefficiencies (such as an index's price being different from the weighted basket of the constituents of the same index) represent rare, fleeting opportunities for riskless profit. But riskless profit, or arbitrage, is not the only—or even primary—way in which quants improve efficiency. The main inefficiencies quants eliminate (and, thereby, profit from) are not absolute and unassailable, but rather are probabilistic and require risk-taking.

A classic example of this is a strategy called *statistical arbitrage*, and a classic statistical arbitrage example is a *pairs trade*. Imagine two stocks with similar market capitalizations from the same industry and with similar business models and financial status. For whatever reason, Company A is included in a major market index, an index that many large index funds are tracking. Meanwhile, Company B is not included in any major index. It is likely that Company A's stock will subsequently outperform shares of Company B simply due to a greater demand for the shares of Company A from index funds, which are compelled to buy this new constituent in order to track the index. This outperformance will in turn cause a higher P/E multiple on Company A than on Company B, which is a subtle kind of inefficiency. After all, nothing in the fundamentals has changed—only the nature of supply and demand for the common shares. Statistical arbitrageurs may step in to sell shares of Company A to those who wish to buy, and buy shares of Company B from those looking to sell, thereby preventing the divergence between these two fundamentally similar companies from getting out of hand and improving efficiency in market pricing. Let us not be naïve: they improve efficiency not out of altruism, but because these strategies are set up to profit if indeed a convergence occurs between Companies A and B.

This is not to say that quants are the only players who attempt to profit by removing market inefficiencies. Indeed, it is likely that any alpha-oriented trader is seeking similar, or at least analogous, sorts of dislocations as sources of profit. And, of course, there are times, such as August 2007, when quants actually cause the markets to be temporarily *less* efficient. Nonetheless, especially in smaller, less liquid, and more neglected stocks, statistical arbitrage players are often major providers of market liquidity and help establish efficient price discovery for all market participants.

So, what can we learn from a quant's approach to markets? The three answers that follow represent important lessons that quants can teach us— lessons that can be applied by any investment manager.

1.1   THE BENEFIT OF DEEP THOUGHT

According to James Simons, the founder of the legendary Renaissance Technologies, one of the greatest advantages quants bring to the investment process is their systematic approach to problem solving. As Dr. Simons puts it, "The advantage scientists bring into the game is less their mathematical or computational skills than their ability to think scientifically."[7]

The first reason it is useful to study quants is that they are forced to think deeply about many aspects of their strategy that are taken for granted by non-quant investors. Why does this happen? Computers are obviously powerful tools, but without absolutely precise instruction, they can achieve nothing. So, to make a computer implement a "black box trading strategy" requires an enormous amount of effort on the part of the developer. You can't tell a computer to "find cheap stocks." You have to specify what *find* means, what *cheap* means, and what *stocks* are. For example, *finding* might involve searching a database with information about stocks and then ranking the stocks within a market sector (based on some classification of stocks into sectors). *Cheap* might mean P/E ratios, though one must specify both the metric of cheapness and what level will be considered cheap. As such, the quant can build his system so that cheapness is indicated by a 10 P/E or by those P/Es that rank in the bottom decile of those in their sector. And *stocks*, the universe of the model, might be all U.S. stocks, all global stocks, all large cap stocks in Europe, or whatever other group the quant wants to trade.

All this defining leads to a lot of deep thought about exactly what one's strategy is, how to implement it, and so on. In the preceding example, the quant doesn't have to choose to rank stocks within their sectors. Instead, stocks can be compared to their industry peers, to the market overall, or to any other reasonable group. But the point is that the quant is encouraged to be intentional about these decisions by virtue of the fact that the computer will not fill in any of these blanks on its own.

The benefit of this should be self-evident. Deep thought is usually a good thing. Even better, this kind of detailed and rigorous working out of how to divide and conquer the problem of conceptualizing, defining, and implementing an investment strategy is useful to quants and discretionary traders alike. These benefits largely accrue from thoroughness, which is generally held to be a key ingredient to investment or trading success. By contrast, many (though certainly not all) discretionary traders, because they are not forced to be so precise in the specification of their strategy and its implementation, seem to take a great many decisions in an *ad hoc* manner. I have been in countless meetings with discretionary traders who, when I asked them how they decided on the sizes of their positions, responded with variations on the theme of, "Whatever seemed reasonable." This is by no means a damnation of discretionary investment styles. I merely point out that precision and deep thought about many details, in addition to the bigger-picture aspects of a strategy, can be a good thing, and this lesson can be learned from quants.

1.2   THE MEASUREMENT AND MISMEASUREMENT OF RISK

As mentioned earlier in this chapter, the history of LTCM is a lesson in the dangers of mismeasuring risk. Quants are naturally predisposed toward conducting all sorts of measurements, including of risk exposure. This activity itself has potential benefits and downsides. On the plus side, there is a certain intentionality of risk-taking that a well-conceived quant strategy encourages. Rather than accepting accidental risks, the disciplined quant attempts to isolate exactly what his edge is and focus his risk-taking on those areas that isolate this edge. To root out these risks, the quant must first have an idea of what these risks are and how to measure them. For example, most quant equity traders, recognizing that they do not have sufficient capabilities in forecasting the direction of the market itself, measure their exposure to the market (using their net dollar or beta exposure, commonly) and actively seek to limit this exposure to a trivially small level by balancing their long portfolios against their short portfolios. On the other hand, there are very valid concerns about false precision, measurement error, and incorrect sets of assumptions that can plague attempts to measure risk and manage it quantitatively.

All the blowups we have mentioned, and most of those we haven't, stem in one way or another from this over-reliance on flawed risk measurement techniques. In the case of LTCM, for example, historical data showed that certain scenarios were likely, others unlikely, and still others had simply never occurred. At that time, most market participants did not expect that a country of Russia's importance, with a substantial supply of nuclear weapons and natural resources, would go bankrupt. Nothing like this had ever happened in modern history. Nevertheless, Russia indeed defaulted on its debt in the summer of 1998, sending the world's markets into a frenzy and rendering useless any measurement of risk. The naïve over-reliance on quantitative measures of risk, in this case, led to the near-collapse of the financial markets in the autumn of 1998. But for a rescue orchestrated by the U.S. government and agreed on by most of the powerhouse banks on Wall Street, we would have seen a very different path unfold for the capital markets and all aspects of financial life.

Indeed, the credit debacle that began to overwhelm markets in 2007 and 2008, too, was likely avoidable. Banks relied on credit risk models that simply were unable to capture the risks correctly. In many cases, they seem to have done so knowingly, because it enabled them to pursue outsized short-term profits (and, of course, bonuses for themselves). It should be said that most of these mismeasurements could have been avoided, or at least the resulting problems mitigated, by the application of better judgment on the part of the practitioners who relied on them. Just as one cannot justifiably blame weather-forecasting models for the way that New Orleans was impacted by Hurricane Katrina in 2005, it would not make sense to blame quantitative risk models for the failures of those who created and use them. Traders can benefit from engaging in the exercise of understanding and measuring risk, so long as they are not seduced into taking ill-advised actions as a result.

1.3   DISCIPLINED IMPLEMENTATION

Perhaps the most obvious lesson we can learn from quants comes from the discipline inherent to their approach. Upon designing and rigorously testing a strategy that makes economic sense and seems to work, a properly run quant shop simply tends to let the models run without unnecessary, arbitrary interference. In many areas of life, from sports to science, the human ability to extrapolate, infer, assume, create, and learn from the past is beneficial in the planning stages of an activity. But execution of the resulting plan is also critical, and it is here that humans frequently are found to be lacking. A significant driver of failure is a lack of discipline.

Many successful traders subscribe to the old adage, "Cut losers and ride winners." However, discretionary investors often find it very difficult to realize losses, whereas they are quick to realize gains. This is a well-documented behavioral bias known as the *disposition effect*.[8] Computers, however, are not subject to this bias. As a result, a trader who subscribes to the aforementioned adage can easily program his trading system to behave in accordance with it every time. This is not because the systematic trader is somehow a better person than the discretionary trader, but rather because the systematic trader is able to make this "rational" decision at a time when there is no pressure, thereby obviating the need to exercise discipline at a time when most people would find it extraordinarily challenging. Discretionary investors can learn something about discipline from those who make it their business.

1.4 SUMMARY

Quant traders are a diverse and large portion of the global investment universe. They are found in both large and small trading shops and traffic in multiple asset classes and geographical markets. As is obvious from the magnitude of success and failure that is possible in quant trading, this niche can also teach a great deal to any curious investor. Most traders would be well served to work with the same kind of thoroughness and rigor as is required to properly specify and implement a quant trading strategy. Just as useful is the quant's proclivity to measure risk and exposure to various market dynamics, though this activity must be undergone with great care to avoid its flaws. Finally, the discipline and consistency of implementation that exemplifies quant trading are something from which all decision makers can learn a great deal.

NOTES

1. Robin Wigglesworth, "Quant Hedge Funds Set to Surpass $1tn Management Mark," FT.com, January 8, 2018.
2. https://www.aurum.com/wp-content/uploads/220928-Aurum-Hedge-Fund-Data-Engine-Strategy-Deep-Dive_Quant.pdf.
3. Lisa Kassenaar and Christine Harper, "Goldman Sachs Paydays Suffer on Lost Leverage with Fed Scrutiny," Bloomberg.com, October 21, 2008.
4. Devika Krishna Kumar and Julia Fanzeres, "Oil's Wild Ride Is Driven by a Disruptive Band of Bot Traders," Bloomberg.com, November 30, 2023.
5. Report attributed to Goldman Sachs and Aite Group, as of 2017, posted on https://analyzingalpha.com/algorithmic-trading-statistics.

6. Terry Hendershott, Charles M. Jones, and Albert J. Menkveld, "Does Algorithmic Trading Improve Liquidity?" WFA Paper, April 26, 2008.
7. www.turtletrader.com/trader-simons.html.
8. Hersh Shefrin and Meir Statman, "The Disposition to Sell Winners Too Early and Ride Losers Too Long: Theory and Evidence," *The Journal of Finance*, 40(3) (1985): 777–790.

CHAPTER 2

An Introduction to Quantitative Trading

*You see, wire telegraph is a kind of a very, very long cat. You pull
his tail in New York and his head is meowing in Los Angeles. Do
you understand this? And radio operates exactly the same way:
you send signals here, they receive them there. The only difference
is that there is no cat.*
  —Attributed to Albert Einstein, when asked to explain the radio

The term *black box* conjures up images of a Rube Goldberg device wherein
some simple input is rigorously tortured to arrive at a mysterious and
distant output. *Webster's Third New International Dictionary* defines a
Rube Goldberg device as "accomplishing by extremely complex roundabout
means what actually or seemingly could be done simply." Many observers
in both the press and industry use markedly similar verbiage to describe
quants. One *Washington Post* article, "For Wall Street's Math Brains,
Miscalculations; Complex Formulas Used by 'Quant' Funds Didn't Add Up
in Market Downturn," contains the following definition: ". . . a quant fund
is a hedge fund that relies on complex and sophisticated mathematical algorithms to search for anomalies and non-obvious patterns in the markets."[1]
In the *New York Post*'s "Not So Smart Now," we learn that "Quant funds
run computer programs that buy and sell hundreds and sometimes thousands of stocks simultaneously based on complex mathematical ratios . . ."[2]
Perhaps most revealing, this view was held even by some of the world's best-
respected investors. The late David Swensen, renowned chief investment
officer of the $17 billion Yale University endowment fund and author of
Pioneering Portfolio Management, said in an interview with *Fortune/CNN*

Money, "We also don't invest in quantitative-black box models because we simply don't know what they're doing."[3]

The moniker *black box* itself has somewhat mysterious origins. From what I can tell, its first known use was in 1915 in a sci-fi serial called *The Black Box,* starring Herbert Rawlinson. The program was about a criminologist named Sanford Quest who invented devices (which themselves were placed inside a black box) to help him solve crimes. Universal Studios, which produced the serial, offered cash prizes to those who could guess the contents of the black box.[4]

This connotation of opaqueness still persists today whenever the term *black box* is used. Most commonly in the sciences and in finance, a black box refers to any system that is fed inputs and produces outputs, but whose inner workings are either unknown or unknowable. Appropriately, two favorite descriptors for quant strategies are *complex* and *secretive.* However, by the end of this book I think it will be reasonably obvious to readers that, for the most part, quantitative trading strategies are in fact *clear* boxes that are far easier to understand in most respects than the caprice inherent to most human decision making. I would argue that the true black box is actually the human mind.

For example, an esoteric-sounding strategy called *statistical arbitrage* is in fact simple and easily understood. Statistical arbitrage is based on the theory that similar instruments (imagine two stocks, such as Exxon Mobil and Chevron) should behave similarly. If their relative prices diverge over the short run, they are likely to converge again. So long as the stocks are still similar, the divergence is more likely due to a short-term imbalance between the amount of buying and selling of these instruments, rather than any meaningful fundamental change that would warrant a divergence in prices. This is a clear and straightforward premise, and it drives billions of dollars' worth of trading volumes daily. It also happens to be a strategy that discretionary traders use, though it is usually called *pairs trading.* But whereas the discretionary trader is frequently unable to provide a curious investor with a consistent and coherent framework for determining when two (or more) instruments are similar or what constitutes a divergence, these are questions that the quant has likely researched and can address in great detail.

2.1 WHAT IS A QUANT?

A *quant* systematically applies an alpha-seeking investment strategy that was specified based on exhaustive research. What makes a quant a quant, in other words, almost always lies in *how* an investment strategy is conceived and implemented. It is rarely the case that quants are different from discretionary traders in *what* their strategies are actually doing, as illustrated by the earlier example of pairs trading and statistical arbitrage. There is almost never any attempt to eliminate human contributions to the investment process; after all, we are talking about quants, not robots. As previously mentioned, though quants apply mathematics and/or computer science to a wide variety of strategies, whether a fund designed to track the S&P 500 (i.e., an index fund), to structure exotic products (e.g., asset-backed securities, credit default swaps, or principal protection guarantee notes) or to design new blockchains or the algorithms that determine how the associated digital assets function, this book will remain focused on quants who pursue *alpha*, or returns that are independent of the direction of any market in the long run (a better definition, in my opinion, is presented in Chapter 3).

Besides conceiving and researching the core investment strategy, humans also design and build the software and systems used to automate the implementation of their ideas. But once the system "goes live," human judgment is generally limited in the day-to-day management of a portfolio. Still, the importance of human discretion in such a setup should not be understated. Good judgment is actually what separates the best quants from the mediocre. Even in the case of machine-learning strategies, almost all examples I've seen require researchers to carefully curate what data and transformations thereof are made available to their algorithms. The kinds of issues listed in the statistical arbitrage example are just a small subset of the kinds of decisions that quants almost always have to make, and these fundamental decisions, above all else, drive the strategy's behavior from that time forward. As such, good and bad judgments are multiplied over and over through time as the computer faithfully implements exactly what it was told to do. This is no different than many other fields. Imagine a guided missile system. If the engineers make bad judgments in the way they design these systems, there can be disastrous results, which are multiplied as more missiles are fired using the faulty guidance systems.

To understand the systematic nature of quants better, it can be helpful to examine the frontiers of the systematic approach—in other words, the situations in which quants have to *abandon* a systematic approach for a discretionary one. When a quant intervenes with the execution of her strategy, it is most commonly to mitigate problems caused by information that drives market behavior but that cannot be processed by the model. For example, the 2008 merger between Merrill Lynch and Bank of America, which caused Merrill's price to skyrocket, might have led a naïve quant strategy to draw the conclusion that Merrill had suddenly become drastically overpriced relative to other banks and was therefore an attractive candidate to be sold short. But this conclusion would have been flawed because there was information that justified the spike in Merrill's price and would not seem to a reasonable person to lead to a short sale. As such, a human can step in and simply remove Merrill from the universe that the computer models see, thereby eliminating the risk that, in this case anyway, the model will make decisions based on bad information. In a sense, this is merely an application of the principle of "garbage in, garbage out." If a portfolio manager at a quant trading shop is concerned that the model is making trading decisions based on inaccurate, incomplete, or irrelevant information, she may decide to reduce risk by eliminating trading in the instruments affected by this information.

Note that in this example, the news of the merger would already have been announced before the quant decides to override the system. Some shops are more aggressive, preemptively pulling names off the list of tradable securities at the first sign of credible rumors. By contrast, other quants do not remove names under any circumstances. Many quants reserve the right to reduce the overall size of the portfolio (and therefore leverage) if, in their discretion, the markets appear too risky. For example, after the attacks of September 11, 2001, many quants reduced their leverage in the wake of a massive event that would have unknowable repercussions on capital markets. Once things seemed to be operating more normally in the markets, they increased their leverage again to normal levels.

Though the operating definition of quants at the beginning of this section is useful, there is a full spectrum between *fully discretionary* strategies and *fully systematic* (or *fully automated*) strategies. The key determination that puts quants on one side of this spectrum and everyone else on the other is whether daily decisions about the selection and sizing of portfolio positions are made systematically (allowing for the exceptions of "emergency" overrides such as those just described) or discretionarily. If both the question of *what positions* to own and *how much* of each to own are usually answered systematically, that's a quant. If either one is answered by a human as standard operating procedure, that's not a quant.

It is interesting to note that, alongside the growth in quantitative trading, there are also a growing number of *quasi-quant* traders. For instance, some of these traders utilize automated systems to screen for potential investment opportunities, thereby winnowing a large number of potential choices down to a much smaller, more manageable list. From there, human discretion kicks in again, doing some amount of "fundamental" work to determine which names selected by the systematic screening process are actually worth owning and which are not. Less commonly, some traders leave the sourcing and selection of trades entirely up to humans, instead using computers to optimize and implement portfolios and to manage risk. Still less commonly, a few traders allow the computer to pick all the trades, while the human trader decides how to allocate among these trades. These quasi-quants make use of a subset of the tools in a proper quant's toolbox, so we will cover their use of these techniques implicitly.

2.2 WHAT IS THE TYPICAL STRUCTURE OF A QUANTITATIVE TRADING SYSTEM?

The best way to understand both quants and their black boxes is to examine the components of a quant trading system; this is the structure we will use for the remainder of the book. Exhibit 2.1 shows a schematic of a typical quantitative trading system. This diagram portrays the components of a live, "production" trading strategy (e.g., the components that decide which securities to buy and sell, how much, and when) but does not include everything necessary to create the strategy in the first place (e.g., research tools for designing a trading system).

The trading system has three modules—an alpha model, a risk model, and a transaction cost model—which feed into a portfolio construction model, which in turn interacts with the execution model. The alpha model is designed to predict the future of the instruments the quant wants to consider trading for the purpose of generating returns. For example, in a trend-following strategy in the futures markets, the alpha model is designed to forecast the direction of whatever futures markets the quant has decided to include in his strategy.

Risk models, by contrast, are designed to help limit the amount of exposure the quant has to those factors that are unlikely to generate returns but could drive losses. For example, the trend follower could choose to limit his directional exposure to a given asset class, such as commodities, because of

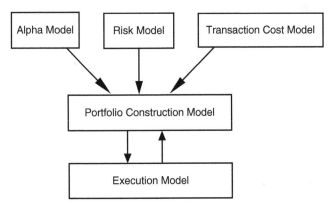

EXHIBIT 2.1 Basic Structure of a Quant Trading Strategy

concerns that too many forecasts he follows could line up in the same direction, leading to excess risk; the risk model would contain the levels for these commodity exposure limits.

The transaction cost model, which is shown in the box to the right of the risk model in Exhibit 2.1, is used to help determine the cost of whatever trades are needed to migrate from the current portfolio to whatever new portfolio is desirable to the portfolio construction model. Almost any trading transaction costs money, whether the trader expects to profit greatly or a little from the trade. Staying with the example of the trend follower, if a trend is expected to be small and last only a short while, the transaction cost model might indicate that the cost of entering and exiting the trade is greater than the expected profits from the trend.

The alpha, risk, and transaction cost models then feed into a portfolio construction model, which balances the tradeoffs presented by the pursuit of profits, the limiting of risk, and the costs associated with trading, thereby determining the best portfolio to hold. Having made this determination, the system can compare the current portfolio to the new target portfolio, with the differences between the current portfolio and the target portfolio representing the trades that need to be executed. Exhibit 2.2 illustrates an example of this process.

The current portfolio reflects the positions the quant trader currently owns. After running the portfolio construction model, the quant trader generates the new target portfolio weights, shown in the New Target Portfolio column. The difference between the two indicates the trades that now need to be executed, which is the job of the execution algorithm. The execution algorithm takes the required trades and, using various other inputs such as the urgency with which the trades need to be executed and the dynamics of the liquidity in the markets, executes trades in an efficient and low-cost manner.

EXHIBIT 2.2   Moving from an Existing Portfolio to a New Target Portfolio

	Current Portfolio	New Target Portfolio	Trades to Execute
S&P500 Index	Short 30%	Short 25%	Buy to Cover 5%
EUROSTOXX Index	Long 20%	Long 25%	Buy 5%
U.S. 10-Year Treasury Notes	Long 40%	Long 25%	Sell 15%
German 10-Year Bunds	Short 10%	Short 25%	Sell Short 15%

The structure shown in Exhibit 2.1 is by no means universal. For example, many quant strategies are run without a transaction cost model, a portfolio construction model, or an execution model. Others combine various components of these models. One can build whatever risk requirements and constraints are considered necessary into the alpha model itself. Another variation is to create more recursive connections among the pieces. Some traders capture data about their actual executions and utilize these data to improve their transaction cost models. However, Exhibit 2.1 is useful because, for the most part, it captures the various discrete functions within a quant trading system, regardless of whether they are organized precisely in this manner.

Exhibit 2.1 captures only part of the work of the quant trader because it considers only the live production trading system and ignores two key pieces required to build it and run it: data and research. Black boxes are inert and useless without data—accurate data, moreover. Quant traders build input/output models that take inputs (data), process this information, and then produce trading decisions. For example, a trader utilizing a trend-following strategy usually requires price data to determine what the trend is. Without data he would have nothing to do, because he'd never be able to identify the trends he intends to follow. As such, data are the lifeblood of a quant and determine much about their strategies. Given data, quants can perform research, which usually involves some form of testing or simulation. Through research, the quant can ascertain whether and how a quant strategy works. We also note that each of the other modules in our schematic, when built correctly, usually requires a great deal of research. We can therefore redraw our diagram to include these other critical pieces, as shown in Exhibit 2.3.

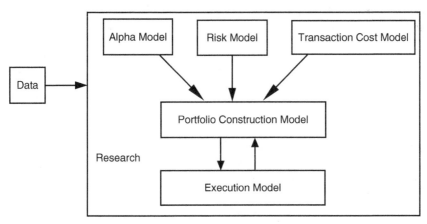

EXHIBIT 2.3 The Black Box Revealed

2.3   SUMMARY

Quants are perhaps not so mysterious as is generally supposed. They tend to start with ideas that any reasonable observer of the markets might also have, but rather than using anecdotal, experiential evidence—or worse, simply assuming that their ideas are true—quants use market data to feed a research process to determine whether their ideas in fact hold true over time. Once they have arrived at a satisfactory strategy, they build their strategy into a quant system. These systems take the emotion out of investing and instead impose a disciplined implementation of the idea that was tested. But this should not be read as minimizing the importance of human beings in the quant trading process. They come up with ideas, test strategies, and decide which ones to use, what kinds of instruments to trade, at what speed, and so on. Humans also tend to control a "panic button," which allows them to reduce risk if they determine that markets are behaving in some way that is outside the scope of their models' capabilities.

Quant strategies are widely viewed by investors as being opaque and incomprehensible. Even those who do focus on this niche tend to spend most of their time understanding the core of the strategy, its alpha model. But we contend that there are many other parts of the quant trading process that deserve to be understood and evaluated. Transaction cost models help determine the correct turnover rate for a strategy and risk models help keep the strategy from betting on the wrong exposures. Portfolio construction models balance the conflicting desires to generate returns, expend the right amount on transaction costs, manage risk, and deliver a target portfolio to execution models, which implement the portfolio model's decisions. All this activity is fed by data and driven by research. From afar, we have begun to shed light on the black box.

Next, in Part Two, we will dissect each of these modules, making our way methodically through the inside of the black box. At the end of each of these chapters, as a reminder of the structure of a quant system and of our progress, we will indicate the topic just completed by removing the shading from it.

NOTES

1. Frank Ahrens, "For Wall Street's Math Brains, Miscalculations," WashingtonPost .com, August 21, 2007, p. A01.
2. Roddy Boyd, "Not So Smart Now," NewYorkPost.com, August 19, 2007.
3. Marcia Vickers, "The Swensen Plan," Money.CNN.com, February 24, 2009.
4. Michael R. Pitts, *Famous Movie Detectives III* (Lanham, MD: Scarecrow Press, 2004), p. 265.

PART TWO

Inside the Black Box

CHAPTER 3

Alpha Models: How Quants Make Money

Prediction is very difficult, especially about the future.

—Niels Bohr

Having surveyed it from the outside, we begin our journey *through* the black box by understanding the heart of the actual trading systems that quants use. This first piece of a quant trading system is its *alpha model*, which is the part of the model that is looking to make money and is where much of the research process is focused. *Alpha*, the spelled-out version of the Greek letter α, generally is used as a way to quantify the *skill* of an investor or the return she delivers independently of the moves in the broader market. By conventional definition, alpha is the portion of the investor's return *not* due to the market benchmark, or, in other words, the value added (or lost) solely because of the manager. The portion of the return which can be attributed to market factors is then referred to as beta. For instance, if a manager is up 12 percent and her respective benchmark is up 10 percent, a quick back-of-the-envelope analysis would show that her alpha, or value added, is +2 percent (this assumes that the beta of her portfolio was exactly 1). The flaw with this approach to computing alpha is that it could be a result of luck, or it could be because of skill. Obviously, any trader will be interested in making skill the dominant driver of the difference between her returns and the benchmark's. Alpha models are merely a systematic approach to adding skill to the investment process in order to make profits. For example, a trend-following trader's ability to systematically identify trends that will persist into the future represents one type of skill that can generate profits.

Our definition of alpha—which I stress is not conventional—is *skill in timing the selection and/or sizing of portfolio holdings*. A pursuit of alpha holds as a core premise that no instrument is inherently good or bad, and therefore no instrument is worth always owning or perpetually shorting. The trend follower determines *when* to buy and sell various instruments, as does the value trader. Each of these is a type of alpha. In the first case, alpha is generated from the skill in identifying trends, which allows the trend follower to know when it is good to be long or short a given instrument. Similarly, a value trader does not say that a given stock is cheap now and therefore is worth owning in perpetuity. In fact, if a stock is always cheap, it is almost certainly *not* worth owning, because its valuation never improves for the investor. When Warren Buffett decided to buy bank stocks during the 2008 financial crisis, after their shares had plunged, he was implying that it was a good time, with the odds stacked in his favor, to make that bet. The idea behind value investing is to buy a stock when it is undervalued and to sell it when it is fairly valued or overvalued. Again, this represents an effort to time the stock.

A somewhat major shift in the marketplace that has occurred over the past 20 years, but which has only become worthy of a name in this context, is the gradual shift of certain strategies from what would be called "alpha" to something else—"risk premia" or "smart beta," being the two most common alternative monikers. But this isn't just an issue of "a rose by any other name." For example, many quants would now consider a longer-term (by which we mean several months to a year) trend/momentum strategy to be more of a risk factor than a source of alpha, even though these strategies are, in fact attempting to generate returns from skill at the timing of the selection, and/or sizing of positions. Perhaps the industry is recognizing a continuum of alpha—there are attempts to simply capture the market without any timing; there are attempts to capture some relatively small amount of skill at timing; and then there are other attempts to capture returns that derive from great and very hard-won skill.

The software that a quant builds and uses to conduct this timing systematically is known as an *alpha model*, though there are many synonyms for this term: forecast, factor, alpha, model, strategy, estimator, or predictor. All successful alpha models are designed to have some "edge," which allows them to anticipate the future with enough accuracy that, after allowing for being wrong at least sometimes and for the cost of trading, they can still make money. In a sense, of the various parts of a quant strategy, the alpha model is the optimist, focused on making money by predicting the future.

To make money, generally some risk, or exposure, must be accepted. By utilizing a strategy, we directly run the risk of losing money when the environment for that strategy is adverse. Returning to the inimitable Warren Buffett, he has beaten the market over the long term, and this differential is (conventionally) a measure of his alpha. But there have been times when he struggled to add value, as he did during the dot-com bubble of the late 1990s. His strategy was out of favor, and his underperformance during this period reflected this fact. In the case of an alpha model, the same holds true: whatever exposures they take on are rewarding if they are in favor, and are costly if they are out of favor. This chapter will address the kinds of alpha models that exist and the ways that quants actually use the forecasts their models make.

3.1 TYPES OF ALPHA MODELS: THEORY-DRIVEN AND DATA-DRIVEN

An important and not widely understood fact is that there are only a small number of trading strategies that exist for someone seeking alpha. But these basic strategies can be implemented in many ways, making it possible to create an incredible diversity of strategies from a limited set of core ideas. This distinction between the idea and how it is implemented is important to understand. Let's take, for example, the idea of correlation. When we discuss correlation, we are really discussing the core concept of *similarity*. But there are many ways to measure similarity—Pearson's rho and Kendall's tau, to name a couple. Each of these is an implementation of the idea of measuring similarity. In many cases, these metrics of similarity, these different implementations, will yield fairly similar results. But not always. For example, Pearson's rho is calcultating the extent to which two variables are moving together at a constant rate—the shape of such a relationship is a straight line. The more the scatterplot of these two variables looks like a straight line (irrespective of the slope), the more indicative Pearson's will be to describe their similarity. Kendall's tau, however, is a *ranked correlation* measure. It is concerned with the extent to which an increase in the first variable is associated with an increase (or decrease) in the second variable. In this case, things are more similar when it can be said that the rankings of the observations align, even if that relationship isn't constant. You can see the difference between these two implementations of the concept of similarity in Exhibit 3.1.

In this example, I created two arbitrary time series of 30 datapoints each. Using Pearson's rho, we compute a correlation coefficient of 0.72. Using Kendall's tau, the correlation coefficient is 0.53. As you can see, there are two trendlines, the two dotted lines on the graph. One is a linear trendline, while the other is polynomial (order 2). You can see that there is in fact a mildly parabolic shape to the relationship between these two variables. Kendall's, in this case, captures that nonlinearity in a way that Pearson's does not.

When to use either (or both) of these metrics is a judgment that the practitioner makes. And it is quite analogous to the kinds of decisions that

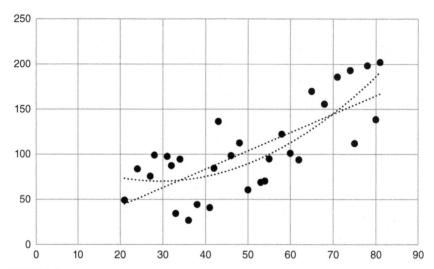

EXHIBIT 3.1   Linearity of a Relationship

quant researchers have to make throughout the investment process—recall, we can't just ask our computer "how similar are apples and oranges?" If we want to ask such a poorly defined question, we either need to give the computer all the relevant features (and deciding what these are is up to the researcher) or give it the tools to figure out the relevant features itself (as in the case of generative AI). But in conventional practice, we would need to specify what apples are, what oranges are, and what we mean, exactly (by formula, embodied into code) by "similar."

With this distinction between concept and implementation in mind, we can tackle another foundational aspect of understanding quant trading strategies: we must first understand the two main approaches quants take on science.

Because many quants are trained first in the sciences and only later in finance, quants' scientific backgrounds frequently determine the approach they take to trading over their entire careers. The two major branches of science, which also serve as a helpful way to differentiate scientists, are theoretical and empirical. *Theoretical scientists* try to make sense of the world around them by hypothesizing *why* it is the way it is. This is the kind of science with which people are most familiar and interact most. For example, viable, controllable, long-distance airplanes exist largely because engineers apply theories of aerodynamics. *Empirical scientists* believe that enough observations of the world can allow them to predict future patterns of behavior, even if there is no hypothesis to rationalize the behavior in an intuitive way. In other words, knowledge comes from experience. The Human Genome Project is one of many important examples of the applications of empirical science, mapping human traits to the sequences of chemical base pairs that make up human DNA. More recently, Chat-GPT is a different sort of empirical science experiment focused on teaching computers to use language as naturally as a human.

The distinction between theoretical and empirical science is germane to quantitative trading in that there are also these two kinds of quant traders. The first, and by far the more common, are theory-driven traders. They start with observations of the markets, think of a generalized theory that could explain the observed behavior, then rigorously test it with market data to see if the theory is shown to be either untrue or supported by the outcome of the test. In quant trading, most of these theories would make sense to you or me and would seem sensible when explained to friends at cocktail parties. For example, "cheap stocks outperform expensive stocks" is a theory that many people hold. This explains the existence of countless "value" funds. Once precisely defined, this theory can be tested.

The second kind of scientist, in a growing minority, believes that correctly performed empirical observation and analysis of the data can obviate the need for theory. Such a scientist's theory, in short, is that there are recognizable patterns in the data that can be detected with careful application of the right techniques. Again, the example of the Human Genome Project is instructive. The scientists in the Human Genome Project did not believe that it was necessary to theorize which genes were responsible for particular human traits. Rather, scientists merely theorized that the relationships between genes and traits can be mapped using statistical techniques, and they proceeded to do exactly that. Empirical scientists are sometimes derisively (and sometimes just as a matter of fact) labeled *data miners*. They don't especially care if they can name their theories and instead attempt to use data analysis techniques to uncover behaviors in the market that aren't intuitively obvious. In the era of generative AI, it is likely that we will see a more rapid increase in the use of data-driven (most frequently referred to as "Machine Learning") approaches to creating alpha models.

It is worthwhile to note that theory-driven scientists (and quants) are also reliant on observations (data) to derive theories in the first place. Just like the empiricists, they, too, believe that something one can observe in the data will be repeatable in the future. Empiricists, however, are less sensitive to whether their human minds can synthesize a "story" to explain the data even if, in the process, they risk finding relationships or patterns in the data that are entirely spurious. And they also generally know that you have to be careful about which data you present to your machine learning algorithm from which to learn. If you are trying to make an algorithm to master chess, you would naturally let it learn from games between grandmasters. You would likely not show it anything to do with checkers or backgammon. Underlying this is a theory: you want only relevant information to determine your data-driven models.

3.2 THEORY-DRIVEN ALPHA MODELS

Most quants (and investors generally) you will come across are theory-driven. They start with some economically feasible explanation of why the markets behave in a certain way and test these theories to see whether they can be used to predict the future with any success. Many quants think that their theories are somewhat unique to them, which is part of why so many of them are so secretive. But this turns out, almost always, to be a delusion. Meanwhile, many outside the quant trading world believe that the kinds of strategies quants use are complex and based on complicated mathematical formulae. This generally also turns out to be false.

In fact—and in defiance of both the presumed need for secrecy and the claims that what quants do cannot be understood by those without doctorate degrees—most of what theory-driven quants do can be relatively easily fitted into one of eight classes of phenomena: trend, mean reversion, technical sentiment, value/yield, growth/sentiment, supply/demand, quality, and tactical/events. It is worth noting that the kinds of strategies that quants utilize are actually exactly the same as those that can be utilized by discretionary traders seeking alpha. These eight categories can be further classified by the data that they use: price-related data and fundamental data. As we will see throughout this book, understanding the inputs to a strategy is extremely important to understanding the strategy itself. If you have a refrigerator full of vegetables, you can make a lot of things, but not fried chicken.

The first two categories of strategies, *trend* and *mean reversion*, are based on price-related data. *Technical sentiment* strategies are less commonly found, but can be thought of as a third class of price-based strategies. The remaining five strategies, *value/yield, growth/sentiment, supply/demand, quality*, and *tactical/events*, are based on fundamental and/or fundamental sentiment data.

The most successful quants utilize more than one type of alpha model in conjunction, but to gain a proper understanding of these strategies, we will first break them down individually and discuss the combination of them afterward. Exhibit 3.2 provides a summary and outline for understanding the types of alpha models that quants use.

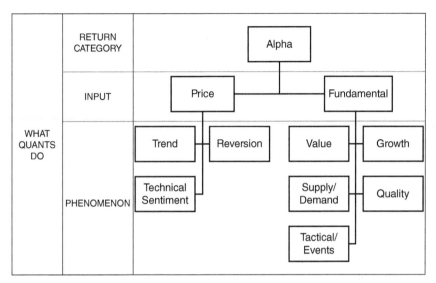

EXHIBIT 3.2 A Taxonomy of Theory-Driven Alpha Models

3.2.1 Strategies Utilizing Price-Related Data

First, we will focus on alpha models that utilize price-related data, which is mostly about the prices of various instruments or other information that generally comes from an exchange (such as trading volume). Quants who seek to forecast prices and to profit from such forecasts are likely to be exploiting one of two kinds of phenomena. The first is that an established trend will continue, and the second is that the trend will reverse. In other words, the price can either keep going in the direction it was going already, or it can go in the opposite direction. We call the first idea *trend following* or *momentum*, and we call the second idea *counter-trend* or *mean reversion*. A third idea will be explored as well, which we refer to as *technical sentiment*, which is far less common, but which deserves some discussion.

3.2.1.1 Trend Following Trend following is based on the theory that markets sometimes move for long enough in a given direction that one can identify this trend and ride it. The economic rationale for the existence of trends is based on the idea of consensus-building among market participants. Imagine that there is uncertainty about the medium-term outlook for the U.S. economy. The labor picture looks fine, but inflation is running rampant and trade deficits are blooming. On the other hand, consumers are still spending and housing is strong. This conflicting information is a regular state of affairs for economies and markets, so that some of the information available appears favorable and some unfavorable. In our example, let's further imagine that the bears have it right—that in fact inflation will get out of control and cause problems for the economy. The earliest adopters of this idea place their trades in accordance with it by, for example, selling bonds short. As more and more data come out to support their thesis and as a growing mass of market participants adopts the same thesis, the price of U.S. bonds may take a considerable amount of time to move to its new "equilibrium," and this slow migration from one equilibrium to the next is the core opportunity that the trend follower looks to capture.

It bears mentioning that there is an alternate explanation of why trends happen; it is affectionately known as the *greater fools theory*. The idea here is that, because people believe in trends, they tend to start buying anything that's been going up and selling anything that's been going down, which itself perpetuates the trend. The key is always to sell your position to someone more "foolish," and thereby to avoid being the last fool. Either theoretical explanation, coupled with the evidence in markets, seems a valid enough reason to believe in trends.

Trend followers typically look for a "significant" move in a given direction in an instrument. They bet that, once a significant move has occurred, it will persist because this significant move is a likely sign of a growing consensus (or a parade of fools). They prefer this significance because a great risk of trend-following strategies is "whipsawing" action in markets, which describes a somewhat rapid up-and-down pattern in prices. If, in other words, you buy the S&P because it was up over the past three months (and, symmetrically, sell short the S&P every time it was down over the three months prior), you need the trend to keep going in the same direction *after* the three-month "observation" period. If the S&P reverses direction roughly every three months, a strategy such as this would lose money on more or less every trade over that period. There are many ways of defining what kind of move is significant, and the most common terms used to describe this act of definition are "filtering" and "conditioning." This turns out to be an important source of differentiation among the various players who pursue trend-following strategies and will be explored further in Section 3.4.

Perhaps the most obvious and well-known example of a strategy that depends on trends is in the world of futures trading, also known as managed futures or commodities trading advisors (CTAs). Exhibit 3.3 illustrates the downward trend in equities that began in the fourth quarter of 2007. One way to define a trend for trading purposes, known as a *moving average crossover* indicator, is to compare the average price of the index over a shorter time period (e.g., 60 days) to that of a longer time period (e.g., 200 days). When the shorter-term average price is below the longer-term

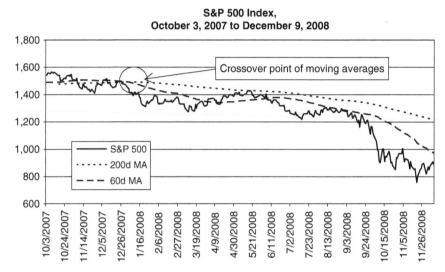

EXHIBIT 3.3 S&P 500 Trend

average price, the index is said to be in a negative trend, and when the shorter-term average price is above the longer-term average, the index is in a positive trend. As such, a trend follower using this kind of strategy might have gotten short the S&P Index around the end of 2007, as indicated by the point at which the two moving averages cross over each other, and remained short for most or all of 2008.

Some of the largest quantitative asset managers engage in trend following in futures markets, which also happens to be the oldest of all quant trading strategies, as far as I can tell. Ed Seykota built the first computerized version of a mechanical trend-following strategy. This was based on the program Richard Donchian created some years earlier, utilizing punch cards on an IBM mainframe in 1970, a year after he graduated from MIT. He was a strong believer in doing ongoing research, and over the course of his first 12 years, he turned $5000 into $15,000,000. He went on to a highly successful three-decades-long career, over which he annualized some 60 percent returns.[1]

Larry Hite represents another interesting example of an early practitioner of trend following. Previously, Hite was a rock promoter in New York who, after experiencing three separate nightclub shootings on a single night, decided a change of career was in order. In 1972, he coauthored a paper that suggested how game theory could be used to trade the futures markets using quantitative systems.[2] After turning his attention to trend following, he created Mint Investments in 1981 with two partners; it became the first hedge fund to manage $1 billion and the first fund to partner with the Man Group, which effectively put Man into the hedge fund business. Mint annualized north of 30 percent per year, net of fees, for its investors over the 13 years it existed under Hite's stewardship. Notably, Mint made some 60 percent in 1987, in no small part by being on the right side of the crash that October.[3]

Lest it seem like this is an overly rosy picture of trend following, it should be stated clearly: These strategies come with a great deal of risk alongside their lofty returns. The typical successful trend follower earns less than one point of return for every point of downside risk delivered. In other words, to earn 50 percent per year, the investor must be prepared to suffer a loss greater than 50 percent at some point. In short, the returns of this strategy are streaky and highly variable.

This is not only true of trend following. Indeed, each of the major classes of alpha described in this chapter is subject to relatively long periods of poor returns. This is because the behaviors they seek to profit from in the markets are not ever-present but rather are unstable and episodic. The idea is to make enough money in the good times and manage the downside well enough in the bad times to make the whole exercise worthwhile.

Perhaps quant trading's most important trend follower in terms of lasting impact was a firm called Axcom, which later became Renaissance Technologies. Elwyn Berlekamp, a Ph.D. in engineering from MIT, in 1986 began to consult for Axcom regarding strategy development. Axcom had been struggling during those years, and Berlekamp bought a controlling interest. In 1989, after doing considerable research, Axcom resumed trading with a new and improved strategy. For its first year, the firm was up 55 percent after charging 5 percent management fees and 20 percent incentive fees. At the end of 1990, Berlekamp sold his interest to Jim Simons for a sixfold profit, which might still have been one of the worst trades in history. Renaissance, as the firm was called by then, is now the most successful quant trading firm and probably the most impressive trading firm of any kind. It has evolved a great deal from the trend-following strategies it used in the mid-1980s and even from the more sophisticated futures strategies it employed in the early 1990s. It stopped accepting new money with less than $300 million in 1992 and went on to compound this money to approximately $5.5 billion some 10 years later, despite eye-popping 5 percent management fees and 44 percent incentive fees. They have annualized approximately 35 percent per year net of these fees, from 1989 onward, and perhaps most astonishingly, have gotten *better* over the years, despite the increased competition in the space and their own significantly larger capital base.[4]

It is worth pointing out that quants are not the only ones who have a fondness for trend-following strategies. It has always been and will likely remain one of the more important ways in which traders of all stripes go about their business. One can find trend following in the roots of the infamous tulip mania of the Dutch in the seventeenth century, or in the dot-com bubble of the late twentieth century, neither of which is likely to have been caused by quants. And, of course, many discretionary traders have a strong preference to buy what's been "hot" and sell what's been "cold."

3.2.1.2 Mean Reversion When prices move, as we have already said, they move in either the same direction they've been going or in the opposite. We have just described trend following, which bets on the former. Now we turn our attention to mean reversion strategies, which bet on prices moving in the opposite direction than that which had been the prevailing trend.

The theory behind mean reversion strategies is that there exists a center of gravity around which prices fluctuate, and it is possible to identify both this center of gravity and what fluctuation is sufficient to warrant making a trade. As in the case of trend following, there are several valid rationales for the existence of mean reversion. First, there are sometimes short-term imbalances among buyers and sellers due simply to liquidity requirements that lead to an instrument being "over-bought" or "over-sold." To return to the example mentioned earlier, imagine that a stock has been added to a well-followed index, such as the S&P 500. This forces any fund that is attempting to track the index to run out and buy the stock, and, in the short term, there might not be enough sellers at the old price to accommodate them. Therefore, the price moves up somewhat abruptly, which increases the probability that the price will reverse again at some point, once the excess demand from index buyers has subsided. Another rationale to explain the existence of mean-reverting behavior is that market participants are not all aware of each other's views and actions, and as they each place orders that drive a price toward its new equilibrium level, the price can overshoot due to excess supply or demand at any given time.

Regardless of the cause of the short-term imbalance between supply and demand, mean reversion traders are frequently being paid to provide liquidity because they are bucking current trends. This is sometimes explicitly true in terms of their execution techniques (which we will discuss in more detail in Chapters 7 and 14). But regardless of execution tactics, mean reversion traders are indeed betting against momentum, and bear the risk of adverse selection.

Interestingly, trend and mean reversion strategies are not necessarily at odds with each other. Longer-term trends can occur, even as smaller oscillations around these trends occur in the shorter term. In fact, some quants use both of these strategies in conjunction. Mean reversion traders must identify the current "mean" or "equilibrium" and then must determine what amount of divergence from that equilibrium is sufficient to warrant a trade.

As in the case of trend following, there are a large number of ways of defining the mean and the reversal. It is worth noting that when discretionary traders implement mean reversion strategies, they are typically known as *contrarians*.

Perhaps the best-known strategy based on the mean reversion concept is *statistical arbitrage* (*stat arb*, for short), which bets on the convergence of the prices of similar stocks whose prices have diverged. While Ed Thorp, founder of Princeton/Newport Partners was probably one of the earliest quantitative equity traders, the trading desk of Nunzio Tartaglia at Morgan Stanley was a pioneer of stat arb and would prove to have a lasting impact on the world of finance. Tartaglia's team included scientists like Gerry Bamberger and David Shaw, and together they developed and evolved a strategy that was based on the relative prices of similar stocks. Stat arb ushered in an important change in world-view, one that focused on whether company A was over- or under-valued *relative to* company B rather than whether company A was simply cheap or expensive *in itself*. This important evolution would lead to the creation of many strategies based on forecasts of relative attractiveness, which is a topic we will address in greater detail shortly.

Exhibit 3.4 shows a simplified example of the mean-reverting behavior evident between similar instruments, in this case, American Airlines (AAL) and Delta Airlines (DAL). As you can see, the spread between these two companies oscillates rather consistently in a reasonably narrow range for

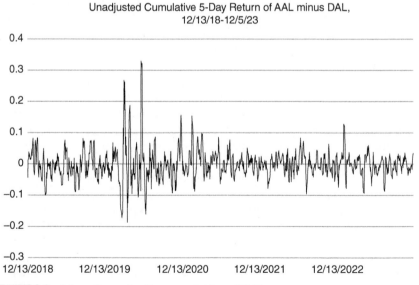

EXHIBIT 3.4　Mean Reversion Between AAL and DAL

long periods. This effect allows a trader to wait for significant divergences and then bet on a reversion back to the equilibrium level.

What you also can observe in this picture is the big pitfall of mean reversion strategies: periods like March 2020 can knock you out entirely. Spreads as severe as what were observed for around six months around the outbreak of the pandemic had not been observed before, nor since. Avoiding these events is a crucial component to success in mean reversion trading.

Trend and mean reversion strategies represent a large portion of all quant trading. After all, price data are plentiful and always changing, presenting the quant with many opportunities to trade. It may be interesting to note that trend and mean reversion, though they are theoretically opposite ideas, both seem to work. How is this possible? Largely, it's possible because of different timeframes. It is obviously correct that both strategies can't possibly be made to be exactly opposite while both making money at the same time. However, there is no reason to create both strategies to be exactly the same. Trends tend to occur over longer time horizons, whereas reversions tend to happen over shorter-term time horizons. Exhibit 3.5 shows this effect in action. You can see that there are indeed longer-term trends and shorter-term mean reversions that take place. In fact, you can also see that the strategies are likely to work well in different regimes. From 2000 to 2002 and again in 2008, a trend strategy likely exhibits better performance, since the markets were trending very strongly during these periods. From 2003 to 2007, mean-reverting behavior was more prevalent. Yet both strategies are likely to have made money for the period as a whole. This can also be examined on other time horizons, and in some cases, mean reversion strategies can work as the longer-term indicator, while momentum can be used as a faster indicator.

3.2.1.3 Technical Sentiment
An interesting third class of price-related strategies tracks investor sentiment—expressed through price, volume, and volatility behaviors—as an indicator of future returns. In some instances, a high degree of positive sentiment in some instrument would indicate that the instrument is already overbought and therefore ready to decline. In others, high positive sentiment would indicate that the instrument has support to move higher. In still others, sentiment is only used as a conditioning variable (this concept will be discussed in more detail in Section 3.4.6), for example, by utilizing a trend-following strategy only if the volumes that were associated with the price movements were significant, whereas a low-volume trend might be ignored. It is this last use of sentiment data that is most common. There are, however, several examples of technical sentiment strategies that can be thought of as standalone ways to forecast future direction.

First is to look at the options markets to determine sentiment on the underlying. There are two separate "straightforward" ideas to explore here.

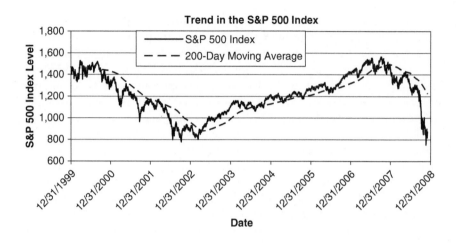

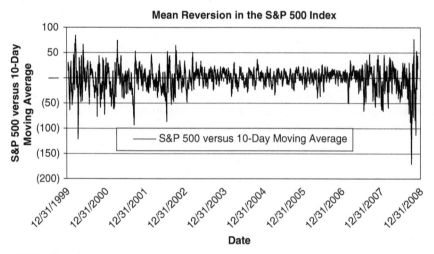

EXHIBIT 3.5 Trend and Reversion Coexisting

One is to look at the volume of puts and calls, and to use this as an indicator of sentiment. If puts have higher volumes relative to calls than they
normally do, it might be an indicator that investors are worried about a
downturn. If puts have lower volumes versus calls than normal, it might be
a bullish sentiment indicator. A second example of options-based sentiment
in equities utilizes the implied volatilities of puts versus calls. It is natural
to see some level of difference in the implied volatilities of puts versus calls.
This is partially in recognition of the habit of stocks to move down quickly
and up slowly, which would indicate that downside volatility is higher than

upside volatility, which in turn causes the seller of a put option to demand a higher price (and therefore implied volatility) than would be demanded by the seller of a call option that is equally far out-of-the-money (or in the case that they are both at the money). If one analyzes the historical ratio of put volatility and call volatility, there will likely be some natural ratio (greater than one, due to the phenomenon just described about upside and downside volatility), and divergences from this natural level might be treated as indicative of sentiment. A related idea would be to use implied volatility or a proxy (e.g., credit default swaps, or CDS for short) as an indicator of investor sentiment.

A second example of a technical sentiment strategy analyzes trading volume, open interest, or other related type of inputs as an indicator of future prices. At the shortest timeframes, some higher frequency traders evaluate the "shape" of the limit order book to determine near-term sentiment. The shape of the order book includes factors such as the size of bids or offers away from the mid-market relative to the size at the best bid/offer, or the aggregate size of bids versus offers. For slightly longer-term strategies, analyses of volume can include looking at the trading volume, the turnover (trading versus float), open interest, or other similar measures of trading activity. As I mentioned at the outset of this section, what to do with this kind of information remains open to debate. It can be used as a contrarian indicator (i.e., high volume or high turnover stocks are expected to underperform, while low volume or low turnover stocks are expected to outperform) or as a positive indicator. Most of the research I have reviewed, however, focuses on the contrarian approach.

3.2.2 Strategies Utilizing Fundamental Data

Most strategies utilizing fundamental data in their alpha models can be easily classified into one of three groups: value/yield, growth, or quality. Though these ideas are frequently associated with the analysis of equities, it turns out that one can apply the exact same logic to any kind of instrument. A bond, a currency, a commodity, an option, or a piece of real estate can be bought or sold because it offers attractive value, growth, or quality characteristics. While fundamentals have long been part of the discretionary trader's repertoire, quantitative fundamental strategies are relatively young.

In quantitative equity trading and in some forms of quantitative futures or macro trading, much is owed to Eugene Fama and Kenneth French (known better collectively as Fama-French). In the early 1990s, they produced a series of papers that got quants thinking about kinds of factors that quants frequently use in strategies utilizing fundamental data. In particular, "The Cross Section of Expected Stock Returns" coalesced more than a decade of prior work in the area of using quantitative fundamental factors to predict stock prices and advanced the field dramatically.[5] Fama and French found, simply, that stocks' betas to the market are not sufficient to explain the differences in the returns of various stocks. Rather, combining betas with historical data about the book-to-price ratio and the market capitalization of the stocks was a better determinant of future returns. It is somewhat ironic that quantitative investing owes so much to Eugene Fama, because Fama's most famous work advanced the idea that markets are efficient. An efficient market cannot be predicted—all information is already accurately and fully incorporated into the current market price. It is clear that our capital markets do not meet this criterion.

3.2.2.1 Value/Yield Value strategies are well known and are usually associated with equity trading, though such strategies can be used in other markets as well. There are many metrics that people use to describe value in various asset classes, but most of them (especially in equities) end up being ratios of some fundamental factor versus the price of the instrument, such as the price-to-earnings (P/E) ratio. Quants tend to invert such ratios, keeping prices in the denominator. An inverted P/E ratio, or an E/P ratio, is also known as *earnings yield*. Note that investors have long done this with dividends, hence the *dividend yield*, another commonly used measure of value. The basic concept of value strategies is that the higher the yield, the cheaper the instrument is considered to be. The benefit of the conversion of ratios to yields is that it allows for much easier and more consistent analysis.

Let's take earnings as an example: Earnings can (and frequently do) range from large negative numbers to large positive numbers and everywhere in between. If we take two stocks that are both priced at $20, but one has $1 of earnings while the other has $2 of earnings, it's easy to see that the first has a 20 P/E and the second has a 10 P/E, so the second looks cheaper on this metric. But imagine instead that the first has −$1 in earnings, whereas the second has −$2 in earnings. Now, these stocks have P/Es of −20 and −10. Having a −20 P/E seems worse than having a −10 P/E, but it's clearly better to only have $1 of negative earnings than $2. Thus, using a P/E ratio is misleading in the case of negative earnings. In the case that a company happens to have produced exactly $0 in earnings, the P/E ratio is simply undefined, since we would be dividing by $0. Because ratios with price in the numerator and some fundamental figure in the denominator exhibit this sort of misbehavior, quants tend to use the inverted yield forms of these same ratios. This idea is demonstrated in Exhibit 3.6, which shows that the E/P ratio is well behaved for any level of earnings per share for a hypothetical stock with a price greater than $1 (in the example, we used $20 per share as the stock price). By contrast, the P/E ratio is rather poorly

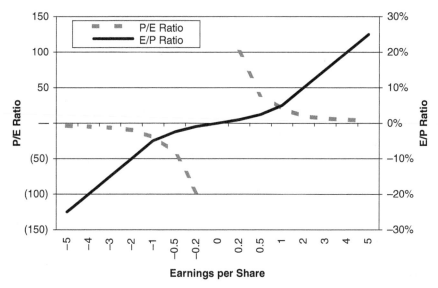

EXHIBIT 3.6 P/E versus E/P ("Earnings Yield")

behaved and does not lend itself well to analysis and is not even properly defined when earnings per share are zero.

There is a bigger theme implied by the example of the treatment of earnings data by quants. Many fundamental quantities are computed or quoted in ways that are not readily used in developing a systematic alpha. These quantities predated the use of computers to trade, and as a result, can have arbitrary definitions and distributions. Quants must transform such data into more usable, well-behaved variables that can lend themselves more readily to systematic trading applications.

Most often, value is thought of as a strategy that is defined by "buying cheap." But this strikes me as being too shallow a definition. In reality, the idea behind value investing is that markets tend to overestimate the risk in risky instruments and possibly to underestimate the risk in less risky ones. Therefore, it can pay off to own the more risky asset and/or sell the less risky asset. The argument for this theory is that sometimes instruments have a higher yield than is justified by their fundamentals simply because the market is requiring a high yield for that kind of instrument at the moment. An investor who can purchase this instrument while it has a high yield can profit from the movement over time to a more efficient, "fair" price. As it happens, instruments don't usually become cheap solely because their prices don't move while their fundamentals improve drastically. Rather, prices are more often the determinant of value than changing fundamentals, and in the case of a cheap instrument, this implies that the instrument's price must have fallen substantially. So in some sense, the value investor is being paid to take on the risk of standing in the way of momentum. Ray Ball, a professor of accounting at the University of Chicago's Booth School of Business, wrote a paper, "Anomalies in Relationships Between Securities' Yields and Yield-Surrogates," which echoes the idea that higher-yielding stocks—those with higher earnings yields—are likely those for which investors expect to receive higher returns and greater risks.[6]

When done on a relative basis, that is, buying the undervalued security and selling the overvalued one against it, this strategy is also known as a *carry trade*. One receives a higher yield from the long position and finances this with the short position, on which a lower yield must be paid. The spread between the yield received and the yield paid is the *carry*. For instance, one could sell short $1,000,000 of U.S. bonds and use the proceeds to buy $1,000,000 of higher-yielding Mexican bonds. Graham and Dodd, in their landmark book *Security Analysis*, propose that value trading offers investors a margin of safety. In many respects, this margin of safety can be seen clearly in the concept of carry. If nothing else happens, a carry trade offers an investor a baseline rate of return, which acts as the margin of safety Graham and Dodd were talking about.

Carry trading is an enormously popular kind of strategy for quants (and discretionary traders) in currencies, where the currency of a country with higher short-term yields is purchased against a short position in the currency of a country with relatively low short-term yields. For example, if the European Central Bank's target interest rate is set at 4.25 percent, whereas the U.S. Federal Reserve has set the Fed Funds rate at 2 percent, a carry trade would be to buy Euros against the U.S. dollar. This is a classic value trade because the net yield is 2.25 percent (4.25 percent gained on the Euro position, less 2 percent paid in U.S. interest), and this provides a margin of safety. If the trade doesn't work, the first 2.25 percent of the loss on it is eliminated by the positive carry. Similar strategies are employed in trading bonds. In fact, this was one of Long Term Capital Management's central trading ideas, until they imploded in 1998.

Note that, in currencies and in bonds, the connection between higher yields and higher risk is more widely understood than in equities. In other words, if some instrument has a higher yield than its peers, there may well be a good reason that investors demand this higher yield. The reason is usually that this instrument is more risky than its peers. This can naturally be seen in the juxtaposition of yields on government bonds, AAA-rated corporate bonds, and various lower-rated corporate bonds. As riskiness increases, so too do yields to compensate lenders.

Another important example of value trading is in equities, where many kinds of traders seek to define metrics of "cheapness," such as earnings before interest, taxes, depreciation, and amortization (EBITDA) versus enterprise value (EV) or book value to price. Book value per share versus price (*book yield* or *book-to-price*) is also a fairly common factor, as it has been among quants since Fama and French popularized it in their papers. Most quant equity traders who use value strategies are seeking relative value rather than simply making an assessment of whether a given stock is cheap or expensive. This strategy is commonly known as *quant long/short* (QLS). QLS traders tend to rank stocks according to their attractiveness based on various factors, such as value, and then buy the higher-ranked stocks while selling short the lower-ranked ones. For example, assume that we ranked the major integrated oil companies by the following hypothetical book-to-price ratios:

Company	Book-to-Price Ratio (Hypothetical) (%)
Marathon Oil (MRO)	95.2
ConocoPhillips (COP)	91.7
Chevron Corp. (CVX)	65.4
Exxon Mobil Corp. (XOM)	33.9

According to this metric, the higher-ranked stocks might be candidates for long positions, whereas the lower-ranked might be candidates for short positions. The presumption is that a stock with a higher book-to-price ratio might outperform stocks with lower book-to-price ratios over the coming quarters.

Value can be used to time any kind of instrument for which valuations can be validly measured. This is easier in instruments like individual equities, equity indices, currencies, and bonds. In the case of most commodities, value is usually thought of more as a "cheap/expensive" analysis, via concepts of the expected supplies of a commodity versus the expected demand for that commodity, rather than being focused on yield. There are classes of strategies in the futures markets (not specifically commodity futures, but most often in that group) which focus on yield explicitly as well. "Roll yield" is the spread between the price of a futures contract with some expiry date in the future, versus that of the spot (or that of a contract with a shorter-dated expiry). In "backward-dated" markets, spot prices are higher than futures contracts as they extend out into the calendar. Because there is a convergence of futures contracts up to the spot price, futures in this situation are considered to have positive roll yield. In "contango" markets, spot prices are lower than futures, and so the yield is considered negative.

3.2.2.2 Growth/Sentiment   Growth strategies seek to make predictions based on the asset in question's expected or historically observed level of economic growth. Some examples of such ideas could be gross domestic product (GDP) growth or earnings growth. That a given stock is a growth asset implies nothing about its valuation or yield. The theory here is that, all else being equal, it is better to buy assets that are experiencing rapid economic growth and/or to sell assets that are experiencing slow or negative growth. Some growth metrics, like the price/earnings-to-growth (PEG) ratio (PE ratio vs. EPS growth rate), are basically a forward-looking concept of value, that is, they compare growth expectations to value expectations to see whether a given instrument is fairly pricing in the positive or negative growth that the trader believes the asset will likely experience. If you expect an asset to grow rapidly but the market has already priced the asset to account for that growth, there is no growth trade to be made. In fact, if the market has priced in a great deal more growth than you expect, it might even be reasonable to short the instrument. But certainly many forms of growth trading are simply focused on buying rapidly growing assets regardless of price and selling assets with stagnant or negative growth, even if they are very cheap (or offer high yields) already.

The justification for growth investing is that growth is typically experienced in a trending manner, either due to changes in market share or to growth in the sector overall. In the case of a company, you could see the case being made that a strong grower is quite likely to be in the process of winning market share from its weaker-growing competitors. This process unfolds over time. Growth investors try to be early in the process of identifying growth and, hence, early in capturing the implied increase in the future stature of a company. We can see examples of both macroeconomic growth strategies and microeconomic growth strategies in the quant trading world. At the macro level, some foreign exchange trading concepts are predicated on the idea that it is good to be long currencies of countries that are experiencing relatively strong growth, because it is likely that these will have higher relative interest rates in the future than weaker-growth or recession economies, which makes this a sort of forward-looking carry trade.

In the quant equity world, the QLS community frequently also utilizes signals relating to growth to help diversify their alpha models. Note that an important variant of growth trading utilized by a wide variety of quants and discretionary equity traders focuses on analysts' earnings estimate revisions (or other aspects of analyst sentiment, including price targets and recommendation levels). Sell-side analysts working at various brokerage houses publish their estimates and release occasional reports about the companies they cover. The thesis is identical to any other growth strategy, but the idea is to try to get an early glimpse of a company's growth by using the analysts' expectations rather than simply waiting for the company itself to report its official earnings results. Because this strategy depends on the views of market analysts or economists, it is called a *sentiment-based strategy*. The quant community does not universally agree that sentiment-based strategies, such as the estimate revision idea just mentioned, are anything more than variants of growth strategies, but it is my experience that these two are highly enough correlated in practice to warrant their being treated as close cousins. After all, too often Wall Street analysts' future estimates of growth look a lot like extrapolations of recent historical growth.

There are also significant numbers of alternative datasets, most of which focus on growth-related alphas. Rather than constituting new types of signals, they're much better described as trying to achieve the same things as traditional datasets, but more accurately and/or more timely. Most of these datasets relate to estimations of key performance indicators (KPIs) of companies' revenues, costs and earnings. For example, if you can analyze credit card transaction data to get an early indication of how much consumers are spending at a store like the Gap, you might have a better chance of making a more accurate forecast of their quarterly financials than the Wall Street consensus. The reason these datasets do not pertain to value is that value strategies are primarily focused on ratios. Being able to forecast earnings for some company better than the market, for example, will not help you forecast the earnings yield of that company, because the price is required to compute the earnings yield. But what alt-data-based strategies are really betting on is that all the amount of growth baked into the current price is inaccurate—it'll either be more growth than expected, or less.

3.2.2.3 Supply/Demand In certain markets, especially commodities, supply and demand strategies are common. For example, it is easy to see that news of an OPEC production cut will have a positive impact on the price of oil. Likewise, news of an extra-cold winter foreshadows increased demand for heating oil and natural gas, which would be bullish for both commodities. Using weather forecast and satellite imagery data, for example, one can forecast supply for agricultural commodities as well, which in turn can inform forecasts for the prices of the relevant commodity futures. Such strategies can also be pursued in most any asset class where supply and/or demand data are available. In bonds, frequently new issuances are themselves interesting for future price, but the auctions also contain data that are used for forecasting purposes. And in equities, secondaries/new issuances, and buybacks can generate signals. In currencies, both fiat and digital, often monetary policy and its analog for digital issuances, can drive expectations for future price action. A subtle distinction between these strategies applied to commodities versus other asset classes is that we use supply and demand data related to the commodities to forecast the prices of instruments linked to the underlying asset (e.g., futures or options). Whereas in other asset classes, we would use supply and demand data related to the asset itself to forecast this same asset (e.g., using expected changes to the supply of shares of a stock to predict price changes of those same shares).

It bears mentioning that these strategies can and often do utilize alternative datasets, for example, weather data or satellite imagery data for the purpose of better assessing supply.

It is debatable whether supply and demand strategies are truly distinct from growth strategies. To be sure, reacting to or predicting demand seems a lot like the work of a growth strategy. But the supply part of the equation appears unlike any other fundamental strategies described here.

3.2.2.4 Quality The fourth kind of theory-driven fundamental alpha is what I call *quality*. A quality investor believes that, all else being equal, it is better to own instruments that are of high quality and better to sell or be short instruments of poor quality. The justification for this strategy is that capital safety is important, and neither growth nor value strategies really capture this concept. A strategy focused on owning higher-quality instruments may help protect an investor, particularly in a stressful market environment. Not coincidentally, these are frequently termed *flight-to-quality* environments. This kind of strategy is easily found in quant equity trading but not as commonly in macroeconomic types of quant trading, probably because, historically, countries were not thought of as being particularly risky. Given the unfolding crisis in Europe, we may begin to see quality models deployed in more macroeconomics-oriented strategies.

I generally find that quality signals fall into one of five categories. First is *leverage*, which would indicate that, based on some measurement of leverage, one should short higher-levered companies and go long less-levered companies, all else being equal. An example from the QLS world might look at the debt-to-equity ratios of stocks to help determine which ones to buy and sell, the idea being that less-leveraged companies are considered higher quality than more-leveraged companies, all else being equal.

A second kind of quality signal is *diversity of revenue sources*, which would find those companies or countries with more diverse sources of potential growth to be of higher quality than those with fewer sources. So, all else being equal, a company that makes money doing a wide variety of things for a variety of customers should be more stable than a company that makes exactly one kind of widget for some narrow purpose. A special case of this relates to the *volatility of revenues* (or, in the case of companies, profits). Here, taking the example of corporate earnings and stock prices, investors would prefer, all else being equal, to own companies whose earnings are more stable (less volatile) relative to companies whose earnings are less stable (more volatile).

A third type of quality signal is *management quality*, which would tend to buy companies or countries that are led by better teams and sell those with worse teams. A great article in *Vanity Fair* relates to this very kind of signal. Entitled, "Microsoft's Lost Decade," several key management missteps (according to the article's author) are highlighted as leading to Microsoft's fall from being the largest market capitalization company in the world to being a "barren wasteland."[7] More recently, one can observe the reaction of Tesla, Inc.'s shares to Elon Musk's purchase and management of Twitter. Tesla's shares reacted negatively as Musk focused more of his energy on the perceived distraction of Twitter. When he announced a new CEO to succeed him at Twitter, Tesla's shares rebounded. As you might expect, given the types of information involved, the data that drive strategies like these are less inherently quantitative and well-structured. We will dig into the issue of the so-called alternative datasets that often fuel fundamental sentiment strategies such as these in Chapter 8. However, there are some that are more readily quantitative in nature. For example, in companies' financial statements, one can consider changes in discretionary accruals (the idea being, the greater the increase in discretionary accruals, the more likely there are problems with the management's stewardship of the company).

A fourth type of quality strategy relates to *fraud risk*, which would indicate to buy companies or countries where the risk of fraud is low, and sell those where the risk is greater. An example of this kind of strategy from the QLS world is an *earnings quality* signal, which attempts to measure how close a company's true economic earnings from its day-to-day operations (as measured by, say, its free cash flow) are to the reported earnings-per-share numbers. Such strategies especially gained prominence in the wake of the accounting scandals of 2001 and 2002 (Enron and WorldCom, for example), which highlighted that sometimes publicly traded companies are run by folks who are trying harder to manage their financial statements than manage their companies.

A final type of strategy relates to the *sentiment* investors have regarding the quality of the issuer of an instrument (again, this can be a company or a country). Generally, quality-related sentiment strategies are focused on a forward-looking assessment of the four quality categories above. In other words, one has a prospective view of changes in leverage, revenue diversity, management quality, or fraud risk. However, this type of strategy is not particularly common, as the signals would appear very sporadically, and because there are relatively few sources of sentiment regarding quality, it is also quite difficult to backtest and achieve any kind of statistical significance. In recent years, the growth of the CDS markets has provided a much more regularly available source of quality-sentiment information. Some investors might also use implied volatility to serve this purpose, but implied volatilities go up because the market itself goes down, because growth expectations are lowered, because a company disappoints expectations on their earnings announcement, or for any number of other reasons unrelated to the quality of the company itself.

Quality's performance over time fluctuates greatly and is highly dependent on the market environment. In 2008, quality was a particularly successful factor in predicting the relative prices of banking stocks. In particular, some quality factors helped traders detect, avoid, and/or sell short those banks with the most leverage or the most exposure to mortgage-related businesses, thereby allowing these traders to avoid or even profit from the 2008 credit crisis. The aforementioned accounting scandals in the early 2000s also would have been profitable for quality signals. However, for all that these strategies profit when things are very dire, they tend to do poorly when the markets are performing well, and terribly when the equity markets go into a state of euphoria.

We now have a summary of the ways that theory-driven, alpha-focused traders (including quants) can make money. To recap, price information can be used for trend or mean reversion strategies, whereas fundamental information can be used for yield (better known as *value*), growth, or quality strategies. This is a useful framework for understanding quant strategies but also for understanding all alpha-seeking trading strategies. The framework proposed herein provides a menu of sorts, from which a particular quant may "order," creating his strategy. It is also a useful framework for quants themselves and can help them rationalize and group the signals they use into families. Quants sometimes fool themselves into thinking that there are a broader array of core alpha concepts than actually exist.

3.2.2.5 Tactical/Events Recent years have seen an increased frequency of high-stakes "one-off" events. The 2016 and 2020 U.S. presidential elections, the 2016 Brexit referendum, the 2020 pandemic, 2014's annexation of Crimea and 2022's invasion of Ukraine by Russia spring to mind. What all of these events had in common was: little or no historical precedent and very high stakes that would drive trends in asset prices for some amount of time. Their first commonality presents a strong challenge to quants, because it makes backtesting somewhere between difficult and impossible.

However, here, Bayesian thinking about priors may unlock the puzzle. For example, you can take as a given that an increased duration or severity of the pandemic-related lockdown—which stifled a significant majority of air travel, cruises, and hotel stays, while dramatically increased demand for certain household products and streaming video services—would have pretty predictable impacts on the likes of Carnival Cruises, American Airlines and Hilton Hotels on one hand, and Proctor & Gamble and Netflix, on the other hand. So, if you had a good model for predicting changes in expectations for the severity or duration of the lockdowns, you might have some pretty reliable forecasts for the performance of the affected stocks.

Similarly strong priors can be easily seen for various sectors and commodity markets as a result of the other events listed. The two U.S. elections had a distinct large-cap versus small-cap impact. It was viewed that, if elected, Biden would pump stimulus that would benefit small cap stocks. As such, if you could model the election outcome, you would be able to bet on large caps versus small cap stocks effectively. The challenge with these strategies is to build models very quickly and without the benefit of much history to validate them, that forecast causal factors like elections or pandemics, while also mapping baskets of securities that stand to benefit or be hurt from the potential outcomes.

While these one-off events are largely sources of risk that requires managing for quants, some offer opportunities to profit as well. You could argue that they're mostly just short-term, catalyzed supply/demand strategies, but they are different enough in the approach to modeling them, and uncorrelated enough from conventional approaches, that it seems worth highlighting them separately.

3.3 DATA-DRIVEN ALPHA MODELS

We now turn our attention to data-driven strategies, which were not included in the taxonomy shown in Exhibit 3.2. These strategies are far less widely practiced for a variety of reasons, one of which is that they are significantly more difficult to understand and the mathematics are far more complicated. Data mining, when done well, is based on the premise that the data tell you what is likely to happen next, based on some patterns that are recognizable using certain analytical techniques.

There are two advantages to these approaches. First, compared with theory-driven strategies, data mining is considerably more technically challenging and far less widely practiced. This means that there are fewer competitors, which is helpful. Because theory-driven strategies are usually easy to understand and the math involved in building the relevant models is usually not very advanced, the barriers to entry are naturally lower. Neither condition exists in the case of data-driven strategies, which discourages entry into this space. Second, data-driven strategies are able to discern behaviors whether they have been already named under the banner of some theory or not, which allows them to discover *that* something happens without having to understand *why*. By contrast, theory-driven strategies capture the kinds of behavior that humans have identified and named already, which may limit them to the eight (and, given the paucity of data associated with tactical/event alphas, probably really only the other seven) categories described earlier in this section.

For example, many high-frequency traders favor an entirely empirical, data-mining approach when designing their short-term trading strategies for equity, futures and foreign exchange markets. These data-mining strategies may be more successful at higher frequencies because there is a lot more data at higher frequencies than at lower. If we have a holding period of one month, we only really have 12 bets per year, whereas if we have a holding period of one hour, we have something like 1,500. In other words, at this shorter timescale there is so much more data to work with that the empirical researcher has a better chance of finding statistically significant results.

If a data-driven strategy is designed well, it is able to discern how the market behaves without having to worry about the economic theory or rationalization behind this behavior. Since there is not much good literature available at this time on the theoretical underpinnings of human and computerized trading behaviors at very short-term time horizons (i.e., minutes or less), an empirical approach may actually be able to outperform a theoretical approach at this timescale.

However, data-mining strategies also have their challenges and shortcomings. One challenge relates to determining how much the researcher influences the model—it is clear that, at a minimum, the researcher must decide what data to feed the model. If he allows the model to use data that have little or no connection to what he is trying to forecast—for example, the historical phases of the moon for every day over the past 50 years as the input to a forecast of the price of the stock market—he may find results that are seemingly significant but are in reality entirely spurious. Furthermore, these are computationally intensive strategies, even if computing costs are ever-decreasing. To run a relatively thorough searching algorithm over, say, two years of intraday tick data, with a handful of inputs, might take a single computer processor about three months of continuous processing before it finds the combinations of data that have predictive power.

If this was not difficult enough, whatever strategies are found in this manner require the past to look at least reasonably like the future, although the future doesn't tend to cooperate with this plan very often or for very long. To adjust for this problem, the data-mining strategy requires nearly constant adjustment to keep up with the changes going on in markets, an activity that has many risks in itself.

The biggest problem, though, is that generating alphas using solely data-mining algorithms is a somewhat dubious exercise. Machine learning has been most successful in domains which are largely immutable, and where data are either extremely abundant or where more can easily be acquired (or even generated). Markets are not like games like chess or go, and they are also not like activities like driving a car or flying a plane. Chess was first mastered by having deep learning algorithms observe games between grandmasters (each move of every game of every major tournament has been recorded in a consistent format for decades), and reverse engineer the strategies that are successful. Then, engineers had the machine play against itself some enormous number of times. If your self-driving car algorithm is underperforming in rainy weather, just take your car to Seattle for a few months. Markets, however, are adversarial and dynamic. They are constantly evolving and, in many ways, that evolution is driven by participants' interactions with the market. If you make a big trade, the market will adjust to you. If you implement some new strategy, over time, the market will catch up to you and render your new strategy less effective.

Compounding the problem that markets are much less stable than many other domains, data are relatively sparse as well. Whereas there are billions of Facebook users for the researchers who target advertisements to study, there are a few thousand stocks in the U.S., and maybe on the order of 10,000 globally. There is also not that much relevant history. In the 1970s, Disney's earnings were predominantly a function of its theme parks. Today, content and merchandising far outweigh theme park performance. So do the data from the 1970s for Disney offer us any use in modeling its price movements?

What both of these problems have in common is that they point to not having enough data to forecast in a world where signal-to-noise ratios are, in the best of cases, very low. When you don't have an awful lot of data to overcome this problem, you end up with a bad answer. As a result, in general, strategies that use data-mining techniques to forecast markets do not work, though there are a few exceptions.

In spite of (or, perhaps, because of) the aforementioned challenges facing data-driven quant strategies, there are some traders who implement them, and it is worthwhile understanding some of what goes into these types of models. Let's first frame the problem broadly. Data-driven strategies look at the current market conditions, search for similar conditions in the historical data, and determine the probability that a type of outcome will occur afterwards. The model will choose to make a trade when the historical probabilities are in favor of doing so, and otherwise will not.

It also bears mentioning that, as much as data-driven quant strategies are often mathematically more difficult to understand, even here there is an analog within the discretionary trading world. Technical analysts, also known as "chartists" because of their use of price and/or volume graphs to detect market patterns, are also looking for repeated patterns in market behavior that lead to predictable outcomes.

So, if data-mining quants are primarily looking at current market conditions, searching the history for similar conditions, determining the probabilities of various outcomes in the aftermath of that "setup," and making trades in accordance with the probabilities, they must, at a minimum, address several questions.

What data will we expose to the machine? As with theory-driven alphas, it is crucial to understand what kinds of inputs these strategies will utilize to make predictions. While raw data can be used in theory, it is far more common to engage in some up-front *feature selection* and/or *feature engineering* before applying a machine-learning model.

Feature selection, in brief, is the choosing of factors or indicators—usually more like the atomic building parts of an alpha model—that you believe should have relevance to the price forecast you're trying to make. For example, a "value" alpha model might consist of a number of indicators of value: earnings yield, cash flow yield, book yield, and so on. Rather than selecting them as an already-assembled strategy, you would select them as features and let the machine-learning algorithm determine which ones to include in the forecast.

Feature engineering is the act of making these indicators better. For example, if you adjust the earnings you use to calculate earnings yield to exclude extraordinary events that the market might also dismiss as irrelevant, or if you normalize your return series when calculating some price-based factor.

It is worth noting that we still care about which raw data are utilized in these endeavors, even if there is a great deal of processing of them that goes into the use of machine learning for alpha.

What defines the "current market condition"? Remember, with a quant trading strategy, there is no leeway to be vague. Telling one's computer to "find me situations in the past that look like the situation right now," isn't enough. One must specify precisely what "current" means and what "condition" means. In the case of "current," and not to get too philosophical about the concept of time, but the present can refer to an instantaneous moment, or the last few minutes, or the last 10 years. There is no standard, and the quant must determine her preference in this regard. So, even in this most empirical, data-driven quant strategy, discretion is a key aspect of the creation of a strategy. In the case of "condition," do we mean merely some aspect of price behavior, or do volumes and/or fundamental characteristics matter also? This is not merely an academic question: it is easy to see that, whether or not one treats the price behavior of two small-capitalization technology companies the same way as one treats the behavior of one of those companies versus that of a mega-cap diversified financial firm is a matter of fundamental beliefs about how the market works.

What is the search algorithm used to find "similar" patterns? Hand in hand with this question is another: **What does "similar" mean?** And, also related: **By what method does the algorithm determine the probability of the outcome?** These are the least easily conceptualized and the most technical questions on the list. I can only say that choosing statistical techniques that are appropriate to the dataset is very obviously critical, and that the quant must be careful. One of the most common follies in quant trading is to apply a statistical tool to the wrong problem. There is a great deal of art and judgment that pertains to this decision, making it difficult to generalize a good answer to this question.

How far into the past will the search be conducted? A decidedly more straightforward question, conceptually, is how far into the past to look for similar patterns. The tradeoff is simple, and it pervades quant research (and discretionary investment management). On the one hand, more recent data matter a lot, because they are the most relevant to the immediate present and near future. While it's debatable whether or not human behavior ever really changes, it's clear that technology, and therefore the way humans interact with one another, do evolve, and not only this, but it evolves faster as more time passes. Market structures, too evolve. How relevant would data from the "Buttonwood Tree" era of the NYSE be to the current world of almost exclusively electronic exchanges? On the other hand, with data-mining techniques applied to such noisy datasets as capital markets in the present, statistical significance is always of paramount importance. The greater the amount of data, the greater one's confidence is in the statistical conclusions drawn from the data, for most types of statistical tests. So, while the more recent past is more relevant, the more data, the merrier. The quant (and the investor examining the quant) must determine the appropriate balance between these conflicting traits of statistical analysis applied to systems with dynamic conditions.

How can we tell what the model is actually doing? As we will discuss in Chapter 6, nonlinear models with many inputs can be rather fickle and difficult to understand. Portfolio optimization models, for example, are by default incredibly sensitive to the inputs they're given. Something with a very slightly higher expected return or very slightly lower expected risk can end up with an exaggerated allocation. As a practitioner (or investor, more generally), you'd ideally want to understand how your model works—why does it make the decisions it does? In machine-learning parlance, this is a question of interpretability. How do we translate the outcomes of our model into something we can rationally understand? The main tool for this task relates to understanding the relative importance of the features to the resulting decisions. This is ascertained, typically, by perturbing these features to different values (or excluding them entirely) to see how much the resulting forecast changes. Let's imagine a human situation. Ten analysts are giving input to a portfolio manager. These inputs range from very bearish to somewhat bullish. We can observe the outcome—the portfolio manager's decision of what level of conviction she may have regarding this security. Now, if we imagine a series of parallel realities, in which we exclude each of the ten analysts, one by one, and see how the portfolio manager reacts, we can get a sense of the sensitivity of the portfolio manager to each analyst. Just so with models, though more reliably—they're computers, and thus should give the same results each time they're given the same inputs with the same underlying model. Why does interpretability matter? Ultimately, we will instill more trust in something when it's doing things that make sense to us. Especially in an environment where we have very low predictive power—as is certainly the case in capital markets—to the extent that we can make sense of decisions and outcomes, it is quite reasonable to give more credence to these than the ones that seem to come out of nowhere, even if the latter have nominally better results in our testing.

3.4 IMPLEMENTING THE STRATEGIES

There are not many ways for alpha-focused traders to make money, whether they are quants or not. But the limited selection of sources of alpha does not imply that all quants choose one of a handful of phenomena and then have a peer group to which they are substantively identical. There is in fact considerable diversity among alpha traders, far more so than may be evident at first glance.

This diversity stems from the way quants implement their strategies, and it is to this subject that we now turn our attention. There are many characteristics of an implementation approach that bear discussion, including the forecast target, time horizon, bet structure, investment universe, model specification, conditioning variables, and run frequency.

3.4.1 Forecast Target

The first key component of implementation is to understand exactly what the model is trying to forecast. Models can forecast the direction, magnitude, and/or duration of a move and furthermore can include an assignment of confidence or probability for their forecasts. Many models forecast direction only, most notably the majority of trend-following strategies in futures markets. They seek to predict whether an asset price will rise or fall, and nothing more. Still others have specific forecasts of the size of a move, either in the form of an expected return or a price target. Some models, though they are far less common, also seek to identify how long a move might take.

The *signal strength* is an important (but not ubiquitous) aspect of quant models. Signal strength is defined by an expected return and/or by a confidence interval. The larger the expected return (i.e., the further the price target is from the current price), the greater the strength of the signal, holding confidence levels constant. Similarly, the more confidence in a signal, the greater the signal strength, holding expected returns constant. In general, though certainly not always, a higher level of signal strength results in a bigger bet being taken on a position. This is only rational. Imagine that you believe two stocks, Exxon Mobil (XOM) and Chevron (CVX), both will go up, but you have either a higher degree of confidence or a larger expected return in the forecast for XOM. It stands to reason that you will generally be willing to take a bigger bet on XOM than on CVX because XOM offers a more certain and/or larger potential return. The same holds for quant models, which generally give greater credence to a forecast made with a relatively high degree of confidence or large expected return. This concept can also influence the approach a strategy will take to executing the trades resulting from signals with varying strengths, which we will address in Chapter 7. However, signal strength also bears some caution. Very large signals are unusual, and therefore there may be less statistical confidence that the relationship between the forecast and the outcome has the same relationship as is the case with smaller signals.

3.4.2 Time Horizon

The next key component to understanding implementation of the alpha model is the time horizon. Some quant models try to forecast literally microseconds into the future; others attempt to predict behavior a year or more ahead. Most quant strategies have forecast horizons that fall in the range of a few days to several months. Notably, a strategy applied to the very short term can look quite different than it would if the exact same idea was applied to the very long term, as illustrated by Exhibit 3.7. As you can see, a "medium-term" version of the moving-average-based trend-following strategy would have been short the S&P 500 index during the entirety of April and May 2008 because of the downtrend in the markets that began in October 2007. By contrast, as shown in the lower graph in Exhibit 3.7, a shorter-term version of the same strategy would have been *long* on the S&P for all but three days in mid-April and for the last days of May. This exhibit illustrates that the same strategy, applied over different time horizons, can produce markedly different—even opposite—positions.

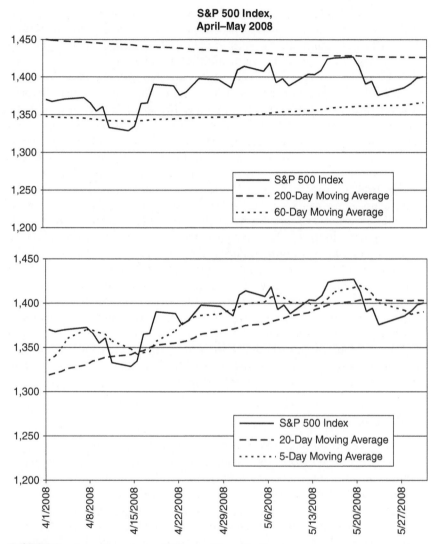

EXHIBIT 3.7 Same Strategy on Different Time Horizons

In general, there is more variability between the returns of a one-minute strategy and a one-hour strategy than between a three-month and a six-month strategy, even though the interval between the latter pair is significantly longer than that between the first pair. Generalized, we find that **differentiation is greater at shorter timescales than at longer ones.** This general rule especially holds true in more risky environments. This happens because the shorter-term strategies are making very large numbers of trades compared to the longer-term versions of the same strategies. Even a small difference in the time horizon of a strategy, when it is being run at a short time scale, can be amplified across tens of thousands of trades per day and in the millions per year. By contrast, three- and six-month versions of the same strategy are simply making a lot fewer trades, so the difference in time horizon does not get amplified. So, for example, a 150-day moving average versus a 300-day moving average trend-following strategy would produce the exact same constant short position in the S&P 500 during April and May 2008 as the trend-following strategy that uses 60- and 100-day moving averages. By contrast, taking merely 10 days off of the longer moving average from the shorter-term system so that it now uses 5- and 10-day moving averages causes the system to be short the S&P for several extra days in mid-April and to add another short trade in mid-May that the 5-/20-day version would not have done. Instead of being short the S&P for eight trading days out of the total of 43 during these two months, the 5-/10-day version would be short for 15 out of the 43 days.

The choice of time horizon is made from a spectrum with a literally infinite number of choices, that is, forecasts can be made for two weeks into the future, or for two weeks and 30 seconds, or for two weeks and 31 seconds, and so on. Yet adding 30 or 31 seconds to a forecast of two weeks might not cause a great deal of differentiation. Along this line of thinking, a classification may be helpful in understanding the distinctions among quant trading strategies by time horizon. *High-frequency* strategies are the fastest, making forecasts that go no further than the end of the current trading day (but generally much shorter than that—strategies have become interesting in the "mid-frequency" space, which holds for many minutes to several hours, perhaps even overnight). *Short-term* strategies, the second category, tend to hold positions from one day to two weeks. *Medium-term* strategies make forecasts anywhere from a few weeks to a few months ahead. Finally, *long-term* strategies hold positions for several months or longer. The lines of demarcation between these groups are arbitrary, but in my experience, this shorthand can be helpful in thinking about how various quant strategies might compare with one another.

3.4.3 Bet Structure

The next key component of an alpha model is the bet structure, which, in turn, is based on how the alpha model generates its forecast. Models can be made to forecast either an instrument in itself or an instrument relative to others. For example, a model could forecast that gold is cheap and its price is likely to rise or that gold is cheap *relative to* silver, and that gold is therefore likely to outperform silver. When looking at relative forecasts, one can forecast the behavior of smaller clusters (e.g., pairs) or larger clusters (e.g., sectors). Smaller clusters have the advantage of being easier to understand and analyze. In particular, pairs are primarily attractive because, in theory, one can carefully select instruments that are directly comparable.

However, pairs have several comparative disadvantages. Very few assets can actually be compared so precisely and directly with one other instrument, rendering a major benefit of pairs trading impracticable. Two Internet companies might each depend significantly on revenues from their respective search engines, but they may differ along other lines. One could have more of a content-driven business while the other uses advertising to supplement the search engine revenues. Meanwhile, one could find other companies with strong advertising or content businesses, each of which shares some characteristics and sector-effects with the first pair. Here the trader is presented with a dilemma: which pairs are actually the best to use? Or to put it another way, how should the trader's pairs best be structured?

Another approach is to make relative bets within larger clusters or groups. Researchers group securities together primarily in an effort to isolate and eliminate common effects among the group. A large part of the point of grouping stocks within their market sector, for example, is to eliminate the impact of a general movement of the sector and thereby focus on the *relative* movement of stocks *within* the sector. It turns out to be extremely difficult to isolate group effects with a group size of merely two. On the other hand, larger clusters allow for a cleaner distinction between group behavior and idiosyncratic behavior, which is beneficial for many quant strategies. As a result, most quants who trade in groups tend to use larger groups than simply pairs when they make relative bets.

Researchers also must choose *how* they create these clusters, either using statistical techniques or using heuristics (e.g., fundamentally defined industry groups). There are many statistical techniques aimed at discerning when things are similar to each other or when they belong together as a group. However, statistical models can be fooled by the data, leading to bad groupings. For example, there may be periods during which the prices of Internet stocks behave like the price of corn. This may cause the statistical model to group them together, but Internet stocks and corn are ultimately more different than they are similar, and most fundamental grouping approaches would never put them together. Furthermore, any time that the market regime changes, the relationships among instruments frequently also change, which can lead the system to mistakenly group things together that no longer will behave like each other.

Alternatively, groups can be defined heuristically. Asset classes, sectors, and industries are common examples of heuristically defined groups.

They have the advantage of making sense and being defensible theoretically, but they are also imprecise (for instance, to what industry does a conglomerate such as General Electric belong?) and possibly too rigid. Rigidity in particular can be a problem because over time, similarities among instruments change. Sometimes stocks and bonds move in opposite directions, and sometimes they move in the same direction. Because the correlation between these two asset classes moves in phases, it can be very tricky to analyze the relationship theoretically and make a static, unchanging declaration that they belong in the same group or in different groups. As a result, most grouping techniques (and by extension, most strategies that are based on *relative* forecasts), whether statistically driven or heuristic, suffer from changes in market regime that cause drastic changes in the relationships among instruments.

In evaluating alpha-oriented strategies, this distinction among bet structures, most notably between directional (single security) bets versus relative (multi-security) bets, is rather important. The behavior of a given type of alpha model is very different if it is implemented on an instrument by itself than it would be if implemented on a group of instruments relative to each other. It is critical to balance the risks and benefits of the various approaches to grouping. In general, relative alpha strategies tend to exhibit smoother returns during normal times than intrinsic alpha strategies, but they can also experience unique problems related to incorrect groupings during stressful periods. Some quants attempt to mitigate the problems associated with any particular grouping technique by utilizing several grouping techniques in concert. For example, one could first group stocks by their sectors but then refine these groupings using a more dynamic statistical approach that reflects recent correlations among the stocks.

Also, it is worth clarifying one piece of particularly unhelpful, but widely used, hedge fund industry jargon: *relative value*. This term refers to strategies that utilize a relative bet structure, but the *value* part of the term is actually not useful. Certainly strategies that make forecasts based on a notion of the relative valuation of instruments are quite common. However, most strategies called relative value have little to do with value investing. Relative mean reversion strategies, relative momentum strategies, and other kinds of relative fundamental strategies are all commonly referred to as relative value.

3.4.4 Investment Universe

A given strategy can be implemented in a variety of instruments, and the quant must choose which ones to include or exclude. The first significant choice a quant makes about the investment universe is *geography*. A short-term relative mean reversion strategy traded on stocks in the United States might not behave similarly to the same strategy applied to stocks in Hong Kong. The researcher must decide where to apply the strategy. The second significant choice a quant makes about the investment universe relates to its *asset class*. A growth strategy applied to foreign exchange markets might behave differently than one applied to equity indices. The quant must decide what asset classes to trade with each strategy. A third significant choice a quant must make about the investment universe relates to the *instrument class*. Equity indices, as accessed through the futures markets, behave differently than single stocks, even though both belong to the equity asset class. Also, the liquidity characteristics and nature of the other participants in a given market differ from one instrument class to another, and these are some of the considerations quants must make regarding what kinds of instruments to trade. There are also tax implications to consider. Finally, in some cases, quants may include or exclude specific groups of instruments for a variety of reasons.

The choice of an investment universe is dependent on several strong preferences that quants tend to have. First, the quant generally prefers liquidity in the underlying instruments so that estimations of transactions costs are reliable. Second, quants generally require large quantities of high-quality data. In general, such data can be found in highly liquid and developed markets. Third, quants tend to prefer instruments that behave in a manner conducive to being predicted by systematic models. For example, some quants exclude biotechnology stocks because they are subject to sudden, violent price changes based on events such as government approval or rejection of their latest drug. Although a physician with a biotech specialization may have some intuitions on this subject, it's simply not something that most quants can model. As a result of these preferences, the most typical asset classes and instruments in which one can find quants participating are common stocks, futures (especially on bonds and equity indices), and foreign exchange markets. Some strategies might trade the fixed income asset class using instruments other than futures (e.g., swaps or cash bonds), though these are significantly less common today than they were in the middle or late 1990s. Geographically, the bulk of quant trading occurs in the United States, developed Europe, and Japan, with lesser amounts done in other parts of North America and developed Asia. Quants are almost completely absent from illiquid instruments, or those traded "over the counter" (OTC), such as corporate or convertible bonds, and are less (but increasingly) common in emerging markets.

This last fact may change going forward as OTC markets become better regulated and electronic. But that also implies that the liquidity of these markets will improve. As such, this notion of liquidity is perhaps the simplest way to summarize in one dimension the salient characteristics of the trading universe for a strategy. After all, more liquid instruments also tend to offer more high-quality data and to be more conducive to being forecast, on average.

3.4.5 Model Specification

An idea for a trading strategy, its core concept, is insufficient for use as a trading strategy: the quant must specifically define every aspect of the strategy before it is usable. Furthermore, any differences in the way a quant chooses to specify or define an idea for her strategy might lead it to behave quite differently than other choices would have. For example, there could be multiple ways to define a trend. Some simply compute the total return of an instrument over some historical period, and if that number is positive, a positive trend is identified (a negative return would constitute a negative trend). Other trend traders use moving average approaches, such as the ones illustrated in Exhibits 3.3, 3.4, and 3.5, to look for prices to rise above or below recent average prices and so determine the presence of a trend. Still other trend strategies seek to identify the breakout of the very early stages of a trend, found using specific price patterns they believe are present in this critical phase, but they do not attempt to determine whether a long-term trend is actually in place or not.

These are but a few of the more common ways a trend can be defined. Just so, each kind of alpha strategy can be defined in various ways, and it is a significant part of the quant's job to decide precisely how to specify the strategy mathematically. This is an area for an investor in quant trading to study carefully because it is often a source of differentiation—and potentially of comparative advantage—for a quant. In Section 3.4.2 of this chapter, we saw that even a specification about the time horizon of a strategy for timing the stock market can have a dramatic impact on whether it is long or short at a given point in time. Given the importance of the time horizon, it is easy to understand the impact of using an entirely different definition of the strategy on its behavior. However, it may be challenging to get a quant to share with an outsider details on exactly how his model is specified. For the nonquant, then, model specification may remain a more opaque aspect of the black box, but exploring this idea as much as possible with a quant trader could, in fact, highlight the reasons for differences in performance that are observed versus the quant's peer group.

One especially important type of specification is in the form of setting parameters for a model. Returning to our trend example, the number of days in each moving average (e.g., a 5-/10-day moving average crossover strategy versus a 5-/20-day moving average crossover strategy) is a parameter.

The specification of parameters is also an area in which some quants utilize machine learning or data-mining techniques. In Section 3.3 we mentioned the idea of fitting models to the data and setting parameter values. This is a problem to which machine-learning techniques, which I described earlier as being neither easily nor commonly applied to the problem of finding alpha, are better suited and more widely used. In essence, machine-learning techniques are applied to determine the optimal set of specifications for a quant model. Machine-learning algorithms are designed to provide an intelligent and scientifically valid way of testing many potential sets of specifications without overfitting.

A subset of the problem of determining parameters relates to how often the models themselves are adjusted for more recent data. This process is known as *refitting* because some of the same work that goes on in the original research process is repeated in live trading in an attempt to refresh the model and make it as adaptive as possible to current market conditions. Because this can be a computationally intensive process, sometimes involving millions or even billions of calculations, many quants refit their models infrequently or not at all. Refitting also leads to a greater risk of overfitting, a very treacherous problem indeed, since spurious and fleeting relationships may be mistaken for valid, lasting ones.

3.4.6 Conditioning Variables

Many strategists (those whose job is to create trading strategies) employ conditioning variables to their strategies. These make the strategies more complex, but they also may increase the efficacy of the forecasts generated. There are two basic types of conditioning variables. One kind is a *modifying conditioner*, which takes a given signal and changes whether or how it is used, generally based on the characteristics of the signal itself or its results. For example, a strategist may find that utilizing a simple trend indicator is not a sufficiently interesting strategy to pursue. After all, there are many false starts to worry about with a trend-following strategy, and many experienced practitioners will admit that, without the "money management" or "risk management" rules they employ, their strategies would be basically un-investable. These rules, and others to be discussed, can properly be thought of as conditioning variables for the trend-following strategy. For example, a "stop-loss" is a common conditioning variable to pair with a trend-following strategy. The idea would be to follow the trend, *unless* that trend has been reversing and causing losses to the position sufficient to trigger a stop-loss. There are numerous kinds of stops: stop-losses, profit-targets (or profit-stops), and time stops. Stop-losses have already been described, and are generally employed when strategies have many "false" signals, but where the "good" signals can yield significant profits. Just so, most directional trend-following strategies make money on a minority of their trades (often less than 40 percent of them!), but the gain on their winners is substantially larger than the losses on their losers (because of stop-loss techniques). Profit-targets are utilized when the strategist believes that the position gets riskier as it generates profits. This is a reasonable enough concept: markets rarely go in the same direction indefinitely, so it may make sense to take profits if they've been going the same way long enough for the strategy to generate significant profits. Finally, time-stops are used to avoid the problem of holding positions on the basis of signals which may have been triggered far enough in the past as to be considered "stale." It's a way of enforcing a refreshing of the bets being taken in the portfolio, among other things.

A second type of conditioning variable is a *secondary conditioner*, which requires the agreement (or some other set of conditions) across multiple types of signals to trigger a tradable forecast. For example, a large portion of fundamental equity analysts are "GARP" devotees, meaning they believe in owning "Growth at a Reasonable Price." If a company is identified as being both growing and inexpensive, it is a candidate to buy. Cheapness on its own would not justify a purchase, just as growth on its own would not. In price-driven strategies, sometimes trend at various timescales, or trend and mean reversion, are combined. For example, a mean-reversion strategy could be conditioned to buy instruments that have experienced price declines, but only when that causes the resulting position to be in the direction of the longer-term trend (i.e., this strategy would buy dips in up-trending markets, or sell short run-ups in down-trending markets).

Utilizing conditioning variables is how most rule-based pattern recognition strategies are designed. Like data-driven strategies, they are looking for repeated patterns in market behavior (basically, more complex patterns than "buy winners/sell losers" or "buy dips/sell run-ups"), but theory-driven pattern-recognition models will begin with pre-defined rules. Data-driven traders rely on their algorithms to determine what a "pattern" is in the first place (though, again, within the bounds specified, as discussed in Section 3.3).

3.4.7 Run Frequency

A final component of building a given alpha model is determining the *run frequency*, or the frequency with which the model is actually run to seek new trading ideas. Some quants run their models relatively infrequently, for example, once per month. At the other extreme, some run their models more or less continuously, in real time. There is an interesting tradeoff that quants must manage here. Specifically, increasing the frequency of model runs usually leads to a greater number of transactions, which means more commissions paid to brokers and higher transaction costs. Also, more frequent model runs lead to a greater probability that the model is moving the portfolio around based on noisy data that don't actually contain much meaning. This, in turn, would mean that the increased transaction costs would cause little or no incremental improvement in the alpha generated by the strategy and would thereby reduce its overall profitability.

On the other hand, less frequent model runs lead to a smaller number of larger-sized trades. These are expensive in a different way, namely in terms of the impact these trades can have on the marketplace. If models are run too infrequently, then at those times when they are run, they could recommend making very significant changes to the currently-held portfolio. This would mean transacting larger blocks of trades, which would likely cost more in terms of "moving the market." Less frequent model runs are also prone to problems associated with the moment of observation of markets. If a strategy is run once a month, it could miss opportunities to trade at more favorable prices that occur during the month while the model is dormant. Alternatively, the model may attempt in vain to trade at attractive, but quickly fleeting, prices that occur if there has been some aberration just around the time of the model being run.

Whether more frequent or less frequent model runs are better depends on many other aspects of the strategy, most especially the time horizon of the forecast and the kinds of inputs. In the end, most quants run their models no less than once a week, and many run continuously throughout the day. The slower-moving the strategy, obviously, the more leeway there is, whereas shorter-term strategies tend toward continuous, real-time runs.

3.4.8   An Explosion of Diversity

We have described a few of the kinds of important decisions that quants must make in building a given alpha model. To succeed in quant trading, each of these decisions requires good judgment on the part of the quant. In short, successful quants are characterized in part by an incredible attention to detail and tirelessness in seeking the right questions to ask and the best solutions to address them. Nevertheless, for those who do not build quant trading systems but who are interested in understanding them, the kinds of issues discussed in this section are straightforward to understand and provide a useful way to distinguish one quant from another.

A final, important implication of these details of implementation is that they lead to an explosion in the variety of quant trading strategies that actually exist. You can easily see that the number of permutations of a strategy focused on the concept of "value," for example, is enormous when accounting for differences in the type, time horizon, bet structure, investable universe, model definition, conditioning variables, and frequency of model run. Just taking the first four types of implementation details listed here and using the simplifying categories we described in this section, there are two types of forecasts (direction and magnitude), four types of time horizon (high-frequency, short-term, medium-term, and long-term), two types of bet structures (intrinsic and relative), and four asset classes (stocks, bonds, currencies, and commodities). Therefore one could build 64 different value models ($2 \times 4 \times 2 \times 4 = 64$ permutations), and this excludes the question of how many ways one can define the idea of value, how one could condition the use of value on other variables, and how often one can look for value. This diversity might seem daunting at first glance, but the framework established here can help anyone interested in understanding what's inside a black box. Exhibit 3.8 revisits the taxonomy of alpha models, expanding it to include the implementation approaches discussed here.

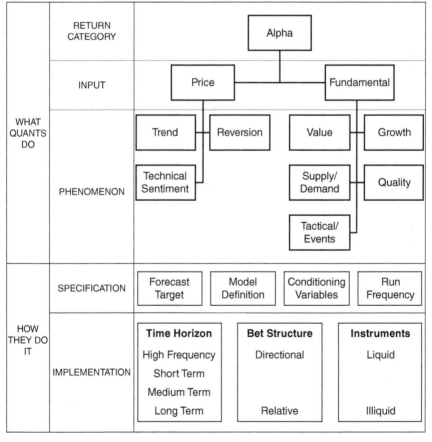

EXHIBIT 3.8 Taxonomy of Theory-Driven Alpha Models and Their Implementations

3.5   BLENDING ALPHA MODELS

Each of the decisions a quant makes in defining a trading strategy is an important driver of its behavior. But there is another extremely important set of choices the quant must make in constructing a trading strategy. Specifically, the quant is not limited to choosing just one approach to a given alpha model. Instead, he is equally free to choose to employ *multiple* types of alpha models. The method used to combine these alpha models is an arena rich with possibilities. The most sophisticated and successful quants tend to utilize several kinds of alpha strategies, including trend and reversion, and various kinds of fundamental approaches across a variety of time horizons, trade structures, instruments, and geographies. Such quants benefit from alpha diversification in exactly the same way that diversification is helpful in so many other aspects of financial life.

Blending or mixing alpha signals has many analogues in discretionary trading (and decision making) in general. Imagine a mutual fund portfolio manager who has two analysts covering XOM. One analyst, focused on fundamental value in the classic Graham and Dodd sense, expects XOM to rise by 50 percent over the next year. The other analyst, taking a momentum approach, thinks XOM is likely to be flat over the next year. What is the net expectation the portfolio manager should have of the price of XOM, given the two analysts' predictions? This is the core problem that is addressed by blending alpha models, each of which can be likened to an analyst.

The three most common quant approaches to blending forecasts are via linear models, nonlinear models, and machine-learning models. There is also a significant fourth school of thought that believes that alpha models should not be combined at all. Instead, several portfolios are constructed, each based on the output from a given alpha model. These factor portfolios are then combined using any of the portfolio construction techniques discussed in Chapter 7.

Each of these four approaches to signal mixing has its disciples, and as with most everything else we've discussed, the best way to blend alphas depends on the model. In general, as in the case of an alpha model, the purpose of a method of mixing alpha models is to find the combination of them that best predicts the future. All other things being equal, it is very likely that any reasonably intelligent combination of alphas will do a better job together than any one of them could do individually over time. Consider Exhibit 3.9. Here we can see that Forecasts A and B each occasionally predict future events correctly. This is illustrated in that there is some overlap between Forecast A and the actual outcome and between Forecast B and the actual outcome. But each forecast has only a small amount of success in predicting the future. However, together, Forecasts A and B are about twice as likely to be correct about the future outcomes as either is separately.

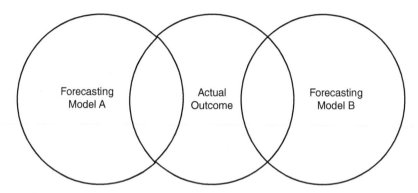

EXHIBIT 3.9 A Visualization of Multiple Forecasts

Linear models are by far the most common way in which quants combine alpha factors to construct a composite forecast. A linear model is a reasonable facsimile for one of the more common ways that humans normally think about cause-and-effect relationships. In linear models, the inclusion of one factor is independent of the inclusion of other factors, and each factor is expected to be additive, independently of the other factors that might be included or excluded. For example, for a high school student trying to get into a good university, she can think of her grades, standardized test scores, extracurricular activities, recommendations, and essays as being these independent factors in the linear model that predicts her odds of gaining admission. Regardless of the other factors, grades are always important, as is each other factor. As such, a linear model is relevant. If, on the other hand, it was the case that, with high enough test scores, her essays wouldn't matter, a linear model is no longer the correct way to predict her chances of getting in.

The first step in using a linear model in this way is to assign a weight to each alpha factor. To return to our example, if we were trying to predict university admissions, this step would require us to define the relative importance of grades versus, say, test scores. This is typically done using a technique known as *multiple regression*, which is aimed at finding the combination of alpha factors that explains the maximum amount of the historical behavior of the instruments being traded. The presumption is that, if a model reasonably explains the past, it has a reasonable chance of explaining the future well enough to make a profit. These weights are then applied to the outputs of their respective alpha factors, which are usually a forecast or score of some kind. The weighted sum of these multiple forecasts gives us a combined forecast. Or, to be more specific, by summing the products of the weights of each factor and the outputs of each factor, we arrive at a composite forecast or score. This composite can then be used to help determine the target portfolio.

Imagine a trading system with two alpha factors. One of the alpha factors focuses on E/P ratios (and is therefore a yield model), and the other focuses on price trends (and is therefore a trend model). The yield factor forecasts a return of +20 percent over the next 12 months for XOM, whereas the trend factor forecasts a return of –10 percent for XOM over the next 12 months. Based on a historical regression, the models are weighted 70 percent toward the yield factor and 30 percent toward the trend factor. Taking their scores and weights together, the total 12-month return forecast of our two-factor model is computed as follows:

70% weight × 20% return forecast for the yield factor comes to + 14%.

30% weight × –10% return forecast for the trend factor comes to − 3%.

The sum of these two products comes to +11 percent, which is the total expected 12-month return for XOM using the example above.

A special case of linear models is the equal-weighted model. Though not highly quantitative, equal-weighting methods abound among quant traders. The general idea behind equal weighting is that the trader has no confidence in his ability to define more accurate weights and therefore decides to give all the alpha factors equal importance. A variant of this approach gives each factor an "equal risk" weighting, which incorporates the concept that giving a dollar to a highly risky strategy is not the same as giving a dollar to a less risky strategy. In Chapter 6 we cover both these approaches in more detail as they apply to portfolio construction. Still another approach would be to give each factor its own weight discretionarily.

There are many forms of nonlinear models that can be used to combine alpha factors with each other. In contrast to linear models, nonlinear models are based on the premise that the relationship between the variables used to make forecasts either is not independent (i.e., each variable is not expected to add value independently of the others), or else the relationship changes over time. As such, the two main types of nonlinear models are conditional models and rotation models. Conditional models base the weight of one alpha factor on the reading of another factor. Using the same two factors as earlier, a conditional model might indicate that E/P yields should drive forecasts, but *only* when the price trends are *in agreement* with the E/P yields. In other words, the highest-yielding stocks would be candidates to be bought only if the price trends of these stocks were also positive. The lowest-yielding stocks would be candidates to be sold short, but only if the price trends of these stocks were also negative. When the agreement condition is met, the yield factor entirely drives the forecast. But if the price trend doesn't confirm the E/P yield signal, the yield signal is ignored entirely. Revisiting the linear factor combination demonstrated earlier, our conditional model would generate no signal for XOM because the price trend forecast a negative return, whereas the yield factor forecast a positive return. If, instead, XOM had a positive return forecast from the trend factor, the combined nonlinear model would have a targeted return of +20 percent over the next 12 months for that stock because this is the return expected by the value factor, which now has been "activated" by its agreement with the trend factor. Note that mixing models in this way is similar to utilizing more conditioning variables in the specification of an alpha model (discussed in Section 3.4.6), though it is not required that the conditional linear model be an "all-or-nothing" type of approach. It is possible to utilize a conditioning variable that simply increases or decreases the weight of a given factor based on the values of other factors at that point in time. An example of a conditional model is shown in Exhibit 3.10.

The second nonlinear way to blend alphas uses a rotation approach. Rather than following trends in markets themselves, this type of model follows trends in the performance of the alpha models. These are similar to linear models except that the weights of factors fluctuate over time based on updated calculations of the various signals' weights. As time passes, the more recent data are used to determine weighting schemes in the hope that the model's weights are more relevant to current market conditions. This method usually results in giving higher weights to the factors that have performed better recently. As such, this is a form of trend following in the timing of alpha factors.

Machine-learning models are also sometimes used by quants to determine the optimal weights of various alpha factors. As in the case of determining optimal parameters, machine-learning techniques applied to the mixing of alpha factors are both more common and more successful than machine-learning approaches used to forecast markets themselves. These techniques algorithmically determine the mix of alpha factors that best explains the past, with the presumption that a good mix in the past is likely to be a good mix in the future. As in the case of rotational models, many machine-learning approaches to mixing alpha factors periodically update the optimal

EXHIBIT 3.10   A Simple Conditional (Nonlinear) Model for Blending Alphas

Value and Momentum Disagree	Value	Momentum	Signal
	Long	Short	None
Value and Momentum Agree	Value	Momentum	Signal
	Long	Long	Long

weights based on the ever-changing and ever-growing set of data available. Unlike the example of using machine learning for the generation of actual alpha signals, applying machine learning to determine the weights of various alpha forecasts is more common and significantly more successful.

We have briefly summarized common approaches to *mixing signals,* or combining alpha forecasts. This is a part of the quant trading process that has received precious little attention in the academic literature and trade press, but personally I find it one of the most fascinating questions about quant trading—or any trading. It is exactly the same problem any decision maker faces when looking at a variety of sources of information and opinions: What is the best way to synthesize all available and relevant information into a sensible decision?

It is worth noting that signal mixing shares some similarities with portfolio construction. Both are questions of sizing and combining, after all. However, they are mostly distinct and separate processes. Signal-mixing models size multiple alpha signals to arrive at one composite forecast per instrument, which is then used in portfolio construction. Portfolio construction models take multiple kinds of signals as inputs, including alpha signals, risk models, and transaction cost models (which we cover in Chapters 4 and 5), and attempt to size individual positions correctly, given these inputs.

3.6 SUMMARY

Having made so many decisions about what sort of alpha should be pursued, how to specify and implement it, and how to combine this alpha with others, the quant is left with an output. The output is typically either a return forecast (expected return = X percent) or a directional forecast (expected direction = up, down, or flat). Sometimes quants add elements of time (expected return over the next Y days) and/or probability (Z percent likelihood of expected return) to help utilize the output effectively in trading decisions. See Exhibit 3.11 for a recap of the structure of a quant trading system. As we continue our progress through the black box, we will highlight the components discussed.

I am consistently amazed by the juxtaposition of the simplicity and relatively small number of concepts used to manage money quantitatively and the incredible diversity of quant trading strategies as applied in the real world. The decisions quants make in the areas discussed in this chapter are major sources of the significant differences in the returns of traders who may be pursuing the same sources of alpha. Those evaluating quant traders (or quants who are evaluating trading strategies of their own) can use

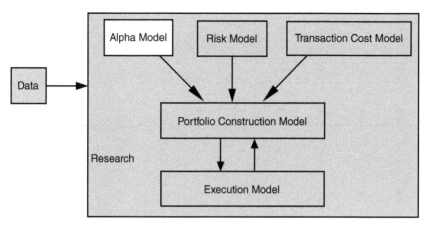

EXHIBIT 3.11   Schematic of the Black Box

the framework provided in this chapter to help determine the nature of the strategies being traded. We now turn our attention to risk modeling, another key component of a quant trading strategy.

NOTES

1. www.turtletrader.com/trader-seykota.html.
2. Larry Hite and Steven Feldman, "Game Theory Applications," *The Commodity Journal*, May–June 1972.
3. Ginger Szala, "Making a Mint: How a Scientist, Statistician and Businessman Mixed," *Futures*, March 1, 1989.
4. Gregory Zuckerman, "Renaissance Man: James Simons Does the Math on Fund," *The Wall Street Journal*, July 1, 2005.
5. Eugene Fama and Kenneth French "The Cross Section of Expected Stock Returns," *Journal of Finance*, 47 (June 1992): 427.
6. Ray Ball, "Anomalies in Relationships Between Securities' Yields and Yield-Surrogates," *Journal of Financial Economics*, 6(2–3) (1978): 103–126.
7. Kurt Eichenwald, "Microsoft's Lost Decade," *Vanity Fair*, August 2012. https://archive.vanityfair.com/article/2012/8/microsofts-lost-decade

CHAPTER 4

Risk Models

*The market can remain irrational longer than you can
remain solvent.*

—John Maynard Keynes

Risk management should not be thought of solely as the avoidance of risk or reduction of loss. It is about the intentional selection and sizing of exposures to improve the quality and consistency of returns. In Chapter 3, we defined *alpha* as a type of exposure from which a quant trader expects to profit. But we also noted that, from time to time, there can be downside to accepting this exposure. This is not what we classify as risk per se. By pursuing a specific kind of alpha, we are explicitly saying that we *want* to be invested in the ups and downs of that exposure because we believe we will profit from it in the long run. Though it would be great fun to accept only the upside of a given alpha strategy and reject the losses that can be associated with it, sadly, that is not possible. However, there are other exposures that are frequently linked to the pursuit of some kind of alpha. These other exposures are not expected to make us any money, but they frequently accompany the return-driving exposure. These exposures are *risks*.

Risk exposures generally will not produce profits over the long haul, but they can impact the returns of a strategy day to day. More important still, the quant is not attempting to forecast these exposures, usually because he cannot do so successfully. But the fact remains that one of the great strengths of quant trading is to be able to measure various exposures and to be intentional about the selection of such exposures. This chapter deals with how quants define, measure, and control risks.

Imagine a relative alpha strategy that focuses on the value (yield) of various stocks, buying higher-yielding stocks and selling short lower-yielding stocks. This strategy clearly loses money if "cheap" (higher-yield) stocks underperform "expensive" (lower-yield) stocks, according to whatever definition the quant chooses for "cheapness" (or yield). That risk is inherent to the pursuit of a value strategy, even if the quant has reason to believe that value strategies should make money in the long term. However, a value strategy without further specification can end up taking significant sector bets in addition to the intentional bet on value. After all, it's easy to see that stocks within a sector tend to move together. So if one technology stock has gotten very cheap, there's a reasonable chance that many other technology stocks have also gotten cheap. This means that an unconstrained value-hunting strategy is likely to end up with a net long position in the technology sector (in this example). But there is no evidence that there exists a long-term benefit of overweighting one industry or sector versus another.

More important, assume that the strategy has neither the intention nor the capability to forecast the performance of various sectors. Therefore, sector exposure would be considered a form of risk in our framework, because sector performance is not being intentionally forecast, but having net exposure to various sectors can alter the strategy's results day to day. So the key to understanding risk exposures as they relate to quant trading strategies is that risk exposures are those that are not intentionally sought out by the nature of whatever forecast the quant is making in the alpha model.

If alpha models are like optimists, risk models are like pessimists. Risk models exist largely to control the size of desirable exposures or to deal with undesirable types of exposures. Their job is to raise hell about things that can cause losses or uncertainty, particularly those bets that are unintentionally made or are incidental byproducts of the alpha model. It both highlights and attempts to remove undesirable exposures from a portfolio. Risk models are also useful for helping explain why profits or losses accrued, especially if they came from some sort of systematic factor exposure that the model captures. Additionally, risk models can be used within the alpha model itself, for example, by computing the residuals of equity returns to the set of factors in the risk model, and then focusing on trying to predict the future path of those residuals.

But back to the main use case of a risk model, especially in the context of this chapter, there are only a few things you can do with a given type of exposure, aside from simply accepting it outright. Mostly you can limit its size or eliminate it altogether. The function of risk management in the investment process is to determine which of these courses of action is most prudent for each kind of exposure and to provide that input to the portfolio construction model. In general, risk models reduce the amount of money a quant can make, but this is a tradeoff many quants are willing to accept. Managing risk has the day-to-day benefit of reducing the volatility of a strategy's returns. But it also has the far more important benefit of reducing the likelihood of large losses. In many ways, the failures of investment managers in general (quant or not) are usually precipitated by failures to manage risk. This can be seen with LTCM in 1998, with Amaranth in 2006, with U.S. quant equity traders in August 2007, with a great many investors in the fall of 2008 and the beginning of the COVID-19 pandemic and lockdown in March 2020.

4.1 LIMITING THE AMOUNT OF RISK

Size limiting is an important form of risk management. It is easy to imagine having a tremendously good trading idea, seemingly a "sure thing," but without some sense of risk management, there can be a temptation to put all one's capital into this single trade. This is almost always a bad idea. Why? Because, empirically, a sure thing rarely exists, so the correct way to size a trade in general is certainly *not* to put all your chips on it. Otherwise it is likely that in the process of "going all in," at some point the trader will go bankrupt. In other words, it is prudent to take just as much exposure to a trade as is warranted by the considerations of the opportunity (alpha) and the downside (risk). Quantitative risk models focused on limiting the size of bets are common, and many are quite simple. The following sections explain how they work.

There are several kinds of quantitative risk models that limit size, and they vary in three primary ways:

1. The manner in which size is limited.
2. How risk is measured.
3. What is having its size limited.

4.1.1 Limiting by Constraint or Penalty

Approaches to the size limits come in two main forms: hard constraints and penalties. Hard constraints are set to "draw a line" in terms of risk. For instance, imagine a position limit that dictates that no position will be larger than 3 percent of the portfolio, no matter how strong the signal. However, this hard limit may be somewhat arbitrary (e.g., imagine a 3.00 percent position size limit; why is a 3.01 percent position so much worse?), so quants sometimes build penalty functions that allow a position to increase beyond the "limit" level, but only if the alpha model expects a significantly larger return (i.e., a much larger expected return than was required to allow the position merely to reach the limit size in the first place). The penalty

functions work so that the further past the limit level we go, the more difficult it becomes to increase the position size additionally. So, using our
example, it would be far easier to see a 3.01 percent position than to see a
6 percent position, because the latter is further from the limit than the former.

In this way, the model attempts to address the idea that an opportunity
can sometimes be so good as to warrant an "exception" to the rule. In a
sense, penalty functions for size limits can be thought of as making rules to
govern exceptions.

The levels of limits and/or penalties can be determined in the same ways
as most other things in the quant world, namely either from theory or from
the data (the latter via data-mining approaches). Theory-driven approaches
mostly look like an arbitrary level that is set, tested, and, if needed, adjusted
until it produces an acceptable outcome. So, to return to the earlier example
of a 3 percent limit on position sizes, the quant researcher could have started
with a risk limit of 5 percent because his experience seemed to dictate that
this was a reasonable level to choose. But through testing and simulating
the historical results of this strategy, he could have come to realize that a
far more appropriate level is 3 percent, which better balances the ability to
make sizeable bets when attractive opportunities appear against the necessity of recognizing that any given trade could easily go wrong. Data-driven
approaches are more varied and can include machine-learning techniques to
test many combinations of limits or simply testing various limit levels and
letting the historical data empirically determine the final outcome. Either
way, these levels and the severity of any penalty functions are parameters of
the risk model that the quant must set, based on either research or heuristics.

4.1.2 Measuring the Amount of Risk

There are two generally accepted ways of measuring the amount of risk
in the marketplace. The first is longitudinal and measures risk by computing the standard deviation of the returns of various instruments over time,
which is a way of getting at the concept of uncertainty. In finance circles, this
concept is usually referred to as *volatility*. The more volatility, the more risk
is said to be present in the markets.[1]

The second way to measure risk is to measure the level of similarity in
the behavior of the various instruments within a given investment universe.
This is frequently calculated by taking the cross-sectional standard deviation
of all the relevant instruments for a given period. The larger the standard
deviation, the more varied the underlying instruments are behaving. This
means that the market is less risky because the portfolio can be made up of a
larger number of diversified bets. This can be seen easily at the extreme: If all
the instruments in a portfolio are perfectly correlated, then as one bet goes,

so go all the other bets. This concept is known among quants as *dispersion*. Dispersion can also be measured by the correlation or covariance among the instruments in a given universe. Here, too, the more similarly the instruments are behaving, the more risky the market is said to be.

There are many other, less commonly utilized, approaches to measuring risk as well. These include the use of measures such as credit spreads or CDS, or the use of implied volatilities.

4.1.3 Where Limits Can Be Applied

Size-limiting models such as these can be used to govern many kinds of exposures. One can limit the size of single positions and/or groups of positions, such as sectors or asset classes. Alternatively, one can limit the size of exposure to various types of risks. For example, in equity trading, one can limit the exposure of a model to market bets (such as a +/-5 percent net exposure limit) or to market capitalization bets. In general, risks that are subjected to limits or penalties are those that are not being forecast explicitly by the alpha model. If an alpha model attempts to forecast individual stocks but makes no attempt to forecast the stock market as a whole, it may be prudent to constrain the size of the bet that the portfolio can ultimately take on the stock market.

Still another component of a risk model may be to govern the amount of overall portfolio leverage. Leverage can be controlled in a variety of ways. For example, one can manage money under the premise that when opportunities abound, more leverage is desirable, whereas when fewer opportunities are present, less leverage is desirable. Alternatively, many quants attempt to offer their investors or bosses a relatively constant level of risk. Using volatility and dispersion as proxies for risk, quants can measure the amount of risk in markets and vary their leverage accordingly to produce a more stable level of risk. The most common tool used for this purpose is known as a *value at risk* (VaR) model, but there are others that are similar philosophically. These models typically consider the dollar amount of exposures in a portfolio and, based on current levels of volatility, forecast how much the portfolio can be expected to gain or lose within a given confidence interval. For instance, most VaR models calculate what a daily single standard deviation move in portfolio returns will be, based on current volatility levels. The way that these models control risk in the face of rising volatility is to reduce leverage. Therefore, in general, the higher the reading of risk in a VaR model, the lower the level prescribed for leverage.

In Chapter 10, we will discuss some of the significant problems with these kinds of risk models. For now I will simply point out that the core purpose of such risk models seems to me to be flawed. Other kinds of investments, such as stocks, bonds, mutual funds, private equity, or fine wine, do not attempt to offer fixed levels of volatility. Why should quants want to manage risk in this manner, or be asked to do so? Furthermore, if a quant is good at forecasting volatility or dispersion, there are far more interesting and productive ways to utilize these forecasts (e.g., in the options markets) than there are in a risk model that governs leverage. These kinds of models often cause traders to take too little risk in more normal times and too much risk in very turbulent times. Nevertheless, they are wildly popular.

A more theoretically sound approach, though substantially harder to implement practically, seeks to increase leverage when the strategy has better odds of winning and to decrease risk when the strategy has worse odds. The trick, of course, is to know when the odds are on one's side. Some quants solve this problem by allowing the level of leverage to vary with the overall strength and certainty of the predictions from the alpha model, which seems to be a reasonable approach.[2]

4.2 LIMITING THE TYPES OF RISK

Though limiting the amount of an exposure is important, some approaches to risk modeling focus on eliminating whole types of exposure entirely. Imagine that an investor's analysis indicates that CVX is likely to outperform XOM. But the trade the investor makes is simply to go long CVX while ignoring XOM. If the market drops precipitously afterward, it is likely that the investor will lose money on the trade, even if his original thesis proves correct. This is because the investor is exposed to market directional risk, even though he didn't have any particular foresight as to where the market was going. The investor could have substantially eliminated the unintentional or accidental market direction risk if he had expressed his analysis by buying CVX and shorting an equivalent amount of XOM. This way, whether the market rises, falls, or does nothing, he is indifferent. He is only affected by being right or wrong that CVX would outperform XOM.

As a general rule, it is always better to eliminate any unintentional exposures, since there should be no expectation of being compensated sufficiently for accepting them. Quantitative risk models designed to eliminate undesired exposures come in two familiar flavors: theoretical and empirical. Each is discussed in detail in the subsequent sections.

It is also worth noting that alpha models can (and often do) incorporate risk management concepts. Let's assume that a quant is building a relative alpha strategy. A significant amount of work is required to match what "relative" means to the exposures he intends to take or hedge. Revisiting an earlier example, if the quant is building a relative alpha strategy to forecast equity returns, he might not believe he has a valid way to forecast the returns of the sectors to which these equities belong. In this case, the quant may design his bet structures so that he is making forecasts of stocks' returns *relative* to their sectors' returns, which means that he never has a bet on the direction of the sector itself, only which stocks will outperform and which stocks will underperform the sector. This, in turn, helps him eliminate sector bets, which is clearly a risk management exercise as much as it is alpha generation. As such, it is theoretically possible (and not infrequently seen in practice) to incorporate all the needed components of his risk model fully into his alpha model by specifying the alpha model such that it only forecasts exactly the exposures from which it expects to make money and structures its bets to avoid exposure to non-forecasted factors. Although not all quant strategies do this, it is worth remembering to look inside the alpha model for elements of risk management, especially for those evaluating a quant strategy.

4.2.1   Theory-Driven Risk Models

Theory-driven risk modeling typically focuses on named or *systematic* risk factors. Just as in the case of theory-driven alpha models, systematic risks that are derived from theory are those for which the quant can make a reasonable, economic argument. Theory-driven risk modeling uses a set of pre-defined systematic risks, which enables the quant to measure and calibrate a given portfolio's exposures.

It is important to note that the use of the term *systematic* in defining risk is completely different from the use of the term *systematic* in describing quant strategies. Systematic risks are those that cannot be diversified away. In the world of single stocks, the market itself is a systematic risk because no amount of diversification among various single stocks eliminates an investor's exposure to the performance of the market itself. If the market is up a lot, it is extremely likely that a portfolio that is long stocks is also going to be up. If the market is down a lot, it is extremely likely that a portfolio that is long stocks will be down. Sector risk is another example of systematic risk, as is market capitalization risk (i.e., small caps versus large caps). A practical example of such a problem, and one that has been well documented by the hedge fund replication crowd, is that an unconstrained market-neutral value model will very likely be making a bet on small caps outperforming large caps.[3]

The world of fixed income, similarly, contains a host of systematic risks. For example, whether one owns corporate bonds or government bonds, owners of these bonds are all subject to interest rate risk, that is, the risk that rates go up, regardless of the level of diversification of the actual portfolio of bonds. Similar examples can be found in any asset class and frequently also across asset classes. Any economically valid grouping of instruments, in other words, can be said to share one or more common systematic risk factors. An investor who traffics in any of those instruments, then, should be aware of this risk factor and should be either making intentional bets on it or eliminating his exposure.

4.2.2 Empirical Risk Models

Empirical risk models are based on the same premise as theory-driven models, namely that systematic risks should be measured and mitigated. However, the empirical approach uses historical data to determine what these risks are and how exposed a given portfolio is to them. Using statistical techniques such as *principal component analysis* (PCA), a quant is able to use historical data to discern systematic risks that don't have names but that may well correspond to named risk factors.[4] For example, a PCA run on bond market data using Treasury bonds across various maturities usually shows that the first (most important) risk factor statistically corresponds to the level of interest rates, or what a theory-driven risk model might call *interest rate risk*. PCA and other statistical models are commonly used in equity markets as well, and these models typically find that the market itself is the first, most important driver of returns for a given stock, usually followed by its sector. These statistical risk models are most commonly found among statistical arbitrage traders, who are betting on exactly that component of an individual stock's returns that is *not* explained by systematic risks. It is important to note that such statistical methods may discover entirely new systematic risk factors, which a reasonable observer might be inclined to acknowledge exist but for which names have not been assigned. On the other hand, statistical risk models are subject to being "fooled" by the data into finding a risk factor that will not persist for any useful amount of time into the future. It is also possible for a statistical risk model to find spurious exposures, which are just coincidences and not indicative of any real risk in the marketplace. This is a delicate problem for the researcher.

4.2.3 How Quants Choose a Risk Model

Quants are attracted to theory-driven risk models because the risk factors they encapsulate make sense. It is hard to make the argument that market risk does not exist as a strong systematic risk factor in equities. Note that this is much the same reasoning that supports theoretical approaches to alpha modeling: Any reasonable person can understand the theory and see that it is likely to be true. This in turn can give the quant faith in the models when it isn't performing very well. Warren Buffett, for example, didn't change his stripes just because he dramatically underperformed the stock market during the Internet bubble. He was able to "keep the faith" in no small part because his approach to markets has very strong theoretical underpinnings.

Quants that choose empirical risk models typically seek the benefits of adaptiveness. Theoretical risk models are relatively rigid, meaning that the risk factors are not altered often (otherwise the theory would not have been very strong in the first place). Yet the factors that drive markets do change over time. For a while in early 2003, daily reports about the prospect, and later the progress, of the U.S. invasion of Iraq drove stock, bond, currency, and commodity markets almost singlehandedly. More recently, in early 2008, commodity prices were a significant factor. At other times, expectations of how much the Federal Reserve might cut or raise rates are the key drivers of market behavior. As markets evolve, the data that the markets produce reflect this evolution, and these data drive empirical risk models. For these reasons, an empirical model may be more adaptive to ever-changing market conditions by detecting through new data whatever factors are implicitly driving markets. There are two stages to this adaptation. During the early phases of a market regime change (e.g., when equity investors rapidly change their behavior from risk seeking to risk aversion), the quant is using now irrelevant historical data to determine relationships and measure risk factors. Thus, during this phase, the empirical risk model will be modeling market risks incorrectly. Later, if the new behavior persists, the empirical risk model eventually will catch up to the newly prevailing theme driving markets and all will be well again.

Besides exhibiting a weakness during a regime change, a basic understanding of statistics reveals another problem with empirical risk models. To achieve statistical significance and reduce the potential for measurement error in computing relationships among various instruments, empirical risk models require a rather large amount of data. But this leads to a tradeoff that could squelch most of the adaptiveness benefits of empirical risk models. The more data that are used, i.e., the further back into history we must look, the less adaptive a model can be, because each new data point is but one of a very large number. If we use two years' worth of rolling daily data, or approximately 520 trading days, each new day adds a new data point and causes the oldest one to fall out of the sample. So for every day that passes, only two days' data have changed out of 520. It will therefore take a long time to "turn the ship" and have the empirical model find the new drivers of risk from the data. However, if the quant attempts to improve adaptiveness by shortening the historical window used, the power of the statistics diminishes significantly so that there cannot be sufficient confidence in the measurements to act on them.

Still, there may be benefits to empirical risk models. If the theoretical risk models are any good at being right, an empirical model should capture these effects without having to know the names of the factors beforehand. If market risk is indeed a big driver of stock prices, an empirical model should pick this up from the data. If the data don't bear it out, what good is the theory? Furthermore, the competing objectives of statistical significance and adaptiveness can be dealt with in part by using intraday data. For example, if a quant uses one-minute intraday snapshots of price activities instead of simply a single closing price for each day, he is able to extract almost 400 data points for *each day* in his sample, which allows him to use far fewer days to achieve the same statistical significance as another quant using a single data point for each day (the closing price).

Ultimately, because of the comfort level with the concepts involved in theory-driven risk modeling, most quants tend to use theory-driven risk models rather than empirical risk models. It is worth noting that these two kinds of risk models are not mutually exclusive. Quants may perfectly reasonably use a combination of both, if they deem it appropriate. A small minority of managers also attempt to use their judgment and discretion to monitor market behavior and, should it become clear to them—for example, from the way that the financial media and their peers in the business are behaving—that there is a "new" risk factor that is driving markets, they build a "made-to-order" risk factor to measure this temporary phenomenon. When they see that the new driver has faded in importance, they can remove it from the risk model, again using their judgment.

It is worth mentioning that quants have the option, as is the case with most of the modules of the black box, to build their own risk model or to purchase one that is "off the shelf." Most premade risk models are not of the empirical variety because empirical solutions require a specifically set universe of instruments, and the analytical techniques are usually relatively easy to implement with simple price data. Also, the vast majority of premade risk models are useful only for equity trading strategies. Several purveyors of risk models—such as BARRA, Northfield, Qontigo/Axioma, and Wolfe Research—have made a healthy business of licensing their software to quant traders. The advantage of buying risk models is that they are ready to be deployed immediately, without extensive R&D by the quant trader, and usually at least reasonably well thought through. However, they are also by nature somewhat generic. There are advantages to building risk models as well, primarily because they can be customized to the specific needs of the particular quant trader.

It is my firm opinion that, to the extent possible, decisions about which exposures to accept, and to what degrees, should be built into alpha models, rather than relying on an overarching risk model fed into an optimizer.

For example, suppose that you have two alpha strategies. One is a deep value strategy, which measures how cheap each stock is (we can ignore the definition of cheap for the moment), and buys or shorts in proportion to cheapness or expensiveness. This strategy is designed to benefit from relative value among closely related stocks—i.e., those within the same industry, general market cap band, etc. The other is predicting earnings surprises and disappointments, and it has the largest signals for the largest deviations from expectations.

This second strategy only engages when there are large deviations from expectations, whereas the first strategy always has a view of the cheapness—and therefore the attractiveness—of every stock, all the time. If we simply mix these two signals together and apply an overarching risk model, we miss something that I believe is crucial: when the second strategy has a prediction of a big event—a large deviation from expectations—it is not so likely that the conventional forces that exert themselves onto stock price movements will be as relevant as they might be in the absence of big news. In other words, the news will drive the stock's price in the near term, not the general, market-wide performance of market-cap, sector, and other common risk factors. So, why control for those factors in that moment, for those stocks being driven almost entirely by big news?

Rather than mixing these signals together and applying a risk model to that blended set of signals (we discuss this in greater detail in Chapter 6), we can think of allocating a certain amount of risk to each of these two strategies. Each strategy has its appropriate risk tolerance baked into the bet structure and/or definition of "relative." The first strategy could, for example, rank stocks that are closely comparable within industries and market cap bins. The second only forces its bets to end up market-neutral in a broad sense—even if that means hedging using an index or a broad basket of stocks (e.g., if there are predominantly positive surprises on a given day, its single-stock bets will be mostly long). In this scenario, risk models could still be useful to ensure that portfolio managers understand the bets their models are taking, and perhaps even within the optimizer, to make sure that some broader bands of risk tolerances aren't breached.

4.3   RISK MANAGEMENT, OUTSIDE OF RISK MODELS

We have described the way that risk models are designed and utilized. But there are significant considerations in the domain of risk management that bear discussion here. In Chapter 3, we proposed a taxonomy of alphas. At the highest level, we distinguished data-driven versus theory-driven alphas. This was useful to understand the alphas, but the risk manager's view of this taxonomy is and should be different.

Let's consider a metaphor. Suppose that we are observing a forest. It is a still, peaceful day. The individual leaves on a tree are moving for largely idiosyncratic reasons—a caterpillar munches on this leaf, a bird's wingbeat moves another. Now, let's imagine a Category 5 hurricane comes through the area. Pretty much every leaf, every branch, every trunk will be straining in the same direction. Now let's apply this to our taxonomy of alphas. We put forth that you can have many definitions of the concept of "value," or "growth," and many ways to implement these signals, for example, in the definition of "relative." In a period where there are no major risks blowing up, it is like the peaceful day in the forest. Each of these variations will have some diversification benefits, moving idiosyncratically. But the more that major risk factors (including and often exclusively ones that are exogenous to one's risk model) are driving markets, the less these variations matter. In fact, it is in scenarios like this that we should consider that we don't have anywhere near seven independent strategies—even if we are actually doing all seven of those named in Chapter 3. Value tends to behave like mean reversion, when push comes to shove. Growth tends to behave like momentum. Supply and demand, quality, technical sentiment strategies, depending on what specific ones we have, might offer some diversification, or might end up correlating to one or another group of strategies. Or, equally possible, such strategies may simply offer no insight into market movements, given whatever risk factors are prevalent. If World War III breaks out, it is pretty unlikely that our technical sentiment or management quality signals have much to do with asset prices.

As such, I encourage portfolio managers to think of how much true diversification they have in their mix of strategies, and to allocate risk accordingly. While this definitely can be modeled, it is not a risk model in the conventional sense.

4.4   SUMMARY

Risk management is frequently misunderstood to be an exercise designed to reduce risk. It is really about the selection and sizing of exposures, to maximize returns for a given level of volatility or downside. After all, reducing risk almost always comes at the cost of reducing return. So, risk management activities must focus on eliminating or reducing exposure to unnecessary risks but also on accepting risks that are expected to offer attractive payoffs. This is true whether one uses a systematic investment process or a discretionary one. The main difference between the two is that quants typically use software to manage risk, whereas discretionary traders, if they use software in the risk management process at all, primarily attempt merely to measure risk in some way, without any systematic process for adjusting their positions in accordance with predefined guidelines.

Whether a quant uses a theoretical or empirical risk model or some hybrid thereof, the goal is the same: The quant wants to identify which systematic exposures are being taken, measure the amount of each exposure in a portfolio, and then make some determination about whether these risks are acceptable. What is good about these kinds of analyses, along with many of the other quantitative risk-modeling approaches, is that they require the quant to be intentional about risk-taking, rather than slapping together some positions that seem like good trades and more or less ignoring the incidental exposures these trades may share. For example, if oil prices become a dominant theme in investors' sentiment about the markets, positions across a variety of sectors and asset classes can be driven by oil. This can lead to significant downside if a previously profitable trend in the price of oil reverses. A risk model may allow the quant to see this kind of exposure and make a choice about whether or not to do something about it. This is an important point. Quantitative approaches to risk management, by virtue of seeking to measure and make explicit which exposures are driving a portfolio, put the power into the hands of the portfolio manager to make rational, intentional decisions. Of course, whether this intentionality is helpful or hurtful depends on the judgment of the portfolio manager, even among quants. But at least quantitative risk management techniques offer the opportunity to see what risks are present in a portfolio and to what extent.

In Chapter 5, we examine transaction cost models, which are the final providers of input to help determine the most desirable target portfolio for a quant. Before doing so, let's look at Exhibit 4.1 to examine our progress through this journey inside the black box.

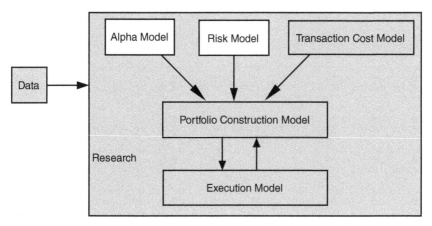

EXHIBIT 4.1   Schematic of the Black Box

NOTES

1. Uncertainty has broadly been adopted as being synonymous with risk. There is usually not much justification for its use, other than expediency for the purposes of relatively easy computations to answer the question, How much risk is there?
2. This concept was formalized in the Kelly criterion, in a paper by John L. Kelly, Jr., in the *Bell System Technical Journal* in 1956. The *Kelly criterion* provides a systematic way of sizing the risk taken on each of a series of bets based on the bettor's edge, which maximizes the expected gains by the end of the series of bets. The edge is defined as a combination of the payoff for winning and the odds of winning. This concept has been widely applied in gambling and somewhat in investing. The noted quant Edward Thorp is credited with first applying the Kelly criterion to trading strategies. However, some critics of the Kelly betting strategy point out that a critical assumption of this criterion is that each bet is expected to be independent of the next, which is true in many forms of gambling, for example. However, in investing, bets can be serially correlated, which is to say that returns to investment strategies tend to be streaky. As such, in general, many investors who believe in the concept of the Kelly criterion use a derivative version of the strategy, such as "half Kelly," to bet less than Kelly suggests. Useful background on Kelly and the criterion can be found on William Poundstone's web site or in his book about Kelly, called *Fortune's Formula*.
3. This phenomenon exists, if for no other reason, because the value investor tends to buy stocks that have fallen in price, which tend therefore to have experienced a shrinkage in their market capitalization. A market-neutral value investor would also tend to sell expensive stocks, which are likely to have rallied and therefore will have experienced market capitalization appreciation as well.
4. *Principal components analysis* (PCA) is a statistical technique used to reduce the complexity of a set of instruments down to a manageable set of "factors," each of which is called a *vector*. Each vector represents a statistically derived systematic risk among the instruments and is derived by analyzing the historical relationships among all the instruments in the set.

CHAPTER 5

Transaction Cost Models

*Without frugality, none can be rich, and with it, very few
would be poor.*

—Samuel Johnson

So far we have examined alpha models and risk models, both critical elements of the black box. The alpha model plays the role of the starry-eyed optimist, and the risk model plays the role of the nervous worrier. In this little play, transaction cost models would be the frugal accountant.

The idea behind transaction cost models is that it costs money to trade, which means that one should not trade unless there is a very good reason to do so. This is not an overly draconian view of trading costs. Many highly successful quants estimate that their transaction costs eat away between 20 and 50 percent of their returns.

In the world of quant trading, there are only two reasons to make a trade: first, if it improves the odds or magnitude of making money (as indicated by the alpha model), or, second, if it reduces the odds or magnitude of losing money (as indicated by the risk model). These reasons, however, are subject to a caveat: A tiny, incremental improvement in the reward or risk prospects of a portfolio might not be sufficient to overcome the cost of trading. In other words, the benefits of the trade need to clear the hurdle of the cost of transacting. Neither the market nor your broker care what the benefits of a trade are. Rather, making a given trade utilizes services that cost the same, regardless of the purpose or value the trade holds for the trader. A transaction cost model is a way of quantifying the cost of making a trade of a given size so that this information can be used in conjunction with the alpha and risk models to determine the best portfolio to hold.

Note that transaction cost models are not designed to minimize the cost of trading, only to inform the portfolio construction engine of the costs of making any given trade. The part of the black box that minimizes costs is the execution algorithm, which we discuss at length in Chapter 7. It is less glamorous to describe costs than it is to minimize them, but the former remains critically important. If a trader underestimates the cost of transacting, this can lead to the system making too many trades that have insufficient benefit, which in turn leads to a problem of "bleeding" losses as a result of the constant acceptance of trading costs. If the trader overestimates the cost of transacting, this can lead to too little trading, which usually results in holding positions too long. Either way, the trader ends up with suboptimal performance, which highlights the importance of correctly estimating transaction costs. But there is also a tradeoff between using more complex models that more accurately describe transaction costs and using less complex models that are faster and less computationally burdensome.

5.1 DEFINING TRANSACTION COSTS

It is useful to understand what the costs of trading actually are, since we are describing ways to model them. Transaction costs have three major components: commissions and fees, slippage, and market impact.

5.1.1 Commissions and Fees

Commissions and fees, the first kind of transaction costs, are paid to brokerages, exchanges, and regulators for the services they provide, namely access to other market participants, improved security of transacting, and operational infrastructure. For many quants, brokerage commission costs are rather small on a per-trade basis. Quant traders typically do not utilize many of the services and personnel of the bank but instead use only the bank's infrastructure to go directly to the market. The incremental cost of a trade to a bank is therefore very small, and even very low commissions can be profitable. Given the volume of trading that quants do, they can be extremely profitable clients for the brokerages, despite the diminutive commissions they pay. Some quants utilize significantly less of the bank's infrastructure and therefore pay even lower commission rates than others who use more and pay higher rates.

Commissions are not the only costs charged by brokerages and exchanges. Brokers charge fees (which are usually a component of the commissions) for services known as *clearing* and *settlement*. Clearing involves regulatory reporting and monitoring, tax handling, and handling failure, all of which are activities that must take place in advance of settlement. Settlement is the delivery of securities in exchange for payment in full, which is the final step in the life of a trading transaction and fulfills the obligations of both parties involved in the transaction. These services take effort and therefore cost money. And, given that many quants are doing tens of thousands of trades each day, there can be a significant amount of work involved.

Exchanges and electronic matching networks provide a different kind of service from conventional brokers, namely access to pools of liquidity. Exchanges must attract traders to their floors for trading, and this trading volume then attracts other traders who are seeking liquidity. Exchanges, too, have some operational effort to make by virtue of their roles, and they also guarantee that both counterparties in a given trade uphold their contractual responsibilities. As such, exchanges also charge small fees for each transaction to cover their costs and risks (and, of course, to profit as a business). More recently, "dark pools," which are effectively matching engines to pair buyers and sellers of the same instrument at the same time within a given bank's customer base, have come into prominence, and now account for a large percentage of all U.S. equity trading volumes (almost 39 percent in 2019, according to the *Wall Street Journal*).[1]

5.1.2 Slippage

Commissions and fees certainly are not negligible. But neither are they the dominant part of transaction costs for most quants. They are also basically fixed, which makes them easy to model. If the all-in commissions and fees add up to, say, $0.001 per share, the quant must simply know that the trade in question is worth more in terms of alpha generation or risk reduction than this $0.001 per-share hurdle. On the other hand, slippage and market impact are considerably trickier to measure, model, and manage.

Slippage is the change in the price between the time a trader (or quant system) decides to transact and the time when the order is actually at the exchange for execution. The market is constantly moving, but a trading decision is made as of a specific point in time. As time passes between the decision being made and the trade being executed, the instrument being forecast is likely to be moving away from the price at which it was quoted when the forecast was made. In fact, the more accurate the forecast, the more likely it is that the price of the instrument is actually going toward the expected price as more time passes. But the instrument makes this move without the trader benefiting, because he has not yet gotten his trade to market. Imagine a trader decides to sell 100 shares of CVX while the price is at $100.00 per share. When the trader finally gets the order through his broker and to the exchange, the price has gone down to $99.90 per share, for a decline of $0.10 per share. This $0.10 per share is a cost of the transaction because the trader intended to sell at $100.00, but in fact the price had already moved down to $99.90. In the event that the price actually moves up from $100.00 to $100.10, the trader gets to sell at a higher price, which means that slippage can sometimes be a source of positive return.

Strategies that tend to suffer most from slippage are those that pursue trend-following strategies, because they are seeking to buy and sell instruments that are already moving in the desired direction. Strategies that tend to suffer least from slippage, and for which slippage can sometimes be a *positive*, are those that are mean-reverting in orientation, because these strategies are usually trying to buy and sell instruments that are moving against them when the order is placed. A quant trader's latency or speed to market has a large effect on the level of slippage his strategy will experience over time. This is because slippage is a function of the amount of time that passes between the order being decided and the order reaching the market for execution. The more latency in a trader's system or communications with the marketplace, the more time passes before her order gets to the market and the further the price of an instrument is likely to have moved away from the price when the decision was made. Worse still, the more accurate a forecast, particularly in the near term, the more damaging slippage will be.

In addition to time, slippage is also a function of the volatility of the instrument being forecast. If we are forecasting 90-day Treasury bills, which tend to move very slowly throughout the day and which can go some weeks without much movement at all, it is likely that slippage is not a major factor. On the other hand, if we are forecasting a high-volatility Internet stock, slippage can be a major issue. Google, Inc. (GOOG), has had an average daily range of 2.6 percent of its opening price, which is about 16 times larger than its average move from one day to the next. Clearly, slippage makes a huge difference if you're trading GOOG.

5.1.3 Market Impact

Market impact, the third and final major component of transaction costs, is perhaps the most important for quants. The basic problem described by market impact is that, when a trader goes to buy an instrument, the price of the instrument tends to go up, partly as a result of the trader's order. If the trader sells, the price goes down as he attempts to complete his trade. At small order sizes, this price movement usually bounces between the current best bid and offer. However, for larger orders, the price move can be substantial, ranging in the extremes, even to several percentage points. Market impact, then, is a measurement of how much a given order "moves" the market by its demand for liquidity. Market impact is normally defined as the difference between the price at the time a market order enters the exchange and the price at which the trade is actually executed.

The basic idea behind market impact is simple enough and is based on the ubiquitous principle of supply and demand. When a trader goes to market to execute a trade for some size, someone has to be willing to "take the other side," or supply the size he is looking to trade. The bigger the size of the demand by a trader, the more expensive the trade will be because the trader must access more of the supply. As simple as the idea of market impact is, quantifying it is actually not so straightforward. One doesn't know how much a particular trade impacts the market until the trade has already been completed, which may be too late to be useful. Also, there are many other factors that can drive a given observation of market impact and that can complicate its measurement. For example, the number of other trades that are being made in the same direction at the same time or whether news in the stock is causing impact to behave differently than normal are both issues that would affect measurements of market impact and are nontrivial to quantify. These other factors are also usually impossible to predict, much less control. Therefore, market impact, as used in transaction cost modeling, usually does not account for these factors but rather focuses on the size of the order relative to the liquidity present at the time. *Liquidity* can be defined in a number of ways, whether by the size available at the bid or offer or by measurements of the "depth of book," which relate to those bids or offers that have been placed away from the best bid/offer prices.

In addition, there could be some interaction between slippage and market impact that makes it tricky to segregate these two concepts in a model. A stock might be trending upward while a trader is trying to sell it, for example. In this case, both slippage and impact could look like *negative* numbers. In other words, the trader might deduce that he was actually *paid*, not charged, to sell the stock. For instance, assume that a trader decides to enter a market order to sell a stock he owns, and at that moment, the stock's price happens to be $100.00. But by the time his order hits the market, the stock, continuing its trend upward, is now trading at $100.05. Slippage is actually *negative* $0.05 because his order entered the marketplace at a more favorable price than the one at which he decided to sell. But now assume that the price continues to drift upward as his order makes its way to the front of the line of sale orders, simply because the marketplace's demand to buy the shares might simply overwhelm the orders, including his, to sell it. The trader ultimately sells his stock at $100.20, generating negative market impact of $0.15 on top of the negative slippage of $0.05. Clearly, entering sell orders does not usually make stocks go up, but in this case, it might not be possible to differentiate impact from slippage or either concept from the move the stock was making independently of the trader's order. Did his sell order slow the rise of the stock somewhat, and, if so, by how much? These are the kinds of complications that traders must account for in building transaction cost models.

Some kinds of trades further complicate the measurement of transaction costs. We have discussed trades that demand liquidity from the marketplace, and these behave as one might expect intuitively: If a trader demands liquidity, there is a cost charged by those providing it. Looking at this from the opposite perspective, someone gets paid to *supply* liquidity. Historically, the party that supplied liquidity was a market maker or specialist whose job it was to make sure that traders can execute an order when they want to. More recently, volumes across many electronically tradable instruments have increased sufficiently to allow for well-functioning marketplaces without the presence of a market maker in the middle.

Alternative Trading Systems (ATS) are less regulated than traditional exchanges. The most common type of ATS is an *Electronic Communication Network* (ECN), which are venues that allow customers to trade directly with one another. The challenge for an ECN is to attract enough customer order flow to show abundant liquidity on their exchange. ECNs also must provide robust technology so that their exchange can continue to function without disruption. To attract providers of liquidity, most ECNs in equity markets have established methods to pay traders who provide liquidity and take payment from traders who demand liquidity. It might cost something like three-tenths of a penny per share for a trader who buys shares at the offer or sells shares at the bid, whereas those providing the bids and offers that are getting hit are earning closer to two-tenths of a penny. The ECN keeps the difference, around one-tenth of a penny per share, as its source of revenue. Some kinds of trading strategies (usually mean reversion strategies) actually call for a mostly passive execution approach in which this act of providing liquidity is modeled as a source of profit due to the rebate programs that ECNs put in place to attract liquidity providers. It is worth noting that some ECNs and exchanges, especially outside of the equities markets, offer no rebates and do not charge customers to take liquidity. There are also inverse exchanges, which pay takers of liquidity and charge providers of liquidity.

Another type of ATS, *dark pools* also allow customers to interact with one another. Dark pools are created by brokers or independent firms to allow their customers to trade directly with each other in an anonymous way. They arose in part because of concerns about the market impact associated with large orders. On a dark pool, there is no information provided about the limit order book, which contains all the liquidity being provided by market makers and other participants. Customers are simply posting their orders to the pool and if someone happens to want to do the opposite side of those orders, the orders get filled. As a result of this anonymous process of matching orders, the market is less likely to move as much as it would in a more public venue, where automated market-making practitioners require compensation to take the other side of large orders. Their invisibility makes dark pools somewhat controversial. They could not exist without the public markets, because the securities traded on dark pools are listed on public exchanges, and the prices at which transactions occur are largely informed by those public (also referred to as "lit") markets. But dark pools do not offer anything to the lit markets in return for this reliance. In addition, they are invitation-only, rather than being totally available to any willing party. These features, while appealing to those who are allowed to participate in these transactions, seem unfair to other investors. As we will see in Part 4, there is plenty of controversy around certain aspects of our markets—particularly U.S. equities. But much of that is misplaced, in my opinion.

5.2 TYPES OF TRANSACTION COST MODELS

There are four basic types of transaction cost models: flat, linear, piecewise-linear, and quadratic—all of which are trying to answer the basic question of how much it will cost to transact a given trade. Some of these costs are fixed and known—for example, commissions and fees. Models of transaction costs use these fixed charges as a baseline, below which the expense of trading cannot go. Other costs, such as slippage and impact, are variable and cannot be known precisely until they have been incurred. Slippage is affected by a number of factors, such as the volatility of the instrument in question (i.e., the higher the volatility, the greater the expectation of slippage) or its prevailing trend (i.e., the stronger the trend, the more slippage is likely to cost if one attempts to transact in the direction of the trend). Impact also has many drivers, including the size of the order being executed, the amount of liquidity that happens to be available to absorb the order, and imbalances between supply and demand for the instrument at the moment. Traders use transaction cost models in an attempt to develop reasonable expectations for the cost of an order of various sizes for each name they trade.

It is worth mentioning that each instrument has its own unique characteristics based on the investor base that tends to transact in it and the amount of liquidity and volatility present in the instrument over time. GOOG doesn't trade exactly like Amazon (AMZN), and CVX doesn't trade exactly like XOM. As a result, in an effort to improve their estimates of transaction costs, many quants build separate models for transaction costs for each instrument in their portfolios and allow each of these models to evolve over time, based on the trading data the quant collects from his execution systems. In other words, many transaction cost models are highly empirical, allowing the actual, observable, recorded transaction data from a quant's own strategy to drive and evolve the model over time.

The total cost of transactions for an instrument, holding all else (such as liquidity, trend or volatility) constant, can be visualized as a graph with the size of the order (in terms of dollars, shares, contracts, or the like) on the x-axis and the cost of trading on the y-axis. It is generally accepted by the quant community that the shape of this curve is *quadratic*, which means that the cost gets higher ever more quickly as the size of the trade gets larger (due to market impact).[2] Certainly many quants do model transaction costs as a quadratic function of the size of the trade (more on this later). However, modeling transaction costs this way can be more complicated and computationally intensive, whereas the other choices of modeling transaction costs are simpler and less intensive.

With advances in computer hardware and processors, the extra computational burdens are now rather easily managed, but that does not alter the fact that a proper quadratic cost function is inherently more complicated. These functions, from the simplest to most complex, are described in the following sections.

5.2.1 Flat Transaction Cost Models

The first kind of transaction cost model is a *flat* model, which means that the cost of trading is the same, regardless of the size of the order. This is extremely straightforward computationally, but it is rarely correct and is not widely used. A graph of a flat transaction cost model is shown in Exhibit 5.1.

As you can see, this graph models the cost of a trade as being fixed, regardless of the size of the trade, which is an assumption that seems obviously incorrect in most circumstances. The main circumstance in which such a model is reasonable is if the size being traded is nearly always about the same and liquidity remains sufficiently constant. In this case, one can simply figure out the total cost of such a trade and assume that it will always cost the same. This assumption is wrong, but being wrong has no consequence because the size of the trade is always the same. Note that where the solid line crosses the dashed line, the model is close to a correct estimate of transaction costs. So, if this point of intersection corresponds to the size of trading normally done, and if the range of that trade size is within the region where the flat line is close to the curved line, a flat t-cost model may not be problematic.

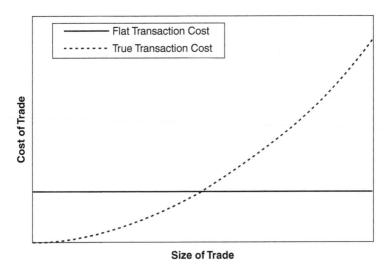

EXHIBIT 5.1   Flat Transaction Cost Function

5.2.2   Linear Transaction Cost Models

The second kind of transaction cost model is *linear*, which means that the cost of a transaction gets larger with a constant slope as the size of the transaction grows larger, as shown in Exhibit 5.2. This is a better fit relative to the true transaction cost, but it is still mostly useful as a shortcut to building a proper model.

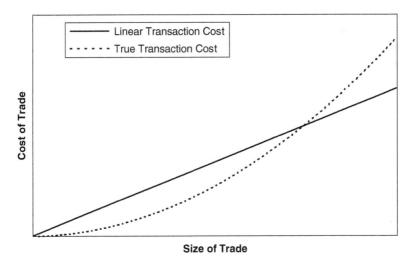

EXHIBIT 5.2   Linear Transaction Cost Function

As you can see, the linear transaction cost model must trade off over-estimating costs at smaller trade sizes with underestimating costs at larger trade sizes. Here, again, the model is correct where the solid line crosses the dashed line and is "close to correct" in the immediate vicinity of that intersection. As with the flat t-cost model, if the trades being done are always within that region, a linear t-cost model is reasonable. In any case, across the curve, it appears to be a better estimator of the real transaction cost than is given by the flat transaction cost model.

5.2.3 Piecewise-Linear Transaction Cost Models

Piecewise-linear transaction cost models are used to help with precision while using reasonably simple formulas to do so. The idea of a piecewise-linear transaction cost model is that, in certain ranges, a linear estimate is about right, but at some point, the curvature of the quadratic estimator causes a significant enough rise in the slope of the real transaction cost line that it is worthwhile using a new line from that point on. This concept is illustrated in Exhibit 5.3.

As you can see, the accuracy of this type of model is significantly better than what can be achieved with flat or linear models across a much wider range of trading sizes; as a result, this model is rather popular among quants as a happy medium between simplicity and accuracy.

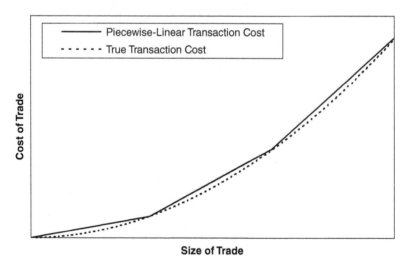

EXHIBIT 5.3 Piecewise-Linear Transaction Cost Function

5.2.4 Quadratic Transaction Cost Models

Finally, quants can build *quadratic* models of transaction costs. These are computationally the most intensive because the function involved is not nearly as simple as what is used for a linear model, or even for a piecewise-linear model. It has multiple terms, exponents, and generally is a pain to build. A plot of a quadratic transaction cost model is shown in Exhibit 5.4.

This is clearly the most "accurate" estimate we have seen of transaction costs. And yet it is not perfect, and it is significantly more difficult to build and utilize than a linear or piecewise linear model. You might be wondering how it is that we have estimated a quadratic function using a quadratic function and still ended up with a less than perfect estimate of the true transaction cost. The reason is that the solid line reflects what is *expected*, whereas the dotted line reflects what is *actually observed* after the fact. This is a significant difference because the solid line must be specified before trading, whereas the dotted line is what is observed empirically after trading. Because the actual transaction cost is an empirically observable fact and any estimation of transaction costs is a prediction, the prediction is unlikely to be perfect. Causes of differences between estimated and realized transaction costs might include changes in liquidity or volatility in the instrument over time or changes in the types of traders (e.g., market makers, hedge funds, mutual funds, or retail investors) who are transacting in the same stock over time. Of course, the quant is trying as hard as possible to make good

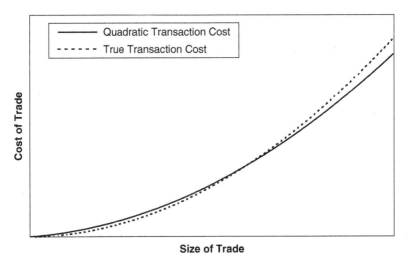

Size of Trade

EXHIBIT 5.4   Quadratic Transaction Cost Function

forecasts, but given that it is known that the forecast is very unlikely to be perfect and that speed and simplicity are both also desirable, the trade-off between accuracy and simplicity is one which requires the judgment of the quant.

Regardless of the type of model used, the quant must describe the cost of trading each instrument in her universe. After all, a less liquid small cap stock is likely to be more expensive to trade than a more liquid mega cap stock, and that must be a factor in deciding how much of each to trade. Furthermore, the quant should refresh empirical estimations of transaction costs both to keep the model current with the prevailing market conditions as well as to indicate when more research is required to improve the model itself.

5.3 SUMMARY

The role of transaction cost models is simply to advise the portfolio construction model how much it might cost to transact. Its job is *not* to minimize the cost of trading, just as the job of the alpha model is not to generate returns but rather to make forecasts and to provide these forecasts to the portfolio construction model. Cost minimization happens in two phases. First, the portfolio construction model, using the input provided by the transaction cost model, accounts for cost in generating a target portfolio. Second, the target portfolio is passed along to the execution algorithms, which explicitly attempt to transact the desired portfolio as cheaply as possible.

There are several kinds of transaction model, ranging from extremely simple to rather complex. The simpler models are useful for traders who either do trades of roughly the same size in a given instrument all the time or who trade in such small size that they can simply assume a modest cost and be close to correct most of the time. The more complex models are useful for quants who have the potential to trade significant, or significantly variable, quantities of a given instrument in a short period. Any of the four models described here can be valid in the right set of circumstances. The question to consider is whether the model chosen fits the application and facts of the situation.

We turn our attention next to portfolio construction models, which utilize the inputs provided by the alpha, risk, and transaction cost models described over the past three chapters, and come up with a target portfolio designed to maximize returns relative to risk. But first we check our progress on the map of the black box in Exhibit 5.5.

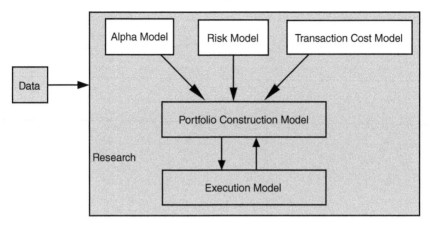

EXHIBIT 5.5   Schematic of the Black Box

NOTES

1. Alexander Osipovich, "'Dark Pools' Draw More Trading Amid Low Volatility," *Wall Street Journal*, May 3, 2019. https://www.wsj.com/articles/dark-pools-draw-more-trading-amid-low-volatility-11556886916

2. While a quadratic cost function is the most commonly agreed upon type, it is not universally accepted. There is good evidence that, at least for U.S. equities, cost per share scales with an exponent of 1.5, or in other words, as the square root of trade size. This empirically seems to be a better fit, while also being supported by the knowledge that many market makers and dealers view their inventory risk as scaling the same way—as the square root of its size. However, compared to linear or quadratic cost functions, this perhaps more accurate one is more computationally intensive and difficult to use.

CHAPTER 6

Portfolio Construction Models

No sensible decision can be made any longer without taking into account not only the world as it is, but the world as it will be.
—Isaac Asimov

The goal of a portfolio construction model is to determine what portfolio the quant wants to own. The model acts like an arbitrator, hearing the arguments of the optimist (alpha model), the pessimist (risk model), and the cost-conscious accountant (transaction cost model) and then deciding how to proceed. The decision to allocate this or that amount to the various holdings in a portfolio is mostly based on a balancing of considerations of expected return, risk, and transaction costs, often coupled with information about the similarities between the assets and any constraints the investor might have. Too much emphasis on the opportunity can lead to ruin by ignoring risk. Too much emphasis on the risk can lead to underperformance by ignoring the opportunity. Too much emphasis on transaction costs can lead to paralysis because this will tend to cause the trader to hold positions indefinitely instead of taking on the cost of refreshing the portfolio.

Quantitative portfolio construction models come in two major forms. The first family is rule-based. Rule-based portfolio construction models are based on heuristics defined by the quant trader and can be exceedingly simple or rather complex. The heuristics that are used are generally rules that are derived from human experience, such as by trial and error.

The second family of quantitative portfolio construction models is optimized. Optimizers utilize algorithms—step-by-step sets of rules designed to get the user from a starting point to a desired ending point—to seek the best way to reach a goal that the quant defines. This goal is known as an *objective function*, and the canonical example of an objective function for an optimizer is to seek the portfolio that generates the highest possible return for a unit of risk (usually, though not necessarily ideally, defined as the standard deviation of returns). By their nature, optimizers can be more difficult to understand at a great level of detail, but they are straightforward conceptually.

As in the case of blending alpha models, discussed in Chapter 3, portfolio construction models are a fascinating area to study. Furthermore, portfolio construction turns out to be a critical component of the investment process. If a trader has a variety of investment ideas of varying quality but allocates the most money to the worst ideas and the least money to the best ideas, it is not hard to imagine this trader delivering poor results over time. At a minimum, his results would be much better if he could improve his approach to portfolio construction. And yet, actual solutions to the problem of how to allocate assets across the various positions in a portfolio are not exceedingly common. This subject receives rather a lot less time and space in academic journals and in practitioners' minds than ways to make a new alpha model, for example. This chapter will give you the ability to understand how most quant practitioners tackle this problem.

6.1   RULE-BASED PORTFOLIO CONSTRUCTION MODELS

There are four common types of rule-based portfolio construction models: equal position weighting, equal risk weighting, alpha-driven weighting, and decision-tree weighting. The first two are the simplest and have at their core a philosophy of equal weighting; they differ only in what specifically is being equally weighted. Alpha-driven portfolio construction models mainly rely on the alpha model for guidance on the correct position sizing and portfolio construction. Decision-tree approaches, which look at a defined set of rules in a particular order to determine position sizing, can be rather simple or amazingly complex. I describe these approaches from simplest to most complex.

6.1.1   Equal Position Weighting

Equal position-weighted models are surprisingly common. These models are used by those who implicitly (or explicitly) believe that if a position looks good enough to own, no other information is needed (or even helpful) in determining its size. There is a further implicit assumption that the instruments are homogeneous enough that they do not need to be distinguished based on their riskiness or otherwise. The notion of the strength of a signal, which, as already discussed, is related to the size of a forecast for a given instrument, is ignored except insofar as the signal is strong enough to be worthy of a position at all. At first glance, this might seem like an oversimplification of the problem. However, some serious quants have arrived at this solution. The basic premise behind an equal-weighting model is that any attempt to differentiate one position from another has two potentially adverse consequences, which ultimately outweigh any potential benefit from an unequal weighting. In other words, they choose an equal-weighting model because of the many disadvantages they see in unequal weighting.

The first (and more significant) potential problem with unequal weighting is that it assumes implicitly that there is sufficient statistical strength and power to predict not only the direction of a position in the future but also the magnitude and/or probability of its move relative to the other forecasts in the portfolio. Quants utilizing equal-weighting schemes believe, instead, that the alpha model is only to be trusted enough to forecast direction, and as long as there is sufficient confidence in a forecast of direction that is sufficiently large to justify trading the instrument at all, it is worth trading at the same size as any other position.

The second potential problem with unequal weighting of a portfolio is that it generally leads to a willingness to take a few large bets on the "best" forecasts and many smaller bets on the less dramatic forecasts. This weighting disparity, however, may lead to the strategy taking excess risk of some idiosyncratic event in a seemingly attractive position. This can be the case regardless of the type of alpha used to make a forecast. For instance, in momentum-oriented strategies, many of the strongest signals are those for which the underlying instrument has already moved the most (i.e., has showed the strongest trending behavior). In other words, it might be too late, and the trader risks getting his strongest signals at the peak of the trend, just as it reverses. Similarly, for mean reversion-oriented strategies, many of the largest signals are also for those instruments that have already moved the most and are now expected to snap back aggressively. But frequently, large moves happen because there is real information in the marketplace that leads to a prolonged or extended trend. This phenomenon is known to statisticians as *adverse selection bias*. Mean reversion bets in these situations are characterized as "picking up nickels in front of a steamroller," which is a colorful way of saying that betting on a reversal against a very strong trend leads to being run over if the trend continues, which it often does. It should be stated that, with care, these issues can be at least partly addressed through techniques such as winsorization, which is simply the act of replacing outlier values on the distribution with some fixed minimum/maximum value. However, this kind of adjustment does not need to be made with equal position sizing schemes.

This last benefit can be seen in other scenarios as well. While practitioners do what they can to clean the data they utilize in trading (which we will discuss further in Chapter 8), there are occasions in which bad data points end up filtering into a trading strategy. Equal weighting positions, in particular if there are many of them, ensure that the risk of loss associated with the large forecasts that could result from significantly wrong data does not get out of hand. For example, if a stock price is off by a factor of 100 (e.g., it is quoted in pence instead of pounds, as happens occasionally in U.K. equities), it is likely that an alpha model might be fooled into wanting to take an enormous position in this ticker. An equal weighting scheme can reduce the size of that position such that it does not end up a catastrophic event.

Indeed, since alphas are generally tested against real datasets, most of their statistical significance and strength generally comes from the meat of a distribution, not from the tails. If we observe a real tail event (not just some accident of a bad data point) that drives a large alpha forecast, this is perhaps a better trade, but it almost certainly involves dramatically higher risk than a more normative level of alpha. Here, too, an equal position weighting scheme can control the risk associated with such tail observations.

Analogous arguments can be made for almost all alpha strategies, making it easy to construct good arguments against unequal weighting positions. Therefore, the basic argument in favor of an equal-weighted approach is one of mitigating risk by diversifying bets across the largest useful number of positions. It is worth mentioning that equal weights are sometimes subject to constraints of liquidity, in that a position is weighted as close to equally as its liquidity will allow. Such liquidity considerations can be applied to each of the other rule-based allocation methodologies discussed in this chapter.

6.1.2 Equal Risk Weighting

Equal risk weighting adjusts position sizes inversely to their volatilities (or whatever other measure of risk, such as drawdown, is preferred). More volatile positions are given smaller allocations, and less volatile positions are given larger allocations. In this way, each position is equalized in the portfolio, not by the size of the allocation but rather by the amount of risk that the allocation contributes to the portfolio. An example is shown in Exhibit 6.1, which shows an example of a two-stock portfolio. As you can see, the more volatile stock (GOOG) gets a smaller allocation in the portfolio than the less volatile stock (XOM).

EXHIBIT 6.1 A Simple Equal Risk Weighted Portfolio

	Equal Weight (%)	Volatility (%)	Volatility-Adjusted Weight (%)
GOOG	50	2.5	39
XOM	50	2.0	61

The rationale is straightforward. A small cap stock with a significant amount of price volatility might not deserve quite the same allocation as a mega cap stock with substantially less volatility. Putting an equal number of dollars into these two positions might in fact be taking a much larger and inadvertent *real* bet on the small cap stock. This is because the small cap stock is much more volatile, and therefore every dollar allocated to that stock would move the portfolio more than the same dollars allocated to the larger cap (and, likely, less volatile) position. As such, some quants who believe that equal weighting is the most appropriate method will utilize an equal risk weighting approach in an effort to improve the true diversification achieved.

However, the equal risk weighting approach also has its shortcomings. Whatever unit of risk is equalized, it is almost always a backward-looking measurement, such as volatility. Instruments with higher volatilities would have smaller allocations, whereas lower-volatility instruments would have larger allocations. But what if the less volatile instruments suddenly became the more volatile? This is not merely a hypothetical question. For many years, bank stocks were very stable. Then, in 2008, they suddenly became highly volatile, more so even than many technology stocks. Any backward-looking analysis of the volatility of stocks that didn't emphasize the last debacle among financial stocks (10 years earlier, in 1998) would likely have been misled by the steady behavior of these stocks for the decade prior to 2008, and therefore an equal risk model is likely to have held much larger positions in banks than were warranted once volatility spiked in 2008.

6.1.3 Alpha-Driven Weighting

A third approach to rule-based portfolio construction determines position sizes based primarily on the alpha model. The idea here is that the alpha model dictates how attractive a position is likely to be, and this signal is the best way to size the position correctly. Still, most quants who utilize this approach would not allow the size of the largest position to be unlimited. As such, they would use the risk model to provide a maximum size limit for a single position. Given the limit, the strength of the signal determines how close to the maximum the position can actually be. This is much like grading on a curve, where the "best score" receives the largest position size, and the scores below the best receive smaller sizes. The types of constraints used with this approach to portfolio construction can also include limits on the size of the total bet on a group (e.g., sector or asset class).

For example, one could constrain individual positions to be less than 3 percent of the portfolio and each sector to be less than 20 percent. There still needs to be a function that relates the magnitude of the forecast to the size of the position, but these functions can be straightforward, and in general, the bigger the forecast, the larger the position. Alpha weighting is favored by some quants because it emphasizes making money, which is, after all, the goal of the whole exercise. However, some quant strategies, such as futures trend following, that utilize this method can suffer sharp drawdowns relatively frequently. This is because these models usually have the largest signals when a price trend is already well established. As the trend proceeds, the size of the position grows, but this will often leave the trader with his largest position just when the trend reverses. Caution is therefore advisable when utilizing an alpha-driven portfolio construction algorithm, because such an approach causes a heavy reliance on the alpha model being right—not only about its forecast of the direction of an instrument but also about the size of the move the instrument will make.

6.1.4 Summary of Rule-Based Portfolio Construction Models

Regardless of which type of rule-based portfolio construction model is used, the alpha model, risk model, and t-cost model can be incorporated in portfolio building. In an equal-weighted model, for example, constraints on the equal weighting can exist because certain instruments are too expensive to transact in, according to the transaction cost model. These considerations can be accounted for within the alpha model itself, for example, by adding a conditioning variable that sets the expected return (or score, or whatever other form of forecast) to "0" if the expected return is less than the expected transaction cost threshold. Thus, any signal that comes out of the alpha model can now be equally weighted. Obviously, the exact nature of the interaction between the other components of the black box and the portfolio construction model depends entirely on the type of portfolio construction model. For example, an equal weighting approach may make use of a risk model in an entirely different way than an alpha weighting approach.

To summarize, rule-based portfolio construction models can be extremely simple (as in the case of an equal-weighted portfolio) or rather complex (in the case of an alpha weighting with many types of constraints). The challenge common to all of them is to make the rules that drive them rational and well-reasoned.

6.2 PORTFOLIO OPTIMIZERS

Portfolio optimization is one of the most important topics in quantitative finance. This is one of the first areas in quant finance to receive the attention of serious academic work; in fact, the case could easily be made that the father of quantitative analysis is Harry Markowitz, who published a landmark paper entitled "Portfolio Selection."[1] He invented a technique known as *mean variance optimization*, which is still ubiquitous today, though much sophistication has been built around its core. In 1990, he shared a Nobel Prize with William Sharpe for both their contributions to the understanding of the quantitative analysis of portfolio construction.

Portfolio optimizers are based on the principles of *modern portfolio theory* (MPT), which are canonical in the asset management industry. The core tenet of MPT is that investors are inherently risk averse, meaning that if two assets offer the same return but different levels of risk, investors will prefer the less risky asset. A corollary is that investors will take on extra risk only if they expect to receive extra return as compensation. This introduced the concept of *risk-adjusted return*. Mean variance optimization is a formal way of building portfolios based on MPT. Mean and variance are two of the inputs to the optimizer, and the output is a set of portfolios that have the highest return at each level of risk. The *mean* in question is the average expected return of each asset being evaluated. *Variance* is a proxy for the expected risk of each asset and is computed as the standard deviation of the returns of the various assets one is considering owning. A third input to the optimizer is the *expected covariance matrix* of these same assets, which relates the variance of each asset to their similarity to each other (measured as correlation, hence co-variance). Using these inputs, the optimizer delivers a set of portfolios that offer the highest possible return for various levels of risk, known as the *efficient frontier*.

Quant trading strategies that utilize risk and transaction cost models, in addition to alpha models, also need to account for the information contained in (and any constraints associated with) those models. For example, the portfolio optimizer might be required to solve for the optimal (i.e., maximum risk-adjusted return) portfolio, which accounts for the expected returns of each potential holding, the variability of those holdings (juxtaposed with the correlation of those holdings to one another), and which minimizes exposure to various pre-specified risk factors, as specified in the risk model. Several additional inputs are utilized by quants in real trading applications, including (a) the size of the portfolio in currency terms; (b) the desired risk level (usually measured in terms of volatility or expected drawdown); and (c) any other constraints, such as a "hard to borrow" list provided by a prime broker in equity trading, which reduces the size of the universe with which the optimizer can work. These inputs are not required by the optimizer, and the first two are also mostly arbitrary, but they help yield a portfolio that is practical and useful to the quant trader.

The reason this technique is known as optimization is that it seeks to find the maximum (optimal) value of a function that has been specified by the researcher. This function is known as the *objective function*, where *objective* is used in the sense of *goal*. The optimizer seeks this goal by an algorithm that conducts a directed search among the various combinations of instruments available to it. As it examines the return and risk characteristics of a given combination, it compares this with previously examined combinations and detects what seems to cause the portfolio's behavior to improve or degrade. By this method, the optimizer is able to rapidly locate a series of optimal portfolios, which are those for which returns cannot be bested by those of any other portfolio at a given level of risk. What is allowed or disallowed is determined by the alpha model, risk model, and transaction cost model. The objective function that many quants use is the same as the original: maximizing the return of a portfolio relative to the volatility of the portfolio's returns. However, an infinite array of objective functions can be used. For example, one could specify an objective function that will cause the optimizer simply to maximize portfolio return, regardless of risk, or to minimize risk, regardless of return. The use of return versus risk is itself entirely optional.

We can graphically illustrate the technique of optimization as shown in Exhibit 6.2. In the graph on the left, we see that on the X (horizontal) and Z (depth) axes of the graph are every possible combination of ownerships of Netflix (NYSE:NFLX) and CVX. The Y-axis (vertical) shows the expected Sharpe ratio of each possible portfolio containing these two stocks. The Sharpe ratio was chosen simply for illustrative purposes, as a typical objective function for an optimizer. The graph on the right is simply a two-dimensional visualization of the same thing, but also showing some specific portfolios. You can see the equal weight and equal risk portfolios, as well as the maximum Sharpe portfolio. Lastly, you can see the search space contained in a long-only version of the same optimization, which we will revisit later.

For simplicity, we chose to use historical returns from December 2019 to December 2023 as expected returns (which is generally a terrible idea in real applications—past asset returns are not good indicators of future returns). Since both CVX and NFLX had positive returns over this period, and since they were only correlated to each other at a relatively low level (about 0.1), the ideal portfolio comes out to be long both names, in relatively equal proportion. The maximum Sharpe portfolio looks like it is about 85 percent CVX and 75 percent NFLX. The reason that this does not sum to 100 percent is that we did not constrain the optimization (we did search only from −100 percent to +100 percent, so, in a sense, you could argue those were the constraints), so it simply looked for whatever proportions gave the best result, as defined by the Sharpe ratio. The optimizer obviously does not look at a graph to pick the point, but this visual can be helpful in illustrating what an optimizer is attempting to achieve.

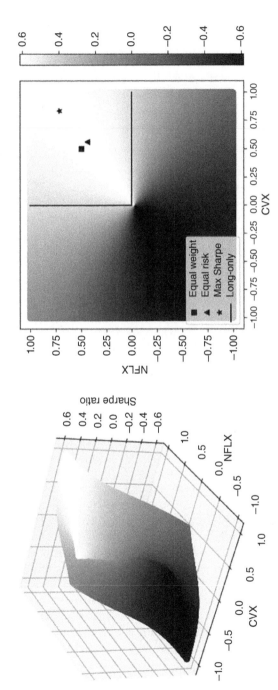

EXHIBIT 6.2 Visual Representations of the Search Space for an Optimization

6.2.1   Inputs to Optimization

The inputs required for an optimizer, as already mentioned, are expected returns, expected volatility, and a correlation matrix of the various instruments to be considered for the portfolio. It is worth understanding where practitioners get the estimates and expectations used in optimization from, since they are critical to the model itself. We consider each of the aforementioned inputs in order.

6.2.1.1   Expected Return   In more traditional finance, such as private wealth management, expected returns are usually set to equal very long-term historical returns because usually the goal is to create a strategic asset allocation that won't need to be dynamically readjusted. By contrast, quants tend to use their alpha models to drive expected return. As we mentioned in our discussion of alpha models, the output of the alpha model typically includes an expected return and/or an expected direction, or some other output which indicates the attractiveness of each potential portfolio holding (e.g., a score). Forecasts of direction can be used as forecasts of return simply by making all positive forecasts equal and all negative forecasts equal (often subject to minimum threshold parameters, so that at least the return forecasts have to be of some significant size before making a bet). In this kind of optimization, it is not important to have a precise forecast of return, but rather a forecast of the attractiveness of each potential position in terms of the expected return. So directional forecasts are indifferent between the expected return of each position, and the only relevant feature of the forecast is its sign.

6.2.1.2   Expected Volatility   Many practitioners, whether in traditional finance or in quant trading, tend to use historical measures for the second input to the optimizer, namely volatility. Some, however, develop and use their own forecasts of volatility. The most common approaches to forecasting volatility utilize stochastic volatility models. Stochastic, in Greek, means *random*. It's worth noting that stochastic volatility models are generally used mostly in strategies that trade options, except for one very specific case we will discuss shortly. In statistics, a stochastic process is one that is somewhat predictable but that has some element of unpredictability or randomness built in. In case you're wondering what statisticians mean by the word "process," they are referring to some continuous series of changes, which is basically a synonym for a time series in this context. The basic idea behind the stochastic family of volatility forecasting methods is that volatility goes through phases in which it is at high levels, followed by periods in which it is at low levels (i.e., the somewhat predictable phases of the volatility cycle), with occasional jumps (the somewhat random and unpredictable part).

The most widely used such technique (particularly in equity trading) is called *Generalized Autoregressive Conditional Heteroskedasticity* (GARCH), which was proposed in 1986 in the *Journal of Econometrics* by the Danish econometrician Tim Bollerslev.[2] Other approaches to stochastic volatility modeling and variants of the original GARCH forecast abound. All these techniques basically share the notion that volatility goes through clustered periods of relative calm, followed by periods of swings, followed by a return to calm, and so forth. This can be seen in Exhibit 6.3 as being a relatively useful way to describe market volatility. From 2000 to 2003, the S&P 500 was rather volatile. This was followed by a period of calm from mid-2003 to mid-2007, and after that by another period of extreme volatility from mid-2007 through 2008. Even during the relatively calm period, short, seemingly periodic bursts in volatility occurred. GARCH types of models do a reasonable job of forecasting volatility in this sort of pattern.

Indeed, there exist many other approaches to forecasting volatility, and they can be understood in much the same way that we evaluated strategies for forecasting price. Indeed, it appears that a much simpler technique than GARCH, an exponentially weighted moving average, or EWMA, may perform just about as well as GARCH while being considerably more elegant and easily computed.[3] EWMA tends to make forecasts based on ideas of trend, reversion, or some fundamental model of volatility; they can be made over various time horizons; they can forecast either the volatility of a single instrument or the relative volatility of more than one instrument, and so

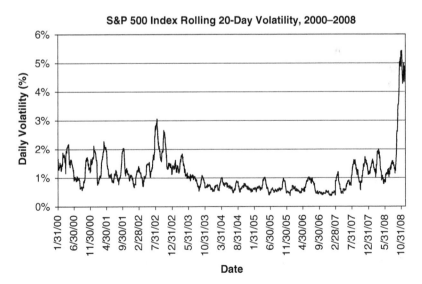

EXHIBIT 6.3 Historical S&P 500 Volatility

forth. GARCH forecasts, for example, are a way of understanding how a time series behaves. The "A" in the acronym GARCH stands for Autoregressive, which is a statistical term that characterizes a mean-reverting process. A negative value for autoregression implies that the time series exhibits trending behavior (which is also called autocorrelative). In this case, the time series relates to the volatility of an instrument.

6.2.1.3 Expected Correlation The third input to the optimizer is the correlation matrix. Correlation is at heart a measure of the similarity of the movements of two instruments, expressed in a number between −1 and +1. A +1 correlation implies exact similarity, whereas a −1 correlation implies that the two instruments are exactly opposite, or *anti*-correlated. A 0 correlation is perfect *non*-correlation and implies that the two instruments are entirely dissimilar, but not opposite. An interesting fact about correlation is that it says nothing about the trend in the instruments over time. For example, imagine two companies in the same industry group, such as airline companies. If the first company is simply out-competing the other and winning market share, the first will likely have a positive trendline, while the second may well have a negative trendline (assuming the overall market is roughly flat). Nevertheless, these two companies will likely have a high positive correlation, because their returns are still driven heavily by the overall market, by their sector, and by their industry, not to mention the more specific market factors associated with being an airline company (e.g., the price of oil).

There are a number of problems with using standard correlation measures in quant trading, most of which we will address at various points later. Most relevant for the moment, the measurement of the relationships between two instruments can be very unstable over time. They can even be unreliable over long time periods. For example, imagine a portfolio with two investments: one in the S&P 500 and one in the Nikkei 225. Taking the data on both since January 1984, we can see that these two indices correlate at a level of 0.37 since inception. The range of correlations observed using weekly returns over any consecutive 365 calendar days (a *rolling year*) is shown in Exhibit 6.4. Please note that we choose to use weekly returns in this case, rather than daily returns, because of the time-zone difference between the U.S. and Japan. In general, there is a one-day lag between the movements that occur in Japan, with respect to the moves that occur in the U.S. This can be handled either by using less frequent than daily returns (as in this example) or by lagging the Japanese returns by a day.

You can see that the level of correlation observed between the S&P 500 and the Nikkei 225 depends quite a lot on exactly when it is measured. Indeed, this correlation reaches the lowest point in the sample (+0.01) in October 1989 and by mid-2008 was at its highest point (+0.66). What's

EXHIBIT 6.4   Rolling Yearly Correlation Between S&P 500 and Nikkei 225

worse, the correlation between these indices went from +0.02 to +0.58, and then back to +0.01 all during the course of about four years, from November 1985 until October 1989. Even using a rolling five-year window, the range is +0.21 to +0.57.

If the strategy specifies appropriate groupings of instruments, as in our earlier example of industry groups, the stability of the correlations over time improves. This specification can be made either in the definition of *relative* in a relative alpha strategy and/or in the specification of the risk model. So, for example, if the model groups together companies such as XOM and CVX, this can be seen as reasonable, because these two companies have much in common. Both have market capitalizations on the same general scale, both are oil companies, both are based in the United States and have global operations, and so on.

Meanwhile, a comparison between XOM and NFLX might be less defensible based on fundamental factors, such as the fact that NFLX is not much like an oil company, even though it has a similar market capitalization. Somewhat obviously, this theoretical difference in the comparability between these two pairs of stocks (XOM vs. CVX, XOM vs. NFLX) also bears out in the data, as shown in Exhibit 6.5.

As you can see, CVX and XOM correlate relatively well over the entire period shown. The lowest correlation level observed between this pair is approximately 0.75, and the highest is 0.92. The correlation over the entire sample of five years is 0.86. Meanwhile, XOM and NFLX correlate poorly, at a level of only 0.12 over the whole sample, with a minimum one-year correlation of −0.17 and a maximum of 0.53. Furthermore, the correlation

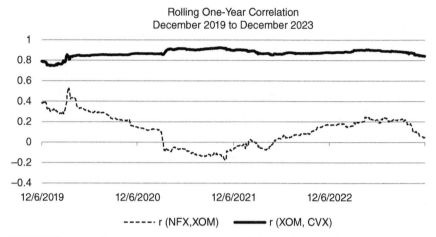

EXHIBIT 6.5 Correlation Over Time Between Similar and Dissimilar Instruments

between CVX and XOM changes more smoothly over time than that between XOM and NFLX. Though both pairs can be said to be somewhat unstable, it is quite clear that grouping CVX with XOM is less likely to be problematic than grouping XOM with NFLX. To be clear, the instability of correlations among financial instruments is more or less a fact of the world. It is not the fault of optimizers, nor of correlation as a statistic, that this happens to be the case in the finance industry.

The main source of this instability is that the relationships between financial instruments are often governed by a variety of dynamic forces. For example, if the stock market is experiencing a significant downdraft, it is probable that the correlation between XOM and NFLX will be temporarily higher than usual—as indeed is easily observed in the spike in correlation in early 2020. If, on the other hand, there is uncertainty about oil supply, this may affect XOM but not NFLX, and correlation may be reduced temporarily. If either company has significant, particularly unexpected, news, this can cause de-coupling as well.

So far, we have been discussing very simple examples of a correlation between two assets. But, in many real-life examples, a portfolio may have thousands of positions—let's just pick 2,000 for the moment. The correlation matrix that describes the relationships among these 2,000 instruments is 2,000 × 2,000. In other words, there are some 4 million figures in the correlation matrix. Now, the correlation of XOM to NFLX is the same as the correlation between NFLX and XOM. The ordering of the pair makes no difference. And the correlation between any instrument and itself—which forms the diagonal from the top left to the bottom right corner of the matrix—is always one—a thing is perfectly correlated to itself. As such, that is really 1,998,000 individual correlation coefficients that we care about. Do we really have a model to predict almost 2 million pairs? That is unlikely. Most quants simply measure the historical relationship and assume that the relationship will hold up in the future (with the caveats mentioned already in this section). However, if you do want to predict correlation, it turns out the EWMA method referenced in Section 6.2.1.2 is equally useful here.[4]

6.2.2 Optimization Techniques

There are many types of optimizers. They range from basic copies of Markowitz's original specification in 1952 to sophisticated machine-learning techniques. This section provides an overview of the most common of these approaches. It is worth reiterating here, that all optimization is focused on one key goal: trading off opportunity, risk, cost, and other constraints (including solvability) to arrive at a reasonable decision for a given moment in time.

Given all the recent advances in machine learning and so-called "artificial intelligence" (which, to me, remains more artificial than intelligence, sorry), it's worth understanding how ML/AI and optimization relate to each other.

Portfolio optimization, in brief, is focused on finding the ideal allocation of weights to assets that optimize the outcome of some objective function. If we get rid of the "portfolio" part of this, we're just focused on assigning weights to whatever we've got (e.g., predictors in a chess match) that determine the best next move, given whatever we've defined as best (note that winning is technically a different objective than not losing, and very different from losing in exactly 100 moves).

Machine learning is often described as function approximation. In other words, an ML model is using historical relationships between inputs and outputs to approximate new outcomes that result from new inputs. The key to understanding how this is an optimization is to understand minimization and maximization, and how they're very similar, outside of the sign we're targeting.

With ML models, we're focused on minimizing error between forecast and reality. There are tradeoffs involved in determining the optimal model, for example, complexity versus robustness. With portfolio optimization models, we're focused on maximizing return versus risk, again with many other considerations.

With that said, generally speaking, we do not see many strictly "machine learning" models for portfolio construction. The state of the art remains portfolio optimization, various flavors of Markowitz's model (including some that are quite sophisticated indeed). It is worth noting that, under the hood, most machine-learning algorithms are utilizing optimization techniques.

6.2.2.1 Unconstrained Optimization The most basic form of an optimizer is one that has no constraints; for example, it can suggest putting 100 percent of a portfolio in a single instrument if it wants. Indeed, it is a quirk of unconstrained optimizers that they often do exactly that: propose a single-instrument portfolio, where all the money would be invested in the instrument with the highest risk-adjusted return.

6.2.2.2 Constrained Optimization To address this problem, quants add constraints and penalties in the optimization process, which forces more "reasonable" solutions. Constraints can include position limits (e.g., not more than 3 percent of the portfolio can be allocated to a given position) or limits on various groupings of instruments (e.g., not more than 20 percent of the portfolio can be invested in any sector). An interesting conundrum for the quant, however, is that, if the unconstrained optimizer would tend to choose unacceptable solutions, to the extent that constraints are applied it can become the case that the constraints drive the portfolio construction more than the optimizer. For example, imagine a portfolio of 100 instruments, with the optimizer limited to allocating no more than 1.5 percent to any single position. The average position is naturally 1 percent (1/100 of the portfolio). So, the very best positions (according to the alpha model) are only 1.5 times the average position, which is relatively close to equal-weighted. This is fine, but it somewhat defeats the purpose of optimizing.

Another class of constraints for optimization involves the integration of risk models. Here, too, there are several ways to implement a constraint (as discussed in Chapter 4), including penalties and hard limits. For example, we could introduce a penalty function that penalizes a small amount of sector risk at a low level (i.e., the expected return needed to overcome this penalty would be itself relatively small); but, as the level of sector risk increases to double the prior level, the expected return needed to justify this increase is substantially larger than double the alpha required at the lower level of sector risk. In other words, the expected marginal reward must increase substantially faster than the expected marginal risk, and the larger the increase in risk, the faster the expected return must increase to make the optimizer accept the tradeoff and allow the increased risk exposure.

Transaction costs, too, can be addressed in various ways. One can build an empirical model of every stock's market impact function and use this set of individual market impact models to feed into the optimizer. Alternatively, one could simply specify a market impact function that takes inputs such as volatility, (dollar) volume, and the order size, and have a generalized solution for a market impact model. These are but two of the many ways that quants can account for expected transaction costs as an input to a portfolio optimization.

The mathematics and programming that achieve optimization are designed to account for the types of inputs mentioned above, iteratively solving for the tradeoff that maximizes the objective function (e.g., the expected return versus the expected volatility) of a portfolio. The optimizer is trying to solve a lot of problems at once, potentially: maximize returns per unit of risk, accounting for correlation and volatility, while staying within various hard limits (e.g., maximum position size constraints), and while accounting for risk factor exposures and transaction costs. While it's complicated, compared to many other aspects of a systematic trading strategy, these are generally very well-understood solutions, and there are many canned, off-the-shelf (including free, open-source codebase) packages that compute these solutions relatively painlessly.

If we think back to Exhibit 6.2., visually, constraining an optimization involves cutting out regions of the surface which do not satisfy the conditions. For example, imagine that we impose a constraint that we cannot hold positions short, we must be long only. In this case, most of the surface will be ignored by the optimizer, and only the parts of the surface that satisfy the long-only constraint are searched. This is illustrated in Exhibit 6.6. You can see that the graph on the right essentially zooms into the square at the top-right quadrant of the one on the left (which we borrowed from Exhibit 6.2). We simply excluded three-quarters of the search space, where either or both stocks would be held short. Note that, since we are limiting the region for the optimizer to search through, it is possible to add so many constraints that there is no solution.

It is also worth recognizing that our example is extremely oversimplified. We have a portfolio of only two assets, high correlation, and one simple constraint. In a more realistic scenario, the surface is unlikely to be so simple-looking, with a clear trend toward a single peak. In a more complex case, there may be many peaks scattered around various regions of the overall space. The algorithm used to seek the optimal outcome must be designed with a specific tradeoff in mind, namely between thoroughness and speed. A faster, less thorough optimization algorithm might find a local peak in the curve and stop looking, even though somewhere else in the universe of possible portfolios, there is an even better portfolio to consider. A more thorough search algorithm might find that "globally optimal" solution, but its search might take far too long to be practicable.

6.2.2.3 Black-Litterman Optimization

Fischer Black, of Black-Scholes fame, and Bob Litterman, of Goldman Sachs, in 1990 produced a new optimization

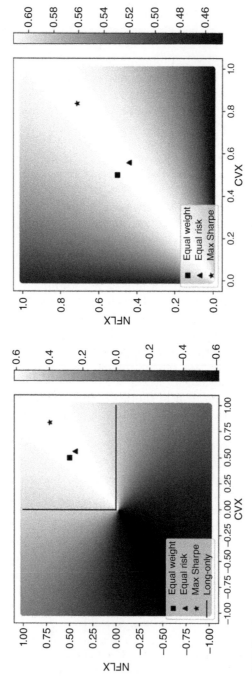

EXHIBIT 6.6   Visual Representation of Constraining the Search Space for an Optimization

method that was first introduced in an internal memo at Goldman but was later published in 1992 in the *Financial Analysts Journal*.[5] Their *Black-Litterman optimizer* addresses some of the problems associated with false precision of the expected return inputs to an optimizer, and the sensitivity of standard optimizers to small perturbations in those expected returns. The two most salient new capabilities that came from their innovation were the ability to specify a default portfolio—a baseline of sorts—and the ability to blend an investor's expectations with a degree of confidence about those expectations with the historical precedent evident in the data. Some quants prefer this method of optimization because it allows for a more holistic approach to combining the alpha model with the other inputs to optimization.

6.2.2.4 Grinold and Kahn's Approach: Optimizing Factor Portfolios Another kind of optimizer that bears mentioning is described in Grinold and Kahn's seminal *Active Portfolio Management*.[6] This kind of portfolio optimization technique is directly aimed at building a portfolio of signals, whereas most optimizers try to size positions. The method of optimizing proposed by Grinold and Kahn is fairly widely used. The idea of this approach is to build *factor portfolios*, each of which are usually rule-based (in fact, very often equal-weighted or equal risk-weighted) portfolios based on a single type of alpha forecast. So, for example, one could imagine building a momentum portfolio, a value portfolio, and a growth portfolio. Each of these portfolios is in turn simulated historically, as though it were making stock picks through the past. For instance, the value factor's portfolio would look back at the historical data and simulate the results it would have achieved by buying undervalued instruments and shorting overvalued instruments through this historical sample, as though it were reliving the past. In this way, a time series of the returns of these simulated factor portfolios is generated. These simulated factor portfolio returns are then treated as the instruments of a portfolio by the optimizer.

One benefit of this approach is that the number of factor portfolios is typically much more manageable, usually not more than about 20, corresponding to the number of individual factors in the alpha model. What is therefore being optimized is not a portfolio of thousands of instruments but rather the mixing of a handful of factor portfolios. This is certainly an easier hurdle to clear in terms of the amount of data needed. Factor portfolio optimization allows for the inclusion of the risk model, transaction cost model, portfolio size, and risk target as inputs, in much the same way as described for other optimizers.

Given the weight of each model, we ultimately need to ascertain the weight of each position. The way that each position's weight is computed in this approach is perhaps easiest to understand by example. Imagine we have two alpha factors, both of which yield only a directional forecast (i.e., +1 for a buy signal or −1 for a sell signal). We have 100 stocks in the factor portfolios, which are equally weighted for simplicity's sake. This means that each stock is 1 percent of each factor portfolio. Let's assume that the factor optimization procedure dictated that we should have a 60 percent weight on the first factor portfolio and a 40 percent weight on the second. The allocation to any stock in this example is 1 percent (the weight of each name in each factor portfolio) times the signal given by that factor (i.e., long or short) times the weight of each factor portfolio. Let's say that the first alpha factor's forecast for a given company is +1, and the second is −1. So the total allocation to the company is

$$[(1\%)*(+1)*(60\%)] + [(1\%)*(-1)*(40\%)] = +0.2\%$$

meaning that we would be long 0.2 percent of our portfolio in this company.

6.2.2.5 Resampled Efficiency In *Efficient Asset Management*, Richard Michaud proposed yet another approach to portfolio construction models.[7] Rather than proposing a new type of optimization, however, Michaud sought to improve the inputs to optimization. His "Resampled Efficiency" technique may address oversensitivity to estimation error. Michaud argues that this is in fact the single greatest problem with optimizers. Earlier, we gave the example of the instability of the correlation between the S&P 500 and Nikkei 225. This implied that, if we used the past to set expectations for the future—in other words, to estimate the correlation between these two instruments going forward—we are reasonably likely to have the wrong estimate at any given time, relative to the actual correlation that will be observed in the future. A quant will have such estimation errors in the alpha forecasts, in the volatility forecasts, and in the correlation estimates. It turns out that mean variance optimizers are extremely sensitive to these kinds of errors in that even small differences in expectations lead to large changes in the recommended portfolios.

Michaud proposes to resample the data using a technique called *Monte Carlo simulation* to reduce the estimation error inherent in the inputs to the optimizer. A Monte Carlo simulation reorders the actually observed results many times, thereby creating a large number of time series all based on the same underlying observations. For example, imagine we are testing a trend-following strategy that is based on the closing prices of the S&P 500 from 1982 through 2008. But now we want to get a sense of how robust the strategy might be if the future doesn't look exactly like the past. So, we can take the return distribution of the S&P 500, which tells us how often the S&P

gains or loses various amounts, and use it to create a large number of alternate histories for the index. By reshuffling the returns in this way, we have less dependence on the past looking just like the future, because we now have thousands of "pasts" over which to test our strategy. Interestingly, the average return and the volatility of returns will remain the same across all these alternate histories because they are based on the same underlying return distribution. But now we can see how often our strategy performs well or poorly across all these hypothetical scenarios and therefore how likely it is to work well or poorly in a future that might not resemble the past precisely. This technique is thought to produce more robust predictions than are possible from simply using only the actual sequence of returns the instrument exhibited, in that the researcher is capturing more aspects of the behavior of the instrument. It is this intuition that is at the heart of Monte Carlo simulations.

A word of warning regarding such resampling techniques, however: re-using an historical distribution is only really useful if you have sufficient confidence that the sample in the historical distribution is a fair representation of the whole population. For example, if you were to use the S&P's daily returns from 1988 through 2006, you might believe you had a very good data sample: approximately 19 years of daily returns. However, you would be missing many of the largest negative observations, because both the 1987 crash and the 2007–2008 bear market would be missing. Specifically, using the 19-year sample, you'd have only nine days in your sample during which the S&P declined by more than 4 percent, and only 11 days where the S&P rose by more than 4 percent. By including those extra three years of data, you would see an extra 19 days on which the S&P declined by more than 4 percent (including one day larger than −20 percent), as well as 16 extra days on which the S&P rose by more than 4 percent (including one day of almost +12 percent).

6.2.2.6 Convex Optimization We saw in Section 6.1 that we don't have to use an optimizer to answer the question of portfolio weights. But if we do choose to use an optimizer, the problem we're solving is usually very complex— in fact, I would argue that optimizers are the most complicated and often difficult to understand pieces of code in the entire black box. This is because they are accounting for many types of variables and constraints: return, risk, various types of costs, limits (or penalties), any other preferences or requirements. Optimization, in many ways, can be thought of as an art as much as a science, with no guarantee that standard methods to solve these problems will find the actual best answer.

But it turns out that many portfolio construction problems can be formulated as optimization problems with a special property: convexity. And for optimization problems that consist of convex functions, a special kind of optimization technique can be employed called *Convex Optimization*, which allows for extremely rapid and flexible solutions—a portfolio optimization problem, with 10,000 assets and a raft of typical constraints, can be solved reliably in about one second!

Convex functions are those which (a) have no holes or gaps, no divots, or other irregularities—they are smooth and continuous; and (b) look either like a smile or a frown—there's a single "highest" or "lowest" point. It doesn't matter if we are interested in finding a minimum (e.g., risk), or a maximum (e.g., return). As long as the function that describes that variable (or constraint) is convex, then it qualifies. Conceptually, if you imagine the expected return of some multi-leg options position, it could be positive in various ranges and negative in various other ranges, and look more like a sine-wave than a smile or straight line. There might be some actual best outcome and some actual worst outcome, but the curve is not convex. This would not be a convex function, and thus convex optimization cannot be utilized.

The details of convex optimization are beyond the scope of this book. But what I can tell you is that this technique allows the solving of extraordinarily complex-sounding problems with great efficiency. For example, let's say that you don't know what the covariance between two of your assets might be. The optimal portfolio, given that fact, is different from the optimal portfolio given some estimate of that covariance. Let's say that your forecasts for each instrument in your universe is a distribution, rather than a point estimate. Again, the optimal portfolio will look different than if you used a point estimate—even if it was the mean or median of the distribution—to determine your weights. And in both of these examples, convex optimization allows you to solve these sophisticated problems relatively quickly and painlessly, through advances in the underlying solving algorithms. Much of this work is owed to Stephen Boyd and Lieven Vandenberghe, and their seminal text, *Convex Optimization*, though, of course, there have been many other contributors over the years.

Given the power and speed of convex optimization, one is well incentivized to utilize this technique. However, first, all relevant functions must be characterized as convex. In some cases, if they are not natively convex, they can be reframed or transformed into convex functions and then utilized in this altered form, so long as they continue to faithfully represent the original. There is a great deal of art that goes into making these transformations, and it proves to be a most valuable skill.

6.2.3 Final Thoughts on Optimization

One interesting byproduct of portfolio optimization is that there are instances in which an instrument that is forecast to have a positive return in the future by the alpha model might end up as a short position in the final portfolio (or vice versa). How can this happen? Imagine we are trading a group of equities in the United States and that one of the constraints imposed on the optimization by the risk model is that the portfolio must be neutral to each industry group. In other words, for every dollar of long positions within, say, the software industry, we must have a corresponding dollar of short positions within the same industry (to create a zero net position in the software industry). But what if we have positive return expectations for every stock in the software industry? The optimizer would likely be long those software companies with the highest positive return expectations and short those software companies with the lowest positive return expectations.

Certainly, among sophisticated quants that use optimizers to build their portfolios, the most simplistic optimization techniques (particularly unconstrained) are in the minority. Still, though the intuition behind optimization is sound, the technique itself is perhaps the most properly labeled "black box" part of the quant trading system. The output is sometimes confusing relative to the inputs because of the complexity of the interactions among an alpha model, a risk model, and a transaction cost model, along with the constraints of size and desired risk level. Compounding the complexity, we have to consider the interaction among various kinds of alpha factors within the alpha model. That said, it is highly likely that the larger positions in the portfolio are those with the strongest expected returns. The strange behavior described here—having a position in the opposite direction as the alpha model's forecast—is observable mainly with the smaller positions in the portfolio because it is among these that the expected returns can be overcome by transaction cost or risk management considerations.

This last phenomenon is sometimes known as the substitution effect. If we have a higher forecasted return for ABC than we do for DEF, it might be expected that our portfolio should reflect this. However, if ABC is also expected to be dramatically more expensive to trade, and if ABC and DEF are reasonably correlated, the optimizer might well choose to invest in DEF instead of ABC.

6.3 OUTPUT OF PORTFOLIO CONSTRUCTION MODELS

Optimizers, as mentioned, solve a problem of balancing various types of inputs, preferences, and constraints, and delivering portfolio weights that result in the best outcome—as defined by the practitioner. This is most often visualized in the so-called Efficient Frontier. Each point on the curve that constitutes the Efficient Frontier is "efficient" because it is the maximum return for the corresponding level of risk. Since it is the maximum, there is nothing better beyond it, hence "frontier."

A classic example of the Efficient Frontier is presented in Exhibit 6.7. In it, a simple, unconstrained mean-variance optimization was run to allocate weights to four ETFs. They were: the S&P 500 (SPY), the MSCI EAFE index (EFA), 7–10-year U.S. Treasuries (IEF) and Gold (GLD). Again, this example used historical returns (for a one-year period) as expected returns. The graph shows the risk and return of owning various portfolios that you might find intuitively interesting. The first thing to note is that none of the individual assets is as good as the combination of them—illustrating the benefits of diversification that motivate the use of optimizers in the first place. You can see the equal-weighted portfolio is also sub-optimal, but seems better than any of the individual options. You can see the lowest risk portfolio, the highest return portfolio, and most importantly, the highest Sharpe portfolio, which is labeled as the "Tangency Portfolio" in Exhibit 6.7.

The Tangency Portfolio, or Maximum Sharpe Portfolio, is the best point on the curve of the best portfolios. If we were able to scale that up by using leverage or down by putting some of our portfolio in cash, as represented by the dashed line, our result would actually be *better* than the Efficient Frontier's portfolios, because we are scaling the single best portfolio on the Efficient Frontier.

Regardless of the type of portfolio construction approach used, the output of the quantitative portfolio construction model is a target portfolio: the desirable individual positions and the targeted sizes of each. This target portfolio is compared to the current portfolio, and the differences are the trades

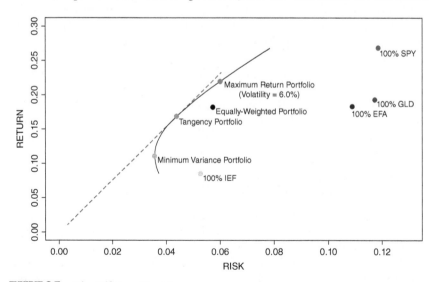

EXHIBIT 6.7   The Efficient Frontier.
Source: Adapted from Daniela Hanicova, "Markowitz Model," www.quantpedia.com/markowitz-model

that need to be done. In the case that a brand-new portfolio is being built from scratch, all the positions recommended by the portfolio construction model will need to be executed. If, instead, the quant is re-running the portfolio construction model as he would do periodically in the normal course of business, he would need to do only the incremental trades that close the gap between the newly recommended portfolio and the existing portfolio he holds.

6.4 HOW QUANTS CHOOSE A PORTFOLIO CONSTRUCTION MODEL

I have observed that the significant majority of quants using rule-based allocation systems seem to take an "intrinsic" alpha approach (i.e., they forecast individual instruments rather than forecasting instruments relative to each other). Most, but not all, of these are actually futures traders. Meanwhile, quants utilizing optimizers tend to be focused on a "relative" alpha approach, most typically found among equity market-neutral strategies. There is no obvious reason for the difference in the preferred portfolio construction approach for relative and intrinsic traders. However, it is likely that quants that use relative alpha strategies already believe implicitly in the stability of the relationships among their instruments. After all, in a relative alpha paradigm, the forecast for a given instrument is as much a function of that instrument's behavior as it is about the behavior of the instruments to which the first is being compared. If these relationships are unstable, the strategy is doomed to start with, because its first premise is that certain comparisons can be made reliably. If the relationships are stable, however, it is entirely logical and consistent that the quant can rely on them for portfolio construction as well.

Meanwhile, if a quant takes an intrinsic alpha approach, he is making an implicit statement that his portfolio is largely made up of a series of independent bets, so relying on a correlation matrix (one of the key inputs to the optimizer) might not be very useful. Instead, this kind of quant would focus efforts more directly on risk limits and alpha forecasts subject to transaction costs. This more direct approach to portfolio construction is usually best implemented with a rule-based model. It is interesting to note that the kind of alpha model a quant builds is likely to impact the choice of portfolio construction model that makes the most sense to use.

6.5 SUMMARY

We have described the two major families of portfolio construction models. Rule-based models take a heuristic approach, whereas portfolio optimizers utilize logic rooted in modern portfolio theory. Within each family are numerous techniques and, along with these, numerous challenges. How does the practitioner taking a rule-based approach justify the arbitrariness of the rules he chooses? How does the practitioner utilizing optimization address the myriad issues associated with estimating volatility and correlation? In choosing the "correct" portfolio construction technique, the quant must judge the problems and advantages of each and determine which is most suitable, given the type of alpha, risk, and transaction cost models being used.

All of these techniques share one common thread, however: they are taking the expected returns (from the alpha model's forecasts) and transforming those into a portfolio. This transformation can be extremely simple or very complex, and the choice is determined by the approach that the quant researcher takes to the problem. However, all of these approaches are attempting to maximize the goodness of the outcome. What determines goodness is also entirely up to the researcher. For example, some seek to maximize the Sharpe ratio, others seek to maximize the ratio of return to maximum peak-to-valley drawdown, and still others might seek to maximize the expected return without consideration given to the level of risk. In each case, the researcher can choose also whether and what to constrain as far as risk exposures. Still, the goal is to maximize the goodness of the outcome, subject to any relevant constraints.

We have completed the penultimate stop on the trip through the inside of the black box, as seen on our roadmap (Exhibit 6.8). Next we will see how quants actually implement the portfolios that they derived using their portfolio construction models.

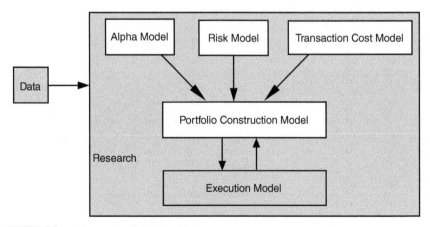

EXHIBIT 6.8   Schematic of the Black Box

NOTES

1. Harry Markowitz, "Portfolio Selection," *The Journal of Finance*, 7(1) (March 1952): 77–91.
2. Tim Bollerslev, "Generalized Autoregressive Conditional Heteroskedasticity," *Journal of Econometrics*, 31 (June 1986): 307–327.
3. Kasper Johansson, Mehmet G. Ogut, Markus Pelger, Thomas Schmelzer, and Stephen Boyd, "A Simple Method for Predicting Covariance Matrices of Financial Returns," *Foundations and Trends in Econometrics* Series, 2023. https://ssrn.com/abstract=4464524
4. Johansson et al., "A Simple Method."
5. Fischer Black and Robert Litterman, "Global Portfolio Optimization," *Financial Analysts Journal* (September–October 1982): 28–43.
6. Richard Grinold and Ronald Kahn, *Active Portfolio Management: A Quantitative Approach for Producing Superior Returns and Controlling Risk* (New York: McGraw-Hill, 1999).
7. Richard Michaud, *Efficient Asset Management: A Practical Guide to Stock Portfolio Optimization and Asset Allocation* (Oxford: Oxford University Press, 2001).

CHAPTER 7

Execution

Quality is never an accident; it is always the result of high intention, sincere effort, intelligent direction and skillful execution.
                                                            —William A. Foster

So far in our tour through the black box, we have seen how quants determine what portfolio they want to own. Quants build alpha models, risk models, and transaction cost models. These modules are fed into a portfolio construction model, which determines a target portfolio. But having a target collection on a piece of paper or a computer screen is considerably different than actually owning that portfolio. The final part of the black box itself is to implement the portfolio decisions made by the portfolio construction model, which is accomplished by executing the desired trades.

There are two basic ways to execute a trade: either electronically or through a human intermediary (e.g., a broker). Most quants elect to utilize the electronic method, because the number of transactions is frequently so large that it would be unreasonable and unnecessary to expect people to succeed at it. Electronic execution is accomplished through *direct market access* (DMA), which allows traders to utilize the infrastructure and exchange connectivity of their brokerage firms to trade directly on electronic markets such as electronic communications networks (ECNs). For ease, I will refer to any type of liquidity pool—whether ECN, exchange or otherwise—as an "exchange," unless a specific point needs to be made about a particular type of market center.

Several points bear clarification. First, DMA is available to any trader, whether quant or discretionary, and in fact, many discretionary traders also utilize DMA platforms offered by their brokers to execute trades. Trades submitted via DMA can still be done manually if so desired, but they are manually entered into computer software, which then directly communicates with the electronic exchanges.

In the past, traders would call their brokers, who would "work" orders, which meant the latter trying to pick the best times, sizes, and prices or occasionally contacting other counterparties to negotiate a better price on a larger block trade. Now, particularly on electronic exchanges, execution algorithms are far more commonly responsible for working orders. Execution algorithms contain the logic used to get an order completed, including: instructions about how to slice up an order into smaller pieces (to minimize market impact), or how to respond to various kinds of changes in the limit order book and price behavior.

One can acquire execution algorithms in one of three ways: build them, use the broker's system, or use a third-party software vendor's system. This chapter will, in part, detail the kinds of things execution algorithms are designed to handle. We will then discuss more recent developments related to the infrastructure quants utilize to execute trades. A more thorough coverage of infrastructure- and execution-related issues, particular to latency-sensitive execution and trading strategies (including high frequency trading) will be addressed in Part IV of this book.

Though most orders executed by quants are algorithmic, traders occasionally utilize a service most brokerages offer, namely, *portfolio bidding*. I describe this idea only briefly, since it is not a particularly quantitative way to execute trades. In a portfolio bid, a "blind" portfolio that the trader wants to transact is described by its characteristics in terms such as the valuation ratios of the longs and shorts, the sector breakdown, market capitalizations, and the like. Based on these characteristics, brokers quote a fee, usually in terms of the number of basis points (100 basis points = 1 percent) of the gross market value of the portfolio being traded. In exchange for this cost, a guaranteed price is given to do the transaction. The quant using this arrangement, in other words, is buying certainty of the prices of his trades and in exchange is paying the broker for providing that certainty. Once an agreement is reached between the broker and the quant, he receives the transactions from the broker at the pre-agreed price, and the broker receives his fee for the service and assumes the risk of trading out of the portfolio at future market prices, which may be better or worse than the prices they have guaranteed. "Human" execution of quant portfolios often looks like a portfolio bid rather than a series of individual orders being worked.

Generally, the workflow for a quant trader is not materially different now than it was in the days that preceded automated execution. Some traders preferred to more actively work their own orders, and many others would outsource order working to brokers. Some firms would outsource their executions to third party execution services firms, who would interface with brokers on behalf of the trader. Today, while some firms continue to employ human traders, more often quant trading firms execute orders through algorithms. As before, some of these firms have their own order working algorithms, while others utilize those offered by their broker or other service providers. In most cases, they still send their orders to a broker for execution. As such, the vast majority of volumes on various exchanges around the developed world are executed by algorithms on behalf of clients. And, just as before, these volumes are a form of currency for the trading firms that drive them. They bring valuable commission dollars to brokers, and in exchange for a trader bringing his business to a particular broker, the broker may be willing to offer research, data, or capital-raising assistance, among other services.[1]

7.1 ORDER EXECUTION ALGORITHMS

Order execution algorithms determine the way in which systematic execution of a portfolio is actually done. We can examine the kinds of decisions the algorithms must make in real time in much the same framework in which we'd think about how discretionary traders implement their orders. The kinds of considerations are the same in both cases, and as has been the theme throughout this book, we find that quants differ here from their discretionary counterparts principally in the mechanics and not so much in the ideas. The principal goal of execution algorithms, and the function of most execution desks in general, are to minimize the cost of trading into and out of positions.

The primary goals of an order execution algorithm are to get the desired amount of a trade done as completely as possible and as cheaply as possible. Each of these goals is equally interesting and important. Completeness is important because the best portfolio is selected by the portfolio construction model, and if those trades are not implemented, then a different portfolio is owned than what was intended. Cheapness is important for all the reasons we described in Chapter 5: in short, if you can save money every time you make a trade, you will be better off. An obvious corollary is: the more you trade, the more important it is to save money on each trade. This statement, simple and obvious as it is, has important implications for how a rational quant trader goes about building an execution capability. For strategies that require infrequent execution, it may be reasonably viewed as overkill to build a very expensive high speed trading infrastructure. After all, the savings of being high speed versus standard speed are very small, so they are only worth pursuing if they can be made up for in frequency.

Cheapness has several facets, including market impact and slippage, as discussed in Chapter 5. However, one driver of both impact and slippage is what is known as a footprint, which refers to a detectable pattern of behavior by a market participant (think of footprints in the same way a tracker does, when hunting some animal in a forest). If an order execution algorithm leaves an obvious footprint, its activities become predictable to other market participants, and these other participants may well react in such a way as to increase the market impact and slippage incurred by such an algorithm.

An important question is how to measure the efficacy of an execution algorithm. There are a few important concepts worth mentioning here. First is the notion of the "mid-market," which is the average of the best bid and the best offer (which is, by definition, the midpoint between those two levels) on an instrument. This is the most standard way to judge the fair price of a given transaction. If, for example, one is able to buy at the best bid, which is obviously below the then-current mid-market, that particular transaction is considered to have been executed at a favorable price (just as a sale at the then-current best offer might be).

Second, the notion of the Volume-Weighted Average Price (VWAP, for short) is the most standard benchmark for judging the quality of an execution algorithm over multiple trades (either within a day or over multiple days). The idea here is that the VWAP may give a fair sense of how the day's volumes were priced. Since this is the weighted average price at which the day's trading was transacted, it is a reasonable start for thinking about the efficacy of an algorithm. The trouble is that some investors may be fooled by looking at VWAP. If a buyer of stock executes huge volumes during some day, his volumes will most likely increase the price of that stock, and the VWAP. As such, his own activities impact the benchmark against which his execution algorithm is measured, making the interpretation of this benchmark tricky.

The major considerations that go into the making of an order working algorithm are as follows: whether to be aggressive or passive; what type of order to utilize; how to determine the ideal order size; and where to send it. We will briefly address each of these issues.

7.1.1 Aggressive versus Passive

There are two general approaches to execution: aggressive and passive. Aggressive orders (most often in the form of market orders) are submitted to the marketplace and are generally unconditional. They can be filled in pieces or in full at whatever price prevails at the market at the time the order's turn is to be executed arrives (within reasonable boundaries, and so long as there is a bid or offer resting in the order book to take the other side of the market order). In contrast, passive orders (a subset of all limit orders) allow the trader to control the worst price at which he is willing to transact, but the trader must accept that his order might not get executed at all or that only a part of it might be executed. There is also a significant problem of adverse selection, which we will describe in further detail in Chapter 14.

The collection of all available bids and offers (all of which are passive orders) for a given security is known as the *limit order book*, which can be thought of as a queue of limit orders to buy and sell. In electronic markets, each order that is placed on the exchange is prioritized. Highest priority is given to orders at the best prices (the best bids for buy orders and the best offers for sell orders), whereas lower priority is given to those who are bidding or offering worse prices. For two traders offering the same price, traders who show their orders are given higher priority (by most exchanges) than those who hide them (more on this shortly), and for traders who are still tied, the tiebreaker is, not surprisingly, (most often) which one came first.

For some markets, rather than time priority, all orders at a given price are given equal priority, but they are filled according to a *pro rata* allocation of any active order. For example, imagine there are two bids on some instrument at $100.00 (which we will assume is the best bid price), one for 100 units and another for 900 units. Now imagine that an active order to sell 100 units comes into the market. The order would be filled at $100.00, and the passive orders would be allocated as follows: 10 units allocated to the 100 unit order, leaving 90 units remaining on the bid at $100.00, and 90 units allocated to the 900 unit order, leaving 810 units remaining at the bid price. Special considerations apply to these markets, namely a tradeoff between oversizing and overtrading.

Oversizing refers to one technique that a trader might consider using to deal with pro rata markets. Since an active trade is allocated to the various relevant limit orders resting in the order book, proportionately to the size of a given limit order versus the other orders resting in the book at the same price, some traders intentionally oversize their limit orders. This will allow that order to get a larger share of any active order that interacts with the order book. However, there is also the risk that the order is so large that it causes the position to be bigger than the passive trader desired.

On the other hand, if the trader sizes his orders smaller, he must deal with placing and canceling large numbers of orders, which is known as overtrading. Imagine some trader wishes to passively buy 100 units of some instrument, and that at the time an active order to sell 100 units comes in, there is another trader's 900 unit order already in the limit order book. He will only receive a 10 unit fill. Depending on the volume of orders that join his limit order price as he awaits a complete fulfillment of his desired size, he runs the risk of having a very large amount of selling needing to take place before his 100 units is finally filled. And, as we will see in more detail in Chapter 14, this means that he runs a severe risk of experiencing adverse selection[2] (i.e., it is often bad news when the fills actually take place, because the price is likely to move against you in the short term by the time that happens). This in turn means that the trader must be quick to cancel orders and replace them as he competes with larger orders. Without high cancelation rates in this type of market, there would be a vicious cycle of oversizing that theoretically might never end. But as traders cancel, an oversized order might need to cancel as well, because it now is vulnerable to being filled at a larger size than the trader intended.

Regardless, the first kind of decision an execution algorithm must make is how passive or aggressive to be. Passivity and aggression represent how immediately a trader wants to do a trade. Market orders are considered aggressive, because the trader is saying to the market that he just wants his order filled immediately, at whatever the prevailing market will bear. As such, a market order to buy is likely to pay at least the offer, whereas a market order to sell is likely to receive, at most, the current best bid. If the order size is larger than the amount available at the current best bid or offer (whichever applies), the transaction will take out multiple bids or offers at increasingly adverse prices. Paying this kind of cost to transact might be worthwhile if the trader really wants the trade done immediately.

Limit orders can be placed at differing levels of aggressiveness as well. For example, a limit order to buy at the current best offer is an aggressive order because it crosses the spread and removes the best offer from the order book (this is also known as *lifting the offer*). By contrast, a limit order to buy at or below the current best bid is passive because the trader is effectively saying he is fine with the lower probability of being executed, but if he does execute, he is at least only paying the price he's specified. In addition to accepting this uncertainty, the passive order is further subject to a serious problem known as adverse selection. A trader who is willing to cross the bid-offer spread by placing an active order may well have information that the trade he is conducting is actually worth paying the bid-offer spread to get put on right away. To complicate matters further, as we discussed regarding transaction cost models, many exchanges actually pay providers of liquidity for placing passive orders while they charge traders for using liquidity being provided. To phrase it another way, orders that *cross the spread* (orders to buy that are executed at the offer, or orders to sell that are executed at the bid) are using, or "taking," liquidity in that each share or contract executed in this manner is taking out a passive order that's been placed by another trader, which reduces the liquidity available for other participants.

The practice of paying for liquidity provision sweetens the deal for a passive order, but only if the order is actually executed. Not only does the passive trader get a better transaction price, but he also receives a commission rebate from the exchange (typically on the order of two-tenths of a cent per share). But again, the tradeoff is a reduction in certainty of being filled and suffering from potential adverse selection. It is worth noting that some exchanges do the opposite: charge providers of liquidity while paying takers of liquidity. Thus, the liquidity provision (or taking) rebate (or fee) factors into the decision of how passive or aggressive to be. This also factors into answering the question of where to route an order, which is a topic we will cover further in Section 7.1.4.

It is generally true that alpha strategies that are based on a concept of momentum will be paired with execution strategies that are more aggressive, because the market can tend to run away from the trader if he is not aggressive. It is also generally the case that mean reversion strategies utilize more passive execution strategies because they are taking the risk that the prevailing trend persists, and at least by executing at a better price, this mitigates the downside risk of "standing in front of the steamroller."

Another factor driving the use of passive or aggressive execution strategies is the strength of the signal and the model's confidence level in the signal. A stronger, more certain signal probably will be executed with greater aggressiveness than a weaker or less certain signal. This idea is easily demonstrated by extreme examples. If you had inside information that a stock was going to double in the next day because some other company was set to announce an acquisition of the stock in question at a large premium, and if trading on inside information was legal (which it, of course, is not), you should be perfectly happy to pay a lot of money to the marketplace to fill a large order to buy this stock. It would be illogical to fret over a few pennies per share when many dollars are the upside. On the other hand, if you have no view on a stock but were being asked what you'd be willing to pay for it by someone who wants to sell it, you are likely to offer a low enough price that there is some margin of safety.

A fairly common "middle ground" is to put out limit orders somewhere between the best current bid and offer (this is only feasible if the spread between the best bid and offer is larger than the minimum tick size). This way, the trader jumps to the front of the queue for executions, and though he pays a bit more than he would have to if he simply waits for his order to get executed passively, the limit order caps the amount by which he is worse off. At the same time, he has a higher probability of execution than he would if he simply added his order to the current best bid or offer. Finally, he is less likely to suffer from adverse selection in this case. In trading parlance, adding an order to the best bid or offer is known as *joining* it; placing an order that constitutes a new best bid or offer is known as *improving*.

As data have been collected and researched by quants on the limit order book, there has been an increase in sophistication of order execution algorithms to adjust passiveness or aggression based on various changes in the "shape" of the limit order book. This is an example of factoring in a so-called *micro price* or fair value for an instrument. The most conventional ways to quote the price of an instrument are either to state its last traded price or its best bid and offer prices. But the last traded price only tells you what someone else just did, not what you can do now, making it of limited use for trading purposes. The best bid and offer are clearly useful, but what if the best bid has 10,000 units quoted, while the best offer has only 1 unit quoted? This clearly implies that the bid price is more relevant than the offer price. As such, many algorithms account for such imbalances by computing a fair price that reflects things like the imbalance between bids and offers in the limit order book.

To summarize, the first characteristic of an order execution algorithm is its level of aggressiveness, and this can be thought of as a spectrum. At the most aggressive end of the spectrum are market orders; at the least aggressive end of the spectrum are limit orders with prices that are far away from the current market. The level of aggressiveness is usually a function of the type of strategy being employed and depends on the strength of the signal, the system's confidence in that signal, and sometimes also on considerations from the order book, such as a micro price.

7.1.2 Other Order Types

Given the plethora of exchanges and their rules, it would not be fruitful to attempt to cover every kind of order possible in this book. This is especially true because new order types are being created by exchanges frequently, and other order types are retired. However, it is worth understanding some of the types common in some of the largest and most active markets. We will outline several such order types in this section.

Hidden orders are a way to mask one's limit orders from the market, at the cost of losing priority versus visible orders at the same price. The goal here is to "hide one's hand" in terms of buy/sell intentions from other market players while still being able to trade. As discussed, any time a trader puts into the queue a visible order—that is, an order that he has allowed the rest of the market to see—he gives away a bit of information. If many units are already being bought, and yet another trader submits another order to buy, you can imagine a scenario where the price goes up quickly, causing the transaction to cost a significant amount more. In other words, the marketplace has a broad-based sense of market impact, based on the total imbalance between the buyers and sellers at the moment. Placing a hidden order provides no information to the market, which helps reduce the market's perception of imbalances. However, it also reduces the priority of the trade in the queue, leading to a lower probability of execution.

One algorithmic trading technique that utilizes hidden orders is known as *iceberging*, which takes a single large order and chops it into many smaller orders, most of which are posted to the order book as hidden orders. In this way, the bulk of the order is hidden from other traders, just as only the tip of an iceberg is visible above sea level. It is worth noting that not all exchanges allow hidden orders.

There are also several versions of market and limit orders, such as "market-on-close" orders or "stop-limit" orders. *Market-on-close orders* instruct the broker to release the order as a market order during the closing auction for that day. *Stop limit orders* instruct the broker to enter a limit order at a pre-determined price, but to wait until the instrument trades at that price before entering the order. There are also modifiers to orders, such as "fill or kill," "all or none," and "good till canceled." A *fill-or-kill order* is a limit order in which all the shares for the order must be filled immediately or the order is automatically canceled. An *all-or-none order* is like a fill-or-kill order without the cancelation feature, so if an order is not immediately completed in its full size, it remains untouched. A *good-till-canceled* order is a limit order that is not automatically canceled at the end of the day but remains in effect for days or weeks, until explicitly canceled by the trader.

Depending on the market and asset class, there are many other kinds of orders. Moreover, order types are regularly introduced and retired based on customer demands and requests. In the process of executing orders, the quant must determine the kind of orders that will be used in various circumstances. The more execution-intensive a strategy is, the more it matters for a given quant to stay abreast of the latest order types available, and how the various exchange's rules work.

One type of order deserves special discussion. *Intermarket Sweep Orders* (ISOs) exist in U.S. equities because of a flaw in Regulation National Market System (NMS). We will discuss NMS further in Section 7.1.4. For the moment, we will simply point out the Reg NMS includes a ban on so-called "locked markets." A market is said to be locked when the best bid for a given ticker is equal to the best offer on that same ticker, but where these two orders do not interact with each other. Theoretically, you might expect that if a buyer is willing to buy shares at $100.00, and a seller is willing to sell the same shares for $100.00, those two traders' orders would interact, and both trades would be filled. However, because of technological weaknesses in the way that the order book is updated by exchanges after a trade has been completed, a market can sometimes look "locked" when it is not.[3]

For example, imagine that a trader enters a limit order to buy 5,000 shares of some stock (we'll call it WXYZ) at $100.00, which happens to be the best offered price at that moment. Further, the best bid at the time is $99.99. There are only 3,000 shares offered at $100.00. What you would think should happen is that the 5,000 share order interacts partially with the 3,000 share order, and that the remaining bid of 2,000 shares of WXYZ at $100.00 would go into the limit order book as the new best bid (because it is a bid to buy WXYZ at a higher price than the former best bid of $99.99). However, because the piece of software that Reg NMS requires exchanges to use to communicate with one another regarding the aggregated limit order book is slow, the 3,000 share offer will not disappear immediately from the consolidated book.[4] And, because of the ban on locked markets, the remaining 2,000 share bid at $100.00 will not be allowed to be posted to the limit order book until after this delay has been overcome.

The problem is that any firm with direct data feeds from each exchange in the consolidated book experiences no such delay in seeing the best offer being taken out of the order book. Furthermore, having noticed that there was a large buy order, they can come in and directly post a bid at $100.00, anticipating that the price of WXYZ is set to rise. Then, once the Reg NMS feed finally allows the original trader's 2,000 share bid at $100.00 to be posted, this order will be lower in priority than the second trader's bid, even though the 2,000 share order actually happened first. We will discuss in more detail in Chapter 14 why this is a problem, but for now, let it suffice to say that it is extremely problematic to be forced to wait to enter an order artificially. To avoid this problem, very sophisticated traders can be granted the right to use ISOs to execute their trades.

Broker-dealers have the right to recognize a given client's ability to be compliant with Reg NMS directly, without the trader having to use the publicly available consolidated limit order book. Instead, these traders have direct feeds from each exchange and build the same limit order book faster than the official one is made. They perform their own compliance checks, and if their brokers believe this is true, then they are allowed to use the ISO flag on their orders, which allows them to post the order correctly. In our earlier example, the trader would have been able to hit the offer of $100.00 on 3,000 shares and immediately be the highest priority, best bid for 2,000 shares at $100.00.

ISOs exist solely because of the ban on locked markets within Reg NMS, coupled with the slow technology that is used by exchanges to remain compliant with NMS. This is a topic we will revisit in the Appendix.

7.1.3 Large Order versus Small Order

Whether for market orders or limit orders, the quant has to determine how much of a total order to send at once. Recall from our discussion of transaction cost models that a large order costs disproportionately more to execute than a small order because demand for liquidity starts eating into more and more expensive supplies of liquidity. As such, a common technique for automated execution involves taking a large transaction for, say, 100,000 shares of a stock, breaking it into 1,000 orders of 100 shares each, and spreading the orders out over a window of time. Of course, by spreading the order out over time, the trader runs the risk that the price moves more while the order is being spread out than it would have if it had been executed right away, even with the extra cost of market impact.

Generally, however, it is agreed that spreading out trades is a useful way to reduce the cost of transacting, and this is an extremely common feature in execution algorithms. The exact size of the chunks that are sent to market to be executed depends on the transaction cost model's estimate of the transaction cost of variously sized orders for the instrument in question. The determination of the size of each order is related to the analysis of the correct level of aggressiveness. Again, a highly attractive trade warrants taking on more of it quickly than a trade that is relatively less appealing.

But if not, this much aggressiveness in the order placement might not be necessary, and the transaction can be executed in a different manner. For example, a trader might find that taking whatever liquidity is available at the best offer (such as on a buy trade) and then waiting for others to step in and offer the same price a moment later, could allow the same volume of shares to be acquired at whatever the best offer was at the time that the first piece of the order was executed, rather than a worse average price achieved by sweeping through multiple levels of the order book.

7.1.4 Where to Send an Order

In some markets, there are several pools of liquidity for the same instruments. For example, BATS and Archipelago are currently two alternative pools of liquidity for trading U.S. stocks. There is a whole field of work in the area of *smart order routing*, which involves determining to which pool of liquidity it is best to send a given order at the current moment. Typically, the determination itself is straightforward. If one pool of liquidity has the units of a security you want for a better price than another pool of liquidity, you are better off routing the order to the first pool.

We described a problem with Reg NMS in Section 7.1.2. The purpose of NMS was to mitigate the perceived problem of having different "best" prices for a given stock in different pools of liquidity, and this regulation was enacted in 2007. One of the consequences of this rule is that the best bid and offer for a stock across any valid pool of liquidity must be displayed by all pools of liquidity concurrently. This somewhat mitigates the purpose of smart order routing in U.S. equities. However, there are many other markets in which a fragmented structure exists, and in those, the importance of smart order routing is unchanged. Further, there remain other temporal or longer-lived differences between the various liquidity pools in U.S. equities. For example, the depth of liquidity for a given name may vary tremendously from moment to moment on various exchanges. There are also differing rebate and fee levels for providing or taking liquidity on various exchanges, so intelligence still needs to be applied to order routing even in the case of the U.S. equity market.

A more recent development in market structure is the increased role of so-called "dark pools" to execute orders, as discussed in Chapter 5. Exchanges can be categorized as being *lit* or *dark*. Lit exchanges show market participants the prices and sizes of bids and offers available in the limit order book. Dark exchanges provide no such information. The most relevant feature of a dark pool is that it facilitates the execution of large orders, because orders placed on a dark pool are not revealed. Instead, if there is a buyer or seller who has placed an offer (for example) that takes the other side a large trade, then the order executes at that price. But no investors other than the two parties that transacted know that the trade has happened. Thinking back to what we described in Section 7.1.1, about the shape of an order book factoring into a prospective participant's trading decision, giving no information about your order to the rest of the marketplace is clearly beneficial. In the U.S. equity market, it is estimated that more than 30 percent of volumes are now transacted on dark pools.[5] Given the rise to prominence of dark liquidity pools, they require consideration in the forming of order routing logic.

It is worth noting that the term *dark liquidity* encapsulates any transactions that do not occur on the lit exchanges. For example, as we will discuss in more detail in Chapter 15, most retail orders are filled by contractual market makers (CMMs), and these orders never actually make it to the exchange. Coupled with dark pool volumes, dark liquidity has been an increasing portion of the volumes in U.S. equities, which has made for an interesting storyline to watch. In some senses, there is a battle being waged between exchanges and dark pools, between exchanges and contractual market makers, and contractual market makers and non-contractual market makers.

7.2 TRADING INFRASTRUCTURE

We have already mentioned that, in order to execute and process electronic trades, connectivity needs to be set up between the trader and the exchange. Furthermore, a protocol for messages between these two parties is required. The hardware and software that quants utilize in implementing their trading strategies are the final pieces of infrastructure. As in most things, quants face a choice between building or buying infrastructure in all three of these areas. Due to regulatory and other constraints, most traders utilize the services of independent brokerage firms that act as the trading agents for their strategies. One of the benefits of using a broker is that the infrastructure requirements are handled by that broker, and this infrastructure can be costly to replicate.

The most common type of exchange connectivity offered to a trader is, as already discussed, DMA access. This involves using the broker's servers and routing orders through them to the various pools of liquidity being traded. However, some quants, especially those engaged in high-frequency strategies, utilize a more recently available form of connectivity called *colocation*. Brokers offer easy access to markets through DMA platforms, but they add a fair amount of latency to the process. Quant strategies that are sensitive to this latency utilize the colocation option as a way of improving their communication speeds. In a colocation setup, the trader attempts to place his trading servers as physically close to the exchange as possible. In many cases, this means hosting servers in the same data centers as those of the exchange. The reason for the desire for proximity is quite literally to cut down to as short as possible the distance that the order must travel—at the speed of light—over the communication lines between the quant's server and the exchange. A typical and relatively high-quality DMA platform tends to cause between 10 and 30 milliseconds of delay between the time the order is sent from the quant's server and the time the order reaches the exchange. By contrast, a well-designed colocation solution can have an order travel from the quant's server to the exchange in a fraction of a millisecond. For latency-sensitive execution strategies, this can be a useful improvement.

In terms of communication, the most important piece of infrastructure in electronic trading is known as the *Financial Information eXchange* (FIX) protocol. The FIX protocol began in 1992 as a communications framework between Fidelity Investments and Salomon Brothers and has grown to become the method of choice for real-time electronic communication among most of the world's banks, money managers using electronic executions, and exchanges offering electronic equities or futures trading. The FIX protocol is a standardized way for various participants in the trading process to communicate information. Considering that the number of order and execution messages is measured in billions per day, it is obviously critical to have a standard format for these communications. The FIX protocol is free and open source, but the software that implements the FIX protocol is known as a *FIX engine*, and not all FIX engines are created equal. Quants must choose whether to build or buy such engines, and a fair number of quants land in each camp. In general, quants who are extremely sensitive to latency, such as high-frequency traders, will likely build their own customized FIX engines to ensure optimal speeds.

The final component of trading infrastructure relates to the hardware and software used. Again, quants can choose to build or to buy various solutions. For example, it is easy to buy computers built with standard hardware (such as microchips, data storage, etc.), utilize off-the-shelf order management systems (which process and manage trades), or utilize third-party execution algorithms. On the other hand, some quant firms have customized their own microchips to perform specialized trading-related functions with greater speed than conventional, commercially available chips. It is generally found that such hardware customization allows greater speeds than any purely software-based solution. However, it is a more rigid process, and unlike software, once hardware is customized, it is difficult to change.

Beyond this, quants attempt to make their algorithms, databases, and execution software leaner, to reduce the internal latency of processing market data and sending an order out to the market. Even the most fundamental choices about computers—for example, the operating system of choice—are considered. For instance, most quants use either Linux or UNIX operating systems because they are more easily configurable and more efficient and therefore provide better computing performance than a PC/Windows configuration. I remember some years ago having a quant firm describe to me their use of the processors from a Sony Playstation 3, because it was a categorically faster processor than what was found in even a powerful PC or server. Since then, Graphics Processing Units (GPUs), which drive the video cards found in our computers, have been pressed into service for many applications, from bitcoin mining to large language models (LLMs) and also to quant investing, because GPUs are designed to operate in a massively parallel manner, which make tasks like training machine-learning models much faster.

7.3 SUMMARY

We have detailed a variety of issues related to the execution of orders for a quant trading strategy. The very first choice the quant must make is whether to build or buy a trading solution. The technical expertise and cost of building a world-class execution infrastructure lead many quants, especially those utilizing longer-term trading strategies or those trading smaller portfolios, to choose the route of buying these services, either from brokers or execution service providers. Both brokers and execution vendors do, in fact, charge for the service of providing execution algorithms and connectivity. This charge normally is made by increasing commission costs. It can often cost five or

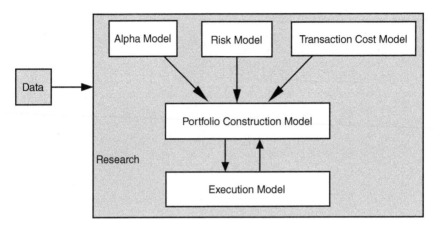

EXHIBIT 7.1   Schematic of the Black Box

more times as much per share to trade through a third party's algorithms than to trade using one's own. Thus, for traders who have expertise in this area and for those managing significant sums, it can be worthwhile building custom execution models and infrastructure.

Execution is where the rubber meets the road for a quant system and how the quant interacts with the rest of the marketplace. This continues to be a fruitful area of research, as it has been ever since markets began to become electronic. This chapter concludes our stroll through inside of the black box, as we can see from Exhibit 7.1. We turn our attention now to understanding the data that feed quant trading strategies.

NOTES

1. In addition to the commissions earned by brokers from customers' trading volumes, brokers have other sources of revenue from the activities of their clients. For example, clearing fees also apply for management of settlement and holding positions for clients as a custodian. Stock loan fees also sometimes create revenue.
2. Adverse selection in the sense that applies to capital markets is defined as a situation in which there is a tendency for bad outcomes to occur, due to asymmetric information between a buyer and a seller. This will be covered in greater detail in Chapter 14.
3. The term "locked" is itself a misnomer. There is nothing frozen about a locked market. It is simply a market with a $0.00 bid/offer spread, which should actually be desirable to encourage.

4. This piece of software in general is called a Securities Information Processor (SIP). The specific SIP used by various U.S. equity exchanges, including Archipelago and INET, is called the UTP Quote Data Feed (UQDF). UTP stands for Unlisted Trading Privilege, which relates to tickers listed on the Nasdaq exchange. The analogous software for stocks listed on the NYSE, AMEX, and some other regional exchanges in the U.S. is known as the Consolidated Quote System (CQS).
5. Matthew Philips, "Where Has All the Stock Trading Gone?" *Business Week*, May 10, 2012. http://www.businessweek.com/articles/2012-05-10/where-has-all-the-stock-trading-gone#p1

CHAPTER 8

Data

I'd sell you my kids before I'd sell you my data, and I'm not selling you my kids.
                                    —Anonymous quantitative futures trader

The old adage is, "garbage in, garbage out," meaning that if you use bad inputs, you'll get bad outputs. This relates to quant trading because most quants utilize some form of *input/output model*, which is a term that comes from computer science (and that has been borrowed by econometricians). It refers to the way in which information processors (such as computers) communicate with the world around them. One of the things we love about input/output models is that if you provide the same input a million times, the output should be consistent every time. The process that transforms an input into an output is typically the part that people call the *black box* in quant trading, and we have seen the inside of this box in the preceding chapters. In this chapter, we will examine the inputs of quant trading models, namely, the data they depend on.

Mechanically, data reach the black box through data servers, which are connected to one or more data sources. On receipt of these data, the black box processes them for use by the alpha, risk, transaction cost, portfolio construction, and execution models that constitute the internal organs of the quant trading machine. These data servers usually process data using software some quants call *data feed handlers,* which are designed to convert the data into a form in which they can be stored and utilized in the modules of the quant system.

8.1   THE IMPORTANCE OF DATA

It is difficult to overstate the importance of data, and it can be seen from many perspectives. First, data, as we know, are the inputs to quant trading systems. It turns out that the nature of the inputs to a system dictates what you can do with the system itself. For example, if you were handed a lot of lettuce, tomatoes, and cucumbers, it would be very difficult to build, say, a jet engine. Instead, you might decide that these inputs are most suited for making a salad. To make a jet engine, you more or less need jet engine parts, or at least materials that can handle high velocities and acceleration, high altitude, and a wide range of temperatures. The same is true with quant systems. To the extent that you are given data that focus on macroeconomic activity, it is extremely difficult to build a useful model that doesn't some-how reflect macroeconomic concepts.

Frequently, many details of the model itself are driven by the characteristics of the inputs that are used. Refining our example, imagine that you are given slow-moving macroeconomic data, such as quarterly U.S. GDP figures; furthermore, you receive them only a week after they are released to the public. In this situation, it is unlikely that you can build a very fast trading model that looks to hold positions for only a few minutes. Also, note that the U.S. data you get might be useful for predicting bonds or currency relationships, but they might not be sufficient to build a helpful model of agriculture markets. U.S. GDP data, even if these give you some small clue about the consumption of corn, will also tell you very little about what is happening in corn futures: besides the small correlation that may exist between GDP growth and corn consumption, there is no information in GDP data about the supply side of the equation.

The nature of the data you are using is also an important determinant of the database technology you would rationally choose for storage and retrieval, a subject we will discuss in greater detail later in this chapter. Data sometimes even drive decisions about what types of hardware and software make the most sense. Again and again, we see that the nature of data—and even how they are delivered—determines a great deal about what can be done and how one would actually go about doing it.

Still another perspective on the importance of data can be understood by examining the consequences of *not* doing a good job of gathering and handling data. Returning to the idea that quant trading systems are input/output models, if you feed the model bad data, it has little hope of producing accurate or even usable results. A stunning example of this concept can be seen in the failure of the Mars Climate Orbiter (MCO) in 1999. The $200 million satellite was destroyed by atmospheric friction because one team of software engineers programmed the software that controlled the craft's thrusters to expect metric units of force (Newtons) while another team programmed the data delivered to the satellite to be in English units (pound-force). The software model that controlled the satellite's thrusters ran faithfully, but because the data were in the wrong units (causing them to be off by a factor of almost 4.5 times), the satellite drifted off course, fell too close to Mars' surface, and ended up being destroyed. In the aftermath, National Aeronautic and Space Administration (NASA) management did not blame the software error but rather the process used to check and recheck the software and the data being fed to it.[1]

Problems, however, can be easy to miss. After all, the results frequently are numbers that can be seen to as many decimal places as you care to see. But this is *false precision*. That we have a number that goes out to several decimal places may not mean that we can rely on this number at all. Because the kind of trading with which we are concerned is all about timing, timeliness is critical. If you build a fantastic model to forecast the price of a stock over the next day, but you don't provide it data until a week later, what good is the model? This is an extreme example, but it is almost exclusively the case that the faster you can get accurate information into a good model, the better off you'll be, at least if succeeding is part of your plan.

Bad data can also lead to countless squandered hours of research and, in extreme cases, even to invalid theorization. Data are generally required to develop a theory about the markets or anything else in science, just as physical scientists utilize their observations of the world to generate their theories. So, if we provide the scientist with incorrect information without her knowledge, she is likely to develop theories that are incorrect when applied to the real world. Bad data lead to bad outcomes. If the data have serious problems, it will be impossible to tell whether a system being tested, no matter how sophisticated the testing nor how elegant the model, is good or bad.

Many quant trading firms recognize this point in their behavior. Most of the best firms collect their own data from primary sources rather than purchasing it from data vendors. They also expend significant resources in the effort to speed up their access to data, to clean data, and even to develop better ways of storing data. Some firms have dozens or even hundreds of employees dedicated exclusively to capturing, cleaning, and storing data optimally.

I close this section with an illustration of the interconnectedness of the various, seemingly disparate pieces of the black box that we have illustrated. I pointed out when I introduced that schematic in Chapter 2 that this schematic is intentionally discretizing what could be more integrated. Just so, an interesting paper connects the public attention to (especially military) satellite launch events to the level of correlation among U.S. equities on those corresponding dates.[2] It is remarkable to consider the fact that public attention focused on satellite launches affects the dispersion of individual stock prices for a few days on either side of the anticipated launches.

8.2 TYPES OF DATA

The two most common and important kinds of data are *price data* and *fundamental data*. Price data is actually not solely related to the prices of instruments; it includes other information received or derived from exchanges or transactions. Other examples of price data are the trading volumes for stocks or the time and size of each trade. Indeed, the entire "order book," which shows a continuous series of all bids and offers for a given instrument throughout the course of a day as well as the amounts of each, would be considered price-related data. Furthermore, we would place anything that can be derived from the levels of various indices (e.g., percent changes computed from the daily values of the S&P 500 index) in the price-related data category, even if the computed value is not the price of a traded instrument.

There is a rather broad variety of fundamental data, which can make it difficult to categorize effectively. In a sense, fundamental data relate to anything besides prices. However, what all types of data have in common is that they are expected to hold some usefulness in helping to determine the price of an instrument in the future, or at least to describe the instrument in the present. Also, we can do a bit more to create a reasonable taxonomy of fundamental data. The most common kinds of fundamental data are financial health, financial performance, financial worth, and sentiment. For single stocks, for example, a company's balance sheet is mostly used to indicate the financial health of the company. Meanwhile, for macroeconomic securities (e.g., government bonds or currencies), budget, trade deficit or personal savings data might serve to indicate the financial health of a nation. Portions of the income and cash-flow statements (e.g., total net profits or free cash flow) are used to determine financial performance; other portions are used to indicate financial health (e.g., ratios of accruals to total revenue or cash flow to earnings). Similarly, the U.S. GDP figure might be an example of macroeconomic financial performance data, whereas the trade balances figure is an example of macroeconomic financial health data. The third type of fundamental data relates to the worth of a financial instrument. Some common examples of this kind of data in the equities world are the book value or the amount of cash on hand. The last common type of fundamental data is sentiment. How analysts rate a stock, the buying and selling activity of company insiders, and information related to the implied volatility of the options on a stock are examples of sentiment data for stocks; economists' forecasts for GDP growth for next quarter are an example of macroeconomic sentiment data.

The third kind of data is what we will refer to as *in-house* data. A small minority of quant practitioners utilize this kind of information, but it remains interesting. One simple example of this type of data would be a history of all trades and their fill prices. It is easy to imagine fine-tuning a transaction cost model with empirical observations of one's own market impact. Similarly, as we will discuss in Chapter 9, assumptions have to be made about how long it takes for your system to detect new information and act upon it (by getting an order into the marketplace). In-house data can be utilized to more accurately assess this duration.

Lastly, we consider *meta-data*. Meta-data often include crucial pieces of information that we require to use other data effectively. For example, most equity strategies require the use of a *security master*, which is used to organize information so that other systems can use it without error. Identifiers for stocks are a good example of this kind of information. While you might think that the ticker symbol is a perfectly good identifier, it in fact has major weaknesses. It is not immutable over time, for example. Citigroup, after merging with Travelers, took on the symbol C, while Exxon, after merging with Mobil, changed from XON to XOM. Facebook simply changed its name and ticker outright, from FB to META. Other times, a symbol ceases to be related to one company and becomes related to another. V used to be Vivendi's symbol, but after they delisted, it became available. Visa Inc stepped in and took over the symbol in March 2008. If you don't carefully track which symbols relate to which underlying companies, you run the risk of applying figures to the wrong companies. Exhibit 8.1 presents a taxonomy of data. I should be very clear: there is no chance this taxonomy is complete (I do not flesh out the nascent category of "healthcare" data), nor is it likely to be totally accurate even for what it is. Plenty of other practitioners would organize data differently, for example, by the sector they relate to. Nonetheless, I think it is useful to get a sense of the scope of the types of data, for a variety of reasons.

We don't want to oversimplify the matter. Clever researchers are constantly looking for new and innovative information that might not be used by other players. Technology advances in the broader marketplace have greatly aided this kind of activity. In the last edition of this book, some examples of what was "cutting edge" were natural language processing of news articles, using GPS tracking of shipping vessels, utilizing credit card data to assess the revenues of retailers, and so on. By now all of these have advanced significantly, and many other innovations and products have been brought to bear in domains such as geospacial data, web scraping, social media, anonymized clickstreams, and phone apps. In addition, prime brokerages and banks have gotten into the business of providing data on their aggregated customers' sentiment or flows to other customers (namely hedge

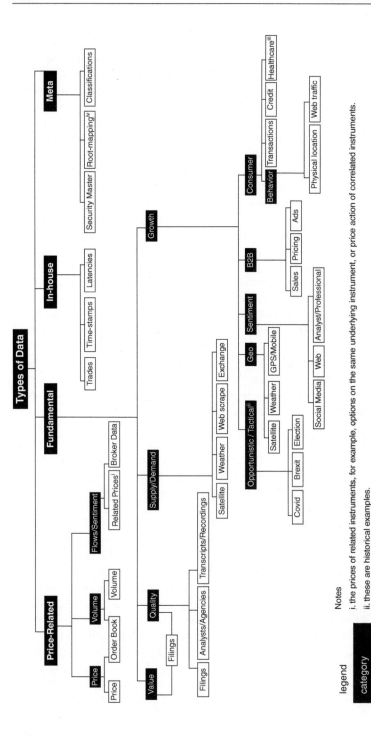

Notes

i. the prices of related instruments, for example, options on the same underlying instrument, or price action of correlated instruments.

ii. these are historical examples.

iii. healthcare data are a newer area, not really available yet, and questionably included in this category.

iv. we mean the mapping of a given instrument to the underlying asset. For example, there may be many bonds issued by a single issuer, but they all need to be mapped back to that issuer.

legend

category

item or source

EXHIBIT 8.1 A Taxonomy of Data

funds, and especially quants). It bears noting that most alternative data so far has been focused on consumer spending or activity. Separately, analyses of audio replays of earnings calls can be used to determine any hidden information in the voices of the speakers (e.g., from subtle cues of intonation), or entire analyst reports can be generated automatically using a large-language model (LLM).

Indeed, machine-learning techniques figure prominently in the acquisition of data for quants. It is likely that this is the arena in which machine learning has had most impact in the quant space. Most of the approaches to collecting these datasets, organizing them, giving them structure, and rendering them useful are wholly dependent on ML techniques, so it is not at all surprising that, as these techniques have advanced and matured, so has the number of potential datasets available to quant firms exploded.

In general, the so-called "alternative data" game remains largely an exercise in getting faster and more robust indicators of sentiment (or other types of fundamentals already described), so we believe that sources such as this are still fundamental in nature. Even in the case that there are potentially revolutionary advances, such as LLMs, in the approach to collecting or transforming such data, the nature of the fundamental information being sought is by no means different than it was. This is not to diminish the ingenuity of those who developed such ideas. We simply point out that our classification scheme seems to do a reasonable job of explaining the kinds of data that exist.

An interesting pattern has emerged in our discussion of data. Much of what we saw in the price category of data tended to focus on shorter time scales. We spoke about daily values and even continuous intraday values. Meanwhile, in the fundamental category, we tend to see new information released on the cadence of weeks, months, or quarters. One implication we can immediately discern from these differing periodicities is that, in general, trading strategies utilizing price-related information have the option to be much faster than those utilizing primarily fundamental information. Again, this is simply because the information we have about the securities is refreshed more frequently with price-related information than it usually is with fundamental data. This statement is not universal, since some fundamental strategies, especially those focused on changes in fundamentals or sentiment, can be very short-term-oriented. However, this statement holds most of the time and is a handy rule of thumb to bear in mind when looking at a quant strategy.

8.3 SOURCES OF DATA

One can get data from many sources. Most direct, but also perhaps most challenging, is to get raw data from the primary sources. In other words, a quant would get price data for stocks traded on the New York Stock Exchange directly from the NYSE. This has the benefit of allowing the quant maximum control over the cleaning and storing of data, and it can also have significant benefits in terms of speed. However, there is also a massive cost to doing things this way. It would require building connectivity to every primary source, and if we are speaking about trading multiple types of instruments (e.g., stocks and futures) across multiple geographical markets and exchanges, the number of data sources can explode. With each, software must be built to translate the primary sources' unique formats into something usable by the quant's trading systems.

Examples of the kinds of primary sources and data types include these:

- **Exchanges:** Prices, volumes, timestamps, open interest, short interest, order book data.
- **Regulators:** Financial statements from individual companies, filings related to large owners of individual stocks as well as insider buying and selling activities.
- **Governments:** Macroeconomic data, such as employment, inflation, or GDP data.
- **Corporations:** Announcements of financial results and other relevant developments (e.g., changes in dividends).
- **News agencies:** Press releases or news articles.
- **Investment banks/brokerages/ratings agencies:** Generally, these will be reports about companies (or macroeconomic forecasts), indicating various expectations for either growth (e.g., revenue or earnings forecasts) or quality (e.g., credit ratings). Some brokerages are now also licensing out (usually selectively) information about client order flows, which help the users of such data determine information relevant to technical sentiment forecasts.
- **Websites:** Social media and other websites provide data, usually unwittingly, to those who have developed tools to "scrape" (which means to extract in a machine-readable form) these websites and analyze the contents. For example, one could develop software to read X (formerly Twitter) posts (Tweets) to determine the sentiment of the public about a new product launch from Nike, or about Nike's stock itself.
- **Tech (or other) companies/alternative data vendors:** Some companies generate data as part of their business, without any regard for its uses for quant investing. For example, a company Envestnet | Yodlee have been aggregating financial data, such as credit card transactions, for some time. Their main customers are banks and other financial institutions looking to gain insights about their own customers. But it turns out that investors might also be interested in these kinds of insights,

because they may give a sneak peak as to which companies are more likely to beat or miss earnings expectations, and to the general volume of economic activity. As such, licensing these datasets to hedge funds became a part of Envestnet | Yodlee's business model. There are innumerable examples: road traffic data, weather station data (e.g., for crop growth forecasts, or for demand for heating oil in the winter), satellite imagery data, geolocation data (e.g., when you allow your phone to report your location to various apps, they can aggregate your location with others' and sell that data to, well, whomever may be interested and able to pay), internet traffic data, and so on. Some of these datasets are, in my mind at least, pretty controversial, but they continue to proliferate, nonetheless.

- **In-house data:** Perhaps the most neglected source of data is generated from the activities of an investor. For example, while quants have transaction cost models, these are largely generic. But there are plenty of transactions that investors make, and these can be used to refine the transaction cost model. More interestingly (and less commonly), one can juxtapose different alpha's signal strengths with the transaction costs of the resulting trades, or even the simple profitability of that trade to garner further insights from such house-generated data. Perhaps most interestingly, you can observe the reactions of the market to your interactions with it, to glean the effects you're having and tune your interactions accordingly.

Because of the scope of the work involved in accessing data directly from primary sources, many firms use secondary data vendors to solve some aspects of the data problem. For example, some data vendors take financial statement data from regulatory filings around the world and create quantified databases that they then license to quant traders. In this example, the data vendor is being paid for having solved the problem of building a consistent framework to house and categorize data from many direct sources. But imagine that the quant firm wants to collect both price and fundamental data about companies around the world. It is frequently the case that entirely different companies provide each of these types of data. For instance, for a given stock, there may be one data vendor providing price data and a completely different one providing fundamental data. These data vendors may also differ in the way they identify stocks. One might use the ticker; another might use a SEDOL code or some other identifier.[3] With two or more different data sets regarding the same security, the quant will have to find a way to ensure that all the data ultimately find their way into the same company's record in its internal database. The tool used to help with this is frequently called a *security master* in that it is the master file mapping the various ways that data vendors identify stocks to a single, unique identifier method that the quant will use in her trading system.

Further complications arise from the way that companies buy and sell assets—and these assets can themselves be companies. Consider that you may be able to use credit card transaction data to see that customers are spending more money than expected at the Olive Garden. That's great, but what does it mean for the bottom line of their owner, Darden Restaurants (DRI)? They also own Ruth's Chris Steakhouse, The Capital Grille, and many other chains. So you would have to aggregate data across all of those brands and roll them up correctly to have a useful guess about DRI. What's more, DRI has owned the Olive Garden since 1995. Before that, General Mills was the owner, so if you're back-testing long enough, you would have to account for this change of ownership (and the resulting change in the mapping of revenues, expenses, etc.).

As you might have guessed, still other firms have cropped up to provide unified databases across many types of vendors and data types. These we can call *tertiary data vendors*, and they are paid to make data easy to access for the quant. They establish connections with many primary and secondary data vendors, build and maintain security masters, and even perform some data-cleaning activities (a subject we will discuss in more detail presently). As a result, they are immensely popular among many firms. However, we should make it clear that as much benefit as they offer in terms of ease, tertiary data vendors do add another layer between the quant and the original data. This layer can result in loss of speed and possibly in less control over the methods used to clean, store, or access data on an ongoing basis.

8.4 CLEANING DATA

Having established the types and importance of data, we now turn to the kinds of problems quants face in managing these raw materials and how they handle such flaws. Despite the efforts of primary, secondary, and sometimes even tertiary data vendors, data are often either missing or incorrect in some way. If ignored, this problem can lead to disastrous consequences for the quant. This section addresses some of the common problems found with errors and some of the better-known approaches used to deal with these challenges. It's worth noting that although some of the following data problems seem egregious or obvious to a human, it can be challenging to notice such problems in a trading system that is processing millions of data points hourly (or even within one minute, as in the case of high-frequency traders).

The first common type of data problem is missing data, as we alluded to already. Missing data occur when a piece of information existed in reality but for some reason was not provided by the data supplier. This is obviously an issue because without data, the system has nothing to go on. Worse still, by withholding just some portion of the data, systems can make erroneous computations. Two common approaches are used to solve the problem of missing data. The first is to build the system so that it "understands" that data can in fact go missing, in which case the system doesn't act rashly when there are no data over some limited time period. For example, many databases automatically assign a value of zero to a data point that is missing. After all, zero and nothing have a lot in common. However, there is a very different implication to the model thinking the price is now zero (e.g., if we were long the instrument, we'd be showing a 100 percent loss on the position) versus thinking that the price is unknown at the moment.

To fix this problem, many quants program their database and trading systems to recognize the difference between zero and blank. This frequently means simply using the last known price until a new one is available. The second approach is to try to interpolate what a reasonable value might be in place of the missing data. This is useful for historical data rather than real-time data, but a variation of the method described here can be used for real-time data as well.

Let's take an example of a semiconductor company's listed stock. Imagine that we know the price of a semiconductor stock immediately before and immediately after the missing data point (this is why this technique is mainly useful to back-fill missing data points in a database). We could simply interpolate the price of the stock as being midway between the price immediately before and immediately after the gap. Imagine further that we know how the stock index, the tech sector, the semiconductor industry, and some close competitors performed for the period that is missing. By combining information about the periods around the missing point and the action of related things during the missing period, it is possible to compute a sensible value for the stock's missing data point. Though we aren't guaranteed and in fact aren't terribly likely to get the number exactly right, at least we have something reasonable that won't cause our systems problems.

A more sophisticated approach might be to utilize correlation matrices to backfill/infill missing data (including to backfill data from before there was any for a given security, with the goal of having the same amount of data for each asset). Let's say you have two assets, A and B. Let's say that the price history for A goes back five years and for B, it goes back 10 years. And let's say that the correlation between A and B is 0.65. You could backfill the missing five years of data for A as simply having zero cumulative return but a 0.65 correlation to the actual price history of B. In so doing, creating uniform numbers of datapoints in the history, certain complex optimizations can be simplified significantly.

A second type of data problem is the presence of incorrect values. For instance, decimal errors are a common problem. To take the example of U.K. stocks, they are sometimes quoted in pounds and sometimes in pence. Obviously, if a system is expecting to receive a figure in pounds and it receives a number that doesn't advertise itself as being anything other than pounds, problems can abound. Instead of being quoted as, say, £10, it is quoted as 1000, i.e., 1000 pence. This can result in the model being told that the price has spiked dramatically upward, which can cause all sorts of other mayhem (e.g., a naïve system without data checks might want to short the stock aggressively if it suddenly and inexplicably jumped 100X in an instant). Alternatively, a price might simply be wrong. Exchanges and other sources of data frequently put out *bad prints*, which are data points that simply never happened at all or at least didn't happen the way the data source indicates.

By far the most common type of tool used to help address this issue is something we call a *spike filter*. Spike filters look for abnormally large, sudden moves in prices and either smooth these out or eliminate them altogether. Further complicating the matter, it should be noted that sometimes spikes really do happen. In these circumstances, a spike filter may reject a value that is valid, either ignoring it or replacing it with an erroneous value. An interesting example of this is shown in Exhibit 8.2. In this case, during the trading day of July 15, 2008, the U.S. dollar's exchange rate with the Mexican peso quickly fell about 3 percent, then regained virtually all that ground in a matter of seconds.

This behavior is not reserved for less commonly traded instruments, however. The 10-year German bund, one of the more liquid futures contracts in the world, dropped about 1.4 percent in a few seconds during the day of March 28, 2008, only to recover immediately (see Exhibit 8.3).

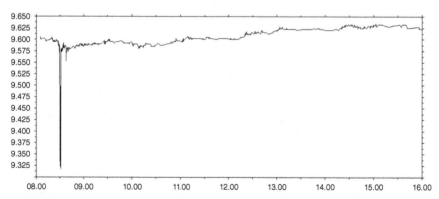

EXHIBIT 8.2   September 2008 Mexican Peso Futures Contract on July 15, 2008

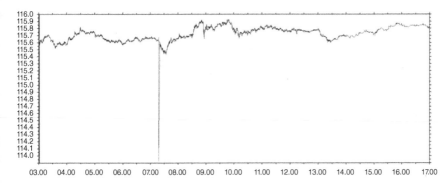

EXHIBIT 8.3 June 2008 German Bund Futures Contract on March 28, 2008

A spike filter might well have called this a bad print, but it really happened. To reduce the impact of this problem, some quants use spike filters to alert a human supervisor to look into the matter further, and the human can then decide, based on what she sees as the facts, on what to do about the strange price. Still another common approach, though useful only if there is more than one source for a given piece of data, is to cross-check a data set given by one provider against one provided by a second source. If they match, it is more likely to be a correct price. If they do not match, one or both of them must be wrong. Of course, what to do when two vendors don't match each other is a whole other ball of wax. A final common approach to cleaning data problems is to utilize the same approach as described earlier in addressing the problem of missing data by looking to the points before and after the "bad" data point and/or by looking to the behavior of related instruments to interpolate an approximate value.

A quant may utilize volume data to assist in dealing with price spikes. Let's imagine that a spike really did happen, but it was driven by a tiny amount of volume at an illiquid period of the day. This price spike may therefore not be actionable, and as a result, you may discount it when forecasting return, risk, or other characteristics of the asset.

Another very common type of data error relates to corporate actions such as splits and dividends. Imagine a ticker that splits 3:1. Generally, the price drops by about two-thirds to offset the threefold increase in the number of shares.[4] Imagine that the data vendor doesn't record this as a split, and therefore doesn't adjust the back-history to reflect this corporate action. In this scenario, the quant trader's system may be misled to believe that the stock simply dropped 67 percent overnight. This is generally handled by independently tracking corporate actions, together with the human-oversight version of a spike filter, described previously.

Another frustrating problem is that the data sometimes contain incorrect timestamps. This is generally a problem with intraday or real-time data, but it has been known to be an issue with other data as well. This is also one of the tougher problems to solve. Obviously, the path of a time series is fairly important, especially since the goal of the quant trader focused on alpha is to figure out when to be long, short, or out of a given security. As such, if the time series is shuffled because of an error in the data source, it can be deeply problematic. A quant researcher could believe her system works when in reality it doesn't,[5] or she could believe her system doesn't work when in reality it does.[6] If the quant trading firm stores its own data in real time, it can track timestamps received versus the internal clocks of the machines doing the storing and ensure that there are correct timestamps, which is perhaps the most effective way of addressing this issue. But to do so requires storing one's own data reliably in real time and writing software to check the timestamp of each and every data point against a system clock in a way that doesn't slow the system down too much, making this a difficult problem to address. It should be noted that this approach only works for those quants who capture and store their own data in real time. For those who are relying on purchased databases, they can only cross-check data from various sources.

Finally, a more subtle type of data challenge bears mentioning here. This is known as *look-ahead bias* and is a subject to which we will devote attention several times in this book. Look-ahead bias refers to the problem of wrongly assuming that you could have known something before it would have been possible to know it. Another way to phrase this is "getting yesterday's news the day before yesterday." We will examine look-ahead bias in Chapter 9 on research, but for now, let's examine a particular form of this bias that comes from the data. Specifically, it derives from asynchronicity in the data.

A common example of asynchronicity can be found in the regulatory filings of financial statements (known as 10-Qs) made by companies each quarter in the United States. Companies report their financial statements *as of* each quarter end. However, these reports are usually released four to eight weeks after the end of the quarter. Let's imagine the first quarter of 2023 has just ended. On May 1, 2023, Acme Concrete Inc. reports that its first-quarter earnings were $1 per share as of March 31. Let's further imagine that the consensus of the analyst community was to expect only $0.50 per share, making the result a strongly positive surprise. Once the data point is available, most data vendors will report that Acme's earnings per share were $1 per share as of March 31, even though the number wasn't released until May 1.

Three years later, a quant is testing a strategy that uses earnings data from this vendor. The data indicate that Acme's earnings were $1 per share for the quarter ending March 31, and her model assumes this to be true, even though in reality she would never have been able to know this until the estimate was released a month later, on May 1. In the back-test, she sees that her model buys Acme in April because its P/E ratio looks appealing from April 1 onward, given the $1-per-share earnings result, even though the model would not have known about the $1 earnings figure until May 1 if she had been trading back then. Suddenly the strategy makes a huge profit on the position in early May, when the world, and her model, actually would have found out about the earnings surprise. This kind of problem also happens with macroeconomic data (such as the unemployment rate), which frequently get revised some months after their initial release. Without careful tracking of the revision history for such data, the quant can be left with the same issue as demonstrated in the equity example: believing that she could have had revised data in the past when in fact she would only have had the less accurate initial data release.

If the quant ignores this data error, she can end up making a Type I error again: believing that her strategy is profitable and sound, even though it may in fact only look that way because she's made a substantial data error. To address look-ahead bias in the data, quants can record the date at which new information is actually made available and only make the data available for testing at the appropriate time. In addition, quants can put an artificial lag on the data they are concerned about so that the model's awareness of this information is delayed sufficiently to overcome the look-ahead bias issues. Note that look-ahead issues with regard to data are specific to research, which we will discuss further in Chapter 9. In live trading, there is no such thing as look-ahead bias, and in fact quants would want all relevant data to be available to their systems as immediately as possible.

Another type of look-ahead bias stemming from asynchronicity in the data is a result of the various closing times of markets around the world. The SPY (the ETF tracking the S&P 500) trades until 4:15 P.M., whereas the stocks that comprise the S&P 500 index stop trading at 4:00 P.M. European stock markets close from 11:00 A.M. to 12:00 P.M., New York time. Asian markets are already closed on a given day by the time New York opens. In many cases, the considerable impact that U.S. news and trading activity have on European or Asian markets cannot be felt until the next trading day.

On Friday, October 10, 2008, for example, the Nikkei 225 fell more than 9 percent for the day. But it was already closed by the time New York opened. European markets closed down between 7 and 10 percent for the same day. At the time of Europe's closing, the S&P 500 was down about 6 percent for the day. Suddenly, however, just after 2:00 P.M. EST on the 10th, with two hours remaining in U.S. trading but the rest of the world already gone for the weekend, the S&P 500 rallied, closing down just over

1 percent. Monday the 13th was a market holiday in Japan. Europe tried to make up ground that Monday, with the key markets closing up over 11 percent but the U.S. market up "only" about 6 percent by midday in New York. However, by the end of the trading day, the U.S. market closed up over 11 percent as well, leaving the European markets behind again. The next day, the Nikkei reopened on the 14th and ended up 14 percent. On their subsequent day, European markets closed up about 3 percent, whereas the U.S. market was down slightly by the end of its own trading day. Ignoring this kind of asynchronicity can be extremely problematic for analyses of closing price data because these closing prices occur at different times on the same day.

These are but a few examples of the many subtle ways in which look-ahead bias seeps into the process of research and money management, even for discretionary traders. A key challenge for the quant is deciding how to manage this problem in its myriad forms.

8.5 STORING DATA

Databases are used to store collected data for later use, and they come in several varieties. The first type of database is known as the *flat file*. Flat files are two-dimensional databases, much like an ordinary spreadsheet. Flat file databases are loved for their leanness, because there is very little baggage or overhead to slow them down. It is a simple file structure that can be searched very easily, usually in a sequential manner (i.e., from the first row of data onward to the last). However, you can easily imagine that searching for a data point near the bottom row of a very large flat file with millions of rows may take rather a long time. To help with this problem, many quants use *indexed flat files*, which add an extra step but which can make searching large files easier. The index gives the computer a sort of "cheat sheet," providing an algorithm to search large sets of data more intelligently than a sequential search.

A second important type of data storage is a relational database. Relational databases allow for more complex relationships among the data set. For example, imagine that we want to keep track of stocks not just on their own but also as part of industry groups, as part of sectors, as part of broader indices for the countries of their domicile, and as part of the universe of stocks overall. This is a fairly routine thing to want to do. With flat files, we would have to construct these groups each as separate tables. This is fine if nothing ever changes with the constituents of each table. But in reality, every time there is a corporate action, a merger, or any other event that would cause us to want to modify the record for a single stock in any one of these tables, we have to remember to update all of them. Instead, in the world of relational databases, we can simply create a database table that contains *attributes* of each stock—for example, the industry, sector, market, and universe it is in. Given this table, we can simply manage the table of information for the stock itself and for its attributes. From there, the database will take care of the rest based on the established relationship. Though relational databases allow for powerful searches, they can also be slow and cumbersome because their searches can span many tables as well as the meta tables that establish the relationships among the data tables.

An important type of relational database is known as a *data cube*, a label I have borrowed from Sudhir Chhikara, the former head of quantitative trading at Stark Investments. Data cubes force consistency into a relational database by keeping all the values for all the attributes of all instruments in a single, three-dimensional table. For a given date, then, all instruments would be listed in one axis of this table. A second axis would store all the values for a given attribute (e.g., closing price for that date) across the various instruments. The third axis would store other attributes (e.g., earnings per share as of that date). This method has the benefit of simplifying the relationships in a way that is rather useful. In other words, it hardwires certain relationships; furthermore, by keeping all attributes of each instrument available every day, there is no need to search for the last available data point for a given attribute and security. For every day, a data cube is created to store all the relevant data. This approach, too, has its potential disadvantages. Hardwiring the relationships leads to inflexibility, so if the nature of the relationships or the method of querying the data changes, it can be problematic.

As newer, and often larger, datasets are being utilized by quants, new challenges also need to be tackled. For example, if you're accessing social media or credit card transaction data coupled with internet traffic data, these are really massive datasets. Sometimes, too large to store even on a single device. Techniques, such as MapReduce, allow the handling of data stored across multiple devices, and which also allow calculations to be split into multiple parallel streams. It is not in the scope of this book to go into the details of MapReduce, but tutorials are readily available on the Internet.

Each of these data storage approaches has advantages and disadvantages. It would be easy to make some assumptions and declare one the "best," but the reality is that the best technique is dependent on the problem that needs to be solved. Here, as in so many other parts of the black box, the quant's judgment determines success or failure.

8.6 SUMMARY

In this chapter, we explained some of the basic concepts of data for use by quant trading systems. Though data are scarcely the most exciting part of a quant strategy, they are so integral and critical to everything quants do and

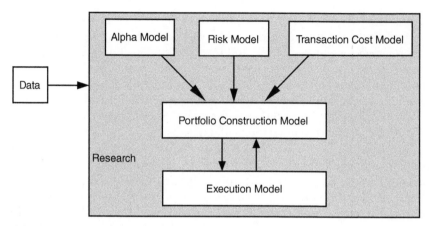

EXHIBIT 8.4   Schematic of the Black Box

inform so much of how to think about a given quant system that they are well worth understanding.

Next we will dive into the research process as our final stop in the exploration of the black box (Exhibit 8.4).

NOTES

1. Greg Clark and Alex Canizares, "Navigation Team Was Unfamiliar with Mars Climate Orbiter," Space.com, November 10, 1999.
2. Hung Xuan Do, et al., "Aerospace Competition, Investor Attention, and Stock Return Comovement." https://papers.ssrn.com/sol3/papers.cfm?abstract_id=4376532
3. SEDOL stands for *Stock Exchange Daily Official List*, which is a list of ostensibly unique security identifiers for stocks in the United Kingdom and Ireland. Other common security identifiers in equity markets are the International Securities Identification Number (ISIN) or Committee on Uniform Security Identification Procedures (CUSIP) number. CUSIPs are primarily relevant for U.S. and Canadian stocks. Many data vendors utilize their own proprietary security identifiers as well.
4. For the sake of simplicity, we are ignoring any "split effect," which many people believe exists; this theory states that stocks tend not to fall as much as expected based on the size of the split because people like to buy nominally lower-priced stocks.
5. In science, this is known as a *Type I error*, which is to accept a false-positive result in testing a hypothesis. This is the error of believing a hypothesis is true when in fact it is false.
6. In science, this is known as a *Type II error*, which is to accept a false-negative result in the outcome of a test. This is the error of believing a hypothesis is false when in fact it is true.

CHAPTER **9**

Research

Everything should be made as simple as possible, but not simpler.
—Albert Einstein

Research is the heart of quant trading. It is in large part because of a well-designed, rigorous, and tireless research program that the best quants earn their laurels. This chapter gives an overview of what research really means for black-box traders. It focuses mostly on research targeted at developing the alpha models of trading strategies. Research is also done with regard to risk models, transaction cost models, portfolio construction models, execution algorithms, and monitoring tools. Relevant research topics in these other areas will be mentioned as necessary, but the general principles from this section hold true throughout the black box.

The purpose of research is to develop and scrutinize a well-conceived investment strategy. A strategy is a long-term course of action designed to achieve an objective, usually success or victory. In most practical settings, strategies are chosen from a limitless number of alternatives. One can find interesting examples in nearly every field: curing cancer, a baseball game, a war, a court case, or financial planning. In each case, one has many choices of strategy; so how is one chosen? In the case of quant trading, a strategy is chosen based on research, which has its roots in the natural sciences.

9.1   BLUEPRINT FOR RESEARCH: THE SCIENTIFIC METHOD

A characteristic shared among well-behaved quants is their adherence to the *scientific method* in conducting research, which is of course the way science is done in every other field of study. This is critical because it forces rigor and discipline into the single most judgment-driven portion of the entire quant trading process. Without such rigor, quants could easily be led astray by wishful thinking and emotion rather than the logic and consistency that make scientists useful to the world in so many other disciplines.

The scientific method begins with the scientist observing something in the world that might be explainable. Put differently, the scientist sees a pattern in her observations. For example, in most circumstances, if something is above the ground and is left unsupported, it falls to the ground. Second, the scientist forms a theory to explain the observations. Sticking with the same theme in our examples, the scientist can theorize that there is something inherent in all things that causes them to move toward each other. This is better known as the *theory of gravity*. Third, the scientist must deduce consequences of the theory. If gravity exists, the orbits of planets should be predictable using the consequences of the theory of gravity. Fourth comes the all-important testing of the theory. But rather than looking to "prove" a theory, properly done science seeks to find the *opposite* of the consequences deduced, which would therefore *disprove* the theory. In the case of gravity, Newton's theory was used to predict the existence of Neptune, based on motions in the orbit of Uranus that could not be explained by other then-known celestial bodies. But this success could at best provide support for Newton's theory and could never actually prove it. Karl Popper, the eminent philosopher of science, labeled this technique *falsification*. A theory that has not yet been disproved can be accepted as true for the moment. But we can never be certain that the next observation we make of the theory will not falsify it. Newton's theory of gravity was never "proved" and in fact was superseded by Einstein's general relativity theory. The latter also has not been proven, and alternatives have been proposed to help explain problems (such as the accelerating expansion of the universe or the unexpectedly high velocities of stars in the outskirts of galaxies) that neither Newton's laws nor Einstein's relativity address in their current form.

Looking at the markets, it is easy to see the parallels with the way quants conduct research. First, let's imagine that a quant researcher observes that the various markets go through phases in which they tend to rise for extended periods, followed by phases in which they tend to fall for a while. She theorizes that a phenomenon called a *trend* exists, which, for whatever reason, causes the future performance of a market to be in the same direction as its recent historical performance. The consequence of this theory would be that she should be able to achieve a better-than-random forecast of how markets will perform, given only information on how these markets have performed before. So, she sets out to test the theory, and lo and behold, she finds that the evidence does not contradict her theory. Using some metric to define the historical trend (such as the moving average crossover example we used in Chapter 3), she sees that she can indeed forecast markets better than random chance is likely to allow. But she can never be sure. At best, she can have enough confidence that her tests were sufficiently rigorous to warrant risking some capital on the validity of this theory.

One important distinction, however, exists between quants and scientists. Scientists conduct research for many purposes, including learning the truth that drives the natural world. And in the natural sciences, a good theory—one that is well supported by the evidence and is widely useful in a variety of practical applications (e.g., Einstein's relativity)—does not require modification to continue to be valid. Quant researchers, by contrast, have no choice but to conduct ongoing research and to take every measure to ensure that their research output is prolific. This is because, though nature is relatively stable, the markets are not. Whether from regulatory changes, the changing whims of the aggregate psychology of investors and traders, the constant competition for alpha among traders, or whatever other phenomena, the markets are in fact highly dynamic processes. For this reason, quant traders must constantly research so that they can evolve with as much rigor and forethought as they used in developing their original strategies.

9.2 IDEA GENERATION

Ideally, quants follow the scientific method in their research. In this regard the development of theories (or theoretically sound approaches to data mining) is the first key step in the research process. We find four common sources of ideas to be observations of the markets, academic literature, migration, and lessons from the activities of discretionary traders.

The main way that quants come up with their own ideas is by watching the markets. This approach most directly embodies the spirit of the scientific method. An excellent example comes from the history of the oldest of quant trading strategies: trend following in futures contracts. Richard Donchian is the father of trend following. He originally traded stocks, but in 1948, he created Futures, Inc., the first publicly held commodity fund. In December 1960, he published his philosophy toward trading in his newsletter, *Commodity Trend Timing*.[1] He observed that there are sweeping moves in many markets that folks tend to call bull or bear markets; he postulated that one could build a system that would detect that these trends had begun and then ride the wave. He translated his philosophy into the following strategy: If a given market's price is above the highest closing price over the past two weeks, buy that market. If its price goes below the lowest closing price over the past two weeks, sell that market short. In the meantime, hold whatever position you have in that market. Using this incredibly simple system, from 1950 to 1970, he built a successful track record and spawned an industry that now manages hundreds of billions of dollars.

The academic literature in quantitative finance, and finance more generally, is replete with papers on a massive array of topics of interest to quant researchers. For example, many finance papers have been written on clever ways in which corporate chief finance officers (CFOs) attempt to "fudge" their companies' earnings and other financial figures to retain the confidence of shareholders. Quant firms have taken note, and several now have strategies in their arsenal that look for the kinds of behaviors described in the academic literature for trading opportunities. Many quant firms spend significant time scouring academic journals, working papers, and conference presentations to glean ideas that can be tested using the scientific method. Such a quant could find papers on topics such as the management of financial statements and could test ideas learned from these papers. Perhaps the most classic example of an academic paper that made massive waves in the quant trading community is Harry Markowitz's paper, modestly entitled *Portfolio Selection*. As discussed in Chapter 6, in "Portfolio Selection," Dr. Markowitz proposed an algorithm to compute the "optimal" portfolio using a technique called *mean variance optimization*. For all the research that has been done on portfolio construction over the decades since Dr. Markowitz's paper was published, his technique and variants of it remain key tools in the toolbox of quant trading. Aside from the literature in finance, quants also frequently utilize the literature from other scientific fields—such as astronomy, physics, or psychology—for ideas that might be applicable to quant finance problems.

Another common source of new ideas is via the migration of a researcher or portfolio manager from one quant shop to the next. Though many firms attempt to make this more difficult via noncompete and nondisclosure agreements, quants can effectively take ideas from one place to another, and this is to be expected. Any rational quant would want to know what the competition are doing, particularly those who are successful. At least part of the attraction of a potential new hire who has worked elsewhere must be the prospect of learning about the activities, and maybe even some secrets, of competitors. There are countless examples of this sort of thing. Goldman Sachs gave birth to AQR's quantitative approach to global tactical asset allocation and global equity market-neutral trading. Richard Dennis trained a group of new traders called the Turtles, none of whom had any trading experience, in trend following as a social experiment and to settle a bet with his friend William Eckhardt. D. E. Shaw was created after its founder cut his teeth at Morgan Stanley's statistical arbitrage prop trading desk and has itself spawned several successful alumni, including Two Sigma. In a fascinating case, Renaissance Technologies, famous for its ability to retain talent partly by having its researchers sign iron-clad noncompete agreements, once lost two of its researchers to Millennium Partners. Renaissance sued Millennium over the incident, and it turned out that the researchers had somehow managed *not* to sign the noncompete agreements while at Renaissance. Nonetheless, the traders were ultimately terminated by Millennium, who simply decided that retaining them was more trouble than it was worth. Sometimes, investors who have peeked behind the curtains as part of their assessment of a given quant shop, and then shared what they've seen with others, act as the carriers of ideas from one quant shop to the next.

Finally, quants learn lessons from the behavior of successful discretionary traders. For example, an old adage among successful traders is, "Ride winners and cut losers." This idea can easily be formalized and tested and has come to be known as a *stop-loss policy*, which involves systematically realizing losses on positions that are not working out. There are many examples of quants working closely with successful discretionary traders in an attempt to codify aspects of the latter's behavior into a trading system. Not all are necessarily bound for success. *Technical trader* is the label applied to a trader who subjectively analyzes graphs of market prices and makes decisions based on "rules" about the implications of various shapes of such graphs. These shapes are given names such as a *head and shoulders pattern* or an *upward triangle pattern*. Many quant funds have come (and mostly gone) that have attempted to recreate such patterns into systematic trading rules. This could be because the idea itself is not based on valid theory, or it might be because the human version is ultimately less rule-based, as one might like to believe, condemning a truly systematic implementation to be unsuccessful. However, even here valuable lessons can be learned: Not all successful traders have skill, and a helpful way to begin figuring out what *really* works and doesn't is to put an idea through the grinder of a research process and see if it's still alive at the end.

With regard to data-driven alphas, even the purest "machine-learning alpha" players tend to agree that feature selection/feature engineering (discussed in Section 3.3) is key. One of the best-respected such quants has been known to say (I paraphrase): "it's important to use everything you know as a researcher, not to discard useful information about what works or doesn't work when you build a machine-learning algorithm to forecast asset prices." Another has said (again a paraphrase): "If you aren't careful about utilizing only those features that have alpha—even if it's not especially strong—then you're doomed. It's a mistake to think that you can take a feature that, on its own, doesn't have predictive power, and somehow it'll be useful by combining it with other features." As such, the ideas that lead to features being selected or engineered are likely to come from the same sources for a data-driven quant as listed above for theory-driven quants.

9.3   TESTING

The process of testing is central to research. At first glance, the most common version of this process looks fairly simple. First, build a model and train it on some subset of the data available (the *in-sample period*). Then test it on another subset of the data to see if it is profitable (the *out-of-sample period*). However, research is an activity that is fraught with peril. The researcher is constantly offered opportunities to forego rigor in favor of wishful thinking. In this section, we address some of the work and challenges inherent in the research process.

9.3.1   In-Sample Testing, a.k.a. Training

In quant trading, models are approximations of the world. They are used to predict the future using data as inputs. The first part of the testing process is to "train" a model by finding optimal parameters over an in-sample period. That sounds rather like a mouthful of marbles, so let's walk through it term by term.

Let's imagine that we want to test the idea that cheap stocks outperform expensive stocks. We even theorize that the metric we will use to define cheapness is the earnings yield (earnings/price), such that a higher earnings yield implies a cheaper stock. But what level of yield is sufficiently high to cause us to think that the stock will outperform? And what level of earnings yield is sufficiently low to imply that a stock is expensive and is likely to underperform? These levels are parameters. In general, the parameters of a model are quantities that define some aspect of a model and can affect its performance. These are variables that can be set at whatever level one chooses, and by varying these levels, the model itself is altered and will provide different results.

Imagine that you hire a consultant to help you buy the ideal "optimal" house. The consultant lists all the relevant variables that might factor into your decision, things like the size of the house, its condition at the time of purchase, and the location and school district. If you do not tell him your ideal levels for each of these variables, he can deduce them by observing your reaction to various houses. A big house in a poor neighborhood might generate a lukewarm reaction, whereas a smaller house in a good neighborhood might generate a higher degree of interest for you. In this way, the consultant can deduce that you dislike the first neighborhood and prefer the second, and furthermore that the neighborhood might be more important to you than the size of the house. If he is able to repeat these "experiments," he can continue to fine-tune the choices he presents to you until he finds the house that matches your desires optimally. To the extent he succeeds in this endeavor, he has performed well.

In this way, optimal parameters in a quant model are those that lead to the best performance based on whatever metrics one chooses to use to measure goodness. Training a model involves simply finding the optimal parameter set, which is usually accomplished by trying a number of them and hoping that at least one set comes out looking appealing. What constitutes appeal is a matter we will discuss in some detail forthwith, but first we consider some other aspects of in-sample research.

In-sample research is, in a sense, fun for a quant. In the real world, the quant's model is constantly buffeted by new information and unpredictable events. But the historical data from the in-sample period are known to the model in their entirety, and nothing about them needs to be predicted. The in-sample period is like the answer key to a test in grade school. It is the model's best chance to work, because it doesn't have to predict anything. The model simply has to do a reasonable job of explaining the in-sample period after the fact, with the whole picture available for review. This is the one part of the research process in which there is a high degree of hope.

An important decision lies in the process of in-sample testing: What exactly constitutes the sample chosen for fitting the model? A sample is characterized by two things: its breadth and its length. Imagine that a researcher plans to build a strategy to trade the almost 4000 listed U.S. stocks and that she has at her disposal data starting in 1990 and ending now. As far as breadth, the researcher must choose how many of the stocks to use and decide how to choose the ones that are used. Should she use a broad cross-section of stocks across sectors and capitalization levels? Should she use a narrower cross-section, or should she choose all the stocks? As to length of time, the researcher must consider what window of data will be available to use for fitting the model. Will it be the most recent data or the oldest data? Will it be a random set of smaller time windows or the entire set of data from 1990 onward? The most common preference among quants would be to use all the instruments for some subset of the time, but this is by no means universal, since there is a tradeoff here to consider.

By using more data, the quant has a broader array of scenarios and market events that the model has to fit itself to, which can help make it more robust. By the time it has to succeed in real conditions, it has already "seen" and been adapted to the scenarios and environments found in the large in-sample period. On the other hand, the more data the model is allowed to see while it is being tuned, the greater the risk of creating a model that is nothing more than a good explanation of the past. For this reason, many quants utilize a reasonable cross-section of the data for the purpose of in-sample testing and model fitting.

9.3.2 What Constitutes a "Good" Model?

Quants utilize a wide variety of metrics to determine the "goodness" of a model. This is true for both the in-sample part of the process and the out-of-sample part of the process, the latter of which we will discuss in Section 9.3.4. I include here a number of statistics (and other output) that quants may use. I illustrate these metrics using a strategy for forecasting the S&P 500. It has a one-day horizon for its forecast, and it uses an adjustment to a well-known idea known as the *equity risk premium*, which is calculated by taking the difference between the earnings yield of the S&P 500 and the 10-year Treasury note each day. If the S&P's yield is higher than the bond's, this is viewed as a signal to be long stocks. If the S&P's yield is lower than the bond's, this is a signal to be short stocks. I built this strategy back in the mid-1990s for tactical asset allocation purposes, but I have never traded it, for reasons that will be obvious after we assess it using these metrics. It is shown simply as a way of illustrating the kinds of tests that a strategy is required to pass before being implemented in the real world, with real money. The results I show for the strategy are based on daily closing prices from June 1982 through December 2000.

9.3.2.1 Graph of the Cumulative Profits Over Time A graph indicating the cumulative profits over time is one of the most powerful pieces of output in a testing process because, as they say, one picture is worth a thousand words. From a graph of cumulative profits, you can see whether the strategy would have made money, how smoothly, and with what sort of downside risk, just to name a few things. As you can see in Exhibit 9.1, the S&P strategy shows as being profitable over the test period, but its return stream is very "lumpy," characterized by long periods of inactivity (several years, in some cases), some sharp losses, and some very steep gains. Immediately a researcher can see that this strategy has some real problems. Is it realistic to want to sit on the sidelines making almost no trades, and certainly no profits, from late 1989 until early 1995?

9.3.2.2 Average Rate of Return The average rate of return indicates how well the strategy actually worked (i.e., how much it might have made) in the past. If it didn't work in the testing phase, it's very unlikely to work in real life. As we will see later, testing offers many opportunities for the researcher to believe that making money in trading is a trivially easy exercise. Sadly, this misperception is mainly due to a wide variety of deadly traps. In our S&P 500 example, the total cumulative profits in the simulation were 746 percent, which comes to an average annual rate of return of 12.1 percent before any transaction costs or fees.

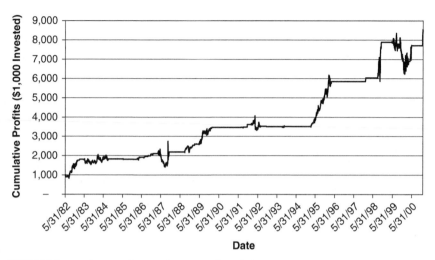

EXHIBIT 9.1 Back-Tested Cumulative Profits of the S&P 500 Strategy

9.3.2.3 Variability of Returns Over Time The variability of returns over time, which describes the uncertainty around the average returns, is helpful in deciding whether the strategy is worth owning. In general, the less the variability for a given level of returns, the better a strategy is considered to be. For example, if a strategy averages 20 percent returns per year, with an annual standard deviation of 2 percent (i.e., 67 percent of the time, the annual rate of return should fall within +/-2 percent of the average 20 percent figure, or between 18 and 22 percent), this would be a better outcome than if the same 20 percent average annual return came with 20 percent annual standard deviation (i.e., 67 percent of the time, returns are within 0 and 40 percent). The idea is that one can have more confidence in a given return if the uncertainty around it is low, and more confidence is a good thing.

At my shop, we look at a statistic we dubbed *lumpiness*, which is the portion of a strategy's total return that comes from periods that are significantly above average. This is another way of measuring consistency of returns. Despite the importance of this metric, it is not always the case that consistency should be a primary goal. Nevertheless, it is good to know what to expect as an investor in or practitioner of a strategy, if for no other reason than to discern when the strategy's behavior is changing. In our S&P 500 strategy, the annualized standard deviation of its daily returns over the entire test period was 21.2 percent.

9.3.2.4 Worst Peak-to-Valley Drawdown(s) This metric measures the maximum decline from any cumulative peak in the profit curve. If a strategy makes

10 percent, then declines 15 percent, then makes another 15 percent, the total compounded return for this period is about +7.5 percent. However, the peak-to-valley drawdown is −15 percent. Another way of stating this is that the investor had to risk 15 percent to make 7.5 percent. The lower the drawdown of a strategy, the better. Many quants measure not just one drawdown but several, to get a sense of both the extreme and more routine downside historical risks of their strategies. It is also typical to measure recovery times after drawdowns, which give the researcher a sense of the model's behavior *after* it's done poorly. Long recovery times are generally disliked because they imply that the strategy will remain in negative territory for quite a while if it does go into a large drawdown at some point. The S&P 500 strategy's worst peak-to-valley drawdown in the back-test was −39.7 percent, and it came from being short the S&P 500 in the summer of 1987, before the crash in October actually made that trade look good.

Drawdown information must be handled with care, however. If we were to look at the returns of a convertible bond arbitrage strategy from 1990 through 1997, eight years of data (which is considered a "long track record" in the hedge fund business) would show you very limited drawdowns. But in 1998, these strategies were badly hurt. The problem was *sample bias*, which means that the sample we used to determine the "worst" drawdown was not a fair representation of the whole array of possible outcomes. Rather, even though it was "long," it covered a period that was almost entirely favorable to this strategy, which would lead to an under-appreciation of the potential downside risks. There's not a great solution to this problem: either the sample over which the drawdown was computed is sufficiently large as to cover a large range of market regimes and both favorable and unfavorable environments (specifically as relate to the strategy being tested), or it doesn't. If the sample cannot be made larger and more representative of all possibilities (the population, in stats-speak), then the quant can only exercise some judgment about how much worse things could look if the environment did turn ugly. This is self-evidently an exercise that depends heavily on the judgment of the researcher, and even then is at best a "ballpark figure."

Furthermore, the worst historical drawdown is merely one potential path that even this biased sample could have produced. Imagine that the historical return distribution of a strategy is like a deck of cards. If we turn the cards over in the order that they are already placed in the deck, we get the historical time series. If, however, we shuffle the deck and then turn the cards over in this new order, we get a different time series from the same return distribution. If we do this over and over, thousands of times, will get many theoretically possible paths from one actual history. This practice is known as *resampling*, and it is done to boost the power of an historical sample. With these thousands of resampled histories, we can compute the worst drawdown(s) of each one, and have a more robust estimate of the potential downside risk of a strategy. It is therefore a sensible practice to recognize again that the deck itself contains only a subset of all the cards that might one day be dealt to us. It may, we worry, contain too many aces and kings, and not enough twos and threes.

9.3.2.5 Predictive Power A statistic known as the *R-squared* (R^2) shows how much of the variability of the thing being predicted can be accounted for by the thing you're using to predict it, or, in other words, how much of the variability in the target is explained by the signal. Its value ranges from 0 to 1, and there are a couple of valid ways to compute it. That said, most statistical packages (including Microsoft Excel) can compute an R^2 with minimal effort on the part of the user. A value of 1 implies that the predictor is explaining 100 percent of the variability of the thing being predicted. In case it's not already clear, when we talk about "the thing being predicted," we are of course referring to a stock or a futures contract or some other financial instrument that we want to trade. In quant finance, we're literally trying to predict the future prices/returns/directions of such instruments, making an R^2 of 1 basically impossible, unless methodological errors are being made. In fact, a superb R^2 in our industry is 0.05 (out of sample, to be discussed later in this chapter). A former employee of mine once said, "If you see an R^2 above 0.15 and it's not because you made a mistake, run the other way, because the SEC will arrest you for insider trading if you use it." Note that an R^2 of 0.15 implies that some predictor describes 15 percent of the *future* variability of the target of the forecast. As another quant trader put it, "People have gotten rich off a 0.02 R^2." Exhibit 9.2 shows that the R^2 of the S&P 500 strategy was less than 0.01 from 1982 through 2000.

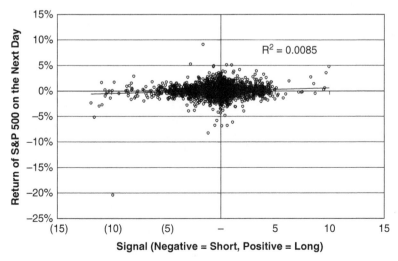

EXHIBIT 9.2 R^2 of the S&P 500 Strategy

Quants frequently utilize an additional approach to ascertaining predictive power. This approach involves bucketing the returns of the instruments included in the test by the deciles (or any other quantile preferred by the researcher) of the underlying forecasts. In general, a model with reliable predictive power is one that demonstrates that the worst returns are found in the bucket for which the worst returns are expected, with each successive bucket of improving expected returns in fact performing better than the prior bucket. If the returns of the instruments being forecast are not monotonically improving with the forecast of them, it could be an indication that the strategy is working purely by accident.

A bar chart showing the quintile study for the S&P 500 strategy is shown in Exhibit 9.3. As you can see, in this study at least, the strategy looks reasonable. The leftmost bucket of signals coincides with an average return in the S&P 500 (on the subsequent day) of −2.35 percent, and indeed, this is the worst average S&P return of any of the buckets. The second bucket from the left shows that the S&P 500 strategy's second most bearish group of forecasts for the S&P averages −0.19 percent. As we move to increasingly bullish signals, the S&P's returns continue to improve in accordance with the bullishness of the forecasts, which is what one would hope for. The fact that each bucket's average return is better than the one previous to it is said to imply a monotonic relationship between our alpha signal (the modified equity risk premium signal described earlier) and the target of our forecasts (the S&P 500 index's return over the next day).

9.3.2.6 Percentage Winning Trades or Winning Time Periods   This percentage is another measure of consistency. It tells the researcher whether the system tends to make

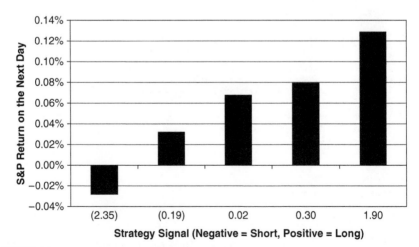

EXHIBIT 9.3   Quintile Study of S&P 500 Strategy's Signals vs. S&P 500 Returns

its profits from a small portion of the trades that happened to do very well or from a large number of trades, each of which might contribute only modestly to the bottom line. Similarly, one can easily measure the total number of winning (positive) periods versus the total number of periods. (This is most often measured by percentage winning, or profitable, days.) In both cases, one tends to have more confidence in strategies with greater consistency. In the S&P strategy, the results of this study are somewhat unusual in that the strategy is not designed to produce a signal every day but instead only when the model perceives that the opportunity is sufficiently attractive to warrant trading at all. As such, the model produces a zero signal 65 percent of the time. It produces winning trades about 19 percent of the time and losing trades about 16 percent of the time. Of the days it actually has a nonzero signal, it wins approximately 54 percent of the time. This, too, is not a terrible outcome for a strategy.

9.3.2.7 Various Ratios of Return versus Risk A great many statistics have been proposed as useful measures of *risk-adjusted return,* which are generally all attempts to measure the "cost" (in terms of risk) of achieving some return. The canonical example is the Sharpe ratio, named after William Sharpe (mentioned earlier in connection with the Nobel Prize in Economics he shared with Harry Markowitz in 1990). The *Sharpe ratio* is computed by taking the average periodic return above the risk-free rate and dividing this quantity by the periodic variability of returns. The higher the Sharpe ratio, the better. Quants (and many in the investment management business) have shortened this moniker by dropping the word *ratio.* A strategy with a 2 *Sharpe* is a strategy that delivers two percentage points of return (above the risk-free rate) for each point of variability (and this is a rather good Sharpe, if you can get it).

A close cousin of the Sharpe ratio is the *information ratio,* which is different from the Sharpe only in that it replaces the risk-free rate with any arbitrary benchmark return—most often zero, which is thus a pure comparison of the total annualized return versus the total annualized risk. The information ratio of the S&P 500 strategy is a mere 0.57, meaning that the investor receives 0.57 percent in return for every 1 percent in risk taken (again, before transaction costs and before any other fees or costs of implementing the strategy). The *Sterling ratio* (average return divided by the variability of below-average returns), the *Calmar ratio* (average return divided by the worst peak-to-valley drawdown), and the *Omega ratio* (the sum of all positive returns divided by the sum of all negative returns) are also widely used among a number of other risk-adjusted return metrics. The S&P 500 strategy from 1982 through 2000 displayed a Sterling ratio of 0.87, a Calmar ratio of 0.31, and an Omega ratio of 1.26. Of these ratios, the most discouraging is the low Calmar ratio, which indicates that the strategy generated only 0.31 percent in returns for every 1 percentage point of drawdown it experienced.

9.3.2.8 Relationship with Other Strategies Many quants utilize several kinds of strategies at once. As such, the quant is effectively managing a *portfolio of strategies*, which can be thought of much like any other kind of portfolio in that diversification is desirable. The quant frequently measures how a proposed new idea will fit in with other, already utilized, ideas, to ensure that the new strategy is in fact adding value. After all, a good idea that doesn't improve a portfolio is not ultimately useful. Though it is common to compute a correlation coefficient between the new idea and the existing portfolio of strategies, many quants measure the value-added of a new strategy by comparing the results of the existing strategy with and without the new idea. A significant improvement in the results indicates that there is a synergistic relationship between the new idea and the existing strategy.

9.3.2.9 Time Decay In testing a strategy, one interesting question to ask is, how sensitive is this strategy to getting information in a timely manner, and for how long is the forecast effect sustained in the marketplace? Many quants will seek to understand what their strategies' returns would be if they must initiate trades on a lagged basis after they receive a trading signal. In other words, if a strategy initiated a signal to sell Microsoft (MSFT) on April 28, 2006, the quant can see what the performance of his strategy would be in MSFT if it was not allowed to sell MSFT for one day, two days, three days, and so on. In this way, he can determine his strategy's sensitivity to the timeliness with which information is received, and he can also gain some information about how crowded the strategy is (because more crowding would mean sharper movements to a new equilibrium, i.e., faster degradation of profit potential). Imagine that a researcher develops a strategy to trade stocks in response to changes in recommendations by Wall Street analysts. Increases in the level of analysts' consensus recommendations for a company lead to a targeted long position in that company, whereas deterioration in the aggregate recommendation level would lead to a targeted short position in the company. This strategy is popular and followed by many quants (and discretionary traders). However, its effects are very short-lived and are very sensitive to the timing of the information received.

An example of this phenomenon is shown in Exhibit 9.4, using MSFT from April through October 2006. As you can see, there were five downgrades on April 28, which caused MSFT to underperform the S&P 500 by about 11.4 percent on the day the downgrades were announced. In fact, the *opening price* of MSFT on the 28th was already down about 11.1 percent because the downgrades all took place before the market opened. As such,

**MSFT versus S&P 500, with Cumulative Analyst Estimate Revisions,
March–October 2006**

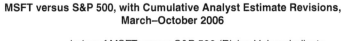

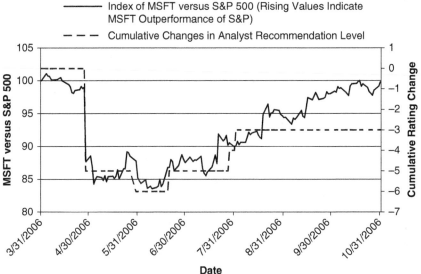

EXHIBIT 9.4   Illustration of Time Decay of Alpha

the quant trader must be careful not to allow his simulation to assume that he was able to transact in MSFT early enough to capture any of the 11.1 percent change. Instead, to be conservative, he can test what his, say, two-week performance on the trade would have been if he initiated the trade on various days *after* the initial ratings change.

If he did this, what he would find is that if he sold MSFT *at any time after* the close of April 27 (the night before the recommendation changes were announced), his trade would have actually been pretty mediocre. He would have made money selling MSFT on at the close on April 28, May 1 (the next business day), or May 2, but from May 3 through May 12 the trade would have been unprofitable. This illustrates the importance of stress-testing a strategy's dependence on timely information, which might not always be available.

Interestingly, delaying the signal's implementation does not always result in a negative outcome. For example, our S&P strategy tends to be "early" on its trades, that is, it tends to be short too early and long too early, even though the market subsequently does move in the direction forecast, on average. As such, delaying its entry by merely one day dramatically improves the total return of the strategy, from 746 percent total (12.1 percent annualized) to 870 percent total (12.9 percent annualized). This does not necessarily bode well for the use of such a strategy. In general, it is not comforting to know that you get a signal from your trading strategy that you not only *can* go without implementing for a little while (which would be the better result) but that you actually are *better off* ignoring for at least a full day after you get the signal.

9.3.2.10 Sensitivity to Specific Parameters It was mentioned earlier that parameters can be varied, and by varying them, differing outcomes are likely. But much can be learned about the quality of a strategy based on how much the outcomes vary based on small changes in the parameters. Let's use our P/E-based strategy from earlier as an example. Imagine that we think that any P/E ratio that is either above 50 or negative (because of negative earnings) should be considered expensive. Meanwhile, we presume that any P/E ratio below 12 is cheap. Assume we test the strategy according to the previously discussed metrics and find that a low P/E strategy with these parameters ($\geq$ 50 implies expensive, $\leq$ 12 implies cheap) delivers a 10 percent annual return and 15 percent annual variability.

Now imagine that we vary the parameters only slightly so that any stock with a P/E ratio below 11 is cheap and any with a P/E ratio that is negative or above 49 is expensive. If this version of the strategy, with slightly differing parameters, results in a significantly different outcome than the first example, we should mistrust both results and use neither in our model. This is because the model has proven to be overly sensitive to a small change in the values of the parameters, which makes little real-world sense. Should there be any great difference between a 10 P/E and an 11 P/E, or between a 50 P/E and a 49 P/E? What many researchers look for is smoothness of the goodness of outcomes with respect to parameter values. Near-neighboring sets of parameters should result in fairly similar results, and if they don't, a researcher should be a bit suspicious about them, because such results may indicate *overfitting*.

The previously described metrics represent a sampling of the kinds that quants use to determine whether a given model is good. These metrics are used to judge the quality of a model, both while it is being created and when it is being used. Indeed, many hedge fund investors look at the majority of these metrics as ways of gauging the performance of various traders.

Quant researchers must evaluate the theories they are testing. This is done using a wide array of measurements and techniques, but ultimately, a significant amount of discretion is used. It is unquestionably the case that what separates a successful researcher from the rest is good judgment about the kinds of issues raised in this chapter. As a general principle, we may note that good researchers must possess sufficient confidence and skill to believe that theories can be developed or improved on. At least as important, researchers must also be skeptical and humble enough to know, and be entirely at peace with the fact, that most ideas simply don't work.

9.3.3   (Over)fitting

For decades, at least in quantitative finance, the worst sin a quant could commit was to overfit. According to the *Oxford English Dictionary*, overfitting is "the production of an analysis that corresponds too closely or exactly to a particular set of data, [*sic*, and tsk. . .this is not even an Oxford comma, which I am also against] and may therefore fail to fit additional data or predict future observations reliably." In a sense, though, it really means expecting too much from the data you have—that you expect some sample to tell you the whole story. Let's say that you are trying to understand the relationship between height and mathematical aptitude. But your dataset is skewed in some way—perhaps it includes children aged 4–15, but without grouping them by age. As a result, you observe some correlation between height and skill in math, but this is confounded simply by age. Your real error, fundamentally, was assuming that your sample represents the whole population. If you had a sample that was much broader—going through, say, the age of 28—you might have drawn a different conclusion (probably none at all). In other words, if you could fit a model on a sample that was really representative of the entire population and future, it's likely that you would not have to worry very much about overfitting. But this ideal situation is impossible, especially with complex, dynamical systems like the capital markets. If you fit a model on data going back to 1950, how relevant is most of that history to today's markets? It is surely a much larger sample of the whole population than using just the last couple of years, but it is also going to give you a false sense of security—you have a lot of data, but it's mostly not useful. And if you use only the last couple of years, while this dataset is surely more relevant to today than the distant past is, it's just not enough data to fit a model in a noisy, chaotic environment.

Fitting is a multi-dimensional problem, ironically, or causally. As such, we will attempt to understand as many aspects of it as I can muster. Consider Exhibit 9.5.

Which of these points would you guess is the best choice for a parameter value? Choice A doesn't look so good, because the strategy seems to do poorly when using it. Choice D seems to have the best outcome, but it is also fairly unreliable, since its near neighbors are universally poor. Just so, choice C looks enticing because it is the highest point of a broad plateau. But it is so near a cliff's edge that we cannot be sure whether we're at risk of picking unwisely. This leaves Choice B as the best. Even though we haven't picked

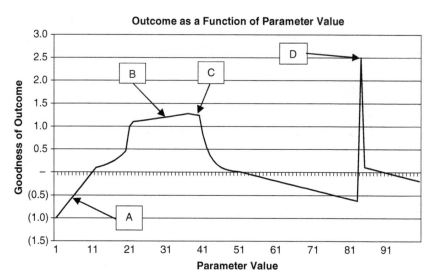

EXHIBIT 9.5   Choosing the Right Parameter Values

the highest point on the plateau, we've picked one with a margin of safety around it on both sides. It bears discussing a bit about why this margin of safety is so important.

When we see a lonely peak like the one represented by Point D in Exhibit 9.5, it is likely that our testing has uncovered some spurious coincidence in the fitting period that makes it especially favorable for that single parameter value. Unfortunately, it is likely that this coincidence will not persist into the future. By selecting Point D, in other words, we are implicitly betting that the future will look *exactly* like the past. Note the parallel here with the beginning of this section: If we had a sample that was really, truly representative of all future possibilities, we might not have to worry about this problem. But we basically never do, at least not in this field. This is not chess or go or language, which either don't change at all, or do so slowly enough that we don't have to worry about it.

You might be familiar with the standard performance disclaimer: "Past performance is not an indication of future results." Yet we all tend to judge the success of a portfolio manager at least partly by performance, which is a way of saying that we believe the past might actually be *some* indication of the future. Similarly, and based on the premises of scientific research in general, all quant trading (and indeed, all science) implicitly assume that the past can have some value in helping us understand the future. This is why the scientific method starts with observations of the world that can be generalized into a theory. But the appropriate way to think about the past is as a *general guide* to the future, not as an exact copy. We build a model that is itself a generalized description of this general guide to the future, and when phrased this way, it is clear that we want our model to err on the side of caution. As such, sensible quants would refer to Point B as being more "robust" than Point D because Point B has a better chance of being good, but not solely as a result of some accident of the sample data used to find it. Any model that explains the past well but is so closely modeled to it that it might be useless for predicting the future has a problem known as *overfitting*, an issue that we will discuss further in Chapter 11.

There remains, however, one more extremely important guiding principle in determining the goodness of a quant strategy, and this is known as *parsimony*. Parsimony is derived from the Latin word *parsimonia*, meaning *sparingness* and *frugality*. Among quants, parsimony implies caution in arriving at a hypothesis. This concept is absolutely central to the research process in quant trading. Models that are parsimonious utilize as few assumptions and as much simplicity as possible in attempting to explain the future. As such, models with large numbers of parameters or trading signals are generally viewed with more skepticism, given the increased risk of overfitting.

Parsimony has its roots in a famous principle of a Franciscan friar and logician, William of Occam, known as *Occam's razor*. Occam's razor is roughly translated from the original Latin as follows: Entities must not be multiplied beyond necessity. In science, this has been understood to mean that it is better to use as few assumptions, and as simple a theory, as possible to explain the observations. Karl Popper pointed out in 1992 that simpler theories are better because they are more easily tested, which means that they contain more empirical value. All around, scientists agree that parsimony, the stripping away of unnecessary assumptions and complexity, is simply better science. Einstein's saying, quoted at the beginning of this chapter, adds an important caveat, which is that oversimplifying an explanation is not helpful either. Looking again at our example of the consultant hired to help you buy a house, if he adds a large number of factors to the mix, such as the color of the guest bathroom tiles or the type of roofing material, given that there is no reason to believe *ex ante* that such factors are top priorities for you as his client, his analysis would become muddled and confused. But if he uses only two factors, the size of the house and its school district, though both of these may be important, this model might not do a good job of predicting your preferences. Similarly, an important part of the quant researcher's job is balancing on the tightrope between trying to explain the past too perfectly and trying to explain it too little. To one side is failure due to overcomplicating the model and to the other is failure due to oversimplifying it.

And here, I want to draw your attention to a seldom-considered parallel between the two major types of scientific errors, Type I and Type II, and overfitting and underfitting errors. A Type I error in science is considered to be when you believe that some result is significant, when in fact it is not; it's a false positive. A Type II error is when you believe a result is *not* significant, when in fact it is—a false negative. When you make an overfitting error, you are fundamentally making a Type I scientific error, believing a result that seems significant, but is in fact not. And, as mentioned above, the main reason for this error is an overreliance on some skewed, biased, not-ultimately-representative sample, which fails to characterize the set of realistic possibilities. For reference, please see Exhibit 9.6.

Up until around the early 2010s, overfitting risk was the main (sole?) preoccupation of most researchers in the quant space. But why? Overfitting is definitely a risk, but so is underfitting. So why would skilled, brilliant researchers focus so heavily on only one side of this problem? I think the answer, funnily enough, relates to supply and demand—specifically the supply of and demand for returns generated from alpha. Recall that, by alpha, we mean returns attributable to skill at timing the selection and/or sizing of portfolio holdings. For many decades, the supply of alpha, relative to the demand for it, was ample. As such, a researcher was more-or-less rational in erring on the side of avoiding Type I (overfitting) errors. However, as competition increased, and as market inefficiencies disappeared for various other reasons as well (e.g., Reg-FD, with regard to U.S. equities), it became harder to make money with broad/universal models, and more and more researchers began to push the envelope of fitting risk, trying to find the balance between overfitting and underfitting, between Type I error risk and Type II error risk.

overfitting ←————————————————→ underfitting

EXHIBIT 9.6 Overfitting (Type I Error) vs Underfitting (Type II Error) Images/ Shutterstock; skynesher/Getty Images

This is an interesting thought: it's easy to ignore the fruit growing way up at the top of a tree when the low-hanging fruits are abundant. But as the low-hanging fruits become scarce, those needing to feed need to go up—where it's more risky. What does this look like in quant investing? Narrower, more fitted models. In the 1990s, most quants would shudder to think about sector-specific models in equities, or asset-class specific models in futures/macro trading. But now it's almost equally obvious that a bank should not be measured and evaluated in the same way as a deep tech company, or a biotech company. There are datasets that apply somewhat narrowly—but significantly—to this or that sector. A 1990s quant would most likely ignore this dataset. And, back then, for good-enough reasons. As it is, we are working in a field with a relative paucity of (relevant) data. It was very important to test ideas out of sample, both longitudinally (over time) and latitudinally (across groups of instruments). Some trend indicator that only worked for treasuries was more likely to be overfit than one that worked well also for all other sectors, even if it worked a little less well in sample than the one that was more narrowly tailored did in just its narrow group. So, one would ignore even readily available data that weren't universally relevant. Inventory isn't relevant for banks, but it is quite important for manufacturers and retailers. R&D expenditures are extremely relevant for biotech companies, but largely irrelevant to travel and hospitality companies. But ideas like earnings yield, book yield, price momentum, mean reversion, put/call ratios—these are quite broadly applicable, and thus give a researcher focused heavily on avoiding overfitting (Type I) errors a little more comfort. I suppose a general model for the "correct" level of fitting, given the availability of alpha, could be summarized in Exhibit 9.7.

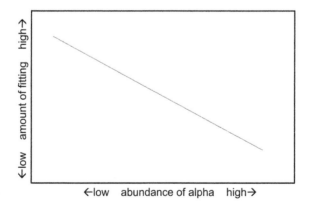

EXHIBIT 9.7   Determining the Correct Balance Between Overfitting (Type I Error) vs Underfitting (Type II Error)

This also relates to modeling approaches. A researcher suggesting use of today's machine-learning techniques would have most likely been laughed out of the meeting in 2005. But today, in no small part because of the relative scarcity of easy alpha, that researcher is now somewhere between common and extremely obvious. The competition for alpha speaks to the demand side of the equation. But there's also a supply side that is relevant. As more and more interesting, "alternative" datasets have become available, as machine learning and statistical techniques generally have advanced, and as compute power has proceeded according to Moore's law, the supply side of the equation has also advanced to render possible, feasible, maybe even straightforward what was once science fiction. World-class research has been formulated into open-source code libraries. The state of the art has been heavily, though not nearly fully, democratized. This, too, has facilitated the use of more fitting in the work of the quant.

Another consideration bears mentioning here. That is the tension between the strength of a prior and the amount of data available to support it, and the implication of this tension on statistical significance (which does not care about the tension, but perhaps should). Let's reflect on the onset of the COVID-19 pandemic in early 2020. It was quite clear that any company that depended heavily on humans traveling or congregating—dine-in restaurants, concerts, airplanes, hotels, office buildings—was in for a world of hurt for some time. Meanwhile, those that offered products or services that catered to isolation or treatment would flourish—for example, makers of home staples like toilet paper, remote-work solutions like Zoom, or vaccine-makers. How much data would you have to test this hypothesis? Almost none. But how clear was it anyway? Very. Perhaps a more common example relates to certain signals derived from alternative data sources, like credit card transaction data. We understand the key performance indicators associated with, say, an online retailer. If sales is one of them, and if some credit card transaction dataset should have a decently representative indication of sales across a decent set of online retailers, we have a good prior that this dataset can give us a headstart at knowing how the company's next announcement will go, and thus position ourselves accordingly now. How long is the history? Not very. Does it matter? Not really. Here, again, we see quant researchers focused more on finding some equilibrium between overfitting and underfitting risks. This consideration, unlike the basic supply and demand one, relates to the strength of a prior relative to the amount of data available to test and/or adjust it.

Nothing discussed here allows the quant to disregard overfitting risk. It simply calls for a healthy balance between taking overfitting and underfitting risks. It is my personal opinion that the correct balance is not exactly in the middle. Perhaps I am simply an outmoded dinosaur, but given the ever-evolving nature of these markets, the scarcity of data even without that dynamic, and the very poor signal-to-noise ratios of even highly successful forecasts, I think that there is a good chance our industry is over-estimating the utility of more fitting—especially outside of the very shortest forecast horizons. Nevertheless, there is some kind of ideal balance at any given moment, in a given circumstance, and I aim mostly to have provided some framework for considering what it is in a given context. What is the supply/demand situation for alpha in this space? What is the strength of my prior? These are highly relevant factors for determining the "correct" balance between overfitting and underfitting risk, between avoiding Type I and Type II errors.

9.3.4 Out-of-Sample Testing

Out-of-sample testing, the second half of the testing process, is designed to tell the researcher whether her formalized theory actually works in real life, without the benefit of seeing the "cheat sheet" provided during in-sample testing. The model's parameters have by now been fixed using a different set of data (from the in-sample testing period), and it's simply a question of whether the model, with whatever parameters are chosen, really works in a new, "out-of-sample" data set. Many of the same kinds of statistics as described in this chapter are utilized to make this judgment.

One additional statistic many quants use is the ratio of the R^2 in the out-of-sample test to the R^2 in the in-sample test. This ratio is another way for the researcher to obtain a sense of the robustness of the model. If the out-of-sample R^2 is relatively close to the in-sample R^2 (i.e., if the ratio is about half or better), that is considered a good thing. If it is significantly smaller, the researcher must be suspicious about the prospects for his model's success.

There are many approaches to out-of-sample testing. The simplest utilizes all the data that was set aside from the in-sample test. Some researchers utilize a *rolling out-of-sample* technique in which the single oldest data point is discarded and one new data point is added to both the fitting (in-sample) and testing (out-of-sample) period. This process is repeated through the entire available sample of data. The rolling out-of-sample technique is thought to help refresh the model over time so that it does not depend on a single set of tests that might have been run some years previously. However, depending on the circumstances, this approach can have the weakness of giving the model the benefit of constant knowledge of the recent past, which could reduce its robustness. This tradeoff is extremely subtle and can be debated in any individual instance, rendering impractical any general judgment about its effectiveness. Still another approach utilizes an ever-growing window of data for ongoing out-of-sample testing as time passes and more data are collected.

Though the objective of out-of-sample testing is clearly a valid and necessary component of research, it turns out to be a rather tricky thing to do correctly. Imagine a researcher who completes the model fitting over the in-sample data. Then, having a model that seems robust, the researcher tests it over the out-of-sample data. But the model fails to deliver a good result on this new data set. The researcher, already having invested a lot of time on the model, decides to examine the reasons for the model's failure over the out-of-sample period and discovers that the environment changed between the in- and out-of-sample periods in such a way that the model was making losing trades during the latter. Having learned a useful lesson, the researcher goes back to the model and alters it to account for this new information. He refits the model in sample, and then retests it out of sample. And, lo and behold, it works much better.

Before we break out the champagne, however, we should consider what the researcher has just done. By learning from the out-of-sample data and using that information to train the model anew, he has effectively used up his out-of-sample data and has caused them effectively to become part of the in-sample data set. In general, going back and forth between the in- and out-of-sample data is a terrible idea. This brings up a still more subtle issue, but one that is closely related.

Often we know enough about what happens in the capital markets during the out-of-sample period that we tend to build models and select parameter sets that we believe are likely to work out of sample anyway. This sullies the purpose of an out-of-sample test because we are, in many respects, looking ahead. For example, we can look back on the Internet bubble of the late 1990s and know that the world and the economy in fact did not change and that negative earnings should not be wildly rewarded in the long run. If we build a strategy today, we can know that it is possible for the Internet bubble to happen but that it eventually bursts. However, we could not have known this with certainty in 1999.

The world finds new and interesting ways to confound our understanding. As such, to test our current best thinking against competition that existed in the past is a form of wishful thinking. This is a subtle and nefarious form of look-ahead bias, which is a critical problem in research. As researchers become more and more familiar with the out-of-sample periods they use to test their ideas' validity, it becomes more likely that they are implicitly assuming they would have known more about the future than in fact they would have known had they been asking the same questions historically. This practice is called *burning data* by some quants.

To mitigate the data-burning form of look-ahead bias, some quant shops take reasonably drastic measures, separating the strategy research function from the strategy selection function and withholding a significant portion of the entire database from the researchers. In this way, the researcher, in theory, cannot even see what data he has and doesn't have, making it much more difficult for him to engage in look-ahead activities. Less draconian, the researcher might simply not be allowed to know or see which data are used for the out-of-sample period, or the portions of data used for in- and out-of-sample testing might be varied randomly or without informing the researcher. Regardless, as you can easily see, the problem of doing testing is tricky and requires great forethought if there is to be any hope of success.

Another approach is to determine that out-of-sample testing is a bit of a myth in the first place, especially for any experienced, observant researcher. As a result, out-of-sample testing is foregone in favor of a combination of extra vigilance regarding the in-sample results, coupled with a minimum of parameter fitting. In this methodology, the quant uses as few parameters as possible, sets the values at some reasonable level, and simply tests the strategy and looks for all those metrics of good performance to have sufficiently high readings.

9.3.5 Assumptions of Testing

Another component in the testing process revolves around the assumptions one makes about trading a strategy that is being tested historically. We discuss two examples here: transaction costs and (for equity market-neutral or long/short strategies) short availability.

We have already discussed transaction costs, of which there are several components: commissions and fees, slippage, and market impact. Interestingly, during the research process there is no empirical evidence of what a trading strategy would actually have cost to implement in the past. This is because the trading strategy wasn't actually active in the past but is being researched in the present using historical market data. Therefore, the researcher must make some assumption(s) about how much his order would really have cost in terms of market impact.

These assumptions can prove critical in determining whether a strategy is good or bad. Let's again look at an extreme case to understand why. Imagine that we assume that transactions are entirely costless. This might make a very high-frequency trading strategy extremely appealing because, as long as it accurately predicts any movement in price, no matter how small, it will seem to have been worthwhile to trade. Imagine that a model is correct 55 percent of the time and makes $0.01 per share when it is correct. It loses 45 percent of the time and loses $0.01 per share when it is wrong. So, for every 100 shares it trades, it could be expected to generate $0.10. But when it is implemented, it turns out that transactions actually cost $0.01 per share across all the components of cost, on average. This would imply that the strategy is actually breakeven on 55 percent of its trades (theoretical profit of $0.01 per share, less the cost of transacting each share of $0.01) and loses $0.02 per share on 45 percent of its trades. As a result, rather than making $0.10 per 100 shares, it is in fact *losing* $0.90, which is obviously a poor outcome. Stated generally, overestimating transaction costs will cause a quant to hold positions for longer than is likely optimal, whereas underestimating transaction costs will cause a quant to turn over his portfolio too quickly and therefore to bleed from the excess costs of transactions. If we have to err in this regard, it makes more sense to overestimate cost than to underestimate, but it is always preferable to get the cost estimation approximately right.

The second kind of assumption a quant must make in testing a market-neutral or long/short strategy in equities relates to the availability of short positions. Imagine a U.S. market-neutral quant trader who, by design, holds a short portfolio that is roughly equal in size to the long portfolio. Over time, the short portfolio adds a significant amount of value by finding overpriced stocks and by making money when the stock market tumbles, thereby reducing the risk inherent in the strategy. However, it turns out that the names the strategy wants to short, and in particular, the most successful short picks, are on *hard-to-borrow lists*. Hard-to-borrow lists are those stocks that are generally restricted from shorting by the broker, because the broker cannot mechanically locate shares to borrow, which is required in the act of shorting. If the shares cannot be located, the trade would be considered a *naked short sale*, which is illegal in the United States. Therefore, the trade wouldn't have been executed as expected by the back-test. If the model is ignorant of hard-to-borrow issues (and making a model aware of this issue in the past is not trivial, since such historical data are hard to come by), the researcher can easily be fooled into thinking that the short portfolio will be able to deliver value that is, in reality, nonexistent. This is because when he goes to implement the live portfolio, he finds that he is unable to put on the best short trades and is forced to replace these with inferior short trades instead.

9.4 SUMMARY

We have only scratched the surface of the work that a quant must do in research, and must do well, to succeed over time. Research is a highly sensitive area within the quant's process. It is where her judgment is most obviously and significantly impactful. Researchers must therefore go about their research with great care because this is the formative stage of a strategy's

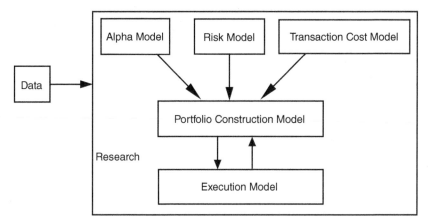

EXHIBIT 9.8 Schematic of the Black Box

life. Mistakes made during research become baked into a strategy for its lifetime, and then the systematic implementation of this error can become devastating. Moreover, the research effort is not a one-time affair. Rather, the quant must continually conduct a vigorous and prolific research program to produce profits consistently over time.

Models are, by definition, generalized representations of the past behavior of the market. More general models are more robust over time, but they are less likely to be very accurate at any point in time. More highly specified models have the chance to be more accurate, but they are also more likely to break down entirely when market conditions change. This tradeoff, between generality and specificity, between robustness and accuracy, is the key challenge faced by quant researchers. While there is no "one-size-fits-all" answer that I'm aware of to address this challenge, I think Einstein's words provide the best guiding principle: "Everything should be made as simple as possible, but not simpler."

We have now completed our tour through the black box (see Exhibit 9.8), both its component models and the key elements—data and research—that drive it. The coming chapters will focus on the evaluation of quant traders and their strategies.

NOTE

1. From Richard Donchian's Foundation website: www.foundationservices.cc/RDD2/

A Practical Guide
for Investors in
Quantitative Strategies

Risks Inherent to Quant Strategies

Torture numbers, and they'll confess to anything.
—Gregg Easterbrook

We have defined two broad classes of exposures: those that generate returns in the long run (alpha and beta) and are intentionally accepted and those that do not generate long-term returns (risks) or are incidental to the strategy. For the kind of quant traders that are the subject of this book, beta exposures are generally avoided (because they can be easily obtained by generic, low-cost index instruments), and therefore we can focus on alpha and risk exposures.

As we have already stressed, the kinds of alpha exposures quants seek to capture are generally exactly the same as those that are sought by discretionary managers. However, with any strategy there is always the possibility that the exposure from which returns are generated is not being rewarded by the marketplace at a given point in time. This risk of "out-of-favor" exposure is shared by both quants and discretionary traders alike.

This chapter will help an investor understand the types of risks that are either unique to quant trading or at least more applicable to quant trading. In a sense, we also are providing a framework for investors to design their own risk models that can be used to help determine how to use quant trading as part of a portfolio of strategies. The latter is a topic we will address again in Chapter 12.

10.1   MODEL RISK

Model risk is the most basic form of risk any quant system brings to an investor. Models are approximations of the real world. If the researcher does a poor job of modeling a particular phenomenon—for example, momentum—the strategy might not be profitable, even in a benign environment for momentum in general. In other words, model risk is the risk that the strategy does not accurately describe, match, or predict the real-world phenomenon it is attempting to exploit. Worse still, model risk need not be evident right away. Sometimes small errors in specification or software engineering lead to problems that accumulate very slowly over time, then suddenly explode on a busy trading day. Additionally, model risk can come from several sources. The most common are the inapplicability of modeling, model misspecification, and implementation errors. It bears mentioning that all types of model risk can occur not only in the alpha model but also from errors in any of the other parts of the strategy. Back-testing software, data feed handlers, alpha models, risk models, transaction cost models, portfolio construction models, and execution algorithms can all have model risk in them.

10.1.1   Inapplicability of Modeling

Inapplicability of modeling is a fundamental error that comes in two forms. The first is the mistaken use of quantitative modeling to a given problem. For example, trying to model the quality of a musician is simply the wrong idea from the start. One could conceive of some relevant factors that correlate with skill in musicianship, such as the source and duration of training. But ultimately, the goodness of a musician is not a question that can be answered with mathematics or computer models. It is an inherently subjective question, and to apply computer models to it is an error.

Mathematical models can lull practitioners into feeling safe because of the precision of their computations. But this feeling is illusory. Indeed, one of the most important tasks of any quant is to sort out what questions he can actually ask using historical data and computer models. The global market turmoil in 2008, which was fueled in part by the securitized mortgage business, could be an example of the problem of the inapplicability of quantitative modeling to a problem. Though these securitized mortgages were not in any way like quant trading strategies, part of their rise to prominence resulted from the quantitative modeling work done by various structured products desks inside a wide variety of banks around the world. They modeled what would happen in various scenarios, and on the back of the comfort gained in the output of these models, they issued AAA-rated bonds backed by instruments that, each on its own, were toxic. It appears that a fundamental error was made (or ignored to rationalize massive greed) in the conceptualization of the problem.

A second type of inapplicability is subtler and, probably because of this subtlety, more common among quant traders. It is the error of misapplication of an otherwise valid technique to a given problem. One example of this type of error, which we have already touched on in the section on risk modeling, is the widespread use of *value at risk* (VaR). Conventional VaR uses correlation matrices and historical volatility to determine the amount of risk in a given portfolio at a point in time. However, there are many assumptions inherent in the use of VaR that are invalid. For example, the use of both correlation matrices and historical volatility (defined as the standard deviation of returns) assumes that the underlying distributions that describe the various elements in a portfolio are normal. But, in fact, market data often exhibit *fat tails*. In other words, there are significantly more observations of extreme values than one would expect from a normal bell curve distribution. A specific example of this situation can be seen with data on the S&P 500. Based on the daily historical index data (excluding dividends) from January 3, 2000 through November 30, 2008, a −4 standard deviation day is one on which the S&P posts a return worse than −5.35 percent. A 4 standard deviation event should occur once every 33,333 trading days (approximately every 128 years, assuming 260 trading days per year) if the S&P's returns are normally distributed. In fact, the S&P has posted a return this poor on average once per 13 *months*, or *119 times more frequently* than you'd be led to believe from a normal distribution.

Furthermore, correlation coefficients (a key ingredient in the computation of VaR measurements) should be used only when a linear relationship exists between the two things being correlated. Instead, many instruments are not linearly related to each other. Exhibit 10.1 shows an interesting contrast between two relationships.

As you can see from the charts, the relationship between XOM and JAVA is not linear. Note that the best day for XOM is actually a fairly poor day (−5 percent or so) for JAVA. Likewise, the best day for JAVA is also a nearly −5 percent loss for XOM. A line that best fits this relationship would look more like the Gateway Arch in St. Louis than a straight line. By contrast, the relationship between XOM and CVX does appear to be reasonably linear. A researcher using correlation to examine the relationship between JAVA and XOM would likely be making a model inapplicability error because the relationship is nonlinear in the first place.

10.1.2 Model Misspecification

The second kind of model risk is *misspecification*. Model misspecification means that the researcher has built a model that badly describes the real world. Practically speaking, a model that doesn't fit the real world at all is unlikely ever to make money and therefore is unlikely to be observable for very long before being shut down. As such, the more prevalent

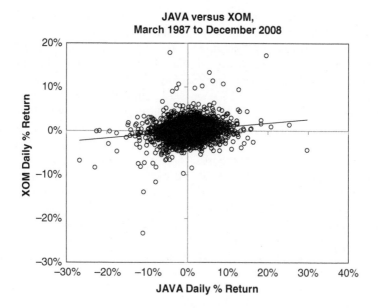

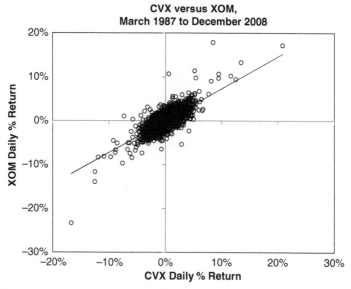

EXHIBIT 10.1   A Demonstration of Nonlinear and Linear Relationships

misspecification errors relate to events that are uncommon. These models work fine most of the time, but they fail when an extreme event occurs. A recent example of this situation can be seen in the aftermath of August 2007, when many quants concluded that they had done a bad job of modeling liquidity risk in large capitalization U.S. stocks. This is because they looked at only the liquidity risk associated with their own holdings in these names. What they learned, however, was that if many large traders liquidate similar holdings at the same time, the aggregate size of these positions matters more than the size any individual trader holds.

As a direct result of this event, some quants discovered risk model or transaction cost model misspecifications and have begun to attempt to correct these flaws. But again, the rarity and unique nature of such events make them extremely difficult to model.

10.1.3 Implementation Errors

The third and perhaps most common variety of model risk is from errors in *implementation*. All quant trading strategies ultimately are pieces of software residing in hardware and network architectures. Implementation errors, or errors in programming or architecting systems, can cause serious risk for the quant trader, and in some cases also for the market at large. For example, imagine that a quant means to have his execution software buy the bid and sell the offer price using limit orders. But he programs his execution software with the signs reversed so that it buys at the offer and sells at the bid. Because of this error, he is now paying the bid/offer spread on every trade—the exact reverse of his intention. This is an example of a programming error. In August 2012, Knight Trading lost more than $400 million in a mere 30 minutes due to a software bug that caused a dormant piece of software to come back online, multiplying order sizes and causing Knight to accumulate massive positions at highly elevated prices. As they sold those positions off, the nine-figure losses mounted. The losses, both in capital and in confidence, have had significant repercussions for Knight. The company nearly went bankrupt and was forced to sell over 70 percent of the firm to a consortium of investors at a steep discount in order to remain afloat. Not to pick on them, but this wasn't Knight's first implementation error. In March 2011, a "process error" at Knight caused the values of some newly created ETFs to drop between 80–100 percent immediately upon their inception (the exchanges canceled those trades).

AXA Rosenberg, too, had a coding error in their risk model, which resulted in a $217 million loss to clients, which AXA eventually repaid to their investors, along with a $25 million penalty paid to the SEC to settle the case. In their case, the error appears to have been introduced in April 2007, but it was not discovered until June 2009, and even after it was discovered, certain AXA executives apparently decided to hide the issue from their CEO, not to disclose it to investors, nor even to fix the issue. AXA did not finally disclose the error to clients until about three years later, in April 2010. In addition to the hefty compensation and penalty AXA paid, their assets under management dropped from $62 billion in March 2010 to $18 billion by the end of June 2012.

In another case, a successful quant trading firm made an architectural error. The firm has separate servers for alpha models and the execution engine. As we discussed earlier, the portfolio construction model looks to the alpha model for information on which positions it should execute on both the long and short sides. At some point during one trading day, there was a need to reboot the servers for the system. But when the servers were restarted, the execution server came online first, and a few minutes later, the alpha model was restored to service. The execution model, seeing that it had no signals whatsoever from the alpha model, rapidly and automatically began liquidating the portfolio of positions in order to eliminate risk. In the few moments before the alpha server came back online, 80 percent of the firm's portfolio was sold off and then had to be reacquired. There was no warning that this error existed until it manifested itself in this unfortunate manner. The strategy was making perfectly good returns but suddenly broke down due to a combination of a specific quirky error and the circumstances of the situation. Given the massive quantities of code that go into a quant trading strategy, such software and architectural errors are unfortunately the most common, but usually least painful (the Knight episode in 2012 notwithstanding), types of errors.

10.2   REGIME CHANGE RISK

Most quant models are based on historical data. Even those using analysts' forecasts or other "sentiment" signals turn out to depend heavily on the past because sentiment usually is biased in the direction of historical trends. Regardless of the type of model, quants use past relationships and behavior to develop theories and build models to help predict the future. If markets have behaved in a particular way for a while, quants will come to depend on that behavior persisting. If there is a regime change, the quant will typically suffer because the relationships and behavior he is counting on are altered, at least temporarily.

Dependence on the past is certainly one of the more interesting problems to consider in analyzing quant strategies and determining how to use them. In some strategies, dependence on the persistence of historical behavior is explicit, as in the case of trend following. Note that this isn't necessarily an indictment of these strategies. Indeed, such strategies have made money for decades and have exhibited better risk-adjusted returns than the stock market by far. However, if an established trend reverses, the trend follower will almost certainly lose money. Ironically, mean reversion-focused quants may also suffer during a large trend reversal, particularly if they are engaged in a *relative* mean reversion strategy. We might expect that if a reversal of trend occurs, this should be good for the mean reversion trader, since he bets against trends. However, if the reversal is also associated with the breakdown of established relationships, this can be quite painful because of the *relative* part of the strategy. Exhibit 10.2 illustrates this point.

As you can see, there are four distinct phases in the relationship between Charles Schwab (SCHW) and Merrill Lynch (MER). From early 1996 until the end of 1997, the stocks were reasonably correlated and showed similar trends. From early 1998 until early 2001, on the other hand, the stocks behaved very differently from one another, and SCHW in particular began

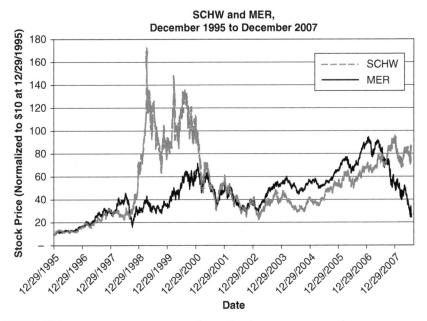

EXHIBIT 10.2   Regime Changes in a Relationship between Two Stocks

to exhibit substantially greater volatility than it had earlier or than it would again later. The Internet bubble appears to be the cause of this shift, during which investors began to treat SCHW as an online broker, and its shares rose and fell with the likes of Ameritrade and E*Trade instead of its more traditional peer, MER. Upon the bursting of the Internet bubble, SCHW reverted uncannily to MER's level and tracked it very closely for some time, from early 2001 until early 2007. Then, in early 2007, you can see another sharp change in the relationship, with MER dramatically underperforming SCHW. This, of course, is due to the banking and credit crisis that traces its roots to early 2007.

A quant betting on this relationship's persistence would have suffered through two reasonably significant periods in the past 10 years in which the relationship did not hold up at all. Whether these stocks have permanently decoupled or will revert again at some point in the future is a matter that is beyond my ability to forecast. But this is precisely what regime change risk is about: A structural shift in the markets causes historical behavior of an instrument or the relationships between instruments to change dramatically and quickly.

Another example of this kind of structural shift can be seen in the relationship between "value" stocks and "growth" stocks, as measured by the IVE and IVW ETFs, which represent S&P 500 Value and S&P 500 Growth, respectively. The historical spread between these two ETFs is illustrated in Exhibit 10.3.

Exhibit 10.3 shows that the S&P Value index outperformed the S&P Growth index by some 29 percent from the start of 2004 until mid-May 2007. The spread then trended a bit lower until mid-July and then rapidly fell as quants unwound their portfolios, which clearly had been betting on Value to outperform Growth. This unwind, combined with the macroeconomic environment,[1] set off a massive rebound in Growth relative to Value.

Note that there are two substantial, short-term reversals of this more recent trend, one in January 2008 and one in July through September 2008, both of which are circled in Exhibit 10.3. These moves are incredibly sharp, actually representing the biggest and fastest moves in this spread in a very long time (certainly going back further than this analysis). In 16 trading days, from January 9 through 31 of 2008, the Value index recovered more than half the underperformance it had experienced in the 160 trading days prior to that point. In other words, the reversal was five times faster than the trend that preceded it. This was another rather painful experience for quants, though not on the order of what was felt in the summer of 2007. Over the subsequent 115 trading days, the Value/Growth spread reversed over 22 percent, all the way back to breakeven, until mid-July 2008.

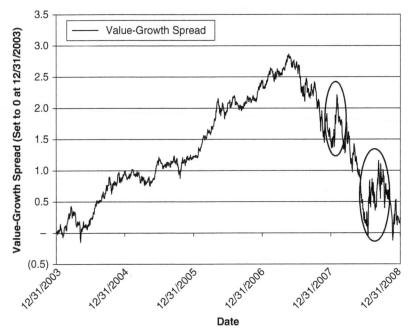

EXHIBIT 10.3 Value/Growth Spread, 2003–2008

At that point, another brief but violent six-trading-day period saw the spread recover almost 40 percent of the lost ground. In other words, the reversal was almost eight times faster than the trend that preceded it. From late August through early September, the spread recovered another 36 percent of its lost ground, and over the 39-day period from mid-July through early September the recovery was more than 50 percent in total.

What's worse, such sharp reversals frequently cause many other types of relationships to falter. For example, the sectors that had been underperforming (such as financial companies or homebuilders) become the new outperformers, while those that had been outperforming (such as technology companies) tend to become the new laggards. Currencies and bonds also tend to reverse, as do commodities (especially over the past five years). An illustration of this last point is shown in Exhibit 10.4.

Note that the OIL ETF moves as almost the mirror image of the Value/Growth spread, experiencing mirroring reversals in early January and mid-July 2008 (again, indicated by the circled periods on the graph) and mirroring trends in between. It is for this reason that regime changes are especially painful for quants: They tend to occur across many levels simultaneously.

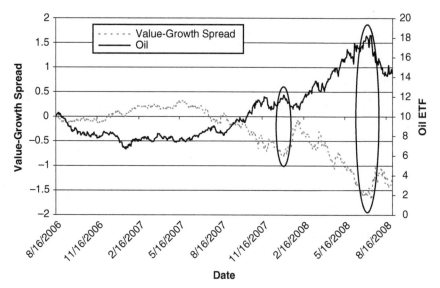

EXHIBIT 10.4   Value/Growth Spreads versus Oil Prices, Normalized to August 16, 2006

10.3   EXOGENOUS SHOCK RISK

The third in the family of quant-specific risks comes from *exogenous shocks*. I refer to them as *exogenous* because they are typically driven by information that is not internal to the market. Terrorist attacks, the beginning of a new war, and regulatory intervention are all examples of exogenous shocks. Because quant models utilize market data to generate their forecasts, when nonmarket information begins to drive prices, quant strategies typically suffer. This is especially true because such shocks usually also result in larger-than-normal moves. So, in situations of exogenous shock, we have big moves that aren't explainable by a reasonable model using market data but rather by information that is entirely external to the markets (see Exhibit 10.5).

The first circled period in the S&P 500 chart in Exhibit 10.5 represents the terrorist attacks on New York and Washington, DC, on September 11, 2001. The market was closed for almost a week, and when it reopened, it dropped precipitously, only to recover much of that ground rather quickly. Ignoring the obviously horrible nature of the attack on civilians, the downward move in markets was actually a continuation of the downward trend in stocks that had begun in March 2000 and therefore benefited trend-following strategies. However, many mean reversion strategies and relative alpha strategies suffered in September 2001 as nonmarket information dramatically and briefly changed the way markets behaved.

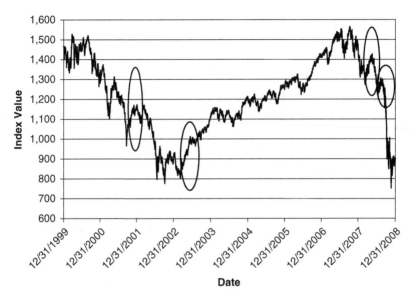

EXHIBIT 10.5   S&P 500 Price Index, December 1999–December 2008

A similarly difficult situation was observable with the start of the Iraq War in early 2003, which is the second circled period. Suddenly global stock, bond, currency, and commodity markets began moving in lockstep with each other, all driven by news reports of the U.S. armed forces' progress through Iraq. This, too, resulted in losses for many quants, including trend followers, since the move resulted in a reversal of the prior trend across several asset classes simultaneously.

The third circled period follows the bailout of Bear Stearns in mid-March 2008. This period was negative for many quant strategies because it was a sharp trend reversal that was caused by information that could not be anticipated by machines. Indeed, even the collapse of Bear might well have been the result of nonmarket "information," and as of this writing, the SEC is supposed to be investigating potential wrongdoing in the rumors that were spread about Bear just in advance of (and which likely contributed to) its collapse.

The final circled period represents another rally in the financial sector in equities, this one set off by the SEC's change in shorting rules, which made it much harder to short battered financial stocks. Though one can argue about whether an SEC intervention or a rumor-based collapse and government-brokered buyout of a major financial institution are endogenous or exogenous to the market, it is unassailably true that the kind of information these events presented to market participants was both unquantifiable and unusual. As such, exogenous shock risk is a significant byproduct of quant investing, one that it is difficult to do anything about (other than with discretionary overrides).

10.4   CONTAGION, OR COMMON INVESTOR, RISK

The newest member of the quant-specific risk family is *contagion*, or *common investor*, risk. By this, we mean that we experience risk not because of the strategy itself but because other investors hold the same strategies. In many cases, the other investors hold these strategies as part of a portfolio that contains other investments that tend to blow up periodically. The first part of this risk factor relates to how crowded the quant strategy in question is. A second part relates to *what else* is held by other investors that could force them to exit the quant strategy in a panic, sometimes called the *ATM effect*. In an ATM effect, significant losses in one strategy cause liquidation of a different, totally unrelated strategy. This happens because investors who have exposures to both, especially if highly levered, reduce their liquid holdings in the face of financial distress and margin calls, since their illiquid holdings are usually impossible to sell at such times. In essence, the good, liquid strategy is exited to raise cash to cover the losses of the bad, illiquid strategy.

This is a particularly challenging type of risk that is certainly not exclusive to quants. However, the clarity with which this risk expressed itself in both August 1998 (easily argued not to be a quant event) and August 2007 (clearly a quant event) demands specific attention. In August 1998, it was not quant trading that suffered but other strategies such as merger arbitrage. We will discuss both of these events in greater detail later, but for the moment, it bears mentioning that there is one striking similarity between the two: In both cases, a credit crisis leading to illiquidity in credit instruments sparked a forced sale of more liquid assets that had nothing to do with the credit crisis.

In 1998, many relative value equity arbitrage positions, which bet on the convergence of share prices between stocks that are either dually listed or else are merging, suffered dramatically as an indirect result of the Russian government's defaulting on its debt obligations. The famous example used by Lowenstein in *When Genius Failed* was Royal Dutch and Shell, a dual-listed company. Royal Dutch had been trading at an 8–10 percent premium to Shell, and the bet was that the two stocks should eventually converge, eliminating the premium. In hopes of this, Long Term Capital Management, or LTCM, (and many others) had long positions in Shell and short positions in Royal Dutch. After all, there was no rational economic reason that a European listing of a given company should outperform a U.S. listing of the same company. Yet because LTCM had to vacate this position at a time when there was little liquidity, the spread widened from 8–10 percent to over 20 percent by the time LTCM was trading out of it. The reason that this position had to be sold is that LTCM also had massive losses on its positions in Russian debt. The Russian bond holdings were part of a relative yield trade that paired a long position in high-yield Russian debt and a short position in lower-yielding U.S. debt (which was a hedge against interest rates moving higher globally and which financed the long Russian position). When Russia defaulted, no one particularly wanted to buy the billions of dollars of their debt that LTCM was stuck with. And so, LTCM was forced to liquidate equity positions such as Royal Dutch and Shell to raise cash in a panic.[2]

It is inaccurate to call the LTCM crisis a quant blowup. To be sure, some of those who worked at LTCM were quite good at mathematics. But ultimately, the strategies in which they were engaged, in particular, the ones that caused the most trouble, were not quant trading strategies. They were engaged in a very broad, cross-border and cross-asset class yield game in which they constantly sought to own risky assets and sell safer ones against them. It was, in most respects, a highly leveraged, one-way bet on ongoing stability and improvement in emerging markets and the markets in general.

10.4.1 The August 2007 Quant Liquidation Crisis

August 2007 was a far different affair and much closer to home for most quant funds. Several drivers coincided, leading to disastrous performance among relative value-oriented quant strategies. The causes were the size and popularity of certain quant strategies, the somewhat poor performance of these strategies for the period leading up to August 2007, the cross-ownership of these strategies with far less liquid ones by many players, and the widespread use of VaR-like models to target constant volatility.

The first driver of the quant liquidation crisis of 2007 was the size and popularity of quantitative long/short trading strategies. From 2004 to 2007, many blue-chip managers launched quant long/short strategies targeted at attracting large pools of investor capital, either large institutions or individual retail investors. The firms launching these products were attracted by the low turnover and longer-term investment horizons of long/short strategies, both of which are necessary for the placement of large sums of capital. Investors were also attracted by the positive returns in quant long/short products from 2004 through the early part of 2007 and by the blue-chip brand-name managers launching the products. In aggregate, it is likely that hundreds of billions in cash were invested in quantitative long/short funds and bank proprietary trading desks, and with leverage, quant long-short traders likely controlled about $1 trillion in gross positions (the value of longs and absolute value of shorts added together). The vast majority of these positions were held in larger-capitalization U.S. securities because the large numbers of deeply liquid stocks allowed for sufficient diversification and size of assets under management to accommodate both the managers' and investors' needs. Even though there was actually a great deal of diversity in the underlying models of the various firms launching these products, enough of them had sufficient overlap to make individual trades get very crowded.

The second driver of the debacle was that many of these operators had already begun to suffer subpar returns for a period leading up to the summer of 2007. Many big-name funds with a U.S. focus were flat or negative year to date before August. This is partly because "value" had underperformed "growth" since at least the end of May 2007, after several years of outperforming growth, as discussed earlier in this chapter. Many multistrategy and prop-trading desks also tend to chase recent performance, adding capital to whatever has been doing well and reducing whatever has been doing poorly. This tendency, coupled with the weak results of quant long/short trading strategies for the few months leading up to summer 2007, is likely to have contributed to especially itchy trigger fingers for risk managers who already felt the need to reduce risk in their broader portfolios.

A third cause, and, in my view, a critically important one, was the widespread practice, especially among banks' proprietary trading desks and multistrategy hedge funds, of either explicitly or implicitly cross-collateralizing many strategies against each other. The huge profits enjoyed by hedge funds and prop-trading desks before this summer attest to their exposure to credit spreads that kept narrowing in early 2008. These credit-based strategies have historically proven to be far less liquid in a crisis than they appear during "normal market conditions," and in July 2007 some credit managers experienced spectacular and sudden losses. This, in turn, drove them to seek to raise cash by selling whatever strategies were still liquid. This ATM effect is the main similarity between the 2007 meltdown and the 1998 situation described earlier.

The fourth factor leading up to the liquidation was *risk targeting* (which we discussed in Chapter 7), whereby risk managers target a specific level of volatility for their funds or strategies. They hope to achieve this "constant risk" by adjusting leverage inversely with the amount of risk their portfolios are taking. The most common tool for measuring the amount of risk in a portfolio is VaR. As already discussed, VaR measures the risk of individual instruments (using the variability of their returns over time) and combines this with how similarly they are trading to each other (a correlation matrix).

With models such as these, risk is computed to be higher when market volatility is higher and/or when correlations among individual instruments are higher. However, note that these two phenomena can be causally linked in that markets tend to become more volatile precisely *because* they are being driven by a risk factor that also leads to higher-than-normal correlation among individual instruments. In other words, both inputs to a VaR risk model can rise simultaneously, and these increases can be driven by the same underlying causes. The decline in market volatility that characterized the period from 2003 through 2006 led to a dramatic increase in the amount of leverage employed in a wide variety of strategies heading into 2007 through two channels. The first was by virtue of the use of risk targeting models for leverage, as described above. When volatility declined, risk targeting models called for increased leverage to keep volatility constant. To deliver the same volatility in early 2007 as was being delivered in, say, 2002 or 2003 would have necessitated increasing leverage by at least one-and-a-half to two times. In other words, what used to be a four-times gross leverage strategy had become a six or eight times leveraged strategy. Second, when volatility declines, opportunity also declines, and returns tend to go down. Strategies that had been reliable producers of double-digit returns in the late 1990s and early 2000s had begun to deliver low single-digit results. Investors and managers both wanted better nominal returns, and thus leverage went up, even with many shops that did not utilize risk targeting approaches. However, in summer 2007, particularly in late July, volatility began to spike dramatically as the credit crisis began in earnest. This led to a requirement for many players to reduce leverage simultaneously because their VaR models reacted very negatively to the simultaneous jumps in correlations and volatility.

To review, there were four main drivers of the crisis quants faced in August 2007: (1) large sums of money invested in value-based quant strategies with at least some similarity to each other, in other words, the "crowded trade" effect; (2) poor year-to-date performance in quant long/short trading in the United States; (3) cross-ownership of illiquid credit-based strategies that were experiencing large losses alongside more liquid quant strategies, causing the latter to be used as an ATM in a time of crisis; and (4) the decline of volatility, which led to increased leverage both because of volatility targeting-based leverage adjustments and the desire to produce higher nominal returns.

It appears that the crisis started when several large multistrategy hedge funds and/or proprietary trading desks began to deleverage their portfolios in response to poor performance in credit-oriented strategies. In addition, market volatility was rising, leading to higher VaR levels and therefore lower leverage targets. The deleveraging began with quant long/short trading in the United States, the most liquid strategy at hand, which also happened to have been underperforming. Managers sold off their longs and covered their shorts, causing substantial market impact. The stocks that had been long positions experienced substantial, fundamentally inexplicable price declines while the stocks that had been short positions experienced similarly violent price increases. This meant that anyone holding any of those stocks in the same direction as they had been held by the liquidators saw large, adverse performance as a result. In many cases, stocks were moving at incredible speed on massively increased volume as quants had to unwind their holdings.

For example, one crowded short trade was in Pulte Homes (NYSE: PHM). Exhibit 10.6 illustrates the issue.

This table contains several fascinating pieces of data. Note that PHM was declining through the early part of the summer on an average volume of 3.5 million shares per day. Then, on July 24, the volume spiked to 7.2 million shares per day, and the stock exhibited an accelerating the price decline. Over the next four trading days, however, volumes increased another 50 percent, and there was a huge reversal in the stock, which recovered about half its 44-day decline in four days (i.e., the stock was moving about 20 times faster than it had been previously). This also happens to be an interesting illustration of the quadratic nature of market impact. The first 100 percent increase in volume was absorbed by the marketplace without a change in the stock's direction. But the next 50 percent increase seemed to be on the wrong side of a tipping point in the market's supply of sellers, and indeed, a trader covering a short position on August 9 was paying as much as 15 percent in market impact, many hundreds of times the average cost to liquidate. As soon as the liquidation pressure subsided, which by all accounts was during the afternoon of August 9, the stock resumed its downward march, falling almost 23 percent on volumes much closer to the average prior to the quant liquidation.

Other types of quant traders, such as statistical arbitrageurs, seemed to provide the necessary liquidity to quant long/short players in late July.

EXHIBIT 10.6   Pulte Homes, Inc. (NYSE: PHM), May 31–August 31, 2007

PHM, Summer 2007	Price Change (%)	Average Daily Volume (millions)
May 31–July 23	−22.0	3.5
July 24–August 3	−12.5	7.2
August 6–August 9	+15.6	10.4
August 10–August 31	−22.6	5.7

Statistical arbitrageurs usually feast on environments like this, and no doubt many were happy to provide liquidity as they bet that prices would eventually converge. Many long positions with relatively attractive valuation characteristics were being sold at extremely depressed levels while expensive, poorer-quality short positions were reaching ever higher prices as a result of the quant long/short liquidations. These stocks had diverged from their peers so significantly that they must have appeared to be excellent trading opportunities to the average stat arb trader, who bets that such stocks will converge again to a "fair" relative value. But at some point, the stat arb traders were also experiencing significant losses by taking on the inventory of other quant funds, inventory which kept flooding the market relentlessly. In front of this tidal wave, stat arb traders could not continue providing liquidity. As they began to experience losses from having acquired these positions, they, too, became anxious to go to cash, adding fuel to the fire.

This was likely the tipping point, and suddenly both stat arb traders and quant long/short traders began to experience significant losses that weren't explained at all by fundamentals but purely by a lack of sufficient liquidity. Thus, by August 7, the situation was starting to get very troubling. A broader set of strategies, such as statistical arbitrage, was losing money at breakneck speed and beginning to liquidate alongside the quant long/short traders. Finally, the dam broke on August 8, with huge losses across many types of strategies and with these strategies responding by suddenly liquidating in an effort to preserve capital. Losses began to spread from U.S. strategies to international strategies, especially those implemented in Japan (which was at that time the most popular non-U.S. market for quant long/short and statistical arbitrage trading).

A wide range of fundamental signals began to lose money as the overlap between the aggregate of all liquidating managers began to overwhelm virtually any level of differentiation between managers. For the first time during this crisis, even growth-based and momentum-oriented factors began to lose money rapidly. Note that these strategies usually hold *opposite* positions from the value-oriented and mean reversion-oriented strategies. Thursday, August 9, was pure bedlam in quant-land. An enormous cross-section of strategies, many of which were extremely far removed from the original losers, began to bleed money. Intraday P&L charts started negative in the morning and literally every minute of the day ticked lower and lower as a huge variety and number of quant equity funds liquidated positions. Whereas a few signals had still been working on August 8, in quant equity trading it was hard to find anything except cash that made money on August 9. It appears that any stock that was attractive for any reason was being sold down, whereas any stock that was unattractive for any reason was running up. In short, most quant equity traders had the worst day in their history, and a great many reduced leverage to extremely low levels, with many shops going completely to cash.

A bit more should be mentioned about why so many managers reacted in the same way, namely by deleveraging and liquidating positions. Early August was a period of exceedingly perverse behavior. Not only were tried-and-true factors not working, they were actually working negatively. And because the primary discretion employed by a great many quant managers is the decision to unwind positions in the event that the models are behaving badly, quant managers did exactly that, leading other managers with any overlap experiencing losses and doing exactly the same thing in response. The losses incurred, it is important to note, were solely the result of market impact.

One of the clearest proofs of this point is that one large, well-known quant firm was suffering like everyone else in early August. On August 9, in a panic, the firm tried to convene its investment committee to determine what to do. But several members of the committee were on their summer holidays, so a meeting was scheduled for Monday, August 13, and in the meantime the lieutenants managing the portfolio day to day kept the fund fully invested. As shown earlier in Exhibit 10.6, prices returned to their previous trends fairly quickly when the liquidations stopped. (PHM, for example, was down about 12.3 percent by the close of business on Monday, August 13, merely two trading days later.) As such, by the time the investment committee met, its fund had recovered a huge proportion of its losses, and the committee elected to hold the course.

Perhaps the greatest irony of the broader situation in August 2007 was that smaller, more boutique quant traders, engaged in less commonplace strategies that had minimal overlap with the more conventional and larger-scale institutional quants, ended up experiencing losses and liquidating their portfolios only very late in the game. As alluded to earlier, managers whose losses began to accumulate only in the middle of the second week of August ended up needing liquidity at the tail end of an already massive deleveraging. This forced them to pay incredible transaction costs (all from market impact) to reduce their leverage. Reports of losses at extremely prestigious funds abounded. The range of losses was wide, from −5 percent to −45 percent, but few equity traders emerged unscathed from this event.

What separated August 2007 from prior market crises, even from the great crash of 1987, was that there was no general market panic during this period. U.S. stocks were approximately flat for the first 10 days of August, whereas stocks internationally were down in the small single digits. What we witnessed in this period was nothing short of a liquidity crisis in the most liquid stocks in the world, driven by market-neutral investors whose hundreds of billions of dollars of position selling led not to a market collapse but to almost no change at all in equity index values. It was a situation where losses were very heavily attributable to the cost of liquidation and market impact, rather than simply "being wrong" about the trade to begin with. This is a fine, mostly academic, distinction, but in dissecting the incident, it bears mentioning. This situation illustrated for the first time that contagion/ common investor risk can appear in liquid quant strategies almost as much as in illiquid or discretionary strategies. For the first time, crowding became a risk of quant trading strategies.

10.5   HOW QUANTS MONITOR RISK

Any discussion of quant-specific risks also merits a discussion of quant-specific tools used to target those risks. Chapter 7 described risk models at some length as models that seek to eliminate or control the size of exposures in a portfolio. But quants also utilize various pieces of software to monitor these exposures, their systems, and the kinds of "quant-specific" risks we have discussed in this chapter. There are several types of monitoring tools, most notably exposure monitoring, profit and loss monitoring, execution monitoring, and systems performance monitoring.

Exposure monitoring tools are straightforward enough. They start with the current positions held and then group and/or analyze these positions for whatever exposures the manager is concerned about. For example, in a futures portfolio, if the manager wants to see how much of his portfolio he has invested in the various asset classes (equities, bonds, currencies, and commodities), this is something he can do with exposure monitoring software. Similarly, one can group instruments by any other sets of characteristics that are of interest, such as their valuation, the level of momentum they have exhibited, their volatility, and so on. Many equity traders (using either proprietary tools or off-the-shelf software such as BARRA or Northfield) monitor their gross and net exposure to various sectors and industries, to various buckets of market capitalizations, and to various style factors such as value and growth. VaR-based tools also measure exposure in terms of the overall, gross level of risk being taken in a portfolio, at least according to that measure of risk. The tools are straightforward, but the art is in how to use them. Experienced managers can discern from the exposures in their portfolios whether the model is behaving as it should be. If exposures are out of line based on either limits or expectations, this can be an early warning that there is a problem with the model or else problematic market conditions.

Profit and loss monitors are similarly straightforward. They also start with the current portfolio, but they then look at the prices at which the portfolio's positions closed the previous day and compare those to the current market prices for the same instruments. Many managers look at charts of the intraday performance of their strategies to determine quickly and visually how the day is going. These tools are also important in watching out for several types of model risk. If the strategy appears to be performing in an unexpected manner, either making money when it should be losing or vice versa, the manager can check the reasons for this anomalous behavior. Or alternatively, the manager can see patterns in his performance that can alert him to problems. We alluded to this idea in discussing the performance of various quant strategies during August 2007, when the intraday performance charts were showing deterioration in the performance with nearly every passing tick. We know of at least one manager who noticed this intraday pattern and, as a result, quickly conducted research that enabled him to reduce his risk much earlier than most, thereby saving him much of the loss experienced by other traders who only acted later.

Other types of profit and loss monitors look at *how* money is being made or lost rather than *whether* money is being made or lost. For example, quants can analyze the realized and unrealized gains and losses of their strategies. Many strategies are constructed to cut losing positions quickly and ride winning positions longer. But if a quant sees that her strategy is holding losers for longer than usual or selling winners more quickly than usual, this can be an indicator that something is wrong and needs to be corrected. This kind of tool also frequently tracks a *hit rate*, which is the percentage of the time that the strategy makes money on a given position. Again, the designer of a strategy usually understands what the hit rate of a trading strategy should look like, and substantial deviations from the norm in this metric can be important indicators of problems.

Execution monitoring tools are usually designed to show the quant trader the progress of his executions. They typically show what orders are currently being worked and which ones recently were completed, along with the sizes of the transactions and prices. Fill rates for limit orders are also tracked to help monitor the execution algorithms' performance, particularly for more passive execution strategies. Some managers specifically measure and monitor slippage and market impact in their order execution monitoring software, which allows them to see whether they are getting the kinds of results from their execution strategies that they would expect.

Finally, *systems performance monitors* are used largely to check for software and infrastructure errors. Quant traders can monitor any aspect of their technology, from the performance of CPUs or the speed of various stages of their automated processes to latency in the communication of messages to and from the exchanges. This kind of monitoring is perhaps the most important for sniffing out systems errors and some types of model risk.

10.6 SUMMARY

Quant trading offers many potential benefits to investors and practitioners. The discipline, computing power, and scientific rigor brought to bear on the challenge of making money in a highly competitive marketplace certainly pay dividends overall. However, quants have their own sets of problems to deal with. Some of these problems are unique to quants (e.g., model risk), but most are simply more significant for a quant strategy than for a discretionary one (e.g., common investor or contagion risk, exogenous shock risk, and regime change risk). Quants utilize various types of tools to monitor their systems and risk, which can help mitigate the downside associated with the risks of quant trading.

Having discussed the challenges facing a quant trader and how the quant faces these challenges, we turn our attention to various criticisms of quant trading that are widely espoused in the marketplace.

NOTES

1. The macroeconomic environment around this time, and for some time thereafter, favored companies that are in "growth" industries. During this period, that meant those positively linked to commodity prices, such as oil companies or gold-mining companies, and those in businesses that are less dependent on economic cycles, such as telecommunications firms.
2. Roger Lowenstein, *When Genius Failed* (New York: Random House Inc., 2000).

CHAPTER 11

Criticisms of Quant Trading

Computers are useless. They can only give you answers.
— Pablo Picasso

People, weirdly, still love to hate quants. The first instance I'm aware of was in 1987, when a sort-of-quant strategy known as *portfolio insurance* was blamed for the crash that occurred that October. Spoiler alert: it wasn't the cause, but it was involved. In 1998, people blamed quant models for the LTCM crisis and the near-collapse of financial markets. Again, in 1998, the proximate causes of the problems were related to excessively easy leverage and naïve assumptions by many parties—regulators, brokers, banks, and also hedge funds of many flavors—not to the existence or validity of systematic investment strategies. In the summer of 2007, though, it might well be that the tide of public opinion turned from leery and suspicious to overtly negative. There could be many and various reasons for this sentiment. Some of the predilection is likely owed to widespread hatred of math classes in grade school, some of it to fear of the unknown, and some to occasional and sensational blowups by one or several black boxes.

As time has passed, and more acceptance of quantitative methods have permeated our society—savvy kids and even adults are totally fine, somehow, with their data being sold, shared, and mined by arguably adversarial agents—the criticisms have slightly abated. Certainly, the inevitability of automation in many previously unthinkable functions has become obvious. When I wrote the first or second edition of this book, the idea of a computerized visual artist or writer would have been unthinkable to almost everyone. Now, with generative artificial intelligence and large language models, no one doubts that machines will pass Turing tests with flying colors. Many of the hardest problems with replacing humans turn out to be related to implementation, not modeling. For example, building a robot soldier is not a theoretical problem so much as it is an engineering one, at this point.

All the same, there remains a very much ingrained fear among our species of things we don't command and understand fully. And so, the arguments against quant trading range from entirely valid to utterly ridiculous. It is worth noting that almost every type of trading in capital markets faces valid criticisms. In other words, quant trading, like any other type of trading, has its pluses and minuses.

This chapter addresses many of the most common criticisms of quant trading and some of my own. Where relevant, I also present counterpoints in defense of quants.

11.1   TRADING IS AN ART, NOT A SCIENCE

The markets are largely driven by humans' responses to the information they receive. Not all this information is understandable systematically. Furthermore, the process by which different people interpret the same piece of information is not systematic. If the CEO of a company is fired, is that good news or bad news? One trader might argue that it shows instability at the highest levels of office and is therefore terrible news. Another might say that the CEO deserved to have been fired, it was a situation well handled by the board of directors, and the company is far better off now. Neither can be proven right *ex ante*. So, critics of quant trading claim, how can anyone believe that you can really model the markets? Their critique is that markets are ultimately driven by humans, and human behavior can't be modeled.

At this point, given the accomplishments of OpenAI, Midjourney, and others—note that the leaders in the field today, in late 2023, might remain dominant players, or might be footnotes in the history of this rather important space—I think the criticism of art being the sole domain of biological humans has been settled pretty squarely. I would also argue that these models are wonderful at translating English words into other things (either more words, or images, or videos, or sounds), but not great at true creativity. For now, anyway. Artificial General Intelligence is probably more of a when than an if. As such, the criticism that investing is somehow impervious to computerized improvement deserves extra skepticism.

The best argument against quant investing is that the markets are quasi-efficient, nonlinear, dynamic, and adversarial systems, which makes it extremely hard to forecast asset prices. That said, there's enough empirical evidence in the sustained performance of the best quant funds to soundly refute that this difficulty is impossible to overcome.

In the end, criticism of quant trading is rather backward, reminiscent of the persecution of scientists such as Galileo and Copernicus for proposing ideas that challenged human authority. Humans have successfully automated and systematized many processes that used to be done by hand, from manufacturing automobiles and flying planes to making markets in stocks. Yes, of course, there is still room for humans to make or do various products or services by hand, but when commerce is the main objective, we typically see that the efficiency and consistency of automated processes outweigh the benefit and cachet of doing things manually.

The idea that human behavior cannot be modeled is a bit less easily dismissed, but it is also unlikely to be true. Consider that quantitative techniques are extraordinarily successful for determining what books you might like at Amazon.com, in mining data in customer relationship management software, and in human resources departments seeking to determine which universities produce the best employees. Code-breaking algorithms also have a very easy time figuring out passwords. Humans are, it seems, significantly less mysterious than we might like to believe. Obviously, as we have already discussed, there is always the risk of trying to get computers to answer questions that shouldn't have been asked of them and of building models that are not good representations of the real world. But in many cases, quant trading included, it is entirely feasible to demonstrate that something humans do with mixed results can be done just as well by computers: to profit from trading the markets.

Indeed, when done well, computerized trading strategies have tended to be exceptional performers over very long periods, as demonstrated by the examples we've used so far (Ed Seykota, Renaissance, Princeton-Newport Partners, D. E. Shaw, and Two Sigma). In the best cases, models are merely simulations of the real world, not replications. So we cannot expect a quant's models to be perfect, just as we cannot expect Amazon.com to recommend exactly the right book every time. However, over time, a well-designed quant strategy can predict enough of the behavior of the markets to generate substantial profit for practitioners, as evidenced by the results of some of the quant firms we highlighted in Chapter 2.

11.2 QUANTS CAUSE MORE MARKET VOLATILITY BY UNDERESTIMATING RISK

This criticism contains components of truth and of falsehood. Many managers, quants included, are subject to a fundamental type of model risk we discussed in Chapter 10, Section 10.1, namely asking the wrong questions and using the wrong techniques. Techniques such as VaR, for example, make numerous wrong assumptions about the market in an effort to distill the concept of risk down to a single number, which is a goal that itself seems mostly pointless. Furthermore, as illustrated by the August 2007 quant liquidation crisis, quants have underestimated the downside risk of being involved in large-scale, crowded trading strategies. This, too, stems from a fundamental flaw of quantitative trading. Computers can be given a problem that is badly framed or makes too many assumptions, and they can come up with an answer that is both highly precise and entirely wrong. For example, I can drum up a model of my wealth that assumes that this book will sell 50 million copies, that I will receive 50 percent of the proceeds, and that I can then invest the proceeds into a vehicle that will earn 100 percent per year, compounded, forever. With this model I can get precise answers to the question of my earnings as far into the future as I want. However, all of my assumptions are highly suspect, at best.

The computer's job is not to judge my assumptions, so this kind of error is ultimately attributable to my poor judgment. Similarly, some quants can be blamed for using quantitative models that are either inappropriate or badly designed to measure risk. That said, they are scarcely alone in making these errors. Indeed, VaR itself was developed to appease risk managers and banking regulators who were interested in having a single number to summarize downside risk, rather than do the difficult and nuanced work of understanding risk from many perspectives. So, though we accept the criticism that quants can underestimate risk or measure it wrongly, it is worth understanding that they are not alone. Decision makers in almost every field commonly manage to underestimate worst-case scenarios, and when they do not, it is usually to overestimate risk in the aftermath of a disastrous event. This is largely because extreme risks are so rare that it is very difficult to forecast their probability or the damage they can cause. So, we find that the statement that quants underestimate risk is likely to be true, but we also find this to be due more to human nature and the circumstances of rare events than to something specific in quant trading.

The idea that this underestimation of risk on the part of quants is somehow responsible for an increase in market volatility is, however, plainly ridiculous. First, we have already shown in Chapter 2 that quants tend to reduce market volatility and inefficiency during normal times. Regardless of what happens in abnormal, chaotic times, this fact should not be simply discounted. Second, extreme events have been happening since people could trade with each other. Preliminarily, we can look at extreme events in stocks and other asset classes. There were five distinct drawdowns in the Dow Jones Industrial Average that were worse than 40 percent before quant trading existed (indeed, before there were computers in general use). The worst of these occurred during the Great Depression, which brought with it a drawdown of almost 90 percent in the Dow and which took until 1954 to recover. The last drawdown in stocks before quant trading became a significant force began in January 1973, reached a nadir of −45 percent in December 1974, and was not fully recovered until November 1982. The next severe drawdown in stocks since then was the bear market of March 2000 through October 2002, which was set off by the bursting of the dot-com bubble. It is ridiculous to claim that a single one of these events of extreme volatility or prolonged pain was owed to quant traders. The same analysis holds for other asset classes. The worst event in recent history in bonds was Russia's default in 1998. This impacted some "quant" firms (though, as mentioned in Chapter 10, I reject wholesale the idea that LTCM was actually a quant trading firm), but was certainly not caused by quants. The currency problems in Mexico and Asia in 1995 and 1997, respectively, were also not the result of quants' activities. In fact, at the time a rather famous *discretionary* macro trader, George Soros, was widely (though not necessarily correctly) blamed by Asian governments for triggering the latter event.

We can also look at the broader question of how quants are related to market crises from the opposite perspective. How does a crisis in quant trading relate to changes in or levels of market volatility? Since we so far have only one example to work from, we will focus on the events of August 2007. The Dow Jones Industrial Average's historical volatility did move up during the two-week period in which quants were experiencing pain that summer. However, the Dow's realized volatility moved from a significantly below-average level to a level that is equal to its average volatility since 1900. From the close of trading on August 3 through August 9, 2007, certainly the worst part of the quant liquidation crisis, the Dow was actually *up* an estimated 1.1 percent—scarcely cause for alarm. Implied volatility, as measured by the VIX index, moved up during this period, from 25.16 to 26.48, but this is by no means a significant change in its level over a four-day period. It would be an impressive stretch of the imagination to attribute any change in market volatility to quant traders. Indeed, of infinitely greater importance to downside risk in markets and upside swings in volatility levels are policymakers' decisions, exogenous shocks (e.g., wars or terrorist attacks), basic economic cycles, and run-of-the-mill manias and panics. With that, I believe that the extraordinary events of 2008 bear discussion.

There is a decidedly better argument that algorithmic trading (and, specifically, market making) create more volatility simply endemically. And this argument is probably true. But, as firms such as Transtrend have been able to figure out, this is not a polemic against high frequency trading or market making. Instead, these algorithms are simply doing more efficiently what their human predecessors were doing slower and a more difficult way previously. Specifically, they are detecting that other traders/investors are piling onto something in a slow-moving train wreck kind of way, and they're simply insisting on being paid to take on that risk. The stock market had a flash crash of sorts in October 1987, with basically no algorithmic trading to point to as a cause. Humans haven't changed, only their efficiency.

11.2.1 The Market Turmoil of 2008

While I was writing the first edition of this book in the summer of 2008, the financial world was suffering in its most challenging environment since the Great Depression. Stocks endured their second distinct 40-plus percent decline in a single decade, and dozens of banks around the world had either gone bankrupt or have been nationalized, including two of the five largest U.S. investment banks. Real estate prices crashed in many parts of the world. Several money-market funds lost all or most of their value. Several of the largest insurance and mortgage companies in the United States were nationalized or required rescuing. The nation of Iceland was effectively bankrupted and actually went to Russia to seek a loan. Record-setting bailout packages and unprecedented, multinational government-backing measures were enacted in an attempt to stabilize the financial system, which U.S. Secretary of the Treasury Henry Paulson reportedly told the U.S. Congress was "days from a complete meltdown." Most forms of financial activity, in particular, credit, were frozen almost entirely. I raise this example of market turmoil for two reasons: (1) to evaluate whether quants can be blamed for it, and (2) to discuss how quants fared.

We now understand a fair amount about what brought us to that precipice, so I think the answer to the first question is widely accepted as a "no" at this point: It was caused by irresponsible banks that lent money without proper diligence to unqualified consumers, who acted with total disregard to their own financial realities; enabled by ratings agencies that had lost all sense of independence and objectivity—though, perhaps more accurately, they only made a breathtakingly clear example of their conflicted interests; and regulators, who ignored and/or exacerbated the situation. Dodgy accounting practices, incredible amounts of leverage, extreme greed, and recklessness among people who should know better, skewed compensation practices, and lofty egos also played significant roles.

Short sellers and hedge funds were widely blamed for causing the crisis at the time, and indeed, it does appear possible that irresponsible rumor-mongering on the Internet might have been partially to blame. (Though I have not seen anyone propose banning the Internet or the kinds of sites that give rumors such wide audiences.) There is no acceptable excuse for those who spread such rumors. But let us be clear and explicit: This was an equally irresponsible attempt to divert attention from the real causes and culprits, many of whom were loudly lobbying for banning short sales and hedge funds. The noise around this has largely died down—*The Big*

Short, a film starring, among others Brad Pitt, Margot Robbie, Christian Bale, Marisa Tomei and Ryan Gosling, and written by our interloping friend Michael Lewis helped, I think.

The facts are unchanged, despite the attempted smokescreen: Many banks did in fact have toxic balance sheets, uncounted and untold billions in losses, and no way to solve the problem. The bailout package passed by Congress in 2008 approved $700 billion of rescue money, and that, coupled with the American Recovery Act and the most benign monetary policy in American history, was enough to stem the pace of the collapse. But various statistical gauges of the U.S. economy indicated that it had not fully recovered until at least 4–5 years after its precipitous occurrence. It was, in short, one hell of a very real mess, not just a rumor-driven illusion. Nonetheless, to appease those railing against hedge funds and short sellers, the U.S. SEC banned all short sales of 799 financial stocks from September 19 to October 8, 2008. During this time, the Financial Select Sector SPDR (NYSEARCA: XLF), an ETF tracking the financial sector, fell another 23 percent (slightly worse, if we exclude a roughly 1 percent dividend issued during this period). By contrast, one week *after* the ban was lifted and financial companies were again allowed to be sold short, XLF *gained* slightly versus its closing price on October 8.

Quants, according to some, are at least partly to blame for the housing bubble which, when it burst, unleashed all this havoc. How? Nonsensical arguments have been made[1] connecting supposedly quant traders like Ken Griffin and Boaz Weinstein to the crisis. These arguments have two major flaws. First, most of those funds that were involved in credit trading are not traded systematically at all. While both Griffin and Weinstein are good at math, their investment strategies are mostly and fully discretionary, respectively. Second, even if we were to call them quants, neither fund's activities in any way precipitated anything associated with the real economic crisis that unfolded in 2008.

It is, in fact, pretty close to inconceivable that anyone could think otherwise. The kinds of credit trading and other arbitrage trading that dominate both Griffin's Citadel and Weinstein's Saba hedge funds are busy looking for trades that take advantage (for example) of mispricings between various tranches of a company's capital structure (equity and various types of debt issuances). The art in these kinds of trades is mostly related to legal and accounting skills, and there is nothing systematic about them whatsoever. Citadel has also made a name buying massively distressed assets, as they did in both the cases of Amaranth and Sowood. Connecting such activities with quant trading is an obvious mistake. But inferring that they were involved in the creation of a crisis is like saying the world is round because California grows good avocados. Yes, Citadel has a sizeable—and very successful—quantitative investing business (alongside their also-very-successful high frequency trading business). But it's also a massive business. It is no more a quant fund than I am the mole on my right shoulder.

Less ridiculous arguments were made about the structured products boom on Wall Street that was far more instrumental in the crisis of 2008. It is clear that many parties were to blame for the credit crisis. The stories of modest income-earners buying fancy houses with no down payments and no proof of financial wherewithal are well known. Regulators and ratings agencies enabled (and quite possibly ensured) irresponsible lending and borrowing that would power the housing bubble. Here, too, other sources are better than this book on this topic.[2] So where do quants come in?

Structured products did play a role in the crisis, making it attractive to lenders to provide loans to utterly unqualified borrowers at massively inflated home values and with little collateral to protect them. This was accomplished by an abuse of the concept of diversification. The thinking was that one bad loan was a bad idea. But making a huge number of equally bad loans was probably a completely fine idea because, it was infamously assumed, not all those loans would go bad all at once. In other words, those who transact in these securities comprised of a bunch of loans were making a convenient, but highly questionable, assumption that there would be no systemic risk that would cause the loans all to go bad at once. How the possibility of a drop in home values or a serious recession was ignored, I'm not sure.

There *is* a tremendous amount of fairly sophisticated mathematics in the determination of the pricing of these securities and analyses of their credit risk.[3] The techniques have names like copulas, Lévy models, saddle-point approximations. But as I indicated from the very beginning, quant trading has little to do with the financial engineering that drives the creation of structured products, and nothing to do with their promulgation throughout the investment community. Yes, both quant trading and financial engineering utilize mathematics in the field of finance. However, that is the extent of the similarity, and it is a microscopic overlap. Quant traders do not originate securities, show them to ratings agencies, market them to pension funds, etc. Financial engineers are not responsible for making forecasts of the future movements of various financial instruments, nor for executing trades. Quant traders don't usually have to think about how to value anything: the prices of the instruments they trade are generally knowable with a high degree of certainty, as they are generally extremely liquid and most often exchange traded.

As a postscript on the 2008 financial crisis, I would like to point out the evidence for game theory for which this event provided such great evidence. People, unsurprisingly much like water, follow the path of least resistance. If you set up a system in which certain behaviors are penalized, others rewarded, and still others are awarded free (to them) do-overs, you will more or less guarantee that, in the aggregate, people will figure out the system and behave accordingly. This actually has wonderfully useful implications for many decisions, including how to set up compensation structures at a quant hedge fund. Selah.

So if quants weren't a cause of the credit crisis, how did they fare through it? In short, better than most. In 2008, many quantitative equity firms struggled, posting losses in the −10 percent range for the year. But a great many quants, using statistical arbitrage, short-term trading and even some longer-term trading strategies, actually made substantial gains. And in other fields of quant trading, 2008 was a banner year. Quantitative CTAs and short-term traders in various asset classes, in particular, performed rather well through the crisis. But even if −10 percent was the norm, why should this be considered a particularly bad outcome, especially compared to the alternatives? Stocks have cut investors' money in half *twice* in the past decade. Many large, storied money market funds have gone bust. To my way of thinking, *these* are examples of extremely risky investments, not quant hedge funds. And, as just mentioned, it is categorically untrue that quants in general struggled in 2008.

This is also not the first time that quants have demonstrated good performance in turbulent times. In the last two severe market dislocations, in the summer of 1998 and in the bear market of 2000 to 2002, quants again proved to be outperformers. Both periods, in fact, were quite good for a great many quants, with some having the best results in their histories during these times. Even in the crash of October 1987, most quantitative trend-following CTAs posted tremendously strong returns. This isn't to say that they are immune from losses or unaffected by market turmoil. The point is that there seems to be an immense double standard applied to quants compared with more traditional markets and even other hedge funds, in terms of what is considered risky.

11.3 QUANTS CANNOT HANDLE UNUSUAL EVENTS OR RAPID CHANGES IN MARKET CONDITIONS

This is perhaps the most valid criticism of quant trading so far. Quants must rely on historical data to make predictions about the future. As a result of this dependence, it is likely that quants will suffer any time there is a significant and sudden change in the way markets behave. It bears repeating and emphasizing that, in order for the event to be of importance to a quant, the regime change must be both large and without much warning. Perhaps the most challenging time for quant trading in its known history has been the period from late July 2007 through August 2008. Over this roughly 13-month window, quants (particularly those implementing equity market-neutral strategies) faced a liquidity crisis and at least three separate episodes of substantial pain. You can see this illustrated in part in Exhibit 11.1.

As you can see from Exhibit 11.1, Value outperformed Growth from mid-2004 through early 2007. There was a reversal of this trend beginning in mid-May 2007, which accelerated aggressively in late July 2007 and was a likely cause of the poor performance among quants that contributed to their liquidation. The trend favoring growth over value from May 2007 to January 2008 is easily seen to be sharper than that which favored value before May 2007. Many quant strategies had adapted to this new regime by the middle of the Fall of 2007, leading to strong performance in the later part of that year. But two other periods catch the eye: one in January 2008, and the other in July 2008, both of which are circled in the chart. These two events were rather violent reversals of the strong trend favoring growth that began in May 2007. These reversals were among the sharpest in the history of this spread, and both were substantial periods of downside risk for many quant traders, particularly those in equities. This is because the prevailing

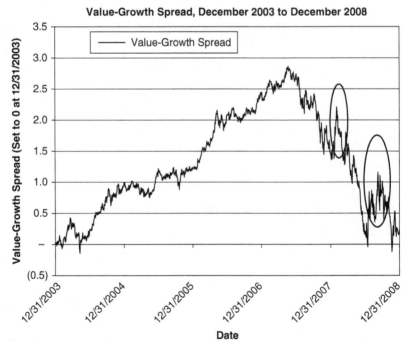

EXHIBIT 11.1   Regime Changes, as Indicated by the Value/Growth Spread

pattern of behavior, on which the quant bases forecasts of future behavior, becomes inverted at such times.

It is worth mentioning that, although the significant majority of quant strategies are negatively impacted by regime changes, a small minority are able to successfully navigate these periods. Some shorter-term strategies specifically seek to profit from short reversals of longer-term trends and the resumption of such longer-term trends. These counter-trend traders have been able to profit in many of the most difficult periods for quants (but certainly not all of them). Others sit on the sidelines during normal times, waiting for large dislocations to signal the beginning of a potentially profitable trading period. This kind of trading is known as *breakout trading*. Both of these styles can be found in any asset class or instrument class but are most generally done with futures instruments in the most liquid markets.

11.4 QUANTS ARE ALL THE SAME

This argument, too, has been widely held to be true, particularly in the wake of the disastrous performance of many quants in August 2007. However, it is a patently false claim, and this I can state with both vehemence and certainty. We will focus again on both theoretical and empirical evidence of this truth, starting with the former.

This book has outlined many of the kinds of decisions each quant must make in the process of building a quant strategy. These decisions include the kinds of instruments and asset classes to trade, the sources of data one will use and how these should be cleaned, ways to research and develop trading strategies, the kinds of phenomena being traded, how these phenomena are specified, ways in which various forecasts are combined, how far into the future forecasts are being made, how bets are structured, ways in which risk is defined and managed, how transactions costs are modeled, how portfolios are constructed, and how trades are executed. The number of degrees of freedom for a quant in building a trading strategy is, in other words, very large. Though the kinds of phenomena are not very numerous, all the other considerations are ways the quant can differentiate his approach from those of others who are ostensibly looking for the same types of anomalies. Depending on the time horizon of the strategy and number of positions it takes, the number of trades per year can easily get into the millions. I know many traders who execute 10,000 to 100,000 trades *each trading day*. As you can imagine, small differences in how one arrives at a single trade are amplified when millions of trades are made in a year.

The empirical evidence is abundant and covers both position data and return information. At my firm, we have separately managed accounts with both quant and discretionary equity firms. On an average day, 30 percent of the quants' positions are held in *opposite directions* on the exact same names. This belies the notion that quants are all the same, especially since only about 75 percent of their positions are even in the same country. In other words, of the positions held in the same country, about 40 percent are held in opposite directions by various quant traders. As the number of traders is increased, this ratio naturally also increases. This has been confirmed by several studies. In 2008, Matthew Rothman, then of Lehman Brothers, produced a study of 25 of the largest quant equity market neutral traders and found that approximately 30 percent of their positions were held in directions opposite those of someone else in the group, on average, using portfolio data spanning over a year. Among smaller firms, the differences are even more noticeable. With a third to a half of all potentially overlapping positions held in opposite directions, it is difficult to accept an argument that quants are all the same. If they were, one quant's long would not be so likely to be another quant's short.

Return data confirm what we see in the position data. I have a sample of a couple of dozen quant managers' daily returns (some going back as far as 1997), and the average correlation of these managers to each other is 0.03. There are only nine pairs of correlations that exceed 0.20, out of 252 pairs in total. And during the heart of the crisis, from September through November 2008, this correlation was merely 0.05. By contrast, the eight HFRX hedge fund indices that have daily returns (i.e., ranging from convertibles to risk arb and macro strategies) correlate at an *average* of 0.21 to each other, and 11 of the 28 pairs correlate at greater than 0.20. Five of the 28 correlate at greater than 0.40, and the maximum correlation is 0.81, between the equity hedge and event-driven styles.

The same basic story is told by monthly return data. Measuring the correlations of some 53 quant equity market-neutral traders with at least 25 months of return history, we find that the average correlation among them is 0.13. Note that we did not even include quantitative futures trading, which would reduce the correlation still further. By contrast, 22 HFRI hedge fund-style indices (excluding the broader HFRI hedge fund and fund of funds indices and excluding the short-selling managers) correlate at an average of 0.48 to each other, and these span styles as diverse as macro and distressed debt. The data are strongly in opposition to the idea that all quants are the same, confirming what we would expect, given a basic understanding of how quant trading strategies are actually developed.

11.5 ONLY A FEW LARGE QUANTS CAN THRIVE IN THE LONG RUN

I've heard this criticism repeated countless times by various observers of the quant trading world. It's actually gotten more prevalent and ingrained, to the point that it has, sadly, affected the industry heavily. The argument is reasonable enough at first glance, and it goes something like this: The largest and best-funded quants can throw the most and best resources at every aspect of the black box, from data to execution algorithms, and can negotiate better terms with their service providers. Based on this premise, it is reasonable to expect that, in the long run, they will outperform their smaller cousins. Ultimately, smaller quant firms will fall by the wayside due to either underperformance or investor attrition. The best shops, furthermore, are so good that they ultimately replace their investors' capital with their own, leaving the investor who desires to invest in quant trading in a quandary: Should she select smaller, inferior shops and be able to keep money with them until they go out of business? Is it better to invest in a handful of the biggest quants while that is still possible, and if they kick out their investors later, so be it? Or is it best to simply avoid this space altogether, since the two other options are unattractive?

This criticism and its corollaries are interesting theoretically but ignore many important facts about quant trading and therefore draw an incorrect conclusion. First, as evidenced very clearly in August 2007 and throughout 2008, having a large amount of money to manage is not always good, because readjustments to such large portfolios can be extremely costly in times of stress. In other words, one sacrifices nimbleness while gaining size and resources.

Second, whole classes of very appealing strategies are made impossible or impractical for the largest quants because the amount of money that can be effectively managed in those strategies is too small to be worth the effort. For example, large quants rarely engage in statistical arbitrage in markets such as Australia or Hong Kong because they cannot put enough money to work there. High-frequency trading in any market has very limited capacity and is therefore a very uncommon component of a large quant trader's portfolio.

Third, there is reasonable evidence that smaller hedge funds actually *outperform* larger funds.[4] Some observers believe this is partly because smaller shops are headed by entrepreneurs who are hungry to succeed rather than already successful managers who can become complacent or uninvolved. Regardless, there isn't a particularly good reason to believe that the lack of resources any small trader faces, relative to those who are much larger and trade similar strategies, is any more an impediment for quants than for discretionary traders. As one small discretionary trader put it, "It's not like I'm going to get the first call when a broker has useful information about a company. I just have to work harder and find things on my own." In other words, though there is evidence that smaller managers outperform larger ones, there is no reason to distinguish smaller quants from smaller discretionary shops. Both face challenges that larger shops don't, and both must find ways to cope with them.

Fourth, smaller managers tend to focus on the kinds of things they know and understand best, whereas larger managers need to diversify into areas that are increasingly far from their core expertise in order to grow to such large size. Most very successful trading strategies have somewhat limited capacity for capital under management. As such, to build on success, a larger trader must incorporate other strategies, which might not be at all similar to the ones in which the original success was achieved. This was certainly the case with LTCM and Amaranth; it is also the case with more successful large hedge funds such as D. E. Shaw, Caxton, and Citadel. Some of these have managed a wide diversity of strategies better than others, but the evidence in favor of large multistrategy hedge funds is mixed at best.

Fifth, and finally, the vast majority of the quality of a quant strategy is determined by the good judgment and sound research process of the people in charge. Therefore, it is absolutely the case that one good quant, with significant applied science and/or trading experience and sound judgment, is worth dozens of Ph.Ds. who lack these traits. The so-called 80–20 rule (that 80 percent of the benefit/value comes from 20 percent of the resources) applies here, too. Sure, a huge firm with tens of billions of assets under management might be able to afford several hundred Ph.Ds., but do all of them add so much value? Or, is it the case that the vast majority of these well-educated individuals are merely there for marketing purposes?

A related point bears mentioning here: ever since the Industrial Revolution, there has been a trend toward specialization in all variety of businesses. In quant trading, this usually means that the bigger firms tend to hire people with very specific skillsets to fill very specific roles. However, I have seen a great deal of (admittedly anecdotal) evidence that this may be suboptimal. Instead of having a mathematician who doesn't understand software development (or hardware issues, or network optimization) and may not have a great deal of trading expertise or experience, it may be better to have senior partners whose skillsets span multiple areas relevant to quant trading (math, computer science, and finance).

There is often a loss of information that accompanies communication between specialists in one area and specialists in another. It is easy to verify this phenomenon by sitting in any meeting that includes participants of widely varying backgrounds. The jargon is almost always different, the approach to communicating can be different, the assumptions are often different, and, perhaps most importantly, the understanding of what problems can be solved (and what can't be solved) by people in other fields is simply not at a high enough level to maximize the efficiency of communication between specialists of differing fields.

I can distinctly remember my first job in the finance industry was as a summer intern in a group that built technology for trading desks.

An enormous amount of energy was expended trying to plug the holes in communication between programmers, statisticians, and traders, and this energy was often spent in vain. This is not an indictment of that particular group: it is a well-known problem endemic to any field which requires expertise from a multitude of disciplines. On the other hand, a great deal of creativity is inspired by the application of techniques from one discipline to another. This is easiest seen in the rise of quant trading itself. Applications of techniques from computer science, physics, statistics, genetics, game theory, engineering, and a huge number of other fields have found their way into the capital markets. Individuals who have expertise in a number of disciplines obviously have an easier time applying techniques across those disciplines.

I have certainly seen first-hand reasonably compelling evidence that a portfolio of boutique quant traders can be built that is productive and competes favorably with a portfolio of larger quant managers. There are also a number of smaller quants who are not among the largest but who certainly have sufficient resources to tackle many of the same advanced problems that the largest shops can consider. For example, the smallest firms most often rely on data vendors, some small boutiques actually collect and clean their own data, something that it is widely assumed that only the largest firms can do. Both theoretically and empirically, there is little evidence to support the idea that only the largest quants can survive.

This is not to say that the largest firms are without advantages. Those pluses outlined at the beginning of this section are certainly valid, for example. But the case in favor of larger quants is far from airtight, and equally strong arguments can be made for boutiques. The good news is that there are many hundreds of them from which to choose. That said, as quant investing has gained traction with previously unwilling investors, the competition for *capacity* has gotten more serious. Investors vie for access to "hot" launches and proven funds that decide to raise capital. While I continue to believe that there is a great deal of opportunity for smaller managers to operate successfully, it is more difficult for smaller *investors* in quant to succeed. And the more constraints these investors have, the greater those difficulties become—to the point of adverse selection or retention.

In short, we find that there is no substantial difference in quality between smaller and larger quants. There are some larger quant firms that invest their resources into better infrastructure. Others may not. If there is empirical evidence to rely on, at this point, it's that the optimal size for a quant fund is somewhere between $500 million and ~$10 billion. But the evidence also favors those below $500 million than those above $10 billion, by a wide margin. There are some smaller firms that have a great deal of expertise and firepower, despite their size. Others suffer from the lack of resources. We find that it boils down to an evaluation of managers "bottom up," and that there is no valid "top down" evidence that either larger or smaller quants have an advantage over the other. The evaluation of managers is a topic we will save for Chapter 12.

11.6   QUANTS ARE GUILTY OF DATA MINING

Data mining is given a fairly bad name in financial circles, though it has come to drive most other industries entirely. It is used interchangeably with another term that is actually deserving of such negative judgment: overfitting. Data mining is an empirical science, to borrow again from the framework of the two major kinds of science we discussed in Chapter 6. Data-mining techniques are generally understood to use large sets of data for the purpose of deriving information about what happens without worrying about *why* it happens. This is the biggest difference between data mining and theory-driven science: Theorists are interested in understanding *why* something happens in order to believe that they can correctly forecast *what* will happen. However, as we already learned, theorists, too, look to historical data for cues about what kinds of theories might explain what has happened. This is a fine line—fine enough that it is not entirely clear that there is a valid difference between well-done empirical science and well-done theoretical science. The only discernible difference is that, in theoretical science, a human is expected to derive an explanation that seems reasonable to other people, whereas in empirical science, the method of analyzing data is the primary subject of scrutiny. In other words, nearly *everyone* mines data, even if only loosely. This is not problematic. We would not have learned that cheap stocks outperform expensive ones unless someone had some data to support the idea. If the data were overwhelmingly opposed to such a statement, no one would espouse it as a valid approach to investing.

Data mining is very successfully used in many industries in the broader economy and society. In the defense industry, data mining is widely used in terrorism prevention. No doubt you have heard of the U.S. government's efforts to scan millions of phone calls and e-mails for information to help predict and therefore help stop terrorist attacks. The government does not have individuals sitting on phones listening into each conversation or at computer terminals reading e-mails. Rather, computer algorithms are used to discern defined patterns that are expected to be fruitful in rooting out potential terrorist activities.

We have already given several other examples of successful data mining in this chapter. Amazon uses data mining to advise you of what kinds of books you might like, given what you've purchased and viewed. Analytical CRM software packages help businesses maximize profit per contact by mining data on these contacts, to allow sales personnel to focus on the most lucrative clients and spend less time on less lucrative prospects. Human resources departments use data-mining tools to discern which universities produce the best employees (the "goodness" of an employee is based on measures of her productivity and quality). Scientists, too, are heavy users of data-mining techniques. This is particularly evident in the field of genomics, where patterns of genetic information lead to linkages between specific genes and human health and behavior. So, it might not be entirely fair to claim that data-mining techniques cannot be used on market data, given their wide use and success in so many social and hard sciences. But, perhaps more importantly, as we showed in Chapter 3, most quants *aren't* interested in data-mining strategies. They are, instead, utilizing strategies based on strong underlying economic principles. Many are very careful about fitting parameters and other aspects of the quant research process that lend themselves to data-mining. In short, data mining doesn't deserve as bad a name in finance as it has received, but it's largely a moot point since most quants aren't data mining in the first place.

Overfitting is another story entirely. *Over*fitting a model implies that the researcher has attempted to extract too much information from the data. With a sufficiently complex model, it is possible to explain the past perfectly. But what is the likelihood that a perfect explanation of the past, using an overly complex model, will have any relevance to the future? It turns out that the answer is, not bloody likely. Imagine that we find out that the S&P 500 dropped an average of 1 percent anytime the Federal Reserve announced a decision during some period. But we have only a handful of observations of the Fed making announcements, and all their announcements during the historical period were of the Fed announcing rate *hikes*. We could, if we were overfitting, draw a conclusion that Fed announcements are always bad, and this conclusion would be successful so long as future Fed announcements are met with the same reaction as past announcements. But what happens if the next Fed announcement is of a lowering of interest rates? It's very likely the strategy would lose money because it was fitted to a sample that primarily included rate hikes. Therefore, we should be concerned about overfitting the data.

As an experiment, I set up a new Amazon account and idly clicked on a handful of books of interest to me. The recommendations that came back were not nearly as good as those that I'm given from my main Amazon.com account, since my main account is based on a lot of real data, whereas the new account is based on information from fewer than 20 observations of my clicking on various titles. The recommendations in this new account are likely to be overfitted, whereas those in my old account are less likely to be overfitted.

To estimate a given parameter of a model, one needs rather a lot of data. Overfitting ignores this basic fact and burdens a limited supply of data too much, asking it to explain more than is realistic, given the amount of data. These models are finely tuned to the past, but the moment that the future is out of step with the past, the model breaks down. In quant finance, the inevitable outcome of overfitting is losing money. There is no question that, when it is found, overfitting should be eliminated. But it is a gross and incorrect generalization that all quants overfit their models. Those most likely to be guilty of overfitting are data-mining quants. And among data-mining strategies, I find that a useful rule of thumb is that shorter time scales tend to be more amenable to data mining than longer time scales.

First, this might be due to the fact that there are so many more observations of trades at short time horizons, and therefore the amount of data available for analysis is increased. If a strategy holds positions for a year, on average, it would take hundreds of years to be comfortable with any substantial statistical analysis of the strategy's returns, because the number of betting periods is so small. If, by contrast, a strategy trading U.S. stocks holds its positions for one minute, there are 390 trading periods per day (because there are 390 minutes per trading day) and about 100,000 trading periods per year (because there are 250–260 trading days per year and 390 minutes per trading day) per stock. If 1000 stocks are traded, there are about 100 million trading periods per year to observe, yielding a great deal more data that can be mined. Remember, the problem of overfitting arises when the model is too complicated for the amount of data available. The more data are made available, the less likely it is that overfitting has occurred for a given level of model complexity.

Second, at very short time scales, it is not clear that theoretical scientists have yet come up with useful explanations of behavior. A practical guideline is that, for strategies with holding periods of less than a day, data-mining strategies might be fairly useful. For strategies with holding periods on the order of a week, a hybrid approach that combines data-mining techniques and sound market theory can be useful. Finally, strategies that expect to hold positions for months or years are not likely to work if they rely on data-mining techniques.

Overfitting models is not only possible, it actually happens among some quant traders. But just as we do not reject analysis because some people are prone to overanalyzing things, we should not so quickly dismiss quantitative modeling (even data mining) just because it is possible (or even easy) for some people to do it badly.

With all of this said, I would like to point back to the points raised in Chapter 9, regarding the (perhaps equally dangerous) pitfalls of *under*fitting, especially in the context of a highly competitive marketplace. The good and bad news of all of this is that it may still come down to skill. The new skill is to finely balance the risks of overfitting and underfitting, whereas the old risk was merely overfitting. But none of this speaks to the prognosis for the activity of *doing* quantitative investing—only to the difficulty of divining who will succeed at it.

11.7 SUMMARY

Quant trading is no magic elixir, and certainly there are quants who are guilty of each or all of the criticisms discussed in this chapter. Some do bad science, underestimate risk, and lose money when market conditions change suddenly. Some implement strategies that are commonplace and crowded, and some overfit their models to limited amounts of data. But most of these criticisms are equally applicable to discretionary traders. Done well, quant trading can produce superior risk-adjusted returns, and substantial diversification benefits.

So, what does it mean to do quant trading well? We will cover this topic in depth in Chapter 12, but let's recap some salient points from this chapter: Quants must be concerned with falling prey to the temptation of false precision, particularly in risk management. A printout with a risk number on it does not imply that the number is accurate or has been properly derived. Quants must also remain aware of relationships within the market and must have a detailed understanding of the kinds of bets they are making and how they are expressing these bets in their portfolios, allowing them to navigate violent regime changes. Quants must conduct innovative research in alpha modeling and across the entire spectrum of the black box, to reduce the risk that there is substantial overlap between their models and those of their peers. Finally, to the extent that data mining is explicitly utilized, it should be done in a manner that does not express overconfidence in the amount and predictive power of historical data.

NOTES

1. Scott Patterson, *The Quants* (New York: Crown Business, 2010).
2. For starters, the Wikipedia entry entitled "Causes of the United States' housing bubble" gives some good color both on the regulatory and other sources of the problem. Another entry entitled "Collateralized debt obligation" gives a good introduction to the structured products that allowed for all those bad loans to be made.
3. An interesting, but technical, primer on this topic, along with a quant's rebuttal of the idea that even financial engineers deserve any blame is provided by Damiano Brigo.

A presentation can be found at: http://www1.mate.polimi.it/ingfin/document/ Crisis_Models_Mip_16_giugno_2010_Brigo.pdf. Damiano Brigo, Andrea Pallavicini, and Roberto Torresetti, *Credit Models and the Crisis: A Journey into CDOs, Copulas, Correlations and Dynamic Models* (Chichester: Wiley, 2010) goes into more depth on this topic.

4. A study by Pertrac, the hedge fund industry's leading database and performance analytics provider, was cited by the Medill Reports' John Detrixhe on August 14, 2008. The article can be found at http://news.medill.northwestern.edu/ washington/news.aspx?id=97223

CHAPTER 12

Evaluating Quants and Quant Strategies

The avocation of assessing the failures of better men can be turned into a comfortable livelihood, providing you can back it up with a Ph.D.

—Nelson Algren

In this chapter we discuss methods of assessing quant strategies and practitioners to separate the good from the mediocre and the mediocre from the poor. As I have said throughout this book, a great deal of the work that quants do has very natural analogues in discretionary trading. There are also significant parallels in the work of a quant trader to the work of a corporate CEO or any other person involved in the allocation of resources. In this regard, the framework presented in this chapter can be used successfully to judge the work of such decision makers. Indeed, one person I trained in this method of assessing quants has adapted it for trading credit markets and now uses the same method to provide a framework for judging the merit of various corporate bond offerings and the companies behind them.

The first challenge an evaluator of quants faces is to pierce the walls of secrecy that quants build around their methods. Though it is fair to say that quants are often secretive, I have had a rather different experience. The vast majority of quants I have evaluated—and there have been many hundreds of them—have been willing to answer most or all of my innumerable questions. The difference is due, at least in part, to the questions we ask at my firm. It also owes to how we ask these questions and how we handle the information we learn from quants. In the next section I describe the principles of my approach to interviewing quants.

Armed with the techniques described in this chapter, the evaluator of a quant has two goals. The first is to understand the strategy itself, including the kinds of risks it is taking and from what sources its returns are generated. This is important because it tells the investor what she owns when she is investing in a given quant strategy. The second goal in the evaluation of a quant is to judge how good the practitioners themselves are. In many respects, a quant trading team is much like an engineering team at an automobile manufacturer. It is fine for the team to build one great engine, but over time, that engine must be improved. As times change, the engine might even need to be redesigned entirely, or other types of engines might need to be designed for other vehicles. It is critical to ascertain whether the quant team is skilled at designing engines, evolving them, and designing new types of engines over time. All these components of the analysis of a quant ultimately serve to help the evaluator answer perhaps the most central question in the evaluation of any kind of trader: Why should I believe that this particular team, utilizing this particular strategy, is actually likely to make money in the future? In hedge fund parlance, what is this manager's "edge"?

Assuming that the investor finds a team and strategy worthy of investment, he must ascertain the integrity of the people involved. After all, skill is a good thing only if it is in the hands of good people. Here I briefly address some thoughts on how to judge the integrity of a trader, although this is not central to quantitative trading. Finally, I provide a few brief thoughts on portfolio construction using the frameworks provided in this book.

12.1 GATHERING INFORMATION

How does one actually go about finding out what a particular quant does? Quants are notorious for their secrecy and paranoia. And this is not without reason. Much of the skill of quant trading comes from experience and knowhow, not from raw mathematical superiority. There is an excellent book called *The Interrogator,* by Raymond Toliver, from which many useful lessons can be learned on how to get information from a quant.[1] The book's subject is Hanns Joachim Scharff, a former World War II Luftwaffe interrogator who succeeded at gathering information from downed Allied pilots without the use of any physical force or psychologically stressful techniques. Instead, Scharff used three major tools: trust building, domain knowledge, and an organized system for tracking and retrieving information.

Before detailing Scharff's techniques, I want to stress that I am no fan of wars or interrogations, nor does the relationship between investor and quant manager closely resemble the relationship between interrogator and prisoner.

But there is one similarity, I believe, that allows lessons from the latter to be useful in the former: In both cases, information that one party is reluctant to provide is needed by the other.

The first technique Scharff used is also the most obvious: He built trust with the pilots he was interviewing. In fact, Scharff remained friends with a great many of them after the war, and they seemed universally to respect and like him. Turning to the quant, trust comes in part from building relationships, but a big chunk of it relates to the behavior of the interviewer. If an investor asks a quant for sensitive information and has either a reputation for talking, or an actual propensity to talk about what other quants do, it is less likely that the quant will or should trust this investor. After all, whatever the quant tells him is likely to get spread around the industry. At my firm, we hold quant managers' strategies in the strictest confidence. Often a quant will ask us what some other quant does. Our answer is universally and always that we will not discuss what others do, just as we do not discuss what the quant who asked us does. However, we've heard numerous stories and witnessed numerous first-hand examples of investors or managers passing along even reasonably proprietary bits and pieces of a quant's strategy to the industry. This is an ugly practice.

The second lesson from *The Interrogator* is that it is hard to feel particularly justified in being secretive with information if the person asking questions already knows most of the possible answers. For example, Scharff knew the name of the pet dog at the home base of one pilot and the names of most of the pilot's colleagues. His goal in a given interview was to learn just a little bit more about his prisoners and their activities. They were frequently lulled into thinking that there was no point in keeping secrets, since their captor knew so much already. Though this never led to blatant "tell-all" behavior, it certainly allowed the interrogator to amass huge amounts of value from the interviews, a little at a time. It is possible to learn a similarly voluminous amount about quant trading without asking any particular quant to teach it to you in a meeting. This is helped along by the fact that most of what an investor needs to understand about a quant can be learned without compromising proprietary information. In this book, for example, we have outlined a great majority of the kinds of approaches quants use. None of this information is especially proprietary to any trader. A quant with any hope of being successful knows most of the material in this book already. In a sense, this book provides you with a great portion of the menu available to a quant. There aren't many dishes he can choose that aren't on this menu, which obviates the need for most of the secrecy. The investor can, in this way, learn about the specific items on the menu that the quant being interviewed has chosen and why these choices were made. For instance, understanding the kinds of alpha models the quant is using, whether they are relative or intrinsic, how fast he trades, and in what instruments and geographies tells the investor a great deal about what risks are being taken. This information is necessary for building a diversified portfolio and is largely sufficient for that exercise.

The third and final lesson of *The Interrogator* is to be organized in the management of information when it is gathered. This greatly supports efforts to get new information but is also useful in ongoing evaluations of the quality of a given practitioner. Scharff's group developed a sophisticated, almost relational database system using index cards and a card catalogue file. (Remember, this was before the computer was invented.) As they got new information, they would organize it by linking it to other relevant cards in the file. For example, if they found out the name of another pilot from a given American base, they would tag that card with references to all the other information, including other pilots, from that base. This way, as they were interviewing a given pilot, they had a dossier that contained an impressive and extensive array of details, well organized and easy to access. These days we have powerful computers and databases to rely on, making such a job easier.

Keeping information organized furthers the goal of developing deep domain knowledge, but it is also quite useful in ascertaining the "goodness" of a quant team over time. If every three months you ask a quant, for example, what types of research projects he is working on and what new pieces he has added to the model over the past three months, over time, you should see a rational life cycle that repeatedly takes a robust research pipeline and turns it into implemented improvements to the strategy. If the quant has a process wherein modules that were not part of the research list from the past suddenly appear in production, this could be evidence of sloppiness in the research process. When visiting a quant's office, it is useful to ask to see firsthand some of the various tools and software that the quant claimed to use or have developed in previous discussions. But, be aware that if you should be asking to see something specific, you have to have carefully managed the information about the nature of these tools and software to begin with.

12.2 EVALUATING A QUANTITATIVE TRADING STRATEGY

In my years of evaluating and creating quant trading strategies, I have noted an extraordinarily interesting fact: The work that a quant does is, in most ways, identical to the work that any portfolio manager, any CEO, or any other allocator of resources must perform. After all, these resources (e.g., time or money) are limited and must be invested in a way that results in maximum benefit. The process used to invest resources—the investment process—contains six major components:

1. Research and strategy development
2. Data sourcing, gathering, cleaning, and management
3. Investment selection and structuring
4. Portfolio construction
5. Execution
6. Risk management and monitoring.

You may note that these activities are closely parallel to the modules of the black box and the activities in and around its construction and management. This is because all these areas must be addressed in order for a quant trading program to function properly over time. One fact about computers, which we've addressed already, is that they do not do a good job of thinking about things you might have missed. As quant trading programs have evolved over time, they have had to address the myriad decisions that any portfolio manager must address. Too often, in discretionary management activities, important aspects of this process are left without sufficient analysis, and an ad hoc approach is taken. I've interviewed scores of discretionary stock pickers who can spin tremendous yarns about why they are long this stock or short another. But when asked how they decide how to size these positions in their portfolios, the answers are often vacuous, given without deep thought or analysis.

Those charged with evaluating managers must thoroughly examine each of these areas. And quants, in general, should be willing to answer questions about each. A few examples of the kinds of questions I ask a quant follow:

- Research and strategy development
  - How do you come up with new ideas for trading strategies?
  - How do you test these ideas?
  - What kinds of things are you looking for to determine whether a strategy works or not?
- Data sourcing, gathering, cleaning, and management
  - What data are you using?
  - How do you store the data, and why that way?
  - How do you clean the data?
- Investment selection and structuring
  - Are your alpha models theory-driven or data-driven?
  - Which alpha strategies are you using (e.g., trend, reversion, value/ yield, growth, or quality)?
  - Are you making relative bets or a bunch of individual bets?
  - If relative, what does relative mean, exactly?

- Over what time horizon, and in what investment universe?
- How are you mixing your various alpha models?
- Portfolio construction
  - How do you do portfolio construction?
  - What are your limits, and why did you set them there?
  - What are the inputs to your portfolio construction?
  - What are you trying to achieve with portfolio construction (i.e., what is your "objective function")?
- Execution
  - What kind of transaction cost model are you using, and why did you choose to model transaction costs the way you did?
  - How are you executing trades—manually or algorithmically?
  - Tell me about your order execution algorithms: What kinds of things did you build into them (e.g., hidden vs. visible, or active vs. passive)?
- Risk management and monitoring
  - What does your risk model account for, and why those things?
  - What are your various risk limits, and why did you set them where you did?
  - Under what circumstances would you ever intervene with your model?
  - What are you monitoring on an ongoing basis?

This is but a small sampling of the hundreds of questions I ask a quant. If he claims that the answers to such questions are proprietary, I do not simply accept that response. Rather, I try to ascertain *why* he thinks the answers are proprietary and try to make him understand *why* I need to know. Most quants I have met are sympathetic to the goals of an investor trying to understand a portfolio's exposures and whether the quant is skilled at his work. It comes back to building trust, having domain knowledge, and being organized in terms of the management of information. As I've said, the menu of things that quants can choose to do is reasonably easy to know. It is largely laid out in this book, and I am certain I've revealed nothing proprietary. A quant generally should not claim that he cannot disclose which items he has chosen from this menu.

The investor has one more tool available for understanding a quant strategy, and that is the footprint left behind by the strategy: its return history. Imagine that an investor learns, by asking many questions such as those I've listed, that a quant is using a trend-following strategy on various individual instruments, with a six-month average holding period. When long-term trends are present, the strategy should do well. When longer-term trends reverse, the investor should see the strategy do poorly. In other words, the strategy's return pattern should corroborate the fundamental understanding that the investor has gained by asking many questions.

12.3 EVALUATING THE ACUMEN OF QUANTITATIVE TRADERS

If I have tried to stress anything in this book, it is that the judgment of a quant trader pervades the strategy she builds. So, an evaluation of the quant's skill and experience in the fields relevant to the trading strategy is obviously important, but it is also easier said than done. This section outlines a few tools that can be used to determine the skill level of quant traders.

The people developing and managing quant strategies should be well trained in the methods they use. At least some members of the team should have substantial live experience in areas of quant trading relevant to the strategy they are currently pursuing. Experience helps drive good judgment, especially in light of the massive array of subtleties and traps inherent in the process of research and trading. From a dispositional standpoint, quants should be careful and cautious in their analysis, and they must be humble about their ability to predict the future. There are considerable hurdles to doing quant trading well, such as polluted data and constantly improving competition. A good quant does not underestimate such challenges. The reality is, however, that evaluating whether scientists know what they are talking about at a deep level is not the easiest task for someone who is not technically proficient. As such, to make a judgment, one may have to rely on the quant's qualifications and experience, reputation, history of success, and analyses of the investment process. Although this is a lot of work, the task is doable for those who want to undertake it.

One of the handiest tricks I know of to evaluate a quant's skill is to dig deeply into the details in a few areas of her process. Why? The difference between success and failure is very commonly found in a large number of highly detailed decisions. If the mechanism used to make these decisions is flawed, the manager has little hope of success in the long run. Thus, an analysis of the investment process, and, by extension, its six major components, is focused on understanding *what* a quant does and, just as important, *why* the quant does it. As discussed throughout this book, a number of approaches to quant trading can work. Momentum and mean reversion strategies can both work, even though they are opposites. Both intrinsic alphas and relative alphas can work. So it is important to understand what a trader does, but why she does it tells you about her judgment, her process, and her potential for future success.

Each decision a quant makes in how she builds a strategy represents a source of potential differentiation from other traders, but also of potential success or failure. And it makes sense that this is the case. Many quants have large numbers of positions, frequently in the thousands, and most engage in strategies that turn these positions over relatively frequently—from once every few minutes to once every few months. If 5000 positions are turned over once a week, for example, this represents about 260,000 individual trades per year. Now imagine two equity traders, Trader A and Trader B. They have remarkably similar strategies, even in the details, and they each manage $500 million. For each dollar managed, they put on $2 of long positions and $2 of short positions so that each trader has a portfolio of $2 billion. Each turns over about 20 percent of her portfolio per day, or $400 million in dollar volume each day. They each average 10 percent returns per year. If Trader A is later able to optimize her executions such that she makes 0.01 percent more per dollar traded than she used to, either by being faster or improving transaction costs or the alpha model, this results in Trader A's annual return improving to 12 percent per year. This is 20 percent, or $10 million per year in profits, better than the result generated by Trader B, which is an enormous difference when compounded over time. Though some quants certainly do things that are plainly incorrect at a high level, the judgment of the quality of a given quant most often comes down to his decisions at a fairly detailed level.

Another reason that the details matter so much is that there is really only a tiny amount of predictability in all the movements of the market. Quants often depend on being right only slightly more often than they are wrong and/or on making only slightly more on winning trades than they lose on losing trades in order to generate profits (though trend-following futures strategies tend to lose as much as 70 percent of the time, with dramatically larger payoffs on the winners than the losses suffered on the losers). As such, small decisions that affect the probability of winning only slightly or those that skew the size of winning trades versus losing trades slightly can dramatically impact the outcome over time.

Finally, if the quant has given deep and well-grounded thought to the details of the few areas that you spot-check, it is more likely that she has given deep thought to other areas of the quant trading process. This, too, improves her probability of success in the future, since we have shown that rigor is a key component of success in quant trading. Though it is likely obvious enough already, I want to make it clear that the fact that a quant has a Ph.D. in physics (or anything else) is no indication of quality or skill. Some of the brightest and most successful quants have no advanced degrees, and some of the biggest failures in quant trading have won Nobel Prizes.

The flaw in focusing on the details of a quant strategy is that such details are less likely to be revealed to an investor during due diligence. Though the higher-level topics discussed in the Section 12.2, "Evaluating a Quantitative Trading Strategy," might be relatively uncontroversial to discuss, the details are not. As I mentioned earlier, it is frequently the details that separate the best traders from the mediocre ones, and these details often boil down to knowhow more than, say, better math skills. So, quants are and probably should be somewhat more reticent to provide such details. Even if they were to provide details, the investor would have to be knowledgeable and proficient enough to pass judgment on them. In other words, to try to divine the quality of a quant's system from clues about its particulars requires significant experience on the part of the quant investor. After all, just as I require experience in my traders, I also benefit from experience in judging them. A great many things that seem plausible enough at first glance simply don't work. For example, just because a quant pays a lot of money to a data vendor for clean data, it doesn't mean that the quant should actually rely on the cleanliness of that data. The saving grace for the non-quantitative investor seeking to evaluate a quant is thoroughness and strong information management in the assessment and due diligence process.

12.4 THE EDGE

In assessing a portfolio manager, including a quant, a key issue to focus on is the idea of an *edge*. We define an edge as that which puts the odds in favor of the portfolio manager succeeding. An edge can come from three sources, listed here in order of commonness: the investment process, a lack of competition, or something structural. In investing and trading, an edge is *not* the same thing as a competitive edge. A trader might have absolutely no competitors, yet still manage to lose money. I've seen that happen more than once. An investment edge is thus more intrinsic than comparative. Still, competition does matter: A valid idea with a valid implementation might make little or no money if there is too much competition, whereas a mediocre strategy might make money if there is none. As such, one must ascertain the sustainability of a given trader's edge. The odds might be in the trader's favor today but against him tomorrow as the world changes or as competition increases, if the trader does not evolve.

An *investment process edge* must come from one or more of the six components of the investment process we just outlined. Too often, when asking a discretionary stock picker what his edge is, we hear him say, "Stock picking." But this is merely a description of the activity, not evidence that the trader is any good at it. One must dig further into the *reason* that the trader claims to have an edge in any of these activities. For quant traders, most often an investment edge comes from experience and skill in conducting research and/or the acquisition or cleaning of data. This is because the goodness of the models for investment selection and structuring, portfolio construction, execution, and risk management is usually determined by the quality of the research and development process that created them. If some modules have not been particularly well researched, there is almost no chance that the trader will have an edge in these areas. An edge in research can derive from superiority in talent or process, but actual experience in conducting successful research in the financial markets is usually critical. In other words, one must have better people and/or a better process to put around these people, but in either case experience is needed.

I have already described a bit about how to assess the people at a quant shop, but one more point bears mentioning. How a quant deals with adversity is critical to understanding his edge and its sustainability. There are times when the model simply doesn't make money. Knowing how and when to react to these episodes is critical. Too often, quants react in a suboptimal manner to losses in their funds, and a knee-jerk reaction can often ruin whatever edge the strategy itself has. A sound approach to managing adversity starts with good monitoring tools, which allow the quant to pinpoint problems and work to solve them rather than panicking. It is unlikely that a trader has an edge because of monitoring, but it is easy to throw away a potential edge through insufficient or badly conceived monitoring processes.

In terms of research, there are several hallmarks of a high-quality process. The process should be vigorous and prolific, and there must be an ability to translate models efficiently from research into production. This is because most quant models eventually decay into mediocrity, and successful ongoing research must be implemented in live trading strategies to stay ahead of this decay. The research process should also deal with issues such as overfitting and look-ahead bias, and the evaluator should ascertain exactly how the quant thinks about and deals with these critical issues. Finally, the process should at least largely follow the scientific method. In evaluating a quant trader, it is useful to ask many questions about how and why various elements of their strategy are the way they are. If a manager says he will close a position if it has moved 10 percent against him, ask him how and why he decided on 10 percent rather than 5 percent or 50 percent. If the quant says he is running a trend-following strategy in certain markets, find out why he picked a trend-following strategy, how he defines the strategy, and why he is using the markets he's using rather than other or simply more markets. These kinds of details will give you insight into the care with which a manager has developed the entirety of an investment strategy.

A *data edge* can come from having proprietary access to some sort of data. Earlier in the book we gave the example of a company that uses geolocational data derived from GPS signals on cell phones to aggregate more real-time macroeconomic indicators. If, in fact, these data prove useful, they might be able to trade using this information, and they might then have a data edge. But in this era of technology and regulation, it is difficult to find sustainable data advantages. It is also possible to build a data edge through superior data gathering, cleaning, and storage techniques. Again, an interviewer should ask questions about where a trader gets his data, what work is done to clean the data, and how and why the data are stored in a certain way. Some answers will be thoughtful; others could indicate carelessness.

This kind of data edge is quite similar to a *lack of competition edge*. But lack of competition is not a long-term plan. It is a truism in economics that, if higher-than-average profit margins can be had in some activity, more and more players will compete until the margins compress and normalize at levels more typical in the broader marketplace. This is likely to have happened already in at least two quant trading spaces: quant long/short and statistical arbitrage. However, once they become more competitive, they also become more cyclical, and there are periods when players vacate the space because it offers too little reward, leaving more of the pie (and therefore better margins again) for the fewer players who remain. It is also important to ascertain *why* there is a lack of competition, when this is found. Some strategies are inherently more difficult for new entrants; others simply have not yet attracted the attention of new entrants. An example of the former, at least historically, can be found in purely quantitative options trading. This is not widely pursued because there are significant challenges associated with acquiring and cleaning data, structuring trades, and modeling the liquidity of options contracts. But this by no means implies that it cannot later become a crowded strategy with many competing firms chasing an ever-shrinking pie.

As an example of the second option, I remember an experienced team that formed a hedge fund to trade corporate credit in Asia back in 2002. They had successfully carried out this strategy as proprietary traders at a bank for several years previously. They had few, if any, competitors, and their early years were very strong. Then, as time passed and more entrants to their niche crowded the field, they had to branch into other areas that were less appealing. Over time their edge, which was largely related to a lack of competition, was eroded. Ultimately the new areas into which competition forced them to participate caused a massive drawdown in their fund. The lack of competition was really due to a lack of discovery of their niche, and these are among the most fleeting kinds of edges.

Structural edges generally relate to something in the market structure that puts the wind in the sails of a market participant. These are usually caused and removed by regulation. I once knew a trader in the pits of the New York Mercantile Exchange who ran a hedge fund that relied on his short-term discretionary trading. Because of his status on the exchange, he was able to supplement a reasonable investment edge with a structural edge that allowed him to transact very cheaply and extremely quickly. Over time, however, his markets went from being pit-traded to electronic, and his structural edge vanished. In quant trading, the most common sort of structural edge comes from liquidity provision, or the rebate, on ECNs. ECNs actually pay market participants for market-making activities by providing commission rebates. In certain cases I have seen the act of transacting become a profitable exercise for the trader, and this too is a structural edge. It is possible that, over time, payments by ECNs for order flow will dwindle, and this edge, too, will be eradicated.

12.5 EVALUATING INTEGRITY

Most quants, and most traders in general, are honest and ethical. Therefore, it is entirely reasonable to work with them on a "trust, but verify" basis. In other words, for most of the evaluation process, it is reasonable to assume that the trader went to school where she claims, got whatever degree(s) she claims, and is generally not a criminal. But before making an investment, most observers would agree that to the extent possible, it's worth verifying a quant's ethics.

Here we have a few tools at our disposal. First, do background checks, education verifications, and reference checks. In the case of backgrounds and education verifications, serious problems in a trader's personal or professional history should probably serve as a red flag. Of course, this is a tricky proposition. The investor must determine whether the mistakes or misdeeds in a quant's past served to "teach her a lesson," or whether they indicate a likely pattern of behavior that will repeat, even if not in exactly the same way. That judgment cannot be made universally for all cases. But I encourage the investor to consider this question only from one specific angle, which might help drive the answer: The job of the investor is not to judge the quant as a person but rather as a potential fiduciary, acting on behalf of the investor. Fiduciaries are bound to act in their clients' best interest and to be very open and upfront about any potential conflicts of interest or anything else that could impede their fulfilling their duties to investors. Using the mentality of the fiduciary as a compass is something I have found helpful in a great many difficult circumstances.

When performing reference checks, I find it useful to request references from existing investors whenever possible and to ask them not only why they like the manager but also what they think her weaknesses are. More helpful still is to seek out references that the manager did not provide herself. It is relatively easy for any trader to find a few people to say something nice about her. But it is much better if the trader is known by others, and those others are likely to provide much more useful input than the references a trader provides for herself. If you cannot locate such references in your own network, it sometimes helps to ask the references provided by the manager whether they know anyone else you can contact.

It turns out that getting into details with quants helps demonstrate their integrity as well. Though even less-skilled quants might have answers at hand for higher-level questions about their strategies and process, even someone intent on deceiving rarely thinks through low-level details sufficiently to be facile in answering questions about them. This is a common and successful interrogation technique in law enforcement. If you ask a suspected criminal where he was last night, it's not surprising to hear him quickly and convincingly provide an alibi, such as "at my girlfriend's house." But if you follow up by asking what time he arrived, how long he stayed, what movie he watched, what he ate and drank while he was there, and so on, he will have to make up answers to these questions he likely has not rehearsed beforehand.

A quant who is lying to cover up a lack of skill would have to be an expert at making up answers to questions about details on the fly to keep up with questions about the details of her strategy. And some people are very good liars, to be sure. However, these answers also have to be able to stand up on their own. Answers that reveal a lack of understanding of the subject matter or answers that are internally inconsistent or are deficient in other ways should not be ignored. They might not lead you to conclude that the manager lacks integrity, but they should be sufficient to conclude that she isn't very good, which is itself sufficient for the purpose of avoiding hiring her. What's more, you can use the same technique of looking for details in assessing a quant's background as in assessing her strategy. If a quant says she completed her Ph.D. at Harvard, you can follow up by asking where she lived while she was there, what her favorite restaurants were, who her dissertation committee included, what her dissertation's title was, how many pages it ended up being, and so on. And again, some of these specifics should be verifiable with her *alma mater*.

It is worth mentioning one more point about selecting managers, whether quant or not: Almost no trader is so special that it is worth investing in her strategy without gaining a reasonably deep understanding of it. It should not take much to say "no," in other words, whereas it should take an incredible amount of confidence to say "yes." Seeing a long and attractive track record should never be sufficient. In fact, I would put forth that it is significantly more important to get good answers to good questions than to see a long track record. If Bernie Madoff and the other scandals that were announced on a nearly weekly basis in late 2008 provide any sort of lesson to investors, it must be that reputation and track record are not enough.

No investor can validly claim that they understood how Madoff could have made such consistently positive returns based on the strategy he is said to have employed. Madoff never addressed questions, maintaining that his strategy (which was discretionary, not systematic) was too proprietary.

Though insufficient to uncover all potentially fraudulent (or simply unprofitable) investments, the tools provided in this chapter can certainly help eliminate a great majority of them. These techniques should be used in conjunction with an equally rigorous operational due diligence process to further reduce the possibility of being victimized by fraud, malfeasance, or other misbehavior on the part of traders.

12.6 HOW QUANTS FIT INTO A PORTFOLIO

Assuming that you find a quant that is worth hiring or investing in, you have to decide how to allocate to this trader. To make this determination, you have to understand how the strategy fits in with the rest of your portfolio. This is largely a question of balancing the levels of various types of exposures. This section details some of the more important kinds of exposures associated with quant investing.

12.6.1 A Portfolio of Alphas

First, it is worth remembering that portfolio construction is about allocating to exposures. A portfolio that contains more kinds of exposures is more diversified than one that is concentrated among a smaller number of exposures. Investors must seek out the appropriate balance of trend, reversion, technical sentiment, value/yield, growth, and quality to achieve optimal diversification. A quant doing trend following is not likely to be so incredibly different, from a portfolio construction viewpoint, than a discretionary trader who is seeking to identify trends. To be sure, the tireless vigilance of a computerized trading strategy might find opportunities that the human trader misses. In addition, the human trader might avoid some bad trades that are taken on by the computerized strategy out of naiveté. But, as trend following in general goes, so it is likely that the human and computerized trader both go. So, at a primary level, the investor must diversify among various alpha exposures. In the evaluation process, the investor should be able to ascertain at least roughly the underlying alpha exposures of the various strategies in a portfolio. Using this information, the investor can allocate capital such that the blended allocations to various types of alpha are in line with the levels that the investor has determined are desirable.

12.6.2 Bet Structures

The second consideration relevant to portfolio construction is bet structure, as described in Chapter 3. Relative bets can behave very differently from single-instrument bets, particularly when these bet structures are used with different types of alpha models. When a quant strategy makes relative bets, it is inherently counting on the stability of the relationships among the instruments that are grouped together. This makes bet structure itself a source of risk in such strategies, and this risk becomes evident when the relationship between the instruments changes. In such environments, for example, relative mean reversion strategies are prone to losses. On the other hand, single-instrument mean reversion frequently *benefits* from large regime changes. This is because this strategy tends to bet against the prevailing trend while remaining indifferent to the destabilizing effects of a large trend reversal on the relationships depended on by a relative alpha strategy. This is but one example of how bet structures can impact results and, as a result, the investor's portfolio. In short, it is worthwhile diversifying across various bet structures as well, even within the same domain of alpha exposure (e.g., relative and intrinsic mean reversion).

12.6.3 Time Horizon Diversification

Finally, the investor must balance her exposure across time horizons. In general, it is my experience that longer-horizon quant strategies—those that hold positions for more than a week or so—tend to go through longer and streakier performance cycles. They can outperform or underperform for several quarters on end, and it can take several years to evaluate whether there is really a problem with the manager. Some longer-term strategies also demonstrated conclusively that they are subject to crowding risk, as seen so vividly in August 1998 and August 2007. While this might make them a bit less desirable, one can manage significantly more money in such strategies, which is sometimes a practical necessity.

Short-term strategies, by contrast, tend to be very consistent performers, but they cannot handle much capital. They are therefore very desirable but also not always practical. Furthermore, when one does find a good short-term trader to invest in, it is not clear that the trader will remain small enough to be effective on short time scales. Many traders are tempted to grow their assets when assets are available, and this demands attention on the part of the investor.

12.6.4 Summary of Portfolio Considerations

Quants can be valuable components of a portfolio. The investor must realize that quants are ultimately not so different than their discretionary counterparts and therefore that the list of things that matter to building a portfolio that includes quants isn't much different than it would be without quants.

As with all things related to portfolios, the key is to build a diversified portfolio that considers three important elements:

1. Various types of alpha exposures
2. Various bet structures
3. Various time horizons.

It is interesting to note that these considerations closely mirror the taxonomy of theory-driven alphas, presented here again as Exhibit 12.1. Equally interesting, I do not believe that the investment universe (asset class, instrument class, or geography) nor various other subtleties about the

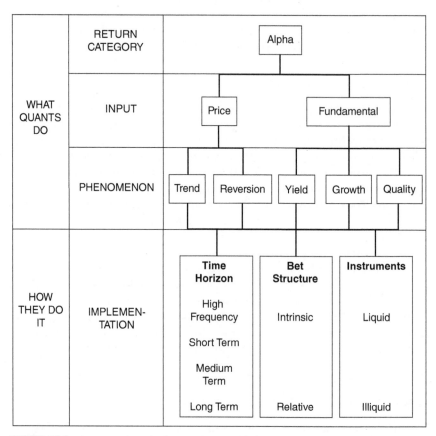

EXHIBIT 12.1   Taxonomy of Theory-Driven Alpha Strategies and Implementation Approaches

models (e.g., model specification or run frequency) are particularly impactful in portfolio construction. These variations add a great deal of diversity when markets are behaving normally, but in stressful times they simply matter a lot less than distinctions along the lines of the three portfolio considerations listed here.

12.7 SUMMARY

To assess a quant trader and a quant strategy, one must understand the strategy being implemented and the quality and vigor of the process that generates strategies. To do this, the investor has three tools at her disposal: building trust, gaining as much knowledge as possible about quant trading, and keeping information she learns as organized as possible. These tools can be used to extract and piece together information on a given quant, and on quant trading generally.

Ultimately, an investor has to determine whether a quant has an edge, what the sources of this edge are, how sustainable the edge is, and what could threaten it in the future. Edges come from people and/or processes, and it is on these areas that the evaluation of a quant must focus. Once quants have been vetted, they should be thoughtfully included in a portfolio. It is important to diversify across different approaches to alpha generation, different time horizons, and bet structures to complement best the other components of the investor's portfolio.

I remember once interviewing a senior employee at one of the best quant shops in the world. I asked him how on earth they had done so well, which of course was a sort of stupid question. His answer, however, was both concise and seemingly on target. To quote him, loosely: "There is no secret sauce. We are constantly working to improve every area of our strategy. Our data is constantly being improved, our execution models are constantly being improved, our portfolio construction algorithms are constantly being improved . . . everything can always be better. We hire the right kinds of people, and we give them an environment in which they can relentlessly work to improve everything we do, little by little."

In closing, some years ago, I was building a training manual for my team, regarding how we do portfolio management at our firm. In it, I included a mind map[2] of our due diligence process. I share that with you here, in Exhibit 12.2. Our version of this process was optimized over the course of many years for our purposes and circumstances. I invite you to reflect on what your ideal version might be.

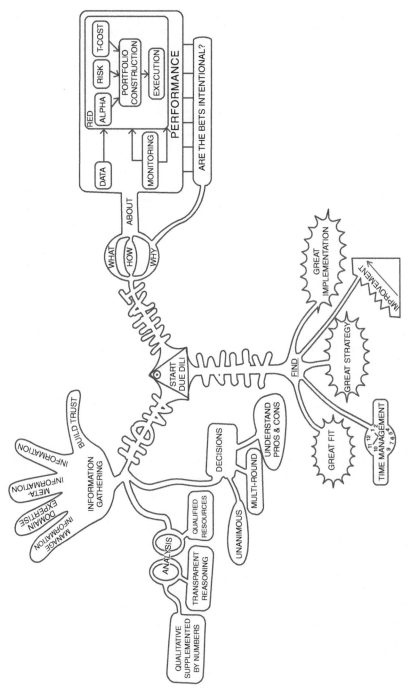

EXHIBIT 12.2 A Mind Map of the Investment Due Diligence Process

NOTES

1. Raymond F. Toliver, *The Interrogator: The Story of Hanns Scharff, Luftwaffe's Master Interrogator* (Atglen, PA: Schiffer Publishing, 1997).
2. The British author Tony Buzan popularized this concept, and I highly recommend his *The Mind Map Book* (London: BBC Active, 2009), but this nonlinear technique for visualizing information dates back at least to Porphyrius's third-century explications of Plato's teachings.

High-Speed and High-Frequency Trading

An Introduction to High-Speed and High-Frequency Trading*

I'm so fast that last night I turned off the switch in my hotel room and was in bed before the room was dark.

—Muhammad Ali

In early 2009, with markets fresh off of a harrying near-Depression experience, news reports began to circulate that among the few winners in financial markets in 2008 was a new breed of trading firms—so secretive as to make quant trading shops look like glass houses—called high-frequency traders (HFTs). It didn't take long for the press, regulators, and some financial firms to begin telling a highly biased, basically fictional tale about high-frequency traders.

Following these stories (which immediately prompted a chorus of cries of "no fair") came an unfortunate incident involving a programmer, Sergey Aleynikov. Aleynikov had left Goldman Sachs to join a then-newly-launched HFT firm called Teza (which itself was formed by former Citadel traders). He was arrested in early July 2009 and accused of stealing code from Goldman to bring with him to Teza. What was most alarming to the public about this case had nothing to do with Aleynikov, Goldman, or Teza (intellectual property theft cases are almost never of interest to the broader public). The prosecuting attorney—in an effort to add weight to Goldman's allegations—said that the software that was allegedly stolen could be used

---

* Important conceptual, empirical, and editorial contributions were made by Manoj Narang throughout Part IV of this book. However, all of the writing was done by Rishi K. Narang, and all opinions contained herein are solely his own.

to "manipulate markets in unfair ways."[1] This was eye-catching for many, because it linked high-frequency trading with market manipulation. Aleynikov ended up being convicted, but had his conviction overturned and vacated by an appeals court after almost three years of appeals and jail time. But the damage was done and the stage was set.

On May 6, 2010, U.S. Equity markets collapsed and recovered dramatically. There was more than a 1,000-point drop in the Dow Jones, with about 600 points of the drop occurring in a five-minute period that afternoon. This was followed by a fierce rally, which wiped out most of the 600-point loss in only 20 minutes. The high-speed nature of this meltdown and recovery came to be known as "the Flash Crash." The Flash Crash was widely blamed on HFTs, though often for contradictory reasons. Some claimed that HFTs caused the crash by virtue of their trades. Others claimed that HFTs caused the crash because they stopped trading once the markets became too panicked. We will address these claims in more detail in Chapter 16, but for now, it suffices to say that the Flash Crash was a major contributor to negative popular opinion about a topic that almost no one understands.

As of 2022, HFTs participate in about 50 percent of all U.S. equity transactions, and about 35 percent of all European equity transactions.[2] But they are active in virtually all markets, including futures, options, cryptocurrencies, foreign exchange, credit, treasuries, and even more esoteric markets like sports betting. One research report pegs the total revenue from HFTs globally at about $8.5 billion in 2021.[3] My own informal survey puts the number quite a bit higher in 2023, likely almost $20 billion. The firms participating in this space are mostly unknown to lay people and even to many financial professionals. Some of the largest in the world are Citadel Securities, Jump, Virtu, Tower Research, Hudson River, DRW, Optiver, Final, and Istra.

So what is high-frequency trading? Just as Parts One and Two showed that quant trading is not some monolithic idea but contains an enormously diverse constituency, it turns out that HFT is not a well-defined, homogeneous activity either. There are multiple kinds of high-frequency traders. But a definition that probably contains most of these kinds of traders is as follows: *High-frequency traders (a) require a high-speed trading infrastructure, (b) have investment time horizons less than one day, and (c) generally try to end the day with no positions whatsoever*. The fastest HFTs (sometimes referred to as ultra-high-frequency traders, or UHFTs) will no doubt scoff at the notion that someone who holds positions for as much as six and a half hours should be considered high frequency. But there is an important distinction between overnight risk and intraday risk, as most news pertaining to tradable instruments (particularly equities) comes out when markets are closed. Any further attempt to narrow down the holding period of an HFT strategy would seem arbitrary: what makes one second "HFT," while one minute is not? Furthermore, our definition specifies that the strategy should require a high-speed infrastructure.

It is worth knowing, however, that HFTs share the high-speed trading infrastructure mentioned above (and described in detail in Chapter 14) with many kinds of algorithmic traders. And high-speed infrastructure does not have only one speed. As we will see in Chapter 14, the challenges facing engineers of such infrastructure are substantial, and in few instances does any "industry standard" exist to meet those challenges.

Within the algorithmic trading community, people tend to think of the users of high-speed infrastructure as falling into four categories: UHFTs, HFTs, medium-frequency traders (MFTs), and algorithmic execution engines. But all of these approaches tend to share commonalities in terms of the definition above (though algorithmic execution engines generally attempt to help acquire longer-term positions, the algorithm itself is usually not interested in what happens tomorrow). As was famously said by Supreme Court Justice Potter Stewart in 1964, "I shall not today attempt further to define the kinds of material I understand to be embraced within that shorthand description; and perhaps I could never succeed in intelligibly doing so. But I know it when I see it..." He was talking about hard-core pornography, of course, but the exact same sentiment applies (in more ways than it should) to HFT.

This act of definition is important for a variety of reasons. First, it allows us to have a common footing when discussing the topic. Second, there are implications to any definition, including this one. This definition of HFT implies that there are several important characteristics of HFTs. First, since HFTs tend to end the day with no positions ("flat," in industry lingo), their buying and selling activity tends to exactly offset. However many shares or contracts were bought of a given instrument had to have been sold as well, otherwise there would be a net position at the end of the day. Second, since there is a desire to be flat at the end of the day, an HFT strategy likely does not seek to accumulate large positions intraday.

As we showed in Chapter 7, accumulating large positions incurs large market impact costs. Unwinding such positions would cause further market impact costs. With an intraday holding period, there is not enough price movement on a typical day to offset the market impact of buying, plus the market impact of selling. Furthermore, since HFTs cannot accumulate large positions, and since price movements during the trading day are of limited magnitude, HFT strategies generally have fairly low profit margins. They must pay the same kinds of costs as other investors and traders—commissions, market impact, and regulatory fees, for example—but they participate in relatively small price moves that occur over very short durations. There are economic incentives associated with higher volumes of trading (such as exchange rebates for providing liquidity or cheaper commission rates from brokers), but the fact is that margins remain very low, and the aggregate cost of technology, commissions, and regulatory fees is usually a large multiple of the net profits after these costs.

Multiple sources have pegged the profitability of an HFT strategy in U.S. equities (in relatively good times) at approximately $0.001 per share (1/10th of a penny). It is instructive to compare this to SEC regulatory fees of $22.40 per million dollars sold. This fee translates to about $0.006 per share for a $70 per share stock, though it applies only to sales. Since HFTs tend to buy as much as they sell, we can divide the fee by two to get a figure that applies to every HFT transaction, and we arrive at a typical SEC fee of approximately $0.003 per share, which is about triple the profit margin for a typical U.S. equity HFT.

It is also worth understanding that an HFT that trades 100,000,000 shares per day is responsible for almost 1 percent of U.S. equity volumes. Its profit, at $0.001 per share, is about $100,000 per day, which comes to $26 million per year. If we multiply this by the 50 percent estimate of the share of HFT volumes versus overall market volumes, we get $1.3 billion in total trading profits for the entire HFT industry for an entire year in the largest equity market in the world. Again, to reconcile these numbers with the larger overall revenue and profit figures industry-wide, one must remember that they are trading in a vast array of markets and geographies.

The reality is that it also costs millions per year for every firm that tries to achieve these revenues, and there are a large number of firms that fail. And since there are a large number of firms competing, even a successful one that accounts for, say, 5 percent of the U.S. equity market's volumes (which would make them an extraordinarily successful outlier) is making something like $65 million per year in revenues, before accounting for the extensive technological, operational, compliance, and human resource costs that are required to compete.

To put this into perspective, Apple, Inc. reported that, for the *quarter* ending June 30, 2023, they had revenues of over $82 *billion* (fun note: this figure is 134 percent higher than it was 11 years ago for the same quarter). One might argue that Apple, the largest market-capitalization in the world at the moment (this was also true 11 years ago), makes an unfair comparison. But even United States Steel Corporation (NYSE:X), a modest $8 billion market cap company at this writing, had quarterly revenues of just over $5 billion for the same quarter as Apple's above (and this is down a little over 20 percent from a year earlier). By comparison, the total revenue I estimated earlier this year across *all* of the largest U.S.-based HFTs (across all of their activities in all markets around the world) combined comes to less than $5 billion per quarter—and about ~$1.75 billion of this alone is attributed to just one firm, Citadel Securities.

In summary, there is clearly "real money" to be made in HFT. However, in the grand scheme of things, HFT revenues are miniscule in comparison to the revenues of many other kinds of companies. Armed with this definition of HFT, and the background knowledge of the economic scope of this activity, we will proceed to explain many aspects of HFT. In Chapter 14, we will explain high-speed trading, which is the basic toolkit for all HFT activity—and a large percentage of all other kinds of trading as well. In Chapter 15, we will outline HFT strategies and explain how they relate to the concepts introduced in Chapter 14. In the Appendix, we will address some of the controversy surrounding HFT and separate truth from myth.

NOTES

1. David Glovin and Christine Harper, "Goldman Trading-Code Investment Put at Risk by Theft," Blooomberg.com, July 6, 2009.
2. Khairul Zharif Zaharudin, Martin R. Young, and Wei-Huei Hsu, "High-Frequency Trading: Definition, Implications, and Controversies," *Journal of Economic Surveys*, 36(1) (2022): 75–107. https://doi.org/10.1111/joes.12434
3. "High-Frequency Trading Market Size in 2023: Growth Opportunities and Future Outlook 2030," 360ResearchReports.com, September 10, 2023.

CHAPTER 14

High-Speed Trading

In skating over thin ice our safety is in our speed.
—Ralph Waldo Emerson

As we delve into the subject of high-frequency trading, we must first clarify a number of important topics. Foremost among these is the difference between high-*speed* trading and high-*frequency* trading. These two concepts are conflated almost continuously by the press, by regulators, and even by reasonably savvy investors. And it is understandable, because the first, which is necessary and inevitable, gives rise very naturally to the second. So high-speed trading and high-frequency trading are cousins, but not synonymous.

High-speed trading is also known as low-latency trading. It refers to the need, on the part of various types of traders, to access the markets with minimal delays, and to be able to act on decisions with minimal delays. In this chapter, we will address why speed is important for many kinds of traders, far beyond high-frequency traders (HFTs), and also what the sources of latency are and how they can be addressed.

Speed has always, throughout the history of any marketplace, been an important part of separating weaker competitors from stronger ones. There is a good, self-evident reason that equity trading firms and brokerage houses established themselves near the exchanges in New York, and that futures trading firms located themselves near the exchanges in Chicago. The same thing can be found in almost every market center in almost every instrument class around the world. Physical proximity is a good start at being fast, and so is having fast communications between market centers. In 1815, Rothschild Bank in London famously used carrier pigeons to find out about Napoleon having lost the battle of Waterloo. They used this information to go short French bonds and made an enormous sum of money. The founder of Reuters, one of the world's leading news and data vendors, got his start in 1845 by setting up a carrier pigeon network in London, and within five years, his service was the lowest-latency source of information about what was happening in Parisian bourses.[1]

14.1 WHY SPEED MATTERS

In modern electronic markets, the best way to understand why speed matters is to see how it matters for various kinds of orders. After all, regardless of the types of alpha, risk, or portfolio construction models, orders are how strategies get implemented. While there are many kinds of orders—especially when we account for all of the various kinds of exchanges around the world—orders can generally be understood as being passive or being active. Furthermore, some orders (passive ones) can be canceled once they are placed. As such, we will describe the three broad cases that capture most of the world's order types as: placing passive orders, placing aggressive orders, and canceling passive orders.

First, a few definitions: *passive orders* are limit orders that cannot be immediately filled. For example, if the best offer on XYZ is 100 shares at $100.01, and a trader enters a limit order to buy 100 shares of XYZ at $100.00 or lower, this is a passive order, because it cannot be immediately filled. An order is labeled aggressive because it is immediately actionable. In most markets, passive orders are aggregated into an exchange's "limit order book," which shows all of the passive orders for a given ticker on the exchange at a single point in time. An illustration of an order book might look something like Exhibit 14.1.

For this hypothetical market, the limit order book shows a price/time priority. This means that the highest priority goes to orders at the best price (highest price for a buy order and lowest price for a sell order). If two orders have the same price, then the time at which they arrived at market is the tie-breaker. Other markets (e.g., Eurodollar futures) have a price/size

EXHIBIT 14.1 Mockup of an Order Book for a Fictitious Ticker

ID	Size	Bid	Offer	Size	ID
Bid1	55	100.00	100.01	2,000	Offer1
Bid2	1,000	100.00	100.02	2,950	Offer2
Bid3	3,100	99.99	100.02	600	Offer3
Bid4	200	99.99	100.03	300	Offer4
Bid5	5,000	99.98	100.04	1,000	Offer5

prioritization, which puts larger orders at a higher priority than smaller orders at the same price (the best price would always be the first test).

Aggressive orders are immediately actionable orders. There are two major types of aggressive orders. Market orders are always aggressive, because they are instructions to buy (or sell) a specific amount, without regard to price. Thus, if the limit order book looks like Exhibit 14.1, and a market order is entered to buy 3,000 shares, there would be two separate fills. First, the market order would use up the 2,000 share offer at $100.01 (Offer1), and then the market order would use up 1,000 of the shares offered at $100.02 (Offer2). Immediately after this trade, assuming no other orders have been filled, the order book would be as shown in Exhibit 14.2.

A second type of aggressive order would be a limit order made at the best offered price (for a buy order). Building from Exhibit 14.2, a limit order to sell 1,000 shares at $100.00 would use up the first 55 shares bid at $100.00, and 945 of the next 1,000 shares bid at $100.00. The order book would now be as shown in Exhibit 14.3, assuming no other orders came in.

In this example, 55 shares (which were from Exch1 in the original example) were filled first, and then the sell order was exhausted by taking 945 of the Exch2's bid at $100.00, leaving 55 shares at $100.00 as the new best bid. This limit order to sell was aggressive, because it was immediately actionable.

EXHIBIT 14.2 Mockup of an Order Book for a Fictitious Ticker After a Large Market Order to Buy

ID	Size	Bid	Offer	Size	ID
Bid1	55	100.00	100.02	1,950	Offer2
Bid2	1,000	100.00	100.02	600	Offer3
Bid3	3,100	99.99	100.03	300	Offer4
Bid4	200	99.99	100.04	1,000	Offer5
Bid5	5,000	99.98			

EXHIBIT 14.3 Mockup of an Order Book for a Fictitious Ticker after a Limit Order to Sell at the Bid

ID	Size	Bid	Offer	Size	ID
Bid2	55	100.00	100.02	1,950	Offer2
Bid3	3,100	99.99	100.02	600	Offer3
Bid4	200	99.99	100.03	300	Offer4
Bid5	5,000	99.98	100.04	1,000	Offer5

A couple of other terms that bear definition are *joining* and *improving*. To join implies that one adds to the size of the best bid (or offer), which is also known as the first level of the order book, or the inside market. An example of joining is shown in Exhibit 14.4, in which we imagine an additional 1,000 shares are added to the offer side of the book at $100.02 (Offer6).

We can see that this new order has a lower priority than the 600 shares that were previously offered at $100.02 (Offer3), because it came in later. This is obviously always true of an order to join: it will always have a lower time-priority. Orders to join are also always passive as they are not immediately actionable.

Finally, we illustrate improving in Exhibit 14.5. Here, we see a new passive limit order to sell (Offer7) which narrows the bid/offer spread by improving the best offer price from $100.02 to $100.01. Because it has the best price of any offer, it receives the highest priority, even though it is the most recent of all of them.

Note that many practitioners tend to confuse passive orders with the notion of providing liquidity, and aggressive orders with the notion of taking liquidity. It is an understandable mistake, because liquidity is often

EXHIBIT 14.4   Mockup of an Order Book for a Fictitious Ticker after a Limit Order to Sell, which Joins the Best Offer

ID	Size	Bid	Offer	Size	ID
Bid2	55	100.00	100.02	1,950	Offer2
Bid3	3,100	99.99	100.02	600	Offer3
Bid4	200	99.99	100.02	1,000	Offer6
Bid5	5,000	99.98	100.03	300	Offer4
			100.04	1,000	Offer5

EXHIBIT 14.5   Mockup of an Order Book for a Fictitious Ticker after a Limit Order to Sell, which Improves the Best Offer

ID	Size	Bid	Offer	Size	ID
Bid2	55	100.00	100.01	2,000	Offer7
Bid3	3,100	99.99	100.02	1,950	Offer2
Bid4	200	99.99	100.02	600	Offer3
Bid5	5,000	99.98	100.02	1,000	Offer6
			100.03	300	Offer4
			100.04	1,000	Offer5

confused with either volume or the size of the order book. However, as we learned from both the flash crash and the August 2007 quant liquidation, increased volumes do not always imply increased liquidity. In fact, in both instances, imbalances in the volumes of buys versus sells led to incredible illiquidity for anyone on the wrong side of those moves (e.g., owners of SPY who wanted to sell into the downdraft on May 6, 2010). On the other hand, aggressive orders to buy units at a time when there are many sellers might be extremely additive to liquidity, even if they technically remove units from the order book. It is our view that this confusion stems from an inaccurate definition of liquidity, and this is itself understandable. Even peer-reviewed academic journals have inconsistent definitions of liquidity, so it is clearly a concept that can be defined many ways.

We define *liquidity* at any point in time as being the *immediate availability of units to be transacted at a fair price*. This is a useful definition because it accounts for all of the important dimensions of the topic—immediacy, size, and a fair price—without being plagued by the problems associated with volume or order book-dominated approaches. It allows us to understand that an execution strategy to acquire a huge position mostly passively is still removing liquidity from the market. On the other hand, an aggressive order, which nominally reduces the number of units in the order book, is sometimes adding liquidity, if it helps push prices toward a fairer level.

Fairness of price deserves a brief explanation. Here, we refer to a price as fair if (1) it is broadly reflective of the fundamentals of the instrument's underlying economic exposure, or (2) it is sensible with regard to other instruments that are similar to it. For example, imagine some company is massively profitable, growing nicely, and trading around $100 per share. If nothing changes in its business, and the price immediately drops to $2 per share, it is highly improbable that the test of fairness was met. In this case, we could say that this company's stock became illiquid when the price moved so far without reason. As to the second test, if the index that the company is a part of, or if the other companies in its sector are moving in a similar way, then the price may well be fair (we will explain this last concept in more detail when we describe HFT arbitrage strategies in Chapter 15).

With this background, we can now illustrate the importance of speed for passive orders to buy, passive orders to sell, and cancelations of passive orders. There is a single, unifying theme that bears mentioning, and it is known as *adverse selection*. This is a concept that has broad applications in finance (and life). Imagine that we post a job listing for a role that sounds perfectly standard. However, the compensation we offer is extremely low relative to other similar job openings that are on the market. It is probable that we will receive resumes mainly from below-average candidates. This is because few self-respecting candidates would apply for an under-paying job.

The better candidates, and even most of the average candidates, will apply for the other job openings. And we, rather than drawing a random distribution of good, bad and average candidates, will be biasing our candidate pool toward the bad side.

Just so, in trading, adverse selection is a significant problem which specifically relates to speed.

14.1.1 The Need for Speed in Placing Passive Orders

Any time one places a passive order there is a risk of adverse selection. Consider what is really happening when you place a passive order: you're showing the world that you're willing to buy, for example, some number of shares of XYZ at $100.00. A prospective seller knows this (because your bid is in the order book), but you don't know what information this seller might possess. That seller's information might make you rue buying those shares. Of course, passive orders give the trader the opportunity to earn the bid-offer spread. Furthermore, some exchanges pay rebates for filled passive orders, and posters of passive orders can earn additional profit by virtue of these rebates. According to internal research conducted by Tradeworx, it is estimated that the average return of all passive orders on the most liquid stocks (above $50 million in dollar volume per day) for the year 2010 was approximately −0.2 cents per share. This assumes that one can exit the trade at no cost (at the mid-market price, which is the simple average of the best bid and the best offer, without regard to the size of the bid or offer) *one minute* after entering it. In other words, buying the bid and selling the offer is a money-losing proposition in the absence of liquidity provision rebates.

So where does the need for speed come into play? Let's start with another imaginary order book for XYZ, as shown in Exhibit 14.6.

Imagine that you place an order to buy 1,000 shares of XYZ at $100.00 (Bid4). Further, let's imagine that there are a large number of shares bid just after yours at the same price (Bid5). This is shown in Exhibit 14.7.

EXHIBIT 14.6 Mockup of an Order Book for a Fictitious Ticker

ID	Size	Bid	Offer	Size	ID
Bid1	3,100	99.99	100.01	2,000	Offer1
Bid2	200	99.99	100.02	2,950	Offer2
Bid3	5,000	99.98	100.02	600	Offer3
			100.03	300	Offer4
			100.04	1,000	Offer5

EXHIBIT 14.7 Mockup of an Order Book for a Fictitious Ticker with Additional Bids

ID	Size	Bid	Offer	Size	ID
Bid4	1,000	100.00	100.01	2,000	Offer1
Bid5	6,000	100.00	100.02	2,950	Offer2
Bid1	3,100	99.99	100.02	600	Offer3
Bid2	200	99.99	100.03	300	Offer4
Bid3	5,000	99.98	100.04	1,000	Offer5

If an aggressive order comes into the market to sell 1,000 shares, you will be filled, and you are now long 1,000 shares of XYZ at $100.00. However, the best bid remains $100.00, because there were other orders behind you indicating a willingness to buy at $100.00. Here, the odds are not bad that you bought at a good price, at least in the extreme near term. This is illustrated in Exhibit 14.8.

But now let's imagine that you place the same 1,000 share order to buy XYZ, and instead of being at the top of the queue, your order is the last one in the book at $100.00, with thousands of shares in front of you. Orders to sell come into the market, and eventually, yours ends up being filled. But now, the best bid is lower, at $0.99 (Bid1), and most likely, the best offer is $100.00 (Offer6). So, yes, you did technically buy at the bid, but the bid immediately went down and the price you received immediately became the subsequent best offer. This is shown in Exhibit 14.9.

The impact of queue placement was examined empirically by Tradeworx. They found that there is approximately a 1.7 cents per share difference in the profitability of being first versus being last at a given price. This is a truly staggering figure, considering that all passive orders average roughly −0.2 cents per share.

EXHIBIT 14.8 Mockup of an Order Book for a Fictitious Ticker After 1,000 Shares Have Been Removed from the Bid

ID	Size	Bid	Offer	Size	ID
Bid5	6,000	100.00	100.01	2,000	Offer1
Bid1	3,100	99.99	100.02	2,950	Offer2
Bid2	200	99.99	100.02	600	Offer3
Bid3	5,000	99.98	100.03	300	Offer4
			100.04	1,000	Offer5

EXHIBIT 14.9   Mockup of an Order Book for a Fictitious Ticker after All $100.00 Shares Have Been Removed from the Bid

ID	Size	Bid	Offer	Size	ID
Bid1	3,100	99.99	100.00	2,000	Offer6
Bid2	200	99.99	100.01	2,000	Offer1
Bid3	5,000	99.98	100.02	2,950	Offer2
			100.02	600	Offer3
			100.03	300	Offer4
			100.04	1,000	Offer5

Thus, when placing any passive order, it is clear that speed is important to the near-term profitability of the trade. It has been argued by some that long-term investors (who hold positions for years and hope for profits on the order of dollars per share) should not care about the loss of a penny or two per share by virtue of being a slow, passive trader. But this is an over-simplification. A pension fund with a multi-year time horizon is making a mistake if it ignores the cost of trading, especially if the number of shares transacted is very large. On the other hand, reaching the top tier of speed for a given market costs a great deal of money, and this does not get factored into simple calculations of cents per share. So there is clearly a tradeoff, and the need for speed among passive orders is a function of:

1. Adverse selection metrics (such as those described here)
2. Volume of shares traded
3. The cost of building and maintaining top-tier speed.

Typically, the smaller and longer-term the investor, the less is the need for higher speed. However, for many strategies (including quantitative alpha strategies, such as those described in this book) and many sophisticated large long-term funds, transaction volumes are sufficiently high as to warrant at least some investment in faster speeds. This explains the boom in the institutional execution technology business that has occurred since approximately 2007.

14.1.2   The Need for Speed in Placing Aggressive Orders

Traders placing aggressive orders are willing to pay the bid-offer spread because they have a reason to get the trade done with more certainty. As we have already shown, there are two kinds of aggressive orders. One is an aggressive limit order, which interacts with an order already resting in the limit order book. The other is a market order. The need for speed is different in each situation, and we will detail both.

In the case of an aggressive limit order, speed is important because you are specifying the price at which you are willing to trade, but others may beat you to that price. As such, the price can move away from you before you are able to complete your trade. Let us begin again with the order book shown in Exhibit 14.6. Imagine that two traders each want to buy 2,000 shares at $100.01 and they both enter limit orders to that effect. The first order to reach the market will interact with the resting $100.01 offer for 2,000 shares. The second offer will not get filled immediately, but will become the new best bid at $100.01 (Bid4). This is illustrated in Exhibit 14.10.

The new best bid belongs to the second order. The first bid interacted with the $100.01 offer of 2,000 shares and was filled completely. If the price continues to climb, and the trader whose order came to market second continues to lag behind other participants, one of three scenarios may apply to his order: (1) it will be filled at $100.01 but is subject to adverse selection biases; (2) it will be filled at a higher price if he cancels and replaces with a higher-priced bid; or (3) it will end up not being filled at all. In any case, this is a bad outcome versus simply having been the first one to bid $100.01.

The second case is that of a market order. Here, we do not have to worry about getting filled, as market orders will basically always be filled. However, with market orders we have very little control over the price of the fill. Speed matters here because a slowly-transmitted market order suffers from adverse selection. If our order to buy is slow in reaching the market, it is less likely that there are other buyers immediately behind us, and we will most likely end up with a worse fill than had we been faster. (This is similar to adverse selection in limit orders.)

In addition, market orders also unfortunately have slippage issues. Let's imagine our order is to buy 2,000 shares of XYZ, and that the order book is that of Exhibit 14.6. Here, if another trader's order (a limit order to buy 2,000 shares at $100.01, or a market order to buy 2,000 shares regardless of price) reaches the queue and gets filled first, our market order incurs

EXHIBIT 14.10 Mockup of an Order Book for a Fictitious Ticker After Two 2,000 Share Bids at $100.01

ID	Size	Bid	Offer	Size	ID
Bid4	2,000	100.01	100.02	2,950	Offer2
Bid1	3,100	99.99	100.02	600	Offer3
Bid2	200	99.99	100.03	300	Offer4
Bid3	5,000	99.98	100.04	1,000	Offer5

slippage and will be filled at $100.02. This may not be a total disaster in a slow-moving market, but as we have seen in any very fast-moving market, getting filled first can have extremely large consequences in the slippage we pay. What's more, the greater the accuracy of the forecasts (from the alpha model) that drove the desire to trade in the first place, the larger our concern over slippage is. After all, a more accurate forecast is more likely to move in the direction we expect, which means that our best trading ideas are also the most important to implement well, when utilizing market orders.

14.1.3   The Need for Speed in Canceling Passive Orders

The cancelation of passive orders that have already been placed is also highly sensitive to latency. If I send a passive limit order to sell 2,000 shares of XYZ at $100.00, this order is simply added to the order book. Let's imagine that the current best offer is to sell at $99.98, two cents better than my offer. I might expect that my order will eventually get filled by virtue of some small fluctuation in XYZ's price. After all, my order is only approximately 0.02 percent away from the current best offer. However, if the market begins moving quickly (as it has a tendency to do at the most inopportune times), it is highly likely that my order will have the same adverse selection problem as any high-latency order that gets placed. Thus, though I would want to lift my order as quickly as possible, by the time I succeed in doing so, XYZ might well be on its way up to well above my $100.00 offer price. Exhibit 14.10 and the accompanying text illustrate this kind of situation. If I'd been able to cancel the 2,000 share order at $100.00 quickly enough and replace it with an offer at $100.01, I would have saved myself money in this scenario. Similarly, if similar or correlated instruments begin to rally (e.g., due to some favorable macroeconomic news), it is highly probable that my offer will be lifted and the price at which I sold at would be inferior to what I could have sold at if I was (1) aware of the upward pressure in these other instruments, and (2) fast enough to cancel my current offer and replace it with a higher-priced one.

Perhaps on one 2,000 share order, this difference is not something I care about. But to repeatedly suffer from adverse selection by virtue of a slow cancelation capability will no doubt cost me dearly over the course of a year. There is some controversy regarding the rate of cancelations in U.S. equities (and some other markets), which we will address in Chapter 16.

14.2   SOURCES OF LATENCY

Having established that it is clearly important for any trader responsible for a reasonably large amount of volume to have access to a low-latency trading platform, we now turn our attention to the potential sources of latency that can be controlled by the trader, and what can be done about each of these sources of latency.

14.2.1   Transmission to and from Market Centers

The first potential source of delay for an algorithmic execution engine comes from the time it takes to get data from and orders to market centers. Much of the work of a good execution engine involves reacting quickly to changes in the marketplace; having as close to a real-time access to those changes is logically the first order of business. Furthermore, getting your orders to the exchange soon after you've decided what to do allows orders to be fresh (as opposed to stale, which is what practitioners call orders that haven't been refreshed very recently).

Information coming from or going to a given venue will arrive fastest if it is going to a location that is physically near the exchange's matching engine itself. The *matching engine* is the software used by the exchange to time-stamp and prioritize all inbound orders, provide the logic that puts buyers and sellers together, and broadcast the data about all of this activity. This software is physically housed on servers in various data centers (there is usually one data center per exchange). These data centers almost always openly offer space within the same physical location to anyone willing to pay for it. When a trading firm colocates its server (which contains its trading algorithms) in the same facility as an exchange's matching engine, the connection between its server and that matching engine is known as a "cross-connect." In some cases—either because a facility does not allow colocation or because it is too expensive to colocate in a large number of data centers—quants can elect to host nearby (with nearby being a totally arbitrary term here). This is known as "proximity hosting."

The difference between being near the exchange and being far away can be material in terms of making sure that the orders that are driven off of that data don't suffer from adverse selection. To put some metrics on it, imagine that a given market's data center is in New York. Rather than colocating your servers alongside the exchange's matching engine in New York, you choose to put your servers in San Francisco. A reasonable expectation of the time for information to travel on a relatively fast fiber optic connection between New York and San Francisco is about 50 milliseconds each way, or about 100 milliseconds round trip. To make a decision and place an order, information has to travel from the exchange to your servers and back to the exchange. Thus the total time needed to place an order is about 100 milliseconds. (It will take some time to process and handle this information, but let's assume that this time is negligible for now. It is in any case a constant whether you colocate in New York or use a data center in San Francisco.)

A lot can happen within these 100 milliseconds. For example, in the space of 100 milliseconds there are between zero and more than 40 messages (at the 99th percentile) posted to the various order books for EBAY (just to take a single example).[2] The largest number of messages are posted during the more liquid times of day. This implies that almost any sensible trading algorithm will concentrate its activities during the times when the number of messages is highest. If your trading algorithm located in San Francisco trades during these times, your orders will be very far behind other orders given the 100 millisecond delay. For this reason, we care far more about the message rate and activity at the 99th percentile than we do about the median level, for example. This is an effect we will describe in more detail in Section 14.2.5.

It also bears mentioning that data handling software, order generation software, and everything in between reside on servers. These servers must be located somewhere. One possibility is to locate them on your own premises. In addition to the problem with latency described above, an office building rarely has adequate power, cooling (servers generate an extreme amount of heat), network speed, and emergency backup capabilities to ensure continuity. As such, most people locate expensive, mission-critical servers in data centers (also known as colocation facilities). If you're going to colocate a server, the least arbitrary and most useful place to do so is at or near the exchange.

14.2.2 Transmission between Market Centers

Another potential source of latency for an algorithmic execution algorithm comes from the aggregation of data between market centers. Even for a single instrument class there are often multiple venues on which to transact these securities. For example, in the case of U.S. equities, there are 13 different official exchanges on which investors can trade, and dozens more (approximately 70 as of the writing of this book) dark pools as well. When information arrives from multiple venues, it has to be aggregated into one big set of data. (Although there are services that consolidate the data for you, these consolidated data feeds contain substantial latency. It is far better to consolidate the data yourself, if you can do it well.) We will address the issue of consolidation separately, but in order to consolidate the data, all of the data has to be in one place physically. The connections between the various exchanges can be visualized as a "mesh." As in Section 14.2.1, the further away a given market's various data centers are from one another in the mesh, the more natural latency there is in the system, and the harder it is to consolidate all of the data into one place physically. All of the points made in Section 14.2.2 apply here: the further away a given market's various data centers are from one another, the more natural latency there will be, and the harder it is to solve this problem.

Let us further look at the problem of consolidating data between market centers. Many strategies look across instrument classes to make trades. For example, most market makers in U.S. equities (which generally trade in the vicinity of New York City) are very keen to know, with minimal latency, what the S&P E-Mini futures contract (called the "ES" futures contract) is doing in Chicago. This is because the ES tends to lead both the SPY (an extremely important ETF that tracks the S&P 500 index) and the independently traded constituents of the S&P 500 index.[3]

The most important long-distance problems in the finance world are getting information back and forth between Chicago and New York, and between New York and London.[4] Data travel at the speed of light, but the problem is that one must transmit data over some medium. Data can't be beamed through the air (in the form of light) in a "straight line" over thousands of miles due to the curvature of the Earth and a wide variety of potential physical obstacles along the way (e.g., buildings, airplanes, birds). If this were somehow possible, it would take just under four milliseconds for data to reach New York from Chicago (and vice versa). As of the writing of this book, a typical commercially available solution for low-latency communications between Chicago and New York has a one-way latency of seven to eight milliseconds. This is over a fiber optic network, which (1) transmits data through glass (the material that fiber optics are essentially made from), and (2) is somewhat circuitous, as there is no telecommunications company with a direct route between Chicago and New York. Light travels about 1.3 times faster through the air than through glass—this explains some of the extra latency. The indirect route a conventional fiber optic network takes between Chicago and New York explains most of the rest, and the small remainder is attributable to sub-optimal hardware.

To solve this problem, a company called Spread Networks undertook a fascinating endeavor to make a much more direct path between Chicago and New York. They leased and bought tracts of land along this path, and found the straightest path possible (cutting through mountains in some cases). They used the best equipment that money could buy. They reportedly employed 126 four-person crews to lay a one-inch-wide line. Ultimately they reduced the distance over which light had to travel by more than 100 miles.[5] In order to use their service (which immediately "sold out"), customers had to sign multi-year contracts rumored to cost on the order of $10 million. In exchange, the one-way latency between Chicago and New York was reduced to about 6.5 milliseconds—1 millisecond faster than the more conventional telecommunications solution described earlier.

But this "arms race to zero" (as the pursuit of minimum latency is less-than-affectionately known) scarcely ended with Spread Networks' unveiling. McKay Brothers launched a microwave solution (which bounces microwave transmissions between towers) in a still-quicker path between Chicago and New York. McKay's solution has a one-way latency of around 4.5 milliseconds. These latencies are achievable because microwaves tend to move faster through the air than photons move through glass (as with fiber optic cables).[6] For a fascinating and extremely in-depth look at microwave towers, their history, and their use in trading, I recommend "Sniper in Mahwah & Friends" blog.[7]

There is some light (no pun intended) at the end of the tunnel, however. The arms race to zero appears to be nearing an end. The potentially-faster microwave solution may not be as reliable as a closely monitored, dedicated fiber optic line, due to weather and other factors. Furthermore, the amount of information that can be transmitted via microwave is also quite small.

The "state-of-the-art" connection between London and New York for some years was Global Crossing's AC-1 transatlantic cable, with one-way transmissions with approximately 65 milliseconds of latency. However, Hibernia Atlantic spent some $300 million laying a transatlantic fiber optic cable which allows for one-way latencies of 59.6 milliseconds. This translates into a latency reduction of approximately 5 milliseconds.[8] The line was activated in May 2012, and reportedly was sold out far in advance to a handful of trading customers. To my knowledge, it remains the fastest line between London and New York.

Other routes have also been optimized, such as between London and Frankfurt, and various Asian markets. In general, the utility for reducing latency in communication between various markets (really, data centers) can be understood to be driven by the relationship between the instruments being traded in those disparate places. The importance of the Chicago-New York connection is related to the fact that the S&P 500 e-mini futures (the most liquid futures contract in the world) is traded in Chicago, while the underlying stocks trade in New York. There is not only a direct, one-to-one correspondence between the weighted sum of the underlying stocks in the index and the futures contract, as well as various ETFs that derive from the S&P 500 index, but also many indirect relationships as well. To the extent that you can garner a speed advantage in having the most relevant information quickly, you stand a better chance of profiting from these relationships.

14.2.3 Building Order Books

The data that a given exchange broadcasts to traders are actually in the form of messages (new orders, cancelations, and trades), not in the form of an order book. It is the job of the quant to build an order book from these messages. This turns out to be a very challenging task. In order to have an accurate order book at a given point in the day, every message from the beginning of the day onward must be processed. There can be no dropped messages. Furthermore, this processing has to be very fast, otherwise latency is introduced. As we all know, there is a tradeoff between speed and accuracy that is difficult to overcome. And this is no exception. Worse still, there are a number of algorithmic solutions that solve this problem, and none are considered "industry standard."

A subtler part of this problem (which relates to our next topic) is timestamping. Each stream of messages from each exchange has its own timestamp. It is crucial to have the sequence of these messages accurately recorded as well. So, not only are we processing the messages themselves, but the timestamps of each message.

14.2.4 Consolidating Order Books

For markets that are fragmented (as in the case of U.S. equities), we have multiple streams of messages that need to be aggregated into one consolidated order book. The challenges described above are compounded by the task of combining these multiple information sources correctly. For example, even if we have an accurate order book for two different exchanges on which XYZ is traded, and even if we have the messages correctly ordered for each of these two, there can still be problems. The messages from the second exchange may be presented to us with greater latency than the first, and this must be accounted for when building the consolidated order book. Otherwise, it will appear that things happened in a sequence that is incorrect.

14.2.5 Data Bursts

One of the most significant (and somewhat unique) challenges facing someone building a high-speed trading infrastructure is the fact that messages do not arrive at an even rate throughout the day. This is an extremely sneaky problem that bears some discussion.

The pioneers of the mathematics of traffic engineering were involved in engineering telephone networks. They assumed that rates of consumption of bandwidth would be basically stationary within some reasonable interval, like minutes or seconds. There is a concept in mathematics called the Poisson-distribution (after a French statistician who invented it in the nineteenth century) that is tailor-made for this application. This assumption made sense in engineering phone networks, where average rates could be assumed to be stationary over some intervals. For example, Mother's Day has an incredibly high average call rate, but basically you could assume that call arrival rate was constant and calls arrived independently over the busiest hour on Mother's Day.

However, in trading, the very action of one person trading causes another to take action (e.g., in the placement or cancelation of orders). This results in a positive feedback loop, and there is absolutely no stationarity in the message rates inside anything that a normal person would consider a reasonable period. To further elaborate, the average of the message arrival rate in the 1-second time frame tells you very little about the arrival rate in the 1-millisecond time frame.

Let's return to the example of EBAY. Exhibit 14.11 shows the number of messages at various percentiles, for various slices of time from 1 second down to 1 millisecond.

What is most interesting about Exhibit 14.11 is that it shows directly and empirically how non-stationary the message rates are. At each percentile, you would expect to see 1/10th the number of messages in one row as in the preceding row. For example, if there are 259 messages per 1 second at the 99th percentile, you would expect to see about 26 messages per 100 milliseconds (because there are 10 separate 100-millisecond periods in each second). Instead, we see that there are 13 messages at the 99th percentile per 100 milliseconds. By contrast, when we get out to the 99.99th percentile, the situation is dramatically different. There are 1755 messages per second in the top 0.01 percent of seconds in the trading day. Thus, you might expect to see 176 or so messages per 100 milliseconds at the top 0.01 percent of millisecond periods during the same trading day. Instead, we see 863, about five times the expectation.

Comparing 1-second intervals to 1-millisecond intervals is even more interesting. At the 99.99th percentile, you would expect about 2 messages per 1 millisecond, given the number of messages at the 99.99th percentile per 1 second (1755 divided by 1000—the number of milliseconds in a single second—is 1.755, which is close enough to 2). In reality, we find that the

EXHIBIT 14.11 Breakdown of Messages at Various Intervals and Percentiles for EBAY on July 20, 2012

	50th Percentile	99th Percentile	99.9th Percentile	99.99th Percentile	99.999th Percentile
1 second	13	259	546	1755	4179
100 milliseconds	0	13	84	863	1306
10 milliseconds	0	1	7	269	557
1 millisecond	0	0	1	56	106

number of messages per 1 millisecond at the 99.99th percentile is 56! Even comparing message rates per 10 milliseconds to message rates per 1 millisecond yields surprising results (around double the number of messages are transmitted at the 1-millisecond level versus what you would expect from looking at the 10-millisecond level.

While it may seem strange to focus on something that happens far less than 1 percent of the time, consider that there are about 23.4 million milliseconds in a day. This means that there are 234,000 observations that occur with 1 percent probability during the day. So a system that is designed to capture "only" 99 percent of all messages transmitted during the day means missing the busiest 234,000 milliseconds worth of data. This should self-evidently be a massive problem for any algorithmic system. There are 2,340 millisecond intervals that comprise the busiest 0.01 percent of observations in a single trading day. This is a huge number. Whereas the tails of the distribution of messages per 10 seconds are relatively well behaved, the tails of the distribution of messages per millisecond are incredibly badly behaved.

Why is this a problem? Because if you are trying to engineer a system to be responsive at a given time scale, you need to be able to handle arrival rates at around the same time scale. So if you only care about millisecond response times, then you can be satisfied with understanding and handling the message rates at the 1-millisecond level. But if you care (as many high-frequency traders do) about tenths of a millisecond, you must be able to handle message arrival rates at the level of tenths of a millisecond. Here the variability is of course even greater. Compounding the problem is the fact that there is a seasonality of busy-ness within each day. On a typical day, the period just before the close is the busiest and the period just after the open is the second busiest. Otherwise things are fairly quiet. This means that on a typical day you have to handle outlier amounts of data simultaneously across all tickers. And during other busy times (e.g. after a Federal Reserve rate announcement or some other big news), the same data-burst problem re-occurs.

A quant system that is able to handle these problems must deal with potential problems in any number of areas: the cross-connect between the server and the exchange's matching engine, the network switch, connections between facilities, the data feed handler, or the code that is used to build an order book—just to name a few. Moreover, bursts of data that might have been handled individually could become overwhelming as one aggregates order books from multiple exchanges.

And if this wasn't enough of challenge already, the models used by HFTs to process the data and come up with trading signals add latency. It takes time to decide exactly what to do. The preferred approach of implementing trading signals is to split them up across multiple servers. But this in itself is a further challenge. There are issues with hardware, software, and network engineering. How do you distribute consolidated data in a timely manner to various servers, for example, when each server is charged with computing and running the actual trading strategy? Distributing data to various servers adds varying amounts of latency. The better one handles these kinds of issues, the less latency introduced during data bursts. The worse one handles them, the more latency there is during times of high message traffic.

14.2.6   Signal Construction

Once data have been properly handled and distributed, a reaction to that data needs to be properly constructed and implemented. Broadly speaking, we can define two categories of strategies that can be implemented within such a system: execution algorithms (covered in Chapter 7) and an HFT strategy. These strategies can be widely varying in the degree of their complexity. For example, an HFT strategy attempting to control for risk factors continuously throughout the day would obviously be more complex than an alpha model with an intraday time horizon but no risk management. Even alpha models with intraday horizons can vary tremendously in their complexity. (We will detail the kinds of strategies that HFTs employ in Chapter 15.) But even if we take two exactly identical HFT strategies, there are (in most cases) multiple algorithms that can be used to calculate the signals. And not all of these algorithms are equally fast.

To give an example, index arbitrage is a widely-known HFT strategy. This strategy involves trading the value of the SPY ETF against the values of the 500 stocks that comprise it. (Note that index arbitrage can be traded on any index versus its constituents, and we use the SPY simply as an illustrative and well-known example.) If you know that the S&P 500 index consists of 500 stocks and 500 weights, you should be able to compute a "bottom-up" estimate of the value of the S&P index. If, however, you find that the actual value of the SPY ETF, after accounting for expense ratios and other similar structural differences between the ETF and a basket of stocks, is trading at a different value, then theoretically free money is to be had by virtue of buying whichever side is under-valued and selling short whichever side is over-valued. However, as you might imagine, there's a lot of competition for free money. This means that you have to make decisions about what is over- or under-valued very quickly. As simple as it sounds, comparing the SPY ETF to the basket of stocks that comprise it is not trivial. There are a number of algorithmic solutions for this, and they don't all do the computations equally fast.

As a sidebar, it is this kind of strategy that you often see in HFT. Very simple ideas, very simple calculations, but which require astoundingly fast infrastructure to actually capture. It is therefore very ironic when we hear the press talk about "sophisticated, complicated algorithms." The difficulty is not in understanding what's being done, but in doing it very quickly.

14.2.7 Risk Checks

The last step before sending an order to the marketplace (in some markets, such as U.S. equities) is submitting the order to what's known as a regulatory risk check. Regulators (under the Market Access Rule) have indicated that broker-dealers (who give trading firms access to the marketplace) are responsible for ensuring that each trade is (1) within the means of the trader, (2) not in error, and (3) compliant with regulatory requirements. They also mandate that the risk-checking software should be in the full and exclusive control of the broker-dealer whose customer is trying to make a trade. This rule was adopted in July 2011 as a response to criticism of HFT and concerns over the stability of a marketplace without such rules. Elaborating a bit further on the kinds of things that need to be checked before an order is sent to market:

- Does the trader's buying power allow for the order(s) in question to be made?
- Does the number of open orders seem to be valid, or does it appear that the trader has a bug that leads to an excessive number of open orders?
- Does this individual trade seem too large to be intentional?

Prior to the adoption of the Market Access Rule, most broker-dealers operated in accordance with the rule anyway. But a small number of very high-volume trading firms operated differently. These firms engaged in what is called "naked access." This meant that customers of the broker-dealer were allowed direct access to the market if the broker was ultimately comfortable enough (after performing many checks of their own) with the client's risk-checking technology. Why does this matter? Because a risk check provided by the broker generally resides on a broker's server. For a trade to go through a risk check, it must be transmitted by the customer to the broker before going out to the market.

This added "hop" (in network engineering terms) adds more latency for two reasons. First, there is another connection between servers that must take place (between the customer's trading server and the broker's risk-checking server). Second, the broker's risk-checking software is generally going to be inferior to that designed by a speed-sensitive trader. This could be for any number of reasons, including the presence of superior talent at the best HFT or quant trading firms versus the typical brokerage firm, or simply different goals.

The broker generally cares a lot more about issues like scalability than being hyper-fast. By contrast, speed-obsessed HFT engineers (who are willing to tackle all the issues above) want the "tick-to-trade" total latency to be as little as 10 microseconds (0.1 milliseconds). They are scarcely going to be satisfied with an added risk-check latency of 50 microseconds.

Thus, some HFT firms opted to send their trades directly to the exchange after utilizing their own in-house risk checks. Not many brokers were willing to accept an arrangement like that because the broker ultimately bears responsibility if there is a problem with the customer's risk check. However some brokers made a business of providing naked access to HFTs, and these firms definitely enjoyed a speed advantage for several years. With the Market Access Rule, the SEC banned this practice, and now one must use a broker-dealer's risk check. This drove some of the largest HFTs to build out their own broker-dealer units so that they could continue to use their own risk checks with additional regulatory overhead. It also drove a new arms race to create the fastest commercial risk checks. As of today's writing, there are roughly three top-tier solutions; the others lag well behind. Solving the "risk check problem" remains an area where some HFTs (and, primarily, their service providers) focus on reducing latency.

14.3 SUMMARY

In this chapter, we have elaborated on the reasons that high-speed (or low-latency) trading matters, as well as the sources of latency. Depending on the type of trade or trading strategy being implemented, there are differing reasons for the emphasis on speed. And, while this has received a significant amount of negative attention in the press, it is absolutely no different than in any other industry. If an advantage can be developed within the rules of a competitive game, then the most competitive players will seek to develop that edge. But, as is the case for quant trading in general, there is clearly a double standard when it comes to HFT and low-latency trading. People seem to be really angry that HFTs, having solved the incredibly difficult problems enumerated above, have achieved a (completely legal, ethical, and fair) competitive advantage over other traders.

The irony, as we will discuss further in the Appendix, is that low-latency trading is like any other enterprise in a reasonably free-enterprise system: taking risk does not imply that one will succeed. Countless HFTs have invested enormous sums of time and money into infrastructure, only to find that they lack the ability simply to generate acceptable returns. Many more HFTs either cannot afford the huge investment of resources, or simply lack the expertise, to create their own infrastructure. A typical "build versus buy" decision is made, and some firms end up utilizing commercial vendors for many or all parts of this infrastructure. Some firms advertise themselves as "HFT-in-a-box" solutions, which allow a strategist with a good idea to implement her strategy without having to build all of these other elements. Unfortunately, few of these vendors deliver what is advertised (just as is true in basically any industry). The result is that when the opportunities to add value are the most plentiful (when trading activity is at its most frenzied level), relatively few vendors are able to deliver true low-latency solutions. To quote Mike Beller, CTO of Tradeworx, "Be suspicious of anyone who quotes averages, or even averages and standard deviations. Responsible people engineer for the 99th percentile."

Even firms that have the resources and that have been successful are subject to substantial risks. While detractors of HFT have pointed to the near-death experience of Knight Capital in 2012 as evidence that HFTs cause instability in the markets, the reality is extremely different: Knight made a change to its software that introduced a bug. It was a mistake of their own doing. And who suffered? Knight. They nearly went out of business and had to secure emergency funding to stay afloat, at the expense of a large portion of the value of their business. While it's sad for Knight and those who own their stock, it is exactly fair. Knight made a mistake, and Knight paid the price. No "mom and pop" investors, no pensioners, no market systems were harmed. And all of this is in pursuit of what amounts to a $0.001 per share profit expectation.

This point is perhaps the most important to remember. A tenth of a penny per share is the expected profit margin of a *successful* U.S. equity high-frequency trader. In exchange for this, these traders take on the risks associated with the capital and time expenditures of competing in a hyper-competitive space. For traders who are expecting to hold positions for a year and make 25 percent or more on that trade, HFTs add liquidity. That they might make $0.001 per share to provide that liquidity is both inconsequential and totally fair. We now turn to the kinds of strategies that HFTs employ.

NOTES

1. Christopher Steiner, "Wall Street's Speed War," *Forbes*, September 27, 2010.
2. All message traffic statistics in this section are courtesy of Tradeworx, Inc. proprietary research, September 2012.
3. In case you were wondering *why* the ES futures tend to lead SPY ETFs, the reason is primarily that the ES futures are where the largest dollar volumes exist. This is probably for two reasons. The first is that ES futures have been around

a lot longer than SPY ETFs, so some of this is just incumbency, both because of habit (once an instrument becomes the instrument of choice for a given exposure, it tends to retain that title with a large amount of inertia on its side), and because it is a pain in the neck to change one's infrastructure to trade stocks (ETFs are listed and traded the same way as stocks, for all intents and purposes) when one is already trading futures. Second, the futures markets do offer a couple of structural advantages over ETFs. Profits on many futures contracts are subject to less onerous taxes than profits on equity or ETF trades. Also, futures contracts offer a fairly substantial amount of leverage, so whether a trader wants to make a big bet or simply doesn't want to spend a lot of money to put on that bet, futures can be an efficient way to implement the trade. However, the gap has been narrowing somewhat, driven by the migration of retail investors away from actively managed mutual funds into passive ETFs, and partially by virtue of the fact that, in many ways, the ETFs are often cheaper (in aggregate) to transact.

4. It is worth noting that, while New York is the city we associate with the U.S. stock market, the realities of the amount of real estate needed for the massive data centers that house stock exchanges are actually mostly located in New Jersey.

5. Melissa Harris, "Some High-Speed Traders Convinced Microwave Dishes Serve Up Bigger Returns," chicagotribune.com, August 19, 2012.

6. Jerry Adler, "Raging Bulls: How Wall Street Got Addicted to Light-Speed Trading," wired.com, August 3, 2012.

7. https://sniperinmahwah.wordpress.com/

8. Matthew Philips, "Stock Trading Is About to Get 5.2 Milliseconds Faster," bloomberg.com, March 29, 2012.

CHAPTER **15**

High-Frequency Trading

If you have a mouse in your hand, you are too late!
—Blair Hull, December 2000

We have described the importance of, components of, and challenges to building a high-speed (low-latency) trading infrastructure. These components are used, primarily, for either HFT applications or for implementing automated execution algorithms. In this chapter, we will focus on HFT, seeking to understand the kinds of strategies employed by these traders and how these techniques relate to the infrastructure we have outlined.

There is no widely accepted classification of HFT strategies. However, we can consider them to fall into one of four broad categories: contractual market making, non-contractual market making, arbitrage, and fast alpha. In this chapter, we will describe each of these kinds of strategies, as well as the risk management and portfolio construction considerations that apply to them.

The types of edges that a successful HFT might have include all of those that pertain to non-HFT quants, but we should add/emphasize one additional type, bringing the total to four: the investment process, a lack of competition, something structural, and technology. We have sufficiently covered the topic of a technology edge in Chapter 14, but it bears discussing how these types of edges typically map to various kinds of HFTs. We will include this information in each subsection below.

15.1 CONTRACTUAL MARKET MAKING

A contractual market maker (CMM) is the class of HFT practitioner that has the closest analog to a traditional feature of the markets. First, we should understand the concept of market making.

The odds that two customers simultaneously want to do exactly opposite things (e.g., customer A wants to buy 2,000 shares of XYZ at $100.00,
while customer B wants to sell 2,000 shares of XYZ at $100.00) are fairly
small. Of course, it is reasonably likely that there is at least some portion of
a customer's desired trade that could be filled by another customer. Taking
our example above, maybe customer A wants to buy 2,000 shares, while
customer B wants to sell 5,000 shares. The balance—a desired sale of 3,000
shares—either goes unfilled until a later time (usually at a time adverse to
the seller), or it can be filled by an intermediary who is willing to take the
risk of buying 3,000 shares for the sole reason that customer B wants to sell
them. Market makers are precisely this kind of intermediary: they provide
liquidity to those who have a utility for it.

An analogy from daily life is useful here. Manufacturers rarely sell their
goods directly to retail customers because, practically speaking, they have
operations lifecycles to manage. They cannot afford to change how much
and what they are supplying at the whims of retail customers. Thus, distributors buy goods from manufacturers and warehouse those goods until
the retail market is ready for them. In the same way, market participants
don't necessarily take investment decisions that coincide perfectly, and market makers get paid to warehouse the risk in the interim.

There are two types of market makers. In this section, we will describe
CMMs, who are sometimes referred to as "order flow internalizers." The
first key to understanding CMMs is to look at the economic and contractual
relationships that CMMs have with the market. The CMM's obligations
vary by market, instrument, and geography, but we can examine U.S. equity
market making as one example. CMMs engage in legal relationships with
various brokerage firms (whose clients wish to make trades), so that the
brokerage routes its customers' orders to the market maker to be executed.
In exchange for the broker sending its retail order flow to the CMM, the
CMM often is required to: (1) pay the broker[1] and (2) fill 100 percent of the
orders that customers send to it. Generally, this last obligation has two different types of commitments to fill: one in the case of small orders and one
in the case of large orders.

CMMs in U.S. equities generally are required to fill 100 percent of
"small" orders on an automated basis (this is aptly known as "autofill").
So, for example, a typical investor in U.S. equities has an account with some
online broker. This investor decides to buy, say, 200 shares of XYZ as a market order. The CMM has agreed with the broker that it will sell 200 shares
of XYZ to this customer at whatever the prevailing market's best offer is.
But interestingly, neither the customer's order to buy nor the CMM's taking
the other side of that trade ever goes into the exchange's limit order book.

The transaction happens away from the exchanges, but it references the activity that is taking place on the exchanges (specifically, the best bid or offer).

The CMM, by virtue of having agreed to this contractual relationship with the broker, gains an advantage that supersedes even the fastest traders. In effect, it doesn't even need to post bids and offers because it passively takes the other side of all customer order flow as it comes in. This happens in the reverse sequence than in a normal market situation: generally a passive order is resting in the limit order book and an active order comes into the market later and takes the liquidity offered by the passive order. In this case, the active order to buy comes to the CMM, and the CMM uses the prevailing best offer from the exchanges to fill the active order. While the CMM's orders are not actually in the queue, there is always at least some support behind their positions. After all, the CMM is piggybacking on whatever the prevailing best offer was at the time the CMM elected to fill the customer order. All that said, so far, it is not at all obvious that the customer is any worse off by virtue of his broker having established this contractual relationship. The customer's order is filled at the prevailing best price available and does not need to compete with other active orders.

We contended in Chapter 14 that trading passively is not necessarily a highly profitable activity (especially before the incentives provided by some exchanges for providing liquidity), because of the problem of adverse selection. However, when facing off against retail order flow, a passive participant enjoys the most favorable selection possible. Retail order flow generally consists of a large number of small orders, and the aggregate of these orders on a given name is usually a fairly small net quantity. This means that there is unlikely to be any significant price impact, which is another important determinant of the level of adverse selection.

For larger orders, CMMs generally have the right to act as an agent of the customer, trying to get the order filled at market, without taking the whole order for itself. So, if the customer wants to buy 10,000 shares of XYZ, the market maker acts on behalf of the customer in attempting to get the order filled. However, here, a perverse incentive may exist. At the very least, it is quite an interesting situation. Let's start with an illustrative order book for XYZ, immediately before the customer's 10,000 share buy order comes in, shown in Exhibit 15.1.

If we imagine the 10,000 share buy order comes in at this moment, the CMM can go to market, lift all 2,000 shares offered at $100.01 (Offer1) and all 4,000 shares at $100.02 (the sum of Offer2 and Offer3). He has now filled 6,000 shares at an average price of $100.0167. Then he can take, say, 3,500 shares of the 4,000 offered at $100.03 (Offer4), and fill the last

EXHIBIT 15.1 Mockup of an Order Book for a Fictitious Ticker

ID	Size	Bid	Offer	Size	ID
Bid1	1,000	100.00	100.01	2,000	Offer1
Bid2	3,100	99.99	100.02	3,000	Offer2
Bid3	2,000	99.99	100.02	1,000	Offer3
Bid4	5,000	99.98	100.03	4,000	Offer4
Bid5	6,000	99.97	100.04	1,000	Offer5

EXHIBIT 15.2 Mockup of an Order Book for a Fictitious Ticker after a Market Order to Buy 10,000 Shares Is Mostly Filled by a CMM Acting as an Agent of the Customer

ID	Size	Bid	Offer	Size	ID
Bid1	1,000	100.00	100.03	500	Offer4
Bid2	3,100	99.99	100.04	1,000	Offer5
Bid3	2,000	99.99			
Bid4	5,000	99.98			
Bid5	6,000	99.97			

500 shares himself. Now that the prevailing best offer is $100.03, he will fill them at $100.03. The order book immediately after this order is filled looks as shown in Exhibit 15.2.

Those first 9,500 shares offered had no idea that the price was about to move up by 2–3 cents immediately. So in this case, since the CMM knew that this customer's order was about to push the price up, he delayed selling until the buy order was almost exhausted. Those last 500 shares, however, are likely to have been profitable to sell. If there was no other buying pressure behind that 10,000 share buy order, the upward move is likely to be immediately reversed, and the offered side of the book is likely to replenish with lower-priced offers than $100.03. This will allow the CMM to exit his position at a profit, and at the expense of those traders whose orders were at lower-priced offers initially.

I mentioned that this is, at the least, an interesting dynamic. It may incentivize the CMM to act in a way that is adverse to the customer, however. If the CMM has the ability to act as an agent of the customer *and* to fill the last portion of a trade, the CMM has an incentive to do the worst possible job of filling the bulk of the customer's order, because it pushes the price to a level that almost certainly makes taking the other side of it very attractive. In other words, the CMM could use a horribly ineffective execution strategy for the first 9,500 shares, specifically designed to get the customer the worst possible price (especially on the last few hundred shares), so that the CMM can come in and take those last few hundred shares into his own inventory at an untenably high price.

Exchanges have begun to fight back against internalization of order flow. Interestingly, the near-destruction of Knight Capital in August 2012 was an indirect result of the NYSE's introduction of a new program designed specifically to combat order flow internalization. This program, called the Retail Liquidity Program (RLP), offers retail orders access to better fill prices than they historically could get. To deal with this change in the market structure, Knight made some changes to its own software. And due to a bug in that new release, Knight's brush with bankruptcy unfolded in merely a half-hour. It is not a coincidence that the roughly 140 stocks that Knight lost money on were all NYSE tickers. That said, programs such as the RLP are not intended to put CMMs out of business. Indeed, thus far, the biggest participants in such programs are the CMMs themselves. The idea is simply to get as much share volume on the lit venues as possible.

As we relate the activities of CMMs to what we showed in Chapter 14 about high-speed trading and the various types of orders, we can see clearly why CMMs need to be fast. While they do not need to compete with other participants for better queue placement in order to get into a position (this comes to them from the brokerage firms directly), they do need: (1) to have a precise, timely estimate of the market in order to fill orders at the correct price; and (2) to be able to exit positions rapidly. They, after all, are taking on the other side of others' trades. And while retail orders may not be the worst kind to take the other side of, there is still a real risk that retail participants move heavily in one direction on a given instrument (e.g., if there is good news about XYZ, our fictitious ticker example, many customers are likely to want to buy it). This can result in the market maker taking on a significant amount of size on the wrong side of the news and short-term momentum in such an instrument, which highlights the need for speed in placing orders to reduce the inventory acquired. All that said, a CMM's need for speed is categorically not at the same level as it is among the HFTs we will describe in the subsequent sections of this chapter.

So how do edge types pertain to CMMs? CMMs typically rely on something structural—a business development edge at closing deals with aggregators of order flow (e.g., brokers and/or exchanges). They couple this with sufficient technology and investment process acumen to be able to deliver on their promises—typically price improvement for the customers of these aggregators and/or payment by the HFT to the aggregator for the order flow—while remaining profitable.

15.2 NON-CONTRACTUAL MARKET MAKING

Non-contractual market making (NCMM) also involves taking the other side of active orders. NCMMs provide bids and offers that rest in the order books of various exchanges, particularly lit exchanges (as described in Section 7.1.4). In many markets, they are incentivized to provide liquidity by virtue of liquidity provision rebates. In other markets, active order flow is sufficiently benign that a fast NCMM can still turn a profit even without any further compensation. In general, an NCMM acquires positions by placing passive orders, waiting for someone to lift his bid or offer. Once acquired, the NCMM may exit passively or actively, depending on liquidity provision rebates and the market's movements.

Given their reliance on passive orders, the biggest risk that any market maker is exposed to is adverse selection. A market maker taking the other side of one order can hope he is able to take the other side of another order immediately, and at a profit that at least equals the bid/offer spread. Or, if the market moves his way, he may be able to exit actively, and make money on the move. This is the embodiment of "buy low, sell high," but modified: "buy low, sell ever-so-slightly higher, very soon, and repeatedly." And indeed, in normal times, in the absence of a very short-term trend, this is at least somewhat achievable.

But first, there is the matter of being fast enough to avoid the adverse selection problems that plague any passive order in the lit markets. As we showed in Chapter 14, this is no small feat in the first place. When we look at the kinds of trades that NCMMs in U.S. equities take the other side of, for example, we find that most of the best order flow is internalized, either by CMMs or by dark pools. This leaves NCMMs to interact primarily with professional investors in the lit exchanges, against whose orders it is dangerous to trade. Thus, while speed matters to any market maker, NCMMs have a particularly acute need to be fast. As an aside, NCMMs do usually have access to dark exchanges as well, and often will route orders through these dark pools first, taking advantage of superior liquidity taking fees, before sending the remainder out to the lit exchanges.

Second, NCMMs must have fast access to information sets that can help them avoid adverse selection problems. We showed in Chapter 14 that the ability to cancel passive orders quickly is critical to a passive trader's likelihood of success. For example, if some stock index's futures contract is rallying sharply, there is a very strong probability that a wide variety of stocks will also rally sharply in the immediate future. A NCMM who cannot access information about the futures market in a timely manner will likely end up failing to cancel his passive offers at the top of the order book, which will cause him to experience adverse selection in the fills he receives on his sell-trades.

A key challenge for NCMMs is how to manage and dispose of the inventory they acquire by virtue of having other market participants lift their bids and offers. This can be particularly challenging when markets are trending, leaving the NCMM with large positions in the opposite direction of the trend. As mentioned earlier, NCMMs bear such substantial risks when holding positions that they sometimes actively exit their trades, even though this means crossing the bid-offer spread and possibly also paying a liquidity taking fee. Another approach to dealing with inventory risk is to take opposing positions in instruments that closely correlate with those in inventory. For example, if UVW is an imaginary company that is a peer of XYZ, in the same industry group, with a similar market capitalization (and so on), it is highly likely that any large, directional move in XYZ will be mirrored in UVW. Thus, if the market maker is filled on a passive bid in XYZ (which makes him long XYZ), his algorithms can consider putting passive offers on UVW, or actively selling it, to hedge his risk that XYZ experiences a large move.

Given the myriad difficulties facing NCMMs, they typically have to have strong edges in both technology and investment process to ensure they can deal with adverse selection on top of the other challenges facing any market maker.

15.3 ARBITRAGE

The word arbitrage connotes riskless profit. This has obvious appeal, and is equally obvious that risk-free profits are hard to come by. Arbitrage opportunities exist when instruments that are *structurally correlated* behave differently. We define structural correlation as a correlation that exists because it must. Instruments that track the S&P 500 index, for example, should all correlate roughly perfectly. If the S&P 500 futures contract (ES) is up 1.00 percent for today, while the SPY ETF (which tracks the S&P 500 also) is up only 0.60 percent, a riskless profit opportunity exists, to go short the futures and go long the ETF. In this way, the trader has virtually guaranteed himself a 0.40 percent profit. These two instruments are both meant to track the performance of the same 500 stocks, and when one is outperforming the other, it is necessarily because there are temporary imbalances in the trading of one versus the other. For example, if a large order to buy the futures suddenly hits the market, moving the futures contract up suddenly, it might take a small amount of time for the passive orders (both bids and offers) in the ETF to cancel and ratchet upward. During that time, a sufficiently fast arbitrageur can pick off a slow-to-cancel passive order and acquire a riskless profit position.

In order to qualify as a true arbitrage, a trade must capture an inefficiency in the marketplace that causes the price of an instrument (or derived version of the instrument) to be different in different locations (e.g., exchanges) or formats (e.g, an ETF versus the stocks that constitute that same ETF) at precisely the same moment. The arbitrageur sells the relatively overpriced one and buys the relatively underpriced one, so that when they converge, he reaps the profit.

The most common form of HFT arbitrage is *index arbitrage*, which is the broader label for our earlier example of S&P futures versus the SPY ETF. This is a strategy that compares the value of an instrument that tracks an index either to another instrument that tracks the same index, or to the value of the constituents of the same index. Take an imaginary futures contract that tracks an index which contains two instruments at a 50/50 weighting. The index can be priced either directly in the futures contract, or indirectly by taking the value of each of the constituents and multiplying that value by the weight (50 percent each, in our example). Because the index trades separately from its constituents (often on different exchanges), the prices of the index traded as a whole versus the index that can be created synthetically by buying its constituents in the correct weighting can and do diverge by small amounts and for short amounts of time.

Another type of arbitrage is *venue arbitrage*, which exists only in fragmented markets. A venue arbitrage takes advantage of a fragmented market structure (which means that there are multiple exchanges that allow trading on the same instrument), which can sometimes cause a price to be different on one venue than another. Here, the instrument isn't merely structurally correlated to another instrument, it is actually the *exact same* instrument traded in more than one place. For the same reason that index arbitrage opportunities can come to exist, these venue arbitrage opportunities also can exist. In U.S. equities, Reg NMS was enacted in 2007 in an attempt to deal with this problem. In certain other markets, venue arbitrage remains a possibility.

In a sense, when a CMM receives customer orders that include requests to buy and sell the same instrument at the same time, he has an arbitrage opportunity, because he can sell the instrument to one party and buy it from another at the same time, at different (advantageous) prices. The buy order is filled at the prevailing best offer, and the sell order is filled at the prevailing best bid (which, by definition, is lower than the offer). To address this extremely obvious inequity, some brokers have begun to require CMMs to fill both such customer orders at the best mid-price when there are matching and opposed orders.

While risk-free profits are undeniably attractive, the cost of remaining at the highest tier of the technological capabilities required to be fast enough to capture such opportunities is substantial. At first glance, it is evident that speed should matter, for the same reason that $100 bills don't get left on the street for very long. If you can cross the bid-offer spread and realize an arbitrage opportunity, then it makes sense to do so. But occasionally, depending on the size of the opportunity, passive orders can be used to improve returns. If the price discrepancy is very large, and if the exchange involved provide liquidity provision rebates, it may be an added benefit to implement an arbitrage trade using limit orders. But, in general, these are active trades. It is better to capture some riskless profit with 100 percent certainty than to risk missing the whole opportunity by trying to make it marginally better.

As a practical matter, not all HFT arbitrages are strictly riskless. In more efficient markets (e.g., U.S. equity indices and single stocks), it is often impossible to do both legs of the arbitrage trade. The opportunity is so fleeting that only one leg at a time can be implemented. So, for example, a strategy that compares ETFs to futures might be able to trade the ETFs only, betting on a lead-lag relationship between the instruments. But the futures might well move again before the trader can lock in a profit. This is still a good trading strategy, but on a given trade, its odds are not substantially better than even. In less efficient markets, there remain opportunities for truly riskless profit.

Arbitrageurs typically have to be extremely fast, thus depending on a technological edge primarily. This can sometimes bleed into a business development (structural) type of edge also—for example, one HFT I examined claimed to have a special relationship with Nvidia, the most prominent maker of GPUs, which are favored for very high-performance computing applications such as HFT. But it typically does not require a great deal of acumen to see if S&P 500 futures on the CME are trading out-of-sync with the SPY ETF.

15.4   FAST ALPHA

The fourth type of HFT strategy we will consider is *fast alpha*. Fast alpha strategies are in essence engaged in the same kinds of strategies as discussed in Chapter 3. They mainly use price-based signals, such as momentum, mean reversion, and technical sentiment. If we consider what we described in Chapter 8, regarding the influence of data types on the kinds of strategies that can be implemented using such data, it makes sense that this is the case. Fundamental information does not change very often. When it does, it usually takes some time (more than a day in most cases) to be fully priced-in. Furthermore, most fundamental information is released during after-hours or pre-trading sessions, when liquidity is poor. However, important (i.e., surprising) fundamental data do have an impact on prices on a very short (intraday) timescale. In 24-hour markets such as currencies, this can be even more true, though there are natural increases in liquidity during certain more conventional market hours. In any case, various growth or value types of strategies can be implemented on an intraday timescale, but this is in the tiny minority of cases. Mostly, fast alpha strategies act on information that changes frequently throughout the trading day: prices, volumes, and limit order book information. Because changes in fundamentals can result in high volumes, HFTs can be quite active when these changes occur, even if they are not explicitly trying to trade based on the fundamental information itself.

Contrasting fast alpha strategies with arbitrage strategies is also useful. Whereas arbitrage strategies are taking advantage of price discrepancies between instruments that are structurally correlated, fast alpha strategies are sometimes looking to profit from price discrepancies on a statistical basis. For example, if XYZ and UVW are two companies in the same industry group that are close peers, with similar market capitalizations and fundamental features, one would expect them to track each other most of the time. If XYZ diverges from UVW, you can reasonably expect that it should converge. But what if the divergence stems from some real information that implies the beginning of a de-coupling between XYZ and UVW? Just as we showed in the example of MER and SCHW in Chapter 10, instruments can go through periods of being closely correlated, and periods of being completely different. In other words, there is no structural reason that correlation between the two instruments must remain related. And, as a result, we are dealing with a statistical relationship, which by definition implies some risk.

This is also true for directional types of forecasts, which look at historical behavior as a guideline for future behavior. There may, for example, be a good chance that, if some instrument makes consecutive new intraday highs several seconds in a row, it will decline briefly thereafter. But this is still a matter of chance. There is no structural relationship between the past performance of the instrument and the future performance of the instrument that causes this setup to remain a return-generating strategy.

Some fast alpha strategies are more passive, for example, intraday versions of statistical arbitrage. They can be considered to be close cousins of NCMMs, in the sense that they are passively placing orders that provide liquidity, but perhaps with a certain selectivity that (hopefully) reduces adverse selection issues. For such strategies, everything we discussed in Chapter 14 regarding the need for speed in placing and canceling passive orders applies. Intraday momentum strategies can also be implemented passively, by canceling passive orders that would take the other side of the prevailing trend and working orders that would get the strategy into a position in the direction of the trend. Obviously, these orders are less likely to be executed, because they are attempting to capture small pullbacks in a trend. Furthermore, adverse selection issues apply, particularly when the trend reverses. As such, the need for speed here stems from a desire to get passive orders to the top of the book, and from the need to cancel stale passive orders to avoid adverse selection issues.

More often, intraday trend following is an actively implemented strategy. These strategies have a particularly difficult challenge because market impact and slippage are both working severely against the strategy's objectives. If an instrument is trending down on a very short timescale, a fast trend-following strategy will naturally want to get short that instrument (or instruments that closely correlate to it). However, any delay in processing data or getting orders back to the marketplace can be detrimental, because the market will not wait for a slow trader to figure out what to do. The trend can move the instrument away from the slow trader, resulting in large slippage costs. Furthermore, because the trader is desiring to buy (or sell) an instrument that has already been going up (or down) for some time, market impact costs are also likely to be more severe in this case. For these reasons, intraday trend following is less common than mean reversion-oriented trading strategies, and requires low-latency capabilities.

These practitioners depend very heavily on an investment-process edge, and the hurdle for being profitable with such an edge, given all the advantages that the other kinds of HFTs bring to bear, is substantial. They also cannot afford to have significant disadvantages in technology versus NCMMs in particular.

15.5 HFT RISK MANAGEMENT AND PORTFOLIO CONSTRUCTION

HFT strategies most often have a different approach to risk management than their slower peers, even for strategies (such as those in the fast alpha category) that share similar underlying themes. Accounting for risk factors, transaction cost models, and various other inputs to an optimizer, for example, takes precious computing time. This would slow down the process of implementing the alpha strategy. Furthermore, most of the kinds of risk factors that longer-term strategies would want to hedge rarely apply to security movements from one moment to the next intraday. For example, some longer-term traders care about neutralizing their exposure to the "size" factor (market capitalization, essentially). They don't want to have a bias of being long small capitalization companies and short large caps (or vice versa). Intraday, this is a dramatically less useful distinction, because the way that this risk factor expresses itself in the markets simply doesn't take place at an (often very short-term) intraday time scale. Another way of thinking of this effect is that statistical correlations are much weaker at shorter timescales than at longer ones, while idiosyncratic (primarily liquidity-driven) considerations are more significant.

There is a further question of applicability of risk models to three of the four types of HFT strategies described above. Arbitrage strategies, for example, clearly require a different type of risk management than is provided by a risk factor model. By design, long positions and short positions are in essentially identical instruments. This leaves no room for conventional risk factor exposures. The kinds of considerations that apply to arbitrageurs relate to sizing their bets to ensure that the temporary variances in the spread between their longs and shorts do not put them out of business. For CMMs and NCMMs, the goal is to unload inventory as quickly as possible, not to worry about risk factor exposures.

The most common approach to risk management for HFT strategies is to control a very small number of very simple-to-calculate risks. For example, limiting the maximum order size on a given ticker, the maximum accumulated position size for a given instrument, the maximum aggregate portfolio size, or the maximum number of open orders on an instrument (or in aggregate) are all very simple risk checks that add virtually no latency. Many will automatically unwind their portfolios and stop trading if they reach a certain predefined loss level. Some HFTs will elect to control their directional exposure as well, limiting their net long or short percentages. Most HFT strategies are concerned with ensuring that hedging trades are put on extremely quickly, and before prices move adversely. For example, if an arbitrage trader sees an opportunity to buy the S&P 500 index and short the underlying stocks, locking in some small profit, it is possible that both legs of this trade will not be implemented at precisely the same moment. After one leg is executed, the trader simply owns a directional bet on the stock market. It is not until the second leg is executed that the trade becomes an arbitrage (and risk-free). As such, if the market moves adversely to the first leg of the trade before the second leg can be put on, not only might the opportunity disappear, but money can easily be lost. This is known as *legging risk*, and many HFTs try to manage it.

Portfolio construction, too, looks very different for HFTs than for longer-term quants. The most obvious example of this is in the case of arbitrage trades. If you have an opportunity to make riskless profits, you should do that trade as large as the market will allow you to do. For both kinds of market makers, they have little control over how many of their passive orders end up being lifted by more active participants. For them, it comes down to simply ensuring that they diversify their risk across names, or to limiting the maximum size of inventory that can be accumulated (since whatever is accumulated must soon thereafter be dispensed). In the case of fast alpha strategies, there is no particularly common theme to how traders size positions. But they tend to use the simpler ideas from among those discussed in Chapter 6. Equal weighting positions, or weighting them based simply on the expected return, are common approaches. But considerations of covariance and volatility rarely factor in, and there is almost no sense in running an optimization or even accounting for risk and transaction cost modeling. All of these things add time to the process of making trades, and so simplifying the calculation of the strategy (as we discussed in Chapter 14) is an important way to reduce latency.

The most surprising thing about HFTs is that, while they trade (hyper) actively, they most often do not account for transactions cost models in their strategies. This seems paradoxical: if transaction cost models are supposed to help you trade in a smarter way, why would the very most active traders eschew them? In some sense, the transaction costs that other investors are paying (bid/offer spreads and liquidity taking fees) are often the main sources of alpha for many HFTs. As such, transaction costs as typically defined are very often negative: they are sources of profit. Obviously, it then becomes desirous to trade as often as possible. This is outside of a passive HFT's control, because they cannot cause someone else to trade actively, but it is an objective for a passive HFT nonetheless.

Active HFT strategies, by contrast, must overcome the same transaction costs as apply to other investors, but without the benefit of holding the position for a very long time. As you can imagine, not nearly as many opportunities exist to hold a position for a short amount of time, say, a few minutes, and generate a profit net of transaction costs. HFTs, thus, tend to consider commissions, regulatory fees and taxes, and the economics of providing or taking liquidity more than market impact and slippage.

15.6 SUMMARY

We have now explored the kinds of strategies that HFTs utilize. You may notice that there are some significant differences between HFT strategies and the kinds of alpha strategies that we described in Chapter 3. Indeed, many HFT practitioners, privately, will tell you they don't think about alpha at all. Even for those that do, it is most often at best secondary to technology concerns. A major risk is losing a speed advantage. And, when you look at both the kinds of strategies being employed and the penalties that accrue to being slow (which we described in Chapter 14), it begins to be clear why this is the case.

It does not take someone particularly clever to say that the S&P 500 index should have basically the same value in every instrument that tracks it.

This is a tautology, in fact. S&P 500 = S&P 500. But it is something else entirely to be able to profit from the extremely fleeting instances where there is a divergence. It is specifically a technological problem, and many of the strategies that HFTs employ are at least as much driven by technology as by a better way of forecasting the future.

NOTE

1. This practice is called "payment for order flow." It carries quite a bit of controversy, because the beneficiary of the payment for order flow is generally the broker, not the broker's customers. It is, of course, the customers who send orders. Despite the well-deserved controversy around this practice, it has remained rather prevalent, spurred on by a trend toward so-called zero-commission stock brokers. But it has been a feature of the capital markets for much longer than HFTs have existed.

CHAPTER 16

Looking to the Future of Quant Trading

All evolution in thought and conduct must at first appear as heresy and misconduct.

—George Bernard Shaw

Black-box investing has existed for over four decades. It is hopefully clearer to the reader that these strategies are not so much black boxes as much as systematic implementations of the kinds of things that human traders and investors have always done. Unfortunately, new things are most often received with a great deal of distress, early on. This is sometimes totally understandable, for example, when a person's occupation is being obviated by automation. Not only should we be concerned about the loss of livelihood in the moment, but also about how this individual can reinvent himself. Other times, ignorance is the main reason for fear. In either case, I believe that the backlash against quants is, at its core, a generational issue. We are just past a point of transition in our marketplace. Automation and computerization in the markets (as in many industries) have pretty much happened. And in the 10 years since I last wrote on this topic, most of those who were poorly equipped to participate profitably in the modern markets have been replaced by newer participants who are perfectly happy to participate in these markets.

I am not a futurist. That said, I see a few trends that bear watching.

16.1 BUSINESS MODELS

First, we address the ongoing and ever-evolving question of which business models are optimal for running a quant strategy. There are at least three distinct elements of this question.

16.1.1   Collaboration versus Competing Pods

The first is the extent to which research is conducted in a collaborative, centralized team versus in competing or at least segregated pods (this is the current industry slang for these silos). Proponents of either approach have valid arguments. Those favoring collaboration point to the benefit of all the great minds you have on your team working together toward solving problems, and also to the ability to align interests with the firm and its investors more effectively. They can also point to case studies of the most successful firms, such as Renaissance and PDT, for evidence. While these are strong arguments, those favoring pods can point to the benefit of diversification of thought, and of the benefit of competition to generating the best outcomes. And there are, in fact, examples, such as Cubist, of firms that have been extraordinarily successful while working in a primarily siloed way. It will be interesting to see how this plays out, but my guess is that the balance will tip toward collaboration.

16.1.2   Standalone Versus Platform

The second business model question is whether standalone quant funds—particularly startups—can compete with the larger, established firms (e.g., Two Sigma, Renaissance) and the multi-manager platforms (e.g., Cubist, Millennium). Let's say that some seasoned researcher has decided to leave her old firm. She has two options. One is to start her own fund, which involves raising capital from investors; finding office space, building relationships with brokers and other service providers; dealing with all the legal, operational, and compliance issues; and in many cases, hiring a team from scratch and rewriting code from scratch as well. The other is to join a platform, which would allow her to focus mostly on the last two issues listed above—which are the closest in kind to the competencies she has already demonstrated, which have put her in the position to have these two options in the first place.

While there are pros and cons to both, the biggest linchpin is often the question of raising capital from investors. As I write today, the situation in our industry has sadly devolved. Largely reputation-risk-averse investors have created a feast-or-famine setup for those seeking to raise capital for a new firm. If the founders are well regarded and come from firms that themselves have a sterling reputation, it is most often the case that such a startup will have many options. If the founders are somewhat unknown, their proposals are rarely evaluated on merits. There is simply no bid. As such, we see the majority of more prominent potential startups taking capital from investors directly, while the less prominent ones go to one or another platform.

There are, however, more layers of questions within this topic.

16.1.2.1 Small versus Large Can small quant funds compete, or has this niche evolved to the point where only those with the most resources can survive? We addressed this in Section 11.5. But, despite my strong opinions, this is not a settled debate. It is also somewhat clear that some minimum level of resource is required to sustain an edge over time, though there is no absolute level that one can reasonably point to. I do believe that it's fair to say that the sweet spot between nimbleness and resources is on the order of $1–10 billion of assets under management, though there is an enormous amount of good work (and commensurate results) being shown by managers with a fraction of the bottom of that range with which to work. I have not seen many (any?) examples of tremendously exciting strategies that are being run at sizes much above $10 billion, though I should clarify something here.

When I speak of exciting strategies, I am primarily referencing either high absolute return levels (e.g., 20 percent or higher, annualized) or high risk-adjusted-returns (e.g., Sharpe ratios above 2), over sustained periods of time. It is a very fair retort that, to generate a 1 Sharpe or a 15 percent annualized return on, say, $30 billion is a tremendously useful and impressive feat. But I don't believe anyone has cracked the problem of generating a high Sharpe on such large sizes, and I furthermore don't believe that there are more than a couple of firms (if even that many) that can boast even a 1 Sharpe on $30 billion.

In other words, size is not linearly beneficial. Instead, the size of assets under management should be sufficient to support the resources necessary to capture edge on the strategies being implemented on those assets. If a firm is trying to trade many strategies in many asset classes, at many time horizons and across many geographies, they will need a lot more resources than someone pursuing a limited number of strategies in one market and a not-particularly-resource-intensive time horizon.

16.1.2.2 A Platform by Any Other Name. . . Lastly, there are some interesting dynamics among the platforms themselves. They are not homogeneous in their approach, nor are they necessarily static over time. Some offer significant amounts of capital to a team, but not much (or any) infrastructure of any kind. They often have an initial period of exclusivity (three or five years is typical), after which the team may raise capital from other investors, with various provisos. Some require every portfolio manager (and their staff) to be full-time employees, who have no intellectual property rights to their work while employed. Others have less of a concern about employment and intellectual property, but only care about having exclusive access (indefinitely) to the capacity of the strategies being implemented. And still others may have preferences regarding these matters, but ultimately can be flexible, so long as the benefit justifies the risk. And the risk, in this case, is the extent to which the platform becomes viewed as simply a fund of funds.

There are also many approaches to hiring, retaining, and terminating portfolio managers among the platforms. Mostly, platforms utilize an unsurprising and unimaginative one: hire those who have attractive, verifiable track records (without much or any curiosity about any of the topics we discussed in Chapter 12). Allocate to them dynamically, in accordance with their recent performance (we call this, pejoratively, performance chasing). And fire them if they either have a drawdown that is in excess of some arbitrary upfront amount, or if their performance doesn't continue to meet some other arbitrary criteria.

This has worked well for ages in discretionary trading, whether on proprietary trading desks or multi-manager platforms. But in quant, it's a recipe for failure. This seems to be gaining some acceptance, though whether this method will become rare instead of nearly ubiquitous remains to be seen. Indeed, those platforms that have demonstrated any kind of sustained success have been headed by "native quants," who understand the importance of both selecting strategies with care, irrespective of their historical track records, developing talent and investing in the resources necessary to allow managers to improve strategies, and taking nuanced approaches to termination.

16.1.3 Build versus Buy

And, finally, we address the way that quants are considering the answer to the question of build versus buy. In most of the discrete parts of the black box, the answers are easy to see and justify. When it comes to data, risk models, portfolio construction models, and execution algorithms, the calculus looks like this: unless you are willing to put quite a lot of work into something special, there are adequate off-the-shelf solutions for these problems. T-cost models are analogous: a standard one is easy enough to build (no need to bother buying), but doing it in the most intelligent manner is quite a bit harder. Quants generally put most of their building effort into their alpha models and the research platforms that enable them to find these alpha models. Two things bear mentioning here, as provisos.

The first is that, in my experience, there are some very interesting things that most quants do not attempt to do in risk modeling, portfolio construction, and execution that aren't particularly hard to do. I have said since the first edition of this book that I find these are likely fruitful areas for research, and I remain convinced that this is the case. The exceptions to the generalization that quants haven't really done much that's interesting in the last 10 years in these three domains are few and far between.

The second is that the licensing of third-party alpha models to supplement and complement one's own is growing in popularity. And I think this, particularly juxtaposed with the dynamic raised in Section 16.1.2.1 relating to investor perception, is an interesting area to watch going forward. Many totally fine quant strategies run by totally fine quant firms are simply not gaining traction with investors. This is mostly because, ironically, they don't already have traction with investors—size begets size, as I am fond of saying. But at least a few of the platforms are headed by people who understand quant trading deeply. And as these platforms compete with each other, and with investors, for talent, these more savvy firms are snapping up those quant funds that are simply small because they are small. But there are a host of other non-investment reasons that there remain plentiful opportunities to find interesting capacity that is not being filled up. So this creates the supply side of the equation. The demand is coming from firms that have more capital than they have great in-house ideas with which to fill that capacity. If you can buy a well-thought-through version of some strategy that you haven't gotten around to developing internally—and you may not even have the right team members in place to adequately pursue it—why not at least consider finding one that might be available due to the inefficiency of the market for quant hedge fund capacity?

Another special case of this topic is that of crowdsourcing. WorldQuant used to talk openly about finding alpha strategies in far-flung parts of the globe, designed by hobbyists or amateurs who aren't employees and may work in domains such as farming as their day job. It is not clear they continue to seek out more such alphas, but the idea of crowdsourcing is clearly tempting. Estimize uses crowdsourcing pretty successfully for earnings predictions (and they, in turn, have some interesting datasets to offer quant funds). But crowdsourcing the alphas themselves has so far been an activity with mixed results. Some highly public efforts have failed and gone away. Others seem to be showing some promise at the time of this writing, but it is far too soon to tell if that is sustainable. And WorldQuant may have abandoned their effort in this regard. Whether it is currently a dead or dying approach or a quietly successful one, it is worth keeping an eye on.

16.2   MACHINE LEARNING AND ARTIFICIAL INTELLIGENCE

Machine-learning alpha strategies have been in use in our industry for more than 15 years, at the time of this writing. And these rely heavily on feature selection and engineering (which is a decidedly human endeavor), particularly for strategies with holding periods longer than about a day or two. Their use in other areas, such as the wrangling of unstructured datasets and allocating to alpha models, is nearly ubiquitous. And their use in execution algorithms and HFT alpha models is also widespread now. However, 2023 has seen what is either a hall-of-fame hype machine or, more likely, a major step forward in the artificial intelligence revolution that most experts agree is coming sooner than later. These tools will have further ramifications for practitioners, but probably marginal compared to what has already transpired.

But how will Large Language Models (LLMs), their more generalized counterparts—which do not yet exist in commercial production—Large Foundation Models (LFMs), and the even more distant prospect of General Artificial Intelligence change the work of the alpha researcher? I am aware of only one credible effort to utilize LLMs in the alpha process, and it is for a very short-term trading strategy. To me, until we get to General Super-Intelligence, all other data-driven approaches will struggle with the same problems that have plagued attempts to be a pure data miner in the capital markets. These are nonlinear, dynamic, adversarial systems, with a serious dearth of data and incredibly low signal-to-noise ratios. The aforementioned are the ingredients for a very high probability of failure in the task.

That said, many of the world's brightest data science minds are now, for better or worse, less focused on improving the targeting of consumer advertisements on social media, or even on problems in quant finance, and rather more focused on solving problems in machine learning. It is difficult to know how things will actually play out. My guess is as stated above, but this is absolutely an area worth watching.

16.3 EXPANSION INTO MORE ASSET CLASSES AND MARKETS

For a variety of reasons, quant strategies have been increasingly applied to more and more asset classes and geographical markets. For example, systematic investing in Chinese equities and futures was basically nonexistent when the second edition of this book came out, but now it is widespread (and being blamed by the Chinese authorities for weakness in the local market). Cryptocurrencies were in their infancy in 2013, but there are now both HFTs and quant funds operating in that domain very actively. This trend will likely only continue.

Assets such as water may be particularly interesting, given global warming. Less exotically (it feels ironic to refer to water as exotic, but in the sense of an asset for trading, I suppose it's an accurate label), I believe quants have not come close to cracking the code fully in asset classes like options or credit. Sports betting is also receiving a good amount more attention than it did previously.

I can also share two specific examples from my own experience. In 2021, AngelList (AL) Ventures launched one of the first (and still one of very few) systematic venture funds, this particular one focused on early-stage companies. I had the pleasure and privilege to work with the AL team on refining these models and getting the fund off the ground. It was a fascinating case study that will be difficult for other firms to replicate, because of the natural advantages AngelList has in the venture ecosystem. Specifically, AL has a fairly accurate, timestamped history of the prices of a huge portion of private companies that receive venture funding. Coupled with this, it has a sister company called Wellfound, which, alongside LinkedIn, is one of the largest job-hunting sites for early-stage companies.

Abe Othman, who headed AL's data science effort, came up with the clever idea that, if you want to see what the most promising companies are, you can follow the "best" talent. If folks that you would generally think are the most attractive candidates (they went to the best schools and worked at the best companies) are hyperactively sniffing at given company's job posting, it may be a good indicator that this company is onto something compelling. If they're ignoring another company's posting, perhaps this company's prospects are dimmer. Othman also did some interesting research around the optimal way to approach early-stage venture as an asset class. He found that it may be a superior strategy to invest very broadly in a large number of promising startups at small size than to worry about ownership percentages, being highly selective, or having rights to invest in follow-on rounds. All of these are pretty heretical views, and time will tell if Othman's research bears out, but either way, it is interesting to see quant methods being applied to what has historically been a decidedly discretionary activity.

Furthermore, I am personally aware that most, if not all, of the largest venture capital funds have been researching the idea of utilizing the huge proliferation of (effectively alt-)datasets to make their work either more systematic or perhaps entirely so.

Another fascinating project is in music royalties investing. One firm, currently on pause, developed a model to identify promising, emerging tracks on Spotify using solely play-count data. I won't share more details on their model, but it seemed to work quite well. They had plans to further explore more spectrographic data—beats per minute, chords, lyrics, and other features—to refine their approach further. Whether by them or others, this is another field that will very likely see more attention from systematic investors.

16.4   DIGITALIZATION AND DATASETS

It is worth briefly addressing something which has already been a huge trend in our industry: the explosion of datasets. As mentioned in Chapter 8, the alternative dataset industry has burgeoned substantially. Most large firms have individuals or teams whose sole function it is to search out new datasets. Some of the more novel strategies we discussed in the previous section are the result of these datasets. As I said, I'm not a futurist, so I am not sure what areas are next, but I do know that our world and all the information in it are rapidly becoming more and more digitized into datasets. Whether these datasets end up in the hands of quant firms is harder to forecast, but the number of opportunities to find new datasets is only going to continue to escalate.

Two potentially near-term examples are in healthcare data and B2B Software-as-a-Service (SaaS) purchase data. Healthcare data in the U.S. is protected by a set of regulations contained within HIPAA (which, true to form for a U.S. law, is inherently an insurance-related regulation, but contains far-reaching implications for the privacy of healthcare data). This presents a serious challenge to attempts to turn it into a dataset. However, the incentive is strong enough to do so that it is at least decently likely that some aggregated, anonymized data will come from the effort.

The B2B SaaS dataset would be, like many other new datasets, the exhaust from an industry's normal work. It would be data that one or more firms would have in the normal course of business—for example, a company that helps other companies rationalize their software stack—might have a lot of insight into the trends in software-as-a-service sales for companies like Intuit or Salesforce.

16.5   MAN AND MACHINE

This has been an area to watch, in my opinion, for more than 10 years, and it remains so. Whether in the role of humans in feature engineering for machine-learning-driven alphas, or in the role of portfolio construction algorithms in the position sizing for discretionary stock pickers, this is already something that quants and discretionary firms are exploring.

One fascinating, if only narrowly applicable, example, is Optios. Imagine any situation in which humans have to make relatively frequent, high-stress decisions. This could be in sports or the military, or in, say, discretionary day-trading. Optios has a portfolio of DARPA-funded intellectual property that is designed to help determine which of these decisions are likely to be successful, based on real-time scanning of brainwaves. It acts as a sort of filter of decisions, only some of which will ultimately be executed. Decisions that are preceded by certain brainwave patterns are "good," and those decisions are allowed through. The rest are discarded. Early results among a cohort of day-traders has been promising, but it's far too early to draw conclusions.

16.6 CONCLUSION

The past decade has seen a lot of advances in the datasets that quants can access, in the methods used to allocate risk to individual alphas, and in the approach to machine learning as a way of discovering alphas. It has seen a lot less advancement in portfolio construction research, risk modeling, and execution. And as an industry, it has seen some reshaping in terms of how investors view and access the space, and especially in the role that multi-manager platforms play. But though there have been many changes, much has stayed exactly the same. The work of a quant remains the work of *how* to invest more than *what* the strategies used to invest are. The types of strategies also remain largely the same. Artificial intelligence may be on the horizon, and how it will affect capital markets generally and quant investing specifically is a significant unknown.

Above and beyond everything discussed so far in this final chapter, we have seen in recent years a higher frequency of significant global geopolitical, health, and climate-driven events than I believe has been true at any point in modern history. That doesn't seem likely to abate anytime soon, and it remains one of the more difficult things for quant strategies to handle. While quants have continued to generate good results overall lately, it is well worth keeping an eye on how they adapt to a world filled with even more high-stakes chaos, catastrophes, and unprecedented events.

Appendix: Controversy Regarding High-Frequency Trading

The major advances in speed of communication and ability to interact took place more than a century ago. The shift from sailing ships to telegraph was far more radical than that from telephone to email!

—Noam Chomsky

As we described at the beginning of Part Four, HFT came into the public's consciousness through controversies surrounding it. Most of the arguments against HFT strike me as being arguments made by people who are either ignorant of the facts or motivated by self-interest to present biased and flawed information to the public. The kinds of criticisms generally ignore the differences between the various types of HFTs, confuse various elements of market structure with the practice of HFT, and conflate high-speed trading (and, often, quant trading in general) with HFT.

The criticisms of HFT seem to gravitate around four major ideas. According to its detractors:

1. HFT represents unfair competition, creating a two-tiered system of "haves and have-nots."
2. HFT manipulates markets and/or engages in front-running other investors.
3. HFT causes structural instability and/or creates additional volatility in markets.
4. HFT has no social value.

We will address each of these arguments in order, with the primary goal of separating fact from fiction.

A.1   DOES HFT CREATE UNFAIR COMPETITION?

In 2009, Andrew Brooks, head of U.S. equity trading for T Rowe Price said, "But we're moving toward a two-tiered marketplace of the high-frequency arbitrage guys, and everyone else. People want to know they have a legitimate shot at getting a fair deal. Otherwise, the markets lose their integrity." The idea behind this argument is that superfast computers, algorithms and telecomm setups, are all very expensive and unavailable to the average person, and they create a two-tiered system where HFTs have a huge advantage. This is not an accurate assessment of the current state of the markets. There are three reasons why, and we will go through each of them here.

A.1.1   The Role of Speed in Market Making

Markets need market makers, just as manufacturers and consumers need distributors. There have always been market makers, and you can't have a properly functioning market without them. Furthermore, market makers have always had to be fast, because of the adverse selection problem associated in with passive trading, which we covered in Chapter 14. In the past, speed advantages were obtained by a privileged tier of traders who were allowed to be insiders of the exchange. They used to be called locals, floor traders, specialists, and so on. Now, speed advantages are earned competitively on a level playing field, and this represents serious progress in leveling the playing field dramatically compared to the state of markets in years gone by.

The markets are more egalitarian today than they ever have been in their history. We have already given the examples from the early 1800s, when a carrier pigeon was winning technology, providing those that invested in it a serious speed advantage. In the early days of Wall Street, firms who were more proximate to the physical exchange had superior speed and access advantages. Later, those that had telephones before others had an advantage. And so on. The advantage that a big bank had over the average investor was bigger by orders of magnitude in 1929 than in 2009. In 2009, the advantage of Getco, among the very fastest in the HFT world, over the average online brokerage customer was on the order of a fraction of a second. Even on a very busy day, the advantage gained by such an edge in speed is trivially small. Compare that with the advantage of a firm that had personnel on the exchange floor 30 years ago, trading in real time, while a typical retail investor would check end-of-day prices the next morning in the newspaper (as my own father did as recently as the early 1990s)!

When advantages are gained in a fair game, on a level playing field, this is not an unfair competition issue, nor is it a two-tiered system issue.

It is a *competitive* advantage. Brooks' comments can be taken to mean that people who are smarter, and who invest capital in expensive infrastructure that makes them better able to compete, have an unfair advantage over everyone else. But by that standard, Warren Buffett has an unfair advantage over everyone else by being earlier to the table on a good idea. He has extra access to information, he is smarter, and has analysts who do a better job than others are able to do of processing information. Why wouldn't that reduce the integrity of the markets? This analogy extends to all fields where competition is present. The New York Yankees can afford to pay any player any amount they want to in order to acquire his services, thereby building a more talented team than many others. Not all players choose to play for them, and the Yankees are clearly not assured of success by virtue of having the highest payroll in their sport. Formula One racing teams are not all equal in funding or talent. Some have better drivers and engineers, engage in better R&D, and they end up winning more races as a result. The reality is that none of this is unfair. It is basic capitalism: if you are willing to take a risk, you might get a reward.

It would be unfair if some players were being prevented from taking risks and having a chance at rewards. But this is clearly not the case with HFT. Anyone can get colocation space for servers. Anyone can get top-of-the-line hardware and fast communications networks. There was an incident in 2012, in which the NYSE was justly punished for making certain datasets available only to some HFTs. But the point is that NYSE was in violation of extant rules (Rule 603(a) of Reg NMS, specifically), which make it clear that *anyone* who wants this special data can get it. They were fined, and the issue has been put to bed.[1] It is clear that someone who wishes to compete must invest a lot of capital in infrastructure. They also have to acquire the skills to compete. But that's true for most any venture.

It is, to my mind, ironic that cries of unfair practices emanate when it comes to refined engineering, but somehow fall silent when invitation-only dark pools are allowed to flourish, pooling selected customers with each other. Or when banks offer data related to their customers' trading activity (aggregated, *of course*) to only certain clientele. Or when Political Action Committees (PACs) and lax regulations around money-for-influence, even at the level of the American Supreme Court, can circumvent campaign finance rules and common sense in ethics, allowing the Harlan Crows and Robert Mercers of the world incredible sway over the world's largest economy and its third most populous. These are all much better examples of two-tiered systems than the existence of firms that pay to be able to trade quickly.

Moreover, investment in massively expensive infrastructure does not guarantee success. I won't name names, but I know many HFTs that have sunk millions of their own and investors' money into infrastructure and have absolutely nothing to show for it except red ink. This demonstrates that paying for the kind of speed we discussed in Chapter 14 does not imply profits. It merely puts a trader on a level playing field with other traders attempting to do similar things. And, as is the case in any fair competition, there are winners and losers. But it's instructive when we see losers, because it demonstrates that there is no "club membership" that an HFT receives by spending large sums of money, which entitle it to low-risk profits. Investment in good real estate, good technology, smart people, and other sources of potential advantage are exactly that: an investment that might pay off or might not.

A.1.2 The Purpose of Speed

The second reason that the claim of a two-tiered system is wrong is that HFTs do not use their fairly earned competitive advantage to compete with investors, but rather with each other. HFTs (particularly market makers) are in the business of facilitating investor orders, which means that they take the opposite side of these orders. As demonstrated in Chapter 14, obtaining a speed advantage over other HFTs is important to managing the adverse selection problems associated with passive trading.

It is incorrect to claim that a trader who does not want to accumulate a significant net position, and who prefers to end the day with no positions at all would be competing with an investor who has a time horizon measured in weeks, months, or years. Indeed, HFTs are enormous net providers of liquidity, while investors are net consumers of it.

This is borne out by the numbers. The enormous energy and cost expended on speed by HFTs can yield a strategy with a speed that can be measured. It comes to around \$0.001 per share in U.S. equities, as mentioned earlier. The fastest traders in the market can earn profits in that range. Yes, of course they trade a lot of shares, but as we showed in Chapter 13, even in aggregate, HFT profits in U.S. equities are just over half of what even a single medium-sized retail U.S. equity brokerage firm earns.

Let's contrast these economics with those of a good statistical arbitrage trader. Such a firm can earn approximately \$0.01 to \$0.02 per share. In this case, the extra \$0.001 per share earned by having better infrastructure is useful, but only at the margin. In the case of a longer-term investor, one with a return target measured in several (or many) dollars and tens of percentage points, earning an extra \$0.001 per share on a typical trade does not move the needle. This is especially true because they don't trade all that often.

Comparing the economics of HFT to the economics of longer-term investors is another way to demonstrate that there is little or no competition across these types of participants. Instead, each has a role in the market's ecosystem. The competition among HFTs exists because they are competing with each other to interact in the least adverse way with non-HFT order flow.

A.1.3 A Philosophical Point

Every advantage in investing, in particular in alpha-driven investing, is about speed. Whether it is getting data faster, processing the information faster (or even processing the information *better*), or executing orders more quickly, investment ideas only make money if other people have similar ideas, *after* you have implemented yours. This is true of deep value investing as much as it is true of HFT investing.

This is a fundamental statement about alpha, and it ties in with the definition of alpha given in Chapter 3: alpha is all about timing. In particular, it is about realizing value before others. Whether you are a long-term active investor like Warren Buffett, a statistical arbitrageur, a trend follower in futures markets, or an HFT, you make money only when your longs go up and/or your shorts go down. This is only the case when other investors, in aggregate, follow in your footsteps. Perhaps this is the most important point to consider of all: successful investing and trading rely inherently on a correct anticipation of the future aggregate behavior of other investors and traders. There is nothing special about anticipating someone's trading (which is focused on short-term price movements), versus anticipating someone's longer-term bets.

In sum, it's hard to see any merit in the idea that HFT is unfair or creates a two-tiered marketplace. HFTs do have some advantages over the average person, but then again, so does every person with an above-average IQ, or even an above-average expenditure of time and money on analysis of investment or trading decisions. That advantage, in every class of active investing from long-term money management to HFT, is fundamentally about speed. Specifically, it is about getting into positions before other people get the same ideas, and getting out before it is too late to retain profits. This leads directly to the second question about HFTs.

A.2 DOES HFT LEAD TO FRONT-RUNNING OR MARKET MANIPULATION?

HFTs are accused of front-running investors. This is a topic that understandably generates a lot of heat. But unfortunately, it also generates very little by way of credible examples to examine. As far as market manipulation, in the rare cases that the arguments get specific, detractors point to such practices as "quote stuffing," which involves placing and canceling huge numbers of orders in order to confound others into making mistakes. Another favorite of critics is that "their [HFTs'] computers can essentially bully slower investors into giving up profits—and then disappear before anyone even knows they were there,"[2] which usually doesn't get further explanation. Events that are entirely unrelated to HFT, such as Facebook's troubled IPO in 2012, have been deemed by some in the press and public to be an HFT manipulation problem.

The manipulation claim seems to have its roots in the case of Goldman Sachs sending the Feds after Sergey Aleynikov (as we described in Chapter 13). That case (until Aleynikov's conviction was dismissed and vacated) gave people who were suspicious about how anyone could make money in 2008 an "aha" moment. In their statements about the sensitivity of the code that was alleged to have been stolen, the indubitable Goldman claimed that "there is a danger that somebody who knew how to use this program could use it to manipulate markets in unfair ways." We will address both claims here.

A.2.1 Front-Running

Let's be really explicit: front-running occurs when a fiduciary uses knowledge of his customer's order to buy or sell to perform that same action before they have the opportunity to do so. But HFTs aren't looking at customer orders and then deciding whether to front-run them. They are forecasting into the extremely near-term future, and sometimes they are speculating about what other traders might do next. But, as we pointed out in the Section A.1, timing is everything for all kinds of alpha-driven investors. But most HFTs are not getting information about customer orders before they go out to the market. Mostly, they are responding to such orders, but that's what most traders have always done, with or without computers.

Some HFTs (arbitrageurs and HFT alpha traders) are reacting to fleeting inefficiencies caused by others' orders to reap profits. NCMMs react to the limit order book and other information to place passive orders. They have no knowledge of the trades that others plan to make and they do not see orders before those orders hit the market. CMMs actually do see customer order flow and have requirements to provide liquidity on that order flow. Ironically, it is here where front-running is actually theoretically possible, in contrast to the other scenarios just mentioned. However, it is rare that a CMM is the subject of the public's ire against HFTs. In fact, some critics want all HFTs to become CMMs, with obligations like those CMMs have. This would have the perverse consequence of giving all HFTs a look at order flow before it hits the tape.

A pet phrase of HFT's detractors is *latency arbitrage*, which is a stylized strategy that is supposed to demonstrate how an HFT can utilize a predatory algorithm to front-run an institutional trader's execution algorithm.[3] It is a story that begins with a premise that an HFT can see a customer order before it hits the tape, and then walks through how this information would be used to front-run an order. It is further claimed that this kind of predatory practice generates $1.5–$3 billion in profits annually for HFTs in the U.S. equity market alone.

It is true that, if an HFT could actually see the order before it hits the tape, they would be able to front-run a customer order. If we grant the premise, the rest of the argument is trivial and follows directly. However, the premise is completely false.

The scenario imagined is that, when this order is placed, it takes some time to be reflected in the NBBO, due to the latency we have described already in updating this centralized data feed. As we have also pointed out, to combat this latency, many HFTs establish direct data feeds from the exchanges. Thus, it is true that they can see the customer's order before it is reflected in the centralized tape. However—and this is the central flaw in the claim being addressed—the customer's order has to already be in the queue at a given exchange for an HFT with a direct data feed to see it.

There is no conceivable way that an HFT could see the order before it happens. It is true that, relative to someone relying on the consolidated tape, the HFT will be able to be better aware of the actual current order book. And there are clearly advantages to having timely information, or else it would be stupid for an HFT to bother establishing expensive and hard-to-manage direct feeds. But this advantage comes at a cost, and it is a cost any participant is welcome to bear for himself to compete. If a trader's strategy requires feeds to be as timely as an HFT, then it is probable he will go through all the trouble. If not, then he will not. But this is no different than establishing any other kind of competitive advantage in any industry (see Section A.1).

It seems to me that HFT's opponents have misunderstood the difference between being faster than others and front-running them. Front-running is illegal, and it basically doesn't occur insofar as HFT is concerned. HFTs are, however, faster than most other market participants. Usain Bolt is faster than most other sprinters. He wins medals, and we marvel at his speed. We are not surprised that a marathoner cannot run 100 meters as quickly as Bolt, and we do not attempt to compare the "fastest man in the world" with the "fastest marathoner in the world." This is because it would be strange to do so: they are competing in different games. Bolt is not trying to outrun Patrick Makau (record-holder for fastest marathon). Just so, HFTs are not trying to front-run pension investors (nor could they, given the basic fact that the pension fund's orders go directly to the market). They are competing in different games.

Imagine a world in which there are no computerized trading strategies, no execution algorithms. In such a world, some traders would still have the ability to access and process information faster and more accurately than others. And those traders would outwit the less capable and make a profit doing so. This is completely normal and acceptable. And the analogy is identical in the case of HFTs. They do not have access to customer order flow before the fact. They can find out what the customer flow was as soon as possible after the fact, and they can attempt to react very quickly to that information. This, too, is completely normal and totally acceptable.

A.2.2 Manipulation and Cancelation Rates

Focusing now on manipulation, some have claimed that HFTs manipulate markets, either by moving prices or as a result of their high order cancelation rates. The troubled Facebook IPO in 2012 has been used as an example of this supposed manipulation by some observers. As it turns out, the problems at the opening of Facebook's IPO were specifically driven by technology problems at Nasdaq. What this has to do with HFTs is not something I have the ability to imagine. It also appears lost on those pointing to the Facebook IPO as evidence of an HFT manipulation problem that the price dropped and remained well below the IPO price for well over a year.

But let's imagine that some bad actor in the HFT world does decide to manipulate markets or engage in quote stuffing. Should someone using a powerful tool for illegal purposes bring judgment on himself or on the tool he used? Should speculative trading be banned because the Hunt brothers cornered and manipulated the silver markets beginning in the 1970s (without the use of any technology more sophisticated than a telephone)? For that matter, should telephones be banned, since they can and have been used for evil purposes?

But we need not grant that HFTs engage in manipulative practices. Manipulation usually requires a trader to acquire large enough inventory of a position to move the market. But considering our definition of an HFT, this is not in line with an HFT's requirement to get out of positions by the end of the day. Inventory, as we've seen, is generally not desirable to an HFT. So there is a logical inconsistency between the contention that HFTs manipulate markets and the fact that they dislike holding positions. The reality is that anyone with sufficient means and motivation can attempt to manipulate markets.

Critics have also pointed to the frequency with which HFTs cancel their orders (known as cancelation rates) as a way to manipulate markets at a micro level. A high rate of entering and canceling orders is referred to as quote stuffing. Opponents of HFT claim that there are two problems with high cancelation rates: first, that high cancelation rates imply that the liquidity that we think we see is either not there at all, or it is of inferior quality; second, that HFTs manipulate markets by overwhelming exchanges with massive message volumes due to placing and canceling too many orders. There are a number of problems with these arguments, but first, let's understand why cancelation rates are and *should be* high, if the market is functioning correctly.

We demonstrated in Chapter 14 the importance of queue placement in placing and canceling passive orders. Time priority markets (such as the U.S. equity markets) require that a passive trader be fast on his feet if he doesn't want to get picked off. Since much of the HFT world is passive, there is a great deal of competition to provide liquidity to active traders. This competition is good for the active trader, because it means that her trade will get done at a good price. Every time the price changes in a market, every time there is a trade, this is new information that must be accounted for by the market maker. This usually means canceling a previously resting passive order and placing a new one. Decimalization of stocks led to an increased frequency of price changes, and this has in turn meant a permanently higher rate of cancelations.

Fragmentation in the U.S. equity market is another important contributor. Because there are over a dozen official exchanges under Reg NMS, and because the formation of the NBBO is so slow (as described in Chapter 14), many HFTs post orders directly to each exchange. But they are posting far more liquidity than they actually want to provide, and once they get filled on the size they are willing to trade, they must cancel the extra orders or risk being run over by active traders. This is some of the basic risk management that we described in Chapter 15, and it is a good thing that HFTs are careful about managing risk.

Finally, many new orders reach the market too late to be at or near the front of the queue. In these cases, allowing those orders to remain in the order book is very risky for market makers, for all the reasons we described in Chapter 14. As such, seeing that an order arrived too late is sufficiently good reason to cancel it.

Opponents of HFT claim that the liquidity being provided is merely a mirage, or if it is real, it is inferior. Unfortunately, there is no evidence to support these claims. But the facts are what they are: the average NBBO quote on SPY, which is the highest volume stock in the world, had an average duration of over 3 seconds in for the first half of 2010. A typical stock has lower volumes and longer NBBO quote durations. These numbers are not different than what opponents claim to have been true in the pre-HFT days of 2004.

HFT's opponents also contend that high message rates (which occur when there are a high volume of orders and cancelations) cause delays for exchanges, which buys the HFT time (to do what, I'm not sure). It is true that, when message volumes spike, exchanges must deal with the same micro-bursting problem (see Chapter 14) as HFTs have to solve, and at the extremes, the exchanges do see delays. But slowing down message traffic would serve no economic purpose for an HFT. Indeed, during the Flash Crash, many HFTs who stopped trading did so specifically because data latencies were getting to such a level that they felt their data quality had deteriorated so much that they couldn't responsibly continue trading. Data latency is an enemy to an HFT, not a friend.

Furthermore, if exchanges were being hampered by HFTs, it is easy enough for them to do something about it. Indeed, exchanges do monitor the message traffic from each participant that connects to them, and they warn, sanction, and, if necessary, ban traders who generate excess traffic. This is a completely rational and acceptable way to handle the situation, because not all exchanges have the same capacity to handle messages. An artificial message limit would be too low for some and too high for others, and would add an arbitrary element to the healthy competition among exchanges.

A minimum resting time, which would disallow the immediate cancelation of an order, has also been suggested. The proximate effect of such a change would be that a large proportion of all orders would be very stale, and that such stale orders would offer new and very fruitful arbitrage opportunities to HFTs. For example, imagine that the NBBO on the SPY shows 1,000 shares bid at $144.20 and 1,000 shares offered at $144.21, and these are freshly made orders that must rest for some time. Now imagine that the S&P futures move rapidly downward just at that time. The trader whose 1,000 share bid at $144.20 is stuck because of a minimum resting time would see it get filled happily by an active order from an index arbitrageur, who would subsequently be able, quite possibly, to immediately buy back the short position at a lower price. Remember, based on what we showed in Chapter 14, the main reason a passive order would get canceled is to avoid being picked off. Requiring that a liquidity-providing passive trader allow himself to be picked off, in order to solve a non-existent problem, doesn't seem likely to be an effective improvement to the current market structure.

As a final note, an academic paper published in September 2012 took the first ever detailed, empirical look at the impact of HFTs on market manipulation.[4] They analyzed 22 stock exchanges around the world from January 2003 through June 2011. Their findings are below:

> *Controlling for country, market, legal and other differences across exchanges and over time, and using a variety of robustness checks including difference-in-differences tests, we show that <u>the</u> presence*

of high frequency trading in some markets has significantly mitigated *the frequency and severity of end-of-day manipulation, counter to recent concerns expressed in the media. The effect of HFT is
more pronounced than the role of trading rules, surveillance, enforcement and legal conditions in curtailing the frequency and severity of end-of-day manipulation. We show our findings are robust
to different measures of end-of-day manipulation, including but not
limited to option expiry dates, among other things.*

A.3 DOES HFT LEAD TO GREATER VOLATILITY OR STRUCTURAL INSTABILITY?

Occasionally, computer software has glitches. When one of those glitches
leads to millions of erroneous orders, causing huge instability in market
prices, people worry. Furthermore, even without the presence of bugs in
someone's code, events like the "Flash Crash" of 2010 lead to speculation
that HFTs are to blame for extreme market volatility. Indeed, it remains
fairly widely asserted that the Flash Crash was a computer-driven event,
despite both an abundance of evidence to the contrary and none in favor
of such a theory. Even an SEC report on the event, which exonerated HFTs
about as clearly as could be done by a government report, made no dent in
the perception that HFTs were to blame.

Aside from the Flash Crash, other events have not helped the public rela-
tions efforts for HFT. For example, an HFT firm named Infinium was probed
in August 2010 for a bug in its HFT programs that led to a $1 increase in the
price of crude oil in about one second. So are HFTs responsible for instability and volatility?

As was the case with the arguments already discussed, HFTs are accused
of things that are equally or more applicable to other forms of trading. For
every HFT problem or computer hiccup, there is a Mizuho securities trader,
who accidentally sold 600,000 shares of a stock at 1 Yen each, instead of 1
share at 600,000 Yen. Not to pick on the Japanese, but another "fat finger"
error only a few months later had another trader buy 2,000 shares of a stock
that traded at 510,000 Yen, instead of 2 shares, costing his firm $10 mil-
lion in losses. An entertaining article in the *Financial Times*, a Dow Jones
publication, from March 2007[5] listed 10 human-driven trading errors of
breathtaking scope, including one for more than $100 billion worth of stock
in a European pharmaceutical; another involving a trader whose elbow
touched an "instant sell" key on his keyboard, leading to massive futures
order in French government bonds; another order where a trader carelessly
attempted to transact more than £8.1 billion worth of shares (nearly four

times the company's market capitalization); and another where someone wrongly entered the 6-digit SEDOL identifier for a stock in the "size" field of an order, leading to a £60 million loss; and so on.

As to whether HFTs cause volatility even in the absence of glitches, this is a somewhat different story. Here, I first have to ask what the problem actually is with volatility. If long-term investors are truly long-term, why should they care about a frenzy of activity in which the market drops by 10 percent and then recovers almost entirely a few minutes later? Why should they care about a glitch at the exchange that led to a less than flawless IPO for a hot tech stock? And it is not clear that most real long-term investors do care about these short-term events.

We have had, and we continue to have, bigger and far more pressing problems weighing on the markets. The 1929 market crash that kicked off the Great Depression, the spike in inflation and bond yields that crushed most assets in the 1970s, the decades-long stagnation in Japan's economy and capital markets, the 1998 LTCM/Russian-driven crash, the dot-com bubble and the subsequent 50 percent decline in stocks that took years to recover, the financial debacle of 2008 (from which we still haven't fully recovered), and the problems in Greek and other Euro-zone sovereigns are all by orders of magnitude more important things to bother ourselves with than a single intraday event. Neither computers nor HFTs play any role in these real economic issues, which seem to be the kinds of things with which real money investors are (and should be) concerned.

A.3.1   An Empirical Analysis of HFTs and Volatility

Empirical analysis supports the claim that HFTs are not responsible for volatility. Critics point out that volatility in the S&P 500 has climbed since HFTs have gained prominence. A September 2011 article in the *New York Times* was titled "Market Swings Are Becoming New Standard."[6] It argues that the stock market is more likely to "make large swings – on the order of 3 percent or 4 percent – than it has been any other time in recent stock market history." It goes on to list HFT as one of the probable causes. In an article for the High-Frequency Traders website, Manoj Narang dissects this argument and provides an empirical study of the sources of volatility.[7] Let's build on that analysis here.

The S&P 500 goes through two distinct phases in any given 24-hour period. The first is the period during which the market is open. We can measure the behavior of the S&P while it's open by comparing the opening price and a closing price. The second period is when the market is closed. To understand the behavior of the market during this period, we can look at one day's closing price and the next day's opening price. These two mutually exclusive segments (open:close and close:open) add up to the behavior of the index from one day's close to the next day's close.

HFTs are active during the trading day. They are almost all dormant overnight (remember, they tend to take home no overnight positions). Much of the news that impacts markets comes out overnight (though some, e.g., the Federal Open Market Committee's announcements are intraday phenomena). As such, we can take as a rule of thumb that overnight (close:open) volatility is unrelated to HFTs, while intraday volatility could be related to HFTs (or other news and events that occur intraday). One of the errors that the aforementioned *New York Times* article makes is to point out that close-to-close volatility has gone up since HFTs have gained prominence. But we can do a better job of understanding the sources of this increase by examining the behavior of the market while it is closed, versus when HFTs are active (while the market is open).

For this analysis, we look at four quantities and compare them during two distinct periods. The first quantity is the absolute value of the percent change in the S&P from one day's close to the next (close:close). The second quantity is the absolute value of the percent change in the S&P from the open to the close of a single day (open:close). The third compares the absolute value of the percent change in the S&P from one day's close to the next day's open (close:open). The final quantity is the absolute value of the percent change from the intraday high to the intraday low for a single day. We took data from January 1, 2000 through September 2012, and drew a dividing line at January 1, 2007. This is because Reg NMS was enacted during 2007, which changed market structure to what it is today. Furthermore, the post-2007 period is clearly when HFTs became most active. If the critics are right, we should see the open:close volatility increase at least as much as the close:close volatility, since that's the only time that HFTs could possibly affect prices.

Comparing the close:close results, we find that the S&P 500 (as measured using the SPY ETF) averaged 0.84 percent changes from 2000–2006, and 1.03 percent changes from 2007–2012. This is a 23 percent increase in the magnitude of the index's movements, and is the primary evidence used to support the contention that HFTs have caused increased volatility. However, if we divide the data into the natural partitions we described (close:open and open:close), we see a different picture. This is shown in Exhibit A.1.

What is clear from Exhibit A.1 is that, while volatility (measured in this way) has increased overall from 2007 onwards, the increase is actually much smaller intraday than it is overnight. The increase in the average of the gap from high to low within a day is also much smaller than the increase in overnight volatility. These data clearly indicate that market volatility has increased for reasons that have nothing to do with HFTs.

EXHIBIT A.1   Average Price Movement in SPY (%)

	2000–2006	2007–2012	% Difference
close:close	0.84	1.03	+23
open:close (intraday)	0.76	0.82	+8
close:open (overnight)	0.37	0.59	+59
high:low	1.47	1.72	+17

EXHIBIT A.2   Median Price Movement in SPY (%)

	2000–2006	2007–2012	% Difference
close:close	0.62	0.67	+8
open:close (intraday)	0.55	0.53	−3
close:open (overnight)	0.26	0.39	+51
high:low	1.26	1.33	+5

Examining the median movements of the S&P instead of the averages shows an even starker contrast, as shown in Exhibit A.2. Here, we see that volatility has actually not increased all that much, and that intraday volatility has actually *contracted* somewhat since the rise of HFTs! By contrast, and consistent with what we saw from the analysis of average movements, overnight volatility has spiked according to this measure as well.

We can also examine whether larger moves have become more frequent. To answer this question, we looked at the frequency of moves of 3 percent or greater in the same way, as shown in Exhibit A.3. Here, we see an increase in volatility measured in each way, but the pattern of increases in overnight volatility far outstripping intraday volatility holds.

It does become more interesting as we examine even larger moves. What we see is that, when counting the frequency of larger moves (4 percent or more), the instances have become more common in the intraday period than in from close to close, while the high versus low volatility increase continues to lag. This is shown in Exhibit A.4.

At these more extreme levels, it appears that overnight volatility plays less of a role than intraday volatility in explaining the increase in the frequency of very large moves since 2007. However, even here, the picture is mixed. First, while the intraday volatility increases more as the magnitude of the move goes up, we see that the high versus low volatility increases at a slower pace overall. Second, as we begin to examine these outlier events, we are dealing with events that happen very infrequently. For example, out of the 1,448 trading days since January 1, 2007, we have seen only 20 instances

EXHIBIT A.3   Frequency of 3% or Greater Moves in SPY (%)

	2000–2006	2007–2012	% Difference
close:close	2.56	5.87	+129
open:close (intraday)	1.53	2.69	+75
close:open (overnight)	0.11	0.83	+629
high:low	6.20	10.91	+76

EXHIBIT A.4   Frequency of 4% or Greater Moves in the SPY (%)

	2000–2006	2007–2012	% Difference
close:close	0.68	2.97	+335
open:close (intraday)	0.28	1.38	+386
close:open (overnight)	0.11	0.48	+325
high:low	1.65	5.73	+248

where intraday moves were at least 4 percent. As such, it would be unwise to draw any serious conclusions from these data.

However, one could contend that HFTs' association with market volatility is as follows: most of the time their activities are coincide with lower volatility, but in the most extreme cases, their activities coincide with higher volatility. Even if we make a grave statistical error and mistake coincidence for causation, the most damning argument against HFTs could be that, in the 20 instances where the market moved at least 4 percent in an intraday period over the last five and a half years, HFTs may have contributed to those large moves to some unknowable degree. Other investors surely will also bear some of the "blame." But for the other 1,428 days, HFTs reduced volatility.

One major reason that the data support the claim that HFTs reduce volatility is that a strategy which buys and sells roughly the same amount during a fixed time period cannot cause any net price impact on the instrument being traded. Whatever price impact was generated on the buying of a position is realized in the opposite direction when selling it. And without impact, the probability that volatility, even measured on the slowest timescale attributable to HFTs (one day) is related to HFTs is effectively nil. The definition of HFTs logically precludes one from drawing such a conclusion.

Furthermore, it is a basic fact of capital markets that posting limit orders, which is a huge part of the activity of HFTs, does not cause volatility, but rather reduces it. Every single order in the order book represents a friction that must be overcome before the market can move through the price levels presented in the order book. Illiquidity breeds volatility, not an abundance of liquidity. This fact seems lost on HFT's opponents. Even in times of duress, when HFTs must trade actively, it is most often to liquidate positions that were acquired passively. This implies that even in stress scenarios, such as the one we will cover in depth next, HFTs are probably no worse than neutral to liquidity. In aggregate, it is extremely clear that they are liquidity providers.

A.3.2　The Flash Crash

It took less than 20 minutes for many blue-chip shares to drop by about 5 percent. In smaller capitalization companies, the moves were worse. Brunswick Corp fell 9.3 percent in 12 minutes (more than 22 percent from its opening price). There was massive volume, enough to cause the NYSE to take almost two and a half hours after the market close to finish reporting floor transactions. Market makers were found to have exacerbated the downdraft by turning from buyers to sellers. There was chaos in the prices of some executions relative to what they should probably have been, given the prevailing market. There was widespread disgust and disappointment in the integrity of capital markets, and many brokerage firms saw reduced volumes and earnings in the wake of this event. These events occurred on May 29, 1962.[8] But they hold some important parallels and equally important lessons in considering the Flash Crash of 2010. The reality is that, just as real, deep crises occur in markets without any help from computers or HFTs, so do rapid fluctuations in prices.

The causes of the 2010 Flash Crash are several. First, and most importantly, the markets were already jittery from a brewing sovereign debt crisis in Europe and a very tentative economic recovery in the U.S. The stock market was already down several percentage points for the day before the first spike down around 2:40PM. The role of negative short-term sentiment on the part of a wide array of market participants should not be discounted. It was the single largest cause of the Flash Crashes of both 1962 and 2010.

Second, Waddell & Reed, an established mutual fund manager, entered a large (somewhat inelegant, and fully discretionary) order to sell S&P futures.[9] The face value of this order was approximately $4.1 billion, and at a time when the market was already down, this order exacerbated price movements enough to trigger further selling, for example, from stop-losses and other kinds of stop-orders. The order was entered around 2:30 PM on May 6, 2010, and at that point, the S&P 500 was already down 2.5 percent for the day. There is little doubt that this 75,000 contract order, which took 20 minutes to execute, was a driver of the volatility that ensued. In particular, their trading algorithm was designed to ignore price movements and merely focus on volume levels as the determinant of the size of each order placed. But since their own order was causing others to panic, volumes increased, and their 75,000 contract order became the center of a snowball. It is important to point out that there is no judgment assigned to these facts. Waddell's order was perfectly legitimate, with no evil intent behind it. It was their right to enter it, and what transpired afterwards has no bearing on that fact.

Third, the inter-connectedness of instruments across various exchanges and instrument classes (e.g., S&P futures to S&P ETFs to the constituents of these ETFs, to the names that are peers of those constituents), in U.S. equities had a role in the propagation of these volatile moves across the marketplace. As we described in talking about index arbitrage in Chapter 15, the prices of structurally correlated instruments will tend to move together. So, when S&P futures fell, the ETFs that track the same index moved in lockstep. So did the stocks that are constituents of the S&P 500 (and the ETFs that contain those). Then, statistical correlations dictated that other, similar stocks should follow suit. There is little judgment on this fact either. It is generally a good thing to have many ways to express an investment idea. Each structure offers some benefits and some drawbacks, and that they tend to move in lock-step with one another does not mean that there is some problem that needs to be solved.

Fourth, the fragmentation of the U.S. equity market played a role. The fragmentation itself was a pro-customer change in market structure that really picked up steam in the late 1990s with the propagation of ECNs. The increased competition with the previously monopolistic stock exchanges drove costs lower and liquidity higher. But in this case, fragmentation did have a hand in the breakdown in liquidity due to the declaration of "self help." Reg NMS allows an exchange to cease participating and sharing information with the other market centers if there is a problem with one or more of them. The NYSE Arca exchange, for example, was alleged to have had problems with its technology, resulting from the huge increase in message traffic (remember our discussion about data bursts in Chapter 14? This is why they matter!). Several exchanges pointed to what they viewed as Arca's problems and declared Self Help, which they are allowed to do if they find that some member of the market system is having problems. This exacerbated the fragmentation problem and reduced liquidity. It was a contributor to the "stub quotes" issue which led to some shares being executed at obviously ridiculous prices.

Finally, the Flash Crash was exacerbated by the extremely reasonable decision by some (not nearly all) HFT speculators to cease trading. They are not required to make markets, and data latency times coming out of exchanges were severe. At a time when the market was clearly broken in several places, there is no judgment that should be cast against any trader who simply wants no part of some craziness in the markets. Note that, nevertheless, volumes during the Flash Crash were spectacularly high, so either non-HFT traders were doing many multiples of their normal order size, or else HFT traders weren't as absent as is widely believed.

In sum, HFTs were not responsible for the Flash Crash, nor are they responsible for the very real economic problems we face currently. Can HFT cause market problems through glitches or misbehavior? Absolutely. But so can a lot of other things that aren't HFTs. No one is talking about banning human traders because they often screw up spectacularly once in a while. Why should we have a double-standard on computerized traders? Regulation is useful here, and there should always be repercussions for costly and careless errors. The first and most appropriate repercussion is that people who make dumb trades tend to lose money for themselves (e.g., Knight Capital). They have their investors to face, as well. But that sort of natural punishment, coupled with any required ex-post enforcement seems perfectly legitimate, given the total lack of other valid options.

A.4 DOES HFT LACK SOCIAL VALUE?

This is perhaps the most disappointing argument I've heard against HFT. Actually its being infuriating has nothing to do with HFT at all. It is problematic in the philosophical outlook it implies, and disappointing in who has furthered its acceptance by many. Paul Krugman, a brilliant Nobel-laureate economist, actually made the argument in an op-ed piece in the *New York Times* that HFT is generally a game of "bad actors," and that it's "hard to see how traders who place their orders one-thirtieth of a second faster than anyone else do anything to improve that social function." Allow me to state this explicitly. This is a catastrophically bad point of view, most especially for a self-described liberal economist.

I don't care about the fact, and it is a clear and indisputable fact despite all the rhetoric to the contrary, that HFTs actually provide an enormous amount of liquidity to the marketplace, which facilitates the trading activities of a great number of other types of players that are judged as having social value by those interested in casting such judgments. It's irrelevant. The problem is far deeper with this argument.

The first question that is begged when someone raises the banner of social value is this: who gets to decide what has social value and what doesn't? What is the minimum holding period for an investor to be judged favorably as improving the social function of markets? Where do we stop with this analysis of social value? What about short-sellers, who were indeed questioned and blamed heavily for the failures of Bear Stearns, AIG, and others in 2008? What about the makers of Bubble-Yum, Snickers bars, Coca-Cola, cigarettes, guns, fighter jets, and nuclear weapons? In short, what kind of fascist, presumptuous thing is it to even raise the question of social value? What's the social value of an economist? What's the social value of Lady Gaga or Metallica, or Brahms or Bach, for that matter?

This is a hideous and damnable line of thinking. It's a free country, so people can say and do what they want, so long as they do not impinge on the rights of others. And this line of thinking leads directly to the impingement of others' pursuits via its fallacious presumptions.

A.5   REGULATORY CONSIDERATIONS

It's true that computers are powerful tools, and that the more powerful a tool is, the greater amount of damage (or good) that it can do. But while that calls for scrutiny and sensible regulation, it does not call for the banning of the use of powerful tools.

Despite the hot-headed talk from some outmoded corners of the marketplace, U.S. regulators have been surprisingly even-headed and downright thoughtful about all this. So far, every real step they've taken with regard to HFT has actually seemed pretty fair. Banning naked access was a reasonable thing to do. The SEC's report on the Flash Crash was even-keeled, pretty accurate, and placed the responsibility (not the blame, which is something needed when there's a real disaster) more or less in the right camps.

One of the most controversial measures being considered in the U.S. is a financial transaction tax (FTT). It is also one of the most stupid ideas regarding HFT and potential improvements to market structure. If the tax is not universal and global, then trading will simply move to markets where taxes are lower or are not applied at all. If taxes are universal and global, and if HFT becomes unprofitable as a result, volumes are likely to plummet, which reduces both the amount collected by the FTT and follow-on impacts to capital gains taxes. Declining volumes will also damage banks and brokerage firms severely, and it is probable that their least risky and most profitable units will be the hardest hit. Banks' prime brokerage units are nearly riskless operations that generate large revenues from customers' commissions. If customers are trading less, banks will make less. This probably implies a substantial loss in jobs, not just at the banks, but also at various trading entities associated with the markets.

None of this has stopped 11 countries in the EU from adopting an FTT, but it will not be surprising if they follow the path Sweden has already been down. In 1984, Sweden enacted an FTT. Trading volumes across various asset classes in Sweden fell dramatically. Futures volumes were off 98 percent, bond volumes dropped 80 percent, and the options market in Sweden disappeared entirely. By 1990, Sweden's equity markets had lost more than half of their volumes to London's exchanges. The fees collected were just over 3 percent of what the Swedish Finance Ministry had forecast, and the FTT actually cost the Swedish Treasury revenue in aggregate, because other taxable revenues on capital gains fell, more than offsetting the miniscule revenues that were achieved. It was repealed in 1991.[10] Needless to say, Sweden also did not join the 11 countries that adopted the FTT in October 2012.

The irony is that the tax is designed to "make the financial firms that got us into this mess pay their share for the recovery." But customers of financial firms (e.g., hedge funds and HFTs) certainly did not cause lax mortgage lending practices, CDOs, bogus AAA ratings, and so on. And it is the customers of financial firms, not the financial firms, who will be paying this tax. It's one thing if it's just HFTs and hedge funds paying the tax. Maybe most people wouldn't care. But, the Dutch Central Bank (DCB), "opposes the introduction of a European financial transaction tax that it estimated would cost the nation's lenders, pension funds and insurers about €4 billion and hurt economic growth." The DCB concluded that more than 40 percent of the annual cost of an FTT in the Netherlands would be borne by pensions (€1.7 billion).[11]

I don't care much about the bluster in the press. I've been involved in hedge funds for over 16 years now, and when I got started, few knew what a hedge fund even was. When they did, it was in the form of vilification (Soros for attacking Asian currencies, LTCM for nearly destroying the financial markets, and so on). We get paid pretty well, and if not being liked by someone who trusts what he reads in the news to be the whole story is the cost of that compensation, I'll take that trade every day. I only hope that those with the power to actually make changes continue to take constructive steps, rather than heeding the biased and/or uninformed voices of a very loud minority with regard to HFT. And certainly, we should be very, very wary of the unintended consequences of taking bad advice from ignorant, short-sighted, or biased people.

Some reasonable ideas to improve market structure do exist. Circuit breakers, which have long been proposed (and used, in markets like futures) are an effective way to cool down overheated markets. Ending the ban on locked markets would go a very long way toward eliminating one of the most severe inefficiencies in the U.S. equity market, which would further eliminate the need for ISO orders (which are, for all practical purposes, unavailable to most investors, since the broker must determine that the investor is capable of complying with Reg NMS, which most investors cannot do). Liquidity provision rebates are currently tiered, so that the most active participants get the best rebate tiers. While rebates themselves are a good thing (as they make it worthwhile to accept the risk of providing liquidity), tiered rebates make it impossible for lower-volume customers to profitably post passive orders. Moving toward a much flatter (or entirely flat) rebate structure would solve this problem. And, finally, it behooves regulators to begin to arm themselves with technology that will enable them to properly monitor and police the markets. This appears to be well understood by now, and we are beginning to see the SEC take significant steps in the right direction.

A.6 SUMMARY

In general, and let me say this clearly, HFTs are not run by evil people. They stay well within both the rules of the markets, and the boundaries of common ethics and good sense. They often self-report any irregularities caused by their trading to the authorities. That the powerful computers and fast communication lines they possess might be used to manipulate the market doesn't mean that legitimate activities undertaken with these tools must be stopped. Just as people are prosecuted for calling in fake bomb threats, so should people be prosecuted for manipulation, front-running, and other bad behaviors in the markets. But there has been no evidence that computerized traders are especially guilty of such activities, and there is certainly no logic to a call to ban their activities because of a few examples of corruption.

Let us remember that some people have to be told what's right and wrong, and they have to be punished for ignoring the rules. We Americans had to be told it was wrong to hold slaves, and wrong to force our children to work as coal miners and chimney sweeps, and so on. That doesn't make farming or all farmers bad. It doesn't make families or all parents bad. It unfortunately makes regulations and their proper enforcement absolutely required, because otherwise some people will go too far. Even with good regulations and enforcement, this still happens. But there's no cure for the vices of humanity.

HFT isn't evil any more than walking your dog is evil. Nor should it be banned any more than walking one's dog should be banned. Yes, some dog owners will let their dog crap on your lawn and simply walk away, leaving the souvenir behind. That doesn't make dogs bad; it makes the dog's owner sort of antisocial, and well-deserving of some punishment. Computers, even when used for trading, are programmed by people. If those people are malicious or careless, they will hurt others, and they should be prosecuted.

But people have been hurting others through malice and carelessness for far longer than we've had computers, ECNs, or dark fiber. To take the attention off of the humans who engage in the activities that are harmful, and to focus on the instrument they use to cause harm, is folly. Furthermore, nearly every single serious academic study undertaken has either demonstrated that HFTs have empirically added liquidity and improved price discovery, or demonstrated that there is no evidence to support the idea that HFTs have created additional volatility or decreased market efficiency. The most critical papers often remark that problems can arise from HFT, but they are quick to note that such problems have arisen before HFT, and continue to arise due to other factors since the advent of HFT. An excellent and recent summary, which is also full of further references, can be found at the Foresight Project, which was conducted by the UK Government Office for Science, using leading academics from 20 countries.[12]

NOTES

Note to the reader: This chapter was originally the fourth and final chapter in the section regarding high-speed and high-frequency trading. It was topical at the time, but I believe most of the noise around the controversies associated with HFT has died down, so I elected not to update it, and to move it to the appendix.

1. http://sec.gov/litigation/admin/2012/34-67857.pdf
2. http://topics.nytimes.com/topics/reference/timestopics/subjects/h/high_frequency_algorithmic_trading/index.html, September 26, 2012. This article starts by conflating high-speed and high-frequency trading. It is a case study in confusing cause and effect, in confusing anything to do with computers with HFT, and with creating a tempest in a teacup (e.g., Knight Capital's near collapse). It's a pretty shabby article, and I say this as someone who *likes* the *New York Times*.
3. Manoj Narang, "What's All the Fuss About High-Frequency Trading Cancellation Rates?," June 24, 2010. www.institutionalinvestor.com
4. Douglas Cumming, Feng Zhan, and Michael Aitken, "High Frequency Trading and End-of-Day Manipulation," September 12, 2012. https://ssrn.com/abstract=2109920 or http://dx.doi.org/10.2139/ssrn.2109920
5. Stacy-Marie Ishmael, "The Curse of the Fat-Fingered Trader," *FT Alphaville*, March 16, 2007. http://ftalphaville.ft.com
6. Louise Story and Graham Bowley, "Market Swings Are Becoming New Standard," *New York Times*, September 11, 2011. http://www.nytimes.com
7. Manoj Narang, "HFT Is NOT Responsible for Market Volatility – You Are!," September 15, 2011. http://www.highfrequencytraders.com
8. Marcy Gordon and Daniel Wagner, "'Flash Crash' Report: Waddell & Reed's $4.1 Billion Trade Blamed for Market Plunge." October 1, 2010. http://www.huffingtonpost.com
9. Jason Zweig, "Back to the Future: Lessons from the Forgotten 'Flash Crash' of 1962," *Wall Street Journal*, May 29, 2010. http://online.wsj.com
10. http://publications.gc.ca/collections/Collection-R/LoPBdP/BP/bp419-e.htm
11. Maud van Gaal, "EU Transaction Tax Is 'Undesirable,' Dutch Central Bank Says," February 6, 2012. http://www.bloomberg.com
12. http://www.bis.gov.uk/foresight/our-work/projects/current-projects/computer-trading/working-paper

About the Author

Rishi K Narang is the Founding Principal of T2AM and manages T2AM's investment activities. Rishi began his career as a Global Investment Strategist for Citibank Alternative Investment in 1996. He then co-founded Tradeworx, Inc., as a quantitative hedge fund manager, in 1999 and acted as its President until his departure in 2002. For three years, he was the co-Portfolio Manager and a Managing Director at Santa Barbara Alpha Strategies before founding T2AM, LLC in 2005. He is Chair of the Board of Directors of Village Health Works, and has acted as an Advisor to DARPA, Planet Labs, AngelList, and numerous others. Mr. Narang completed his BA in Economics from the University of California at Berkeley.

Index